The Grasping Hand

The Grasping Hand

Kelo v. City of New London
and the Limits of Eminent Domain

I L Y A   S O M I N

THE UNIVERSITY OF CHICAGO PRESS   CHICAGO AND LONDON

A CATO INSTITUTE BOOK

Ilya Somin is professor of law at the George Mason University School of Law. He is the author of *Democracy and Political Ignorance: Why Smaller Government is Smarter* and writes regularly for the popular *Volokh Conspiracy* blog.

The University of Chicago Press, Chicago 60637
The University of Chicago Press, Ltd., London
© 2015 by The University of Chicago
All rights reserved. Published 2015.
Printed in the United States of America

24 23 22 21 20 19 18 17 16 15   1 2 3 4 5

ISBN-13: 978-0-226-25660-3 (cloth)
ISBN-13: 978-0-226-25674-0 (e-book)
DOI: 10.7208/chicago/9780226256740.001.0001

Library of Congress Cataloging-in-Publication Data
Somin, Ilya, author.
  The grasping hand : Kelo v. City of New London and the limits of eminent domain / Ilya Somin.
        pages   cm
  "A Cato Institute book."
  Includes bibliographical references and index.
  ISBN 978-0-226-25660-3 (cloth : alkaline paper)—ISBN 0-226-25660-X (cloth : alkaline paper)—ISBN 978-0-226-25674-0 (e-book)—ISBN 0-226-25674-X (e-book)   1. Eminent domain—United States—Case studies.   2. Zoning law—United States—Case studies.   3. Land use—Law and legislation—United States—Case studies.   4. Kelo, Susette—Trials, litigation, etc.   5. New London (Conn.)—Trials, litigation, etc.   I. Title.
  KF5599.S66 2015
  343.73'0252—dc23   2014042602

♾ This paper meets the requirements of ANSI/NISO Z39.48-1992 (Permanence of Paper).

TO MY WIFE ALISON

Contents

Acknowledgments

This book has been in the works for a long time. In the process of research and writing, I have incurred many debts.

My greatest obligation is to the participants in the *Kelo* story who generously took the time to recount their experiences to me. Some of those who took part in these events could not be located or were unwilling to be interviewed about what, for many, were very difficult times. I owe a great deal to those who were both willing and able to speak.

Members of five of the families whose land was taken recounted their stories to me in detail: Richard Beyer, Michael Cristofaro, Matthew Dery, Susette Kelo, and Bill Von Winkle. I am deeply grateful for their time and consideration in going over what, for most of them, were extremely painful memories.

Marguerite Marley recounted her family's experience of "voluntarily" selling their home in the redevelopment area, under the looming threat of condemnation. Frederick Paxton and Peter Kreckovic described to me their roles in helping to organize public opposition to the New London takings. Connecticut lawyer Margaret "Peggy" Little recounted to me her reasons for having to refuse to take the Fort Trumbull property owners' case, despite her sympathy for their cause.

I am also grateful to Claire Gaudiani, former president of the New London Development Corporation, for agreeing to be interviewed and explaining her perspective on these events. Although Professor Gaudiani was not willing to be quoted on the record, her account did much to help me better understand her side of the story.

I learned a great deal from my interviews with lawyers for both sides. Wesley Horton, who represented the City of New London in the Supreme Court, twice took time away from his busy practice to discuss with me his ultimately successful legal strategy in the case. Dana Berliner and Scott Bullock of the Institute for Justice, who represented the property owners throughout the litigation, generously submitted to multiple interviews and provided much useful information about the case and Institute for Justice's approach to public interest property rights litigation more generally. All three advocates also gave me useful comments on the manuscript and helped me avoid potential mistakes.

I am also grateful to Dana for helping to inspire my interest in public use issues when I worked at the Institute for Justice as a law student summer clerk under her direction in 1998. This was before the Institute's involvement with the *Kelo* case began, so I had no role in their later handling of that litigation. But I came away from that summer with great respect for the Institute's work, an abiding interest in the Public Use Clause, and a sense that legal scholars had not paid adequate attention to the constitutional questions it raises.

I owe a debt to the late Jane Jacobs, the legendary urban development theorist on whose behalf I wrote an amicus brief in the *Kelo* case when it reached the Supreme Court in 2004. Representing her was an honor. It also gave me a greater appreciation for the ways in which this case often cut across conventional ideological divisions.

Several George Mason University School of Law students served as outstanding research assistants. They include Ryan Eric Facer, Nate Pettine, Mariam al Koshnaw, Matt Lafferman, Audrey Johnston, and Noah Oberlander. Susan Courtwright-Rodriguez helped design some of the tables included in chapters 5 and 6 and the appendix. Paul Haas and Cattleya Concepcion of the George Mason law library also were instrumental in helping secure research materials.

A number of scholars reviewed and critiqued substantial parts of the manuscript or offered valuable suggestions, including Bruce Ackerman, Jack Balkin, Will Baude, David Bernstein, Josh Blackman, Yun-Chien Chang, Eric Claeys, Steve Eagle, James Ely, Richard Epstein, Rick Hills, Julia Mahoney, Michael McConnell, Yxta Murray, Michael Rappaport, and two anonymous reviewers. They helped save me from many errors.

I should also acknowledge other scholars and audience members who provided comments and suggestions when I presented parts of the manuscript at the University of San Diego Law School Originalism Works-in-Progress Conference, the New York University/University of Vermont Takings Conference, the Oklahoma City University School of Law, the law faculty at Zhenghzou University in China, and the Unirule Institute of Economics in Beijing.

Christopher Rhodes of the University of Chicago Press improved the manuscript in numerous ways and provided invaluable support for this project from the first day when he took over as its editor. I am also grateful to David Pervin, who initially endorsed the book proposal for publication by the Press.

David Boaz and Ilya Shapiro of the Cato Institute also offered valuable editorial suggestions. I am grateful to them and to Cato generally for their support of this project.

At George Mason University, Dean Daniel Polsby and my other law school colleagues provided a wonderful atmosphere for research and writing. GMU's Law and Economics Center contributed important financial assistance. My assistant Katherine Hickey helped address a variety of logistical issues.

The Saint Consulting Group deserves thanks for allowing me to use polling data from their 2005 and 2006 Saint Index surveys, and particularly for agreeing to include two questions about post-*Kelo* eminent domain reform in their 2007 survey. Nathaniel Persily generously shared with me polling data on public attitudes toward *Kelo* from his 2009 Knowledge Networks survey on public attitudes on constitutional issues, coauthored with Stephen Ansolabehere.

Journalist and photographer Jackson Kuhl deserves credit for permitting me to reprint his March 2011 photo of one of the feral cats residing on the condemned New London properties.

Several academic journals granted permission to reprint parts of articles previously published by them. Portions of "Controlling the Grasping Hand: Economic Development Takings After Kelo," 15 *Supreme Court Economic Review* 183 (2007), were included in chapters 3, 4, and 8; parts of "The Limits of Backlash: Assessing the Political Response to Kelo," 93 *Minnesota Law Review* 2100 (2009), were incorporated into chapters 5 and 6; parts of "The Judicial Reaction to *Kelo*," 4 *Albany Government Law* 1 (2011) were included in chapter 7; excerpts from "Federalism and Property Rights," 2011 *University of Chicago Legal Forum* 53 (2011), were included in chapters 4 and 8.

As always, my greatest debt is to my wife Alison. The dedication to this book is a far from adequate recognition of her amazing support over the course of many months of work on this project.

Last but not least, Alison and I wish to acknowledge the invaluable insight and abundant good cheer provided by our golden retriever Willow. Her skillful and unrelenting efforts to appropriate "abandoned" burgers for public use have done much to enhance our understanding of property rights.

Introduction

Our Constitution places the ownership of private property at the very heart of our system of liberty. — Barack Obama[1]

The right to private property is a central part of the American constitutional tradition and of our political culture. Politicians, judges, business leaders, activists, and ordinary citizens all claim to support it—at least in principle. But for many decades, federal courts—and especially the Supreme Court—have given constitutional property rights far less protection than that routinely granted to other constitutional rights. To a large extent, they have left those rights at the mercy of the very government officials that they are supposed to protect us against. This trend was usually tolerated and sometimes actively supported by politicians in both parties and by influential business interests. And, despite occasional protest, it was for many years largely ignored by the general public. Nowhere was the low status of constitutional property rights more clear than in the court's and society's toleration of the government's use of eminent domain to take private property and transfer it to other private interests, on the theory that such policies might provide often vague and uncertain benefits to the public.

In *The Wealth of Nations,* Adam Smith famously argued that private property and decentralized market transactions generate prosperity as if "by an invisible hand."[2] The use of eminent domain to promote "economic development" is based on the exact opposite assumption: that resources will often fail to generate as much wealth as they should unless their allocation is controlled by government. Instead of the invisible hand of the market, eminent domain relies on the grasping hand of the state. Over the last century, state and local governments have greatly expanded their use of that grasping hand. The expansion was significantly facilitated by judicial decisions that reinterpreted state and federal constitutions to allow the condemnation of private property for almost any purpose.

Kelo and the State of Constitutional Property Rights

The contradiction between our supposed devotion to constitutional property rights and the federal courts' reluctance to enforce them was laid bare to much of the public by the Supreme Court's 2005 decision in *Kelo v. City of New London*,[3] the subject of this book. The Court ruled that it was permissible for the government to condemn private property and transfer it to other private parties in order to promote "economic development," despite the fact that the Fifth Amendment's Public Use Clause permits takings only for "public use."[4] So long as the government paid "fair market value" compensation, it could take private property for almost any purpose that might create some sort of public benefit. The Court therefore upheld the condemnation of fifteen residential properties in order to facilitate a private development project in New London, Connecticut.

Ironically, the Court's ruling in *Kelo* came at a time when protection for property rights was experiencing a modest revival in the federal judiciary and a more significant one at the state level. The very fact that *Kelo* was a close 5-4 decision was itself an important sign of change. Twenty or thirty years earlier, the outcome would probably have been far more lopsided, perhaps even a unanimous victory for the government. Justice Sandra Day O'Connor, author of the principal dissent in *Kelo*, had previously written a leading decision where a unanimous Court had allowed government to condemn property for almost any reason "rationally related to a conceivable public purpose."[5] As we shall see, even the majority opinion in *Kelo* was slightly more protective of property owners than previous precedent, which had already largely gutted the Public Use Clause as a meaningful constraint on takings.[6]

Even so, by holding that government could condemn property for virtually any "public purpose," without having to provide any substantial evidence that the supposed public purpose would actually be achieved,[7] *Kelo* perpetuated the Court's long-standing failure to enforce the Public Use Clause of the Fifth Amendment and the more general second-class status of constitutional property rights. While the Court ruled that the clause gives property owners a right not to have their property taken for other than a "public use," it left the definition of "public use" almost entirely up to state and local governments.

Few, if any, other rights protected by the Bill of Rights have been so completely left to the tender mercies of the very governments that they are intended to protect us against. As Justice Clarence Thomas put it in his dissenting opinion, federal courts protect individual rights "when the issue is only whether the government may search a home. Yet today the Court tells us that we are not to 'second-guess the City's considered judgments,' . . . when the issue is, instead, whether the government may take the infinitely more intrusive step of tearing down . . . homes. . . . Though citizens are safe from the government in their homes, the homes themselves are not."[8]

The aftermath of *Kelo* was in some ways even more striking than the decision itself. The ruling led to an unprecedented political backlash. Polls showed that over 80 percent of the public disapproved of the Court's ruling, and it was also denounced by politicians, activists, and pundits from across the political spectrum.[9] In the years following the decision, both the federal government and forty-five states passed new laws limiting the using of eminent domain. No other Supreme Court decision has ever led to such a broad legislative reaction. And, arguably, none has been so widely unpopular. The decision was also negatively received by most of the state Supreme Courts that have considered whether *Kelo* should served as a guide to the interpretation of their state constitutions' public use clauses, many of which have wording similar to the federal one.[10]

At the same time, however, many of the new state laws supposedly limiting the use of eminent domain turn out to impose few or no genuine constraints on governments' power to condemn property. The *Kelo* backlash led to significant gains for property rights but not nearly as many as first appears.

Moreover, many jurists and a substantial majority of constitutional law scholars continue to believe that *Kelo* was rightly decided and that a contrary decision would have been wrongheaded and dangerous. Many academics and land-use planners also contend that *Kelo*-like takings are a valuable tool for alleviating blight and promoting development.

The debate over property rights stimulated by *Kelo* continues and shows no sign of definitive resolution. This work is the first book-length treatment of that debate by a legal scholar.[11] While giving serious consideration to opposing views put forward by many respected jurists and scholars, I conclude that the *Kelo* decision was a major error that the Court should eventually overrule. Both originalist and many "living Constitution" theories of constitutional interpretation point in that direction.

I also argue that stronger judicial enforcement of public use limits on takings has important practical benefits. In many cases, it is the only way to protect poor and politically weak property owners against takings instigated by politically powerful interest groups. The property saved often has great value for its current occupants that goes well beyond its market price. Such is regularly the case with homes, small businesses, houses of worship, and other types of property that are often targeted by economic development and blight condemnations.

Far from being essential to development, *Kelo*-style condemnations often harm communities more than they benefit them. By destroying homes, small businesses, schools, and other preexisting uses of land, and by undermining the security of property rights, economic development takings routinely destroy more economic value than they create. As we shall see, such has been the fate of the Fort Trumbull neighborhood in New London, where the condemned land still lies empty some ten years after the Supreme Court ruled that the homes that once stood there could be taken as part of what Justice John Paul Stevens's majority opinion called a " 'carefully considered' development plan" intended to boost the local economy.[12] Most of the time, private property rights and economic development are not competing values, but mutually reinforcing ones. A major lesson of modern development economics is that secure property rights are an essential building block of long-term growth.[13]

This book does not attempt to provide a comprehensive theory of constitutional property rights. It also does not examine all aspects of the Takings Clause of the Fifth Amendment, which states that "nor shall private property be taken for public use, without just compensation."[14] For example, I do not address the question of what kinds of government restrictions on the use of property qualify as "takings" that require compensation under the amendment.[15] Instead, I use the *Kelo* case as a vehicle for examining the more limited but still vital issue of what kinds of takings are forbidden by the federal Constitution because they are not for a "public use."

To avoid terminological confusion, I will use the term "Takings Clause" to refer to the takings provisions of the Fifth Amendment as a whole, including the requirement of just compensation for takings of private property and the requirement that any taking be for a public use. I utilize

"Public Use Clause" to specifically indicate the prohibition against takings that are not for a public use.

Outline of the Book

Chapter I describes the origins of the *Kelo* case. It briefly tells the story of how the use of eminent domain for a development project in a small Connecticut city led to a case that reached the Supreme Court and became a national sensation. I do not attempt anything close to a complete retelling of every aspect of the Fort Trumbull story.[16] But it is important to understand why the New London authorities sought to condemn the property in question, why the owners decided to resist, and how they were able to continue the fight all way to the Supreme Court.

The New London Development Corporation, a government-sponsored nonprofit agency granted the power of eminent domain by the city, sought to condemn the properties because they genuinely believed that it would benefit the community to transfer the land to a private developer who might then build new office space and other facilities that might promote economic development in the area. At the same time, however, the nature of the plan was greatly influenced by Pfizer, Inc., which hoped to benefit from the condemnation, and with which NLDC leaders had close ties.

Most accounts of the *Kelo* litigation and other takings cases focus on those property owners who choose to resist condemnation and fight the issue in court, while largely ignoring those who "voluntarily" choose to sell under threat of eminent domain rather than resist. But it is also important to consider the latter. In many cases, their decision was anything but genuinely voluntary. New London authorities used a variety of pressure tactics to compel owners to give up their land without a fight.

Seven of the targeted property owners nonetheless chose to resist the takings. They rejected the NLDC's offers because they preferred to keep their land, and believed that the process by which the condemnations were decided on and implemented was unjust. Despite their dedication and commitment, the resisters would almost certainly have had to give in quickly if not for the intervention of the Institute for Justice, a libertarian public interest law firm with a long-standing commitment to property rights issues. It was IJ's involvement that enabled the targeted owners to contest the takings in state court and in the court of public opinion, and ultimately to reach the federal Supreme Court.

Chapter 2 steps back from the immediate circumstances of *Kelo* and traces the process by which we got to a point where most experts believed that the federal courts would not and should not provide effective protection for the *Kelo* plaintiffs and others like them. At the time of the Founding, the dominant view was that there are strict limits to the power of government to condemn property for transfer to private interests. This was even more clearly the case at the time the enactment of the Fourteenth Amendment made the Bill of Rights—including the Fifth Amendment—applicable against state government in 1868.

Although expert opinion was far from unanimous, the majority of state supreme court decisions of the era ruled that "public use" encompassed only condemnation of property for government-owned facilities or private ones that the general public had a legal right to utilize, such as common carriers or public utilities. Leading nineteenth-century legal treatise writers, such as Michigan Supreme Court Justice Thomas Cooley, held similar views. In addition, allowing states to condemn property for any purposes they wanted was profoundly antithetical to the main reason why the framers of the Fourteenth Amendment sought to apply the Takings Clause to the states in the first place: the fear that hostile southern state governments would otherwise violate the property rights of African Americans and white Unionists in the south.

Late nineteenth and early twentieth century federal court decisions were also largely consistent with a narrow view of "public use." This point is much misunderstood, because both the *Kelo* Court and some academic commentators have mistakenly conflated "public use" decisions with cases where takings were reviewed under the Due Process Clause of the Fourteenth Amendment. In the early twentieth century, the Supreme Court had not yet concluded that the Fifth Amendment applies to state governments. So cases challenging state takings in federal court could only proceed on the basis of claims that they violated the Due Process Clause's prohibition on state action depriving individuals of "life, liberty, or property" without "due process of law."[17] The early twentieth-century Court was often deferential to the states in assessing such claims. But it was much less deferential in assessing federal government takings, to which the Fifth Amendment did apply.

By the mid-twentieth century, however, the Supreme Court had reinterpreted the Public Use Clause as allowing almost any condemnations authorized by the legislature. This change reflected the devaluing of property rights brought on by the rise of Progressive and New Deal ideology, and the experience of the Great Depression. The new consensus on public use was not seriously challenged for many years. Nonetheless, the previous history suggests there is a strong originalist case for a less deferential judicial approach to public use issues. Scholars and jurists who believe that the Constitution should be interpreted in accordance with its original meaning at the time of enactment should be sympathetic to the idea of overturning *Kelo*.

Chapter 3 explores the real-world effects of a broad interpretation of "public use," which gives free rein to economic development takings and "blight" condemnations. Such condemnations have allowed politically influential interest groups to forcibly displace hundreds of thousands of people, most of them poor or politically weak. In addition, they often create more harm than benefit from the standpoint of promoting economic development. Some blight and economic development takings might be defensible on the grounds that they are needed to overcome "holdouts" who would otherwise block beneficial development projects. On the whole, however, they tend to destroy far more than they create.

The real-world effects of economic development and blight condemnations suggest that there is a strong "living Constitution" case for overruling *Kelo*, as well as an originalist one. Many judges and legal scholars who reject originalism have good reason for rejecting *Kelo* as well.

There are a number of different variants of living Constitution theory, not all of which have the same implications for public use doctrine. But some of the most influential versions emphasize the need to use judicial review to protect groups that lack influence in the political process, especially when they are threatened with severe harm by government policy.[18] Others emphasize the need to adjust judicial doctrine to modern conditions by taking due account of new information and societal change, much as courts make similar adjustments in common law cases.[19] Under either or both of these approaches, there is a strong argument for enforcing tighter limits on economic development takings and blight condemnations. Such takings have seriously harmed the poor, racial minorities, and the politically weak. And modern experience increasingly suggests that they cause more harm than good and that the political process cannot control them on its own.

There is also a strong case against *Kelo* from the standpoint of "popular constitutionalism," the theory which holds that constitutional interpretation should be influenced by public opinion and social movements;[20] few if any Supreme Court decisions have generated as much sustained public opposition as *Kelo*. Similarly, there is a strong living constitution argument against *Kelo* based on Ronald Dworkin's influential view that the Constitution should be interpreted in light of liberal moral theory.[21]

In chapter 4, I consider the reasoning of the Supreme Court's majority, concurring, and dissenting opinions in *Kelo*. While the decision was in line with existing precedent, it had few other virtues. Much of its reasoning is flawed, internally contradictory, or fails to take account of the way eminent domain functions in the real world.

Surprisingly, even Justice John Paul Stevens, author of the Court's opinion has admitted that his ruling was in part based on an "embarrassing to acknowledge" error: conflating nineteenth- and early twentieth-century Due Process Clause cases with Public Use Clause precedents.[22] While Stevens continues to believe the outcome in *Kelo* was justified on other grounds, his admission undercuts the claim that the ruling was required by adherence to "a century" of precedent.[23] Justice Anthony Kennedy's crucial concurring opinion also has important shortcomings. The dissenting opinions of Justices Sandra Day O'Connor and Clarence Thomas make some important and valid points. But they are not without noteworthy flaws of their own, especially in the case of Justice O'Connor's efforts to reconcile her position in *Kelo* with her own opinion for the Court in the 1984 *Midkiff* case.

Chapter 5 considers the dramatic political reaction to *Kelo*, which generated a wider backlash and more state legislation than almost any other decision in modern Supreme Court history. The massive political and legislative reaction to *Kelo* was an important boost for the cause of property rights. The issue attracted more public attention than ever before, and a number of states passed strong reform legislation, particularly those that enacted it by referendum. But a majority of the new reform laws actually did little or nothing to meaningful constrain economic development takings, despite overwhelming public support for banning them.

In chapter 6, I address the question of why the legislation inspired by public revulsion against *Kelo* was often ineffective. Several factors account for this result. But a particularly important one was widespread political ignorance. Survey data shows that the vast majority of voters had little understanding of the reform laws passed in their states. This enabled legislators to pass off cosmetic reforms as genuine constraints on eminent domain, an opportunity that many were inclined to take so as to simultaneously satisfy both the demands of the public and those of influential interest groups who benefit from relatively unconstrained use of eminent domain. As we shall see, political ignorance also helps account for two other important aspects of the *Kelo* backlash: the fact that it happened at all, and the relatively greater effectiveness of reforms enacted through the referendum process, as opposed to ordinary legislation. The history of the *Kelo* backlash undercuts long-standing claims that judicial intervention is not necessary to ensure protection of constitutional rights that enjoy broad majority support.

Chapter 7 focuses on the judicial reaction to *Kelo* in state and lower federal courts. Although less well known than the high-profile political backlash, the judicial reaction has important implications for the future of property rights. Since *Kelo*, several state supreme courts have considered whether or not that decision's interpretation of the Public Use Clause of the federal Constitution should guide their own interpretations of similar clauses of their respective state constitutions. Overwhelmingly, the answer has been "no." The supreme courts of Ohio, Oklahoma, and South Dakota have all repudiated *Kelo* and endorsed narrower interpretations of public use.[24] Post-*Kelo* state supreme court decisions in several other states have imposed tighter constitutional scrutiny on takings than *Kelo* does, even though they did not directly repudiate it. This reaction is in sharp contrast to the reception that greeted earlier Supreme Court decisions interpreting public use broadly, most notably the 1954 case of *Berman v. Parker*,[25] which was soon adopted by many state courts as a guide to interpreting state public use clauses.

State and federal courts have also struggled to make sense of *Kelo*'s admonition that "pretextual" takings are unconstitutional, since the government is not "allowed to take property under the mere pretext of a public purpose, when its actual purpose was to bestow a private benefit."[26] The *Kelo* Court was extremely vague on the question of how judges are to distinguish a pretextual condemnation from a legitimate one. Since 2005, state and federal decisions have come up with at least five different approaches to this issue. Each of them has notable shortcomings. Eventually, the division of judicial opinion on this issue will probably have to be resolved by the Supreme Court. It could well be the vehicle for bringing the Public Use Clause back to the high court once again.

In chapter 8, I consider some possible strategies for alleviating eminent domain abuse. Scholars and others have proposed a variety of ways to curb harmful and inefficient takings without categorically banning blight and economic development condemnations. These include increasing the compensation paid to property owners whose land is taken, subjecting such condemnations to "heightened scrutiny," giving homes greater protection against takings than that extended to other property owners, and giving local communities a stronger say in condemnation decisions.

Many of these reform proposals have merit. But a categorical ban on economic development and blight condemnations is still likely to be better than any of them. Some of the proposed alternative reforms might also have unanticipated negative side effects. For example, increasing compensation too much could lead politically influential property owners to actually lobby for the condemnation of their land.

In contrast to critics who argue that a ban on economic development and blight condemnations goes too far, some contend that it is likely to do little good because it does not go far enough, thereby enabling government to engage in much the same kinds of abuses by other means. I contend that such criticisms are too pessimistic. While banning blight and economic development takings will not end all harmful uses of eminent domain, it would be a major improvement over the status quo.

The conclusion summarizes the key lessons of the *Kelo* story and its implications for the future of constitutional property rights. Although the *Kelo* decision was a significant setback for property rights supporters, it was also an important sign of progress for them. Critics of *Kelo* have not won a definitive victory in the ongoing debate over public use and still face strong opposition. But the question is now a live controversy among scholars, judges, and other experts. Among the general public and a wide range of activist groups, opposition to *Kelo* is both broad and deep. It is one of the rare issues that cuts across racial and ideological lines. Since *Kelo*, it can no longer be said that the revival of public use constraints on takings is a hopeless cause supported only by a few quixotic extremists. The decision and its aftermath also reinforce the important lesson that effective constitutional reform movements require both litigation and political action. The two are mutually reinforcing rather than mutually exclusive strategies for change.

The debate over *Kelo*, property rights, and public use will surely continue. This book is unlikely to definitively resolve a conflict that has continued in various forms for some two hundred years. But I hope it will make a contribution to the discussion.

The Trouble in Fort Trumbull

The case that led to one of the most controversial decisions in modern Supreme Court history arose from unlikely origins in the little-known Fort Trumbull neighborhood of New London, Connecticut. It began with a small group of property owners who decided to resist the condemnation of their homes and other properties as part of a development plan intended to promote economic growth. Under normal circumstances, their case might never have gotten to court at all, as those targeted by eminent domain might not have had the time, energy, and resources needed to fight a prolonged legal battle. If it nonetheless had resulted in litigation, it could easily have ended at the state level in a decision that would have attracted little attention beyond Connecticut.

That the case became nationally famous was due to the dogged perseverance of the property owners whose land was threatened, the intervention of a major public interest law firm, and what many considered to be the surprising willingness of the Supreme Court to reopen an issue that expert opinion believed to be long settled: the power of the government to condemn private property for purposes of transferring it to other private owners. The seemingly local conflict that began in Fort Trumbull would ultimately trouble the conscience of an entire nation.

The history of the Fort Trumbull takings has already been effectively recounted in an excellent book by journalist Jeff Benedict.[1] But Benedict's main interest was in telling the story on the ground rather than exploring the constitutional and policy questions raised by the case. This chapter builds on his work, emphasizing those points that are most relevant to the broader issues that were eventually implicated by the Supreme Court's decision.

Bulldozing a Path to Prosperity

The Fort Trumbull peninsula of New London, Connecticut had once been a moderately prosperous area. But the area's economy was heavily dependent on the Naval Undersea Warfare Center located on the peninsula. It began to fall on relatively hard times in the 1990s around the time the center was closed as a result of post–Cold War defense cuts in 1995.[2] Both area residents and city officials hoped to revitalize the region.

Despite the difficult economic conditions, some residents—including those who later played a major role in the *Kelo* case—believed that Fort Trumbull could recover and that it remained an attractive place to live and do business. Richard Beyer, who had grown up in New London, bought two small properties in Fort Trumbull in 1994, in which he and a business partner then invested a substantial amount of money to refurbish them for use as rental units.[3] Although he acknowledges that economic conditions were difficult, Beyer believed that "without question," the area had potential, so much, in his view, that "[y]ou really can't lose" by investing there.[4] Bill Von Winkle, another future *Kelo* plaintiff, had a similar story. He too had grown up in the area, and purchased several properties to refurbish as rental units in the 1990s, and also lived in one of them for a time.[5] All told, he had owned property in the area for twenty-four years, and had a total of twelve apartment rental units, a commercial building, and a restaurant.[6] At the time the *Kelo* condemnations began, he had recently spent some $300,000 on renovations.[7]

Susette Kelo, the EMT who became nationally famous because her name was listed first among the plaintiffs in the Supreme Court case, bought a home in Fort Trumbull in 1997.[8] Although the house needed work, she fell in love with its impressive "water view" and what she called its "pizzazz."[9] This was the home that later became famous as the "little pink house" that became an iconic image of the struggle over the Fort Trumbull condemnations.[10] Byron Athenian, owner of an autobody shop, had purchased a house in the same area in the late 1980s, where he lived with his family, including three children.[11] He too liked the area and did not wish to move.

Others had lived in Fort Trumbull for many years and had deep attachments to the community. Pasquale and Margarita Cristofaro, an elderly Italian American couple, had purchased a house in Fort Trumbull in 1972, after their previous residence had been condemned as part of

FIGURE I.I Susette Kelo's famous "little pink house." (Credit: Photo by Isaac Reese, 2004. Courtesy of Institute for Justice.)

FIGURE I.2 The Cristofaro house. (Credit: Photo by Isaac Reese, 2004. Courtesy of Institute for Justice.)

an urban renewal taking.[12] The Cristofaros, whose son Michael spoke for them in the *Kelo* litigation, were dead set against losing yet another house to eminent domain.[13] By the late 1990s, the elder Cristofaros had moved to a different location, though they continued to own the house, which was now occupied by Michael's elder brother and his family. He had recently retired after twenty-three years of service in the U.S. Air Force, and, according to his brother, "hope[d] that this was his last move and [he] would finally be able to settle down."[14]

Matthew Dery came from a family that had owned property in Fort Trumbull since 1890.[15] As of the late 1990s, they owned four houses in the area, one in which Dery lived with his family; two rental units; and one where Dery's elderly parents, Charles and Wilhelmina, lived.[16] Now in her eighties, Wilhelmina Dery had been born in that house in 1918, had never lived elsewhere, and ardently wished to continue living there for as many years as she had left.[17]

While the future *Kelo* plaintiffs liked living in the Fort Trumbull area and believed it was a good community, they also recognized that it had significant economic problems in the wake of the closure of the Naval Undersea Warfare Center. Richard Beyer, for example, told me that there was "a lot of negativity" in the air about the local economy in the 1990s and that "nothing was being done" to improve it.[18] In addition to the area's general economic doldrums, a nearby old city-owned sewage plant periodically emitted a terrible odor that annoyed many residents.[19]

New London city officials also recognized the economic difficulties the area faced. They hoped to revitalize it, as well as the city in general. In 1997, they reestablished the New London Development Corporation, which the Supreme Court would later describe as a "private nonprofit entity established . . . to assist the City in planning economic development."[20] The NLDC would ultimately produce the plan that resulted in the Fort Trumbull condemnations.

The NLDC was reestablished after a period of dormancy, under the leadership of a new president, Claire Gaudiani, an academic and president of Connecticut College with a long history of involvement in philanthropic and social justice causes.[21] The NLDC's resuscitation occurred in large part at the behest of the administration of Republican Connecticut Governor John Rowland. The Republican administration hoped to increase its political support by promoting economic development in overwhelmingly Democratic New London, but wanted to do it by working through an agency that was not controlled by the City's Democratic elected government, which was generally hostile to the governor.[22] The administration recruited Gaudiani to become the new president of the NLDC because of her prestige as the president of the area's most prominent academic institution, her leadership skills, and her interest in community development.[23]

Although this was not the reason for her selection to lead the NLDC, Gaudiani was also the wife of Dr. David Burnett, a high-ranking employee of Pfizer, Inc., then the world's largest pharmaceutical producer.[24] Her knowledge of Pfizer led Gaudiani to recruit Pfizer executive George Milne to join the NLDC board, in part because she hoped that having a prominent corporate leader as a member would help attract investment to New London.[25] But Gaudiani also hoped it would facilitate bringing Pfizer to the area, since she knew that the firm was in search of a location where it could build additional office space for a new headquarters, and New London fit the firm's needs.[26]

In the fall of 1997, Gaudiani and Milne initiated discussions with Pfizer urging them to move to a former mill site location that had become available in New London.[27] Pfizer began to show interest, and the firm and the NLDC engaged in further discussions with state officials, led by Peter Ellef, director of the state's Department of Economic Cooperation and Development, and an important adviser to Governor Rowland.[28] As a condition of moving to the New London site, Pfizer insisted that the city and state acquire ninety acres of property in Fort Trumbull—including the former naval research facility and some sixty acres of other property—in order to turn them into upscale housing, office, space, a conference center, a five-star hotel, and other facilities that would be useful to the corporation and its employees who would work in the area.[29] While Pfizer would not be the new owner of the properties in question, it expected to benefit from their redevelopment.

Throughout the course of the *Kelo* litigation, Pfizer and NLDC representatives insisted that the firm was not involved in initiating the effort to condemn and redevelop the Fort Trumbull properties and that it had not made such redevelopment a condition of its decision to open up a new headquarters facility in New London.[30] But evidence introduced at the trial, as well as additional documentation uncovered by an investigative reporter for the New London newspaper *The Day* in late 2005, several months after the Supreme Court's *Kelo* decision was issued, shows that Pfizer "ha[d] been intimately involved in the project since its inception" and that the NLDC development plan and associated condemnations were "a condition of Pfizer's move" to New London.[31]

Documents obtained by *The Day* through state Freedom of Information Act requests show that the NLDC condemnations were undertaken in large part as a result of extensive Pfizer lobbying of state and local officials.[32] Pfizer representatives did indeed demand the redevelopment plan and its associated takings as a quid pro quo for its agreement to build a new headquarters in New London.[33] In the fall of 1997, Pfizer had had a consulting firm prepare a design sketch for the proposed redevelopment of the Fort Trumbull area, which included proposals for the construction of a "high end residential district" and other facilities that would be of use to the firm and its employees.[34] These ideas became the basis of an eventual agreement between Pfizer and state officials under which the firm agreed to establish a new headquarters in New London in exchange for some $118 million in state government subsidies and an additional $73 million allocated for the clearing and redevelopment of the Fort Trumbull area.[35] State officials claimed that the combination of Pfizer's move and the redevelopment project would generate some two thousand new jobs in New London.[36] While much evidence of Pfizer's involvement in the taking was already known before the 2005 revelations, and introduced in court, the 1997 design and its role in the planning process was not.[37]

Most of the specific facilities that Pfizer wanted built could probably have been constructed without eliminating all the houses in the area.[38] But NLDC leaders and Pfizer officials also believed that it was essential to wipe out all the existing buildings for aesthetic reasons. David Burnett, a high-ranking Pfizer employee and husband of Claire Gaudiani, told a reporter that the houses had to be destroyed because "Pfizer wants a nice place to operate," and "we don't want to be surrounded by tenements."[39] Gaudiani herself stated that the houses had to be knocked down because otherwise they would have looked "ugly and dumb."[40] In 2005, NLDC lawyer Ed O'Connell told the *New York Times* that the homes owned by the preexisting owners had to be torn down in order to make way for "housing at the upper end, for people like the Pfizer employees . . . They are the professionals, they are the ones with the expertise and the leadership qualities to remake the city—the young urban professionals who will invest in New London."[41]

Even before these revelations, the resisting New London property owners and other critics of the project believed that it was undertaken for the purpose of benefiting Pfizer. Richard Beyer, for example, thought the whole project was an "organized land grab" undertaken for the firm's benefit.[42] Bill Von Winkle similarly contends that the project was "Pfizer, 100% Pfizer, wanting us out of our homes."[43] Journalist Jeff Benedict, author of by far the most detailed account of the development of the Fort Trumbull project, concluded that Gaudiani, Milne, and other NLDC leaders genuinely believed that the plan would benefit the people of the city.[44]

It is extremely difficult to divine their subjective motivations with any certainty. My own view, however, is closer to Benedict's than Beyer's. Having interviewed Gaudiani, I am convinced that she genuinely believed that she was acting for the public good and was not simply trying to advance the private interests of Pfizer.[45]

But it is nonetheless problematic that a city redevelopment plan that was closely based on Pfizer's demands was produced by an agency headed by the wife of a high-ranking Pfizer employee and including a Pfizer executive on its board. At the very least, this created a potential conflict of interest. And even if Gaudiani and Milne genuinely believed they were acting in the public good, it is hard not to wonder whether their perception of where the public good lies was affected by their respective connections to Pfizer. People have an understandable tendency to believe that their own interests coincide with the public good,[46] and the NLDC leadership may not have been immune to this common pattern.

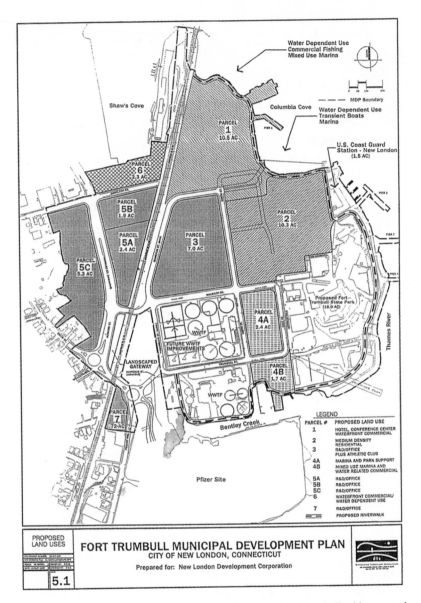

FIGURE I.3 1999 NLDC Municipal Development Plan map of Fort Trumbull, with proposed future uses. The Athenian, Beyer, and Cristofaro properties were on Parcel 3. The Dery, Guretsky, Kelo, and Von Winkle properties were on Parcel 4A. (Source: *Kelo v. City of New London*, No. 104-08, U.S. Supreme Court, Joint Appendix, Vol. I, p. 212.)

In February 1998, Pfizer officially announced its plan to open up the new headquarters in New London. There was great optimism about the potential impact on the community. When the facility officially broke ground in September 1998, Connecticut Governor John Rowland, whose administration had provided crucial support for the venture, called it "without a doubt the most exciting partnership we have seen in the State of Connecticut," one that "will change the landscape of this community for the next 100 years."[47] Claire Gaudiani hailed the event as "the beginning of a whole new day for New London," and George Milne promised that "[t]his is done with the commitment that if we turn this shovel, there'll be no turning back."[48]

The NLDC meanwhile, prepared a municipal development plan that outlined an ambitious proposal to rebuild Fort Trumbull, while meeting Pfizer's requirements.[49] The plan called for the leveling of all the structures in the entire development area and their replacement with a variety of facilities, including a marina, a park, a hotel, office space, and upscale housing.[50] Despite former Mayor Lloyd Beachy's opposition, the New London City Council ultimately approved the plan in a 6-1 vote in January 2000, and authorized the NLDC to use eminent domain to acquire any property in the area whose owners were unwilling to sell.[51]

Condemnation

Even before the city council officially gave it the power to use eminent domain, NLDC representatives began to work to persuade Fort Trumbull property owners to sell their land, often threatening to use eminent domain against them if they refused.[52] Defenders of the New London condemnations argue that most Fort Trumbull residents agreed to sell their property voluntarily. NLDC Director John Brooks claims that "the vast majority of the properties were acquired in a friendly way."[53] It is indeed true that only seven of the ninety property owners in Fort Trumbull ultimately chose to contest the NLDC's efforts to acquire their land.[54] But the voluntariness of the transactions by which the others gave up their property is at the very least extremely questionable.

The threat of eminent domain often played a key role in inducing "voluntary" sales. As New London's lawyer Wesley Horton noted in oral argument at the Supreme Court, "[t]he large share of [the Fort Trumbull property acquisitions] was [voluntary], but of course, that's because there is always in the background the possibility of being able to condemn . . . that obviously facilitates a lot of voluntary sales."[55] When the possibility of using eminent domain to displace Fort Trumbull residents was first publicly discussed in early 1998, numerous residents wrote letters to the state Department of Economic and Community Development indicating that, though they might support redevelopment, they had a strong preference for remaining in their homes. As *The Day* reported in January 1999, "among the letters were comments such as 'I am a senior citizen who has lived here 27 years and am not about to move'; 'I am not interested in selling my home'; and 'I've lived here since 1958 and *I do not want to move.*' "[56]

Interviews with the *Kelo* plaintiffs and other Fort Trumbull property owners confirm that the NLDC used the threat of eminent domain to persuade them to sell "voluntarily."[57] One owner who ultimately agreed to a sale, told me that NLDC representatives had informed her and her husband that "that they could use eminent domain if we did not agree to sell."[58]

The coercion involved in acquiring the "voluntarily" sold properties was not limited to the threat of eminent domain. The *Kelo* plaintiffs and other property owners who were reluctant to sell were also subjected to other forms of pressure.

In late 2000, Bill Von Winkle was sent a letter by the NLDC claiming that it now owned his property and that his tenants' rent payments should be turned over to the NLDC. A few days later, NLDC representatives entered one of his buildings, forced the tenants to leave, and padlocked the doors in order to prevent them from returning, despite the cold winter weather.[59] Von Winkle recalls that the NLDC "evicted [the tenants] physically," and "put people in the street with their socks with no shoes."[60] The NLDC also "put cement barriers in front of the house that made it impossible to rent."[61]

Richard Beyer's tenants were handed eviction notices by city officials and were repeatedly harassed by police officers and other city employees. Some chose to leave because they "wanted to live their life peacefully."[62] Matthew Dery recalls that city employees demolished the already sold building behind his house in a way that caused its wall to collapse onto his garage, thereby destroying it.[63] Michael Cristofaro told me that he and his parents were repeatedly "harassed" by NLDC representatives, including by means of "constant telephone calls late at night" that he believes were intended to intimidate the family.[64]

Susette Kelo remembers similar incidents. "Every day," she said, "we were pressured" to leave. "The wolves were at our door . . . They did everything they could possibly do" to force reluctant homeowners to sell.[65] On one occasion, Byron Athenian arrived at home and discovered that dump trucks had "unloaded tons of dirt in the street right in front of his house," making it impossible for him to move his handicapped granddaughter's wheelchair from the house to the road and creating an overwhelming cloud of dust that covered the inside of his house.[66] Bill Von Winkle stated that the harassment "went on for seven years on a daily basis."[67]

Some of those property owners who did agree to sell were subjected to similar pressures. Marguerite Marley told me that her family, too, was harassed and that neighbors' homes were "broken into." They found the experience "intimidating" and ultimately agreed to sell in part because of such tactics.[68] When they finally did sell, on a Friday, city officials shut off the utilities by Monday, even though they had given the family a week to move.[69]

A 2002 *Wall Street Journal* article recounted interviews with several elderly residents who ended up selling despite the fact that they preferred to stay.[70] One bitterly lamented that he was forced to leave an area where he had lived for seventy-five years; another elderly resident—a World War II veteran—stated that he wished he could have resisted the NLDC, but could not put up a fight because "I am old."[71] Scott Sawyer, a lawyer who later helped file a lawsuit challenging the NLDC plan on environmental grounds, recalled that the residents "were mostly elderly, and they were scared to death."[72] One elderly longtime resident told Sawyer that he did not wish to resist "because I do not have the fight in me."[73] Erika Blescus, a neighbor of Susette Kelo's who had lived in the area for 28 years, agreed to sell after resisting for over a year because, according to *The Day*, she had come to believe that further resistance was likely to be futile.[74]

Michael Cristofaro notes that those who ultimately resisted the takings were all either relatively young themselves or had younger relatives to uphold their interests, as in the case of his own parents and the Derys. Other elderly residents, he believes, did not "have the strength" to fight back and "make it last for 6–7 years."[75]

There is no way to know for sure how many of Fort Trumbull property owners would have been willing to sell their land in the absence of the threat of eminent domain and other coercive tactics used against them.

I do not doubt that at least some would have been willing to sell without any coercive inducement.[76] But it seems likely that at least a substantial minority would have refused to sell at the prices offered. The fact that the NLDC believed that the threat of eminent domain was a necessary tool and that they resorted to other forms of coercion is in itself suggestive.

Whether voluntarily or not, most of the property owners in the Fort Trumbull area eventually agreed to sell their land to the NLDC. But seven refused: Susette Kelo, the Cristofaros, the Derys, Richard Beyer, Bill Von Winkle, Byron Athenian and his mother, and Laura and James Guretsky.[77] A combination of attachment to their properties and anger at the strongarm tactics used by the NLDC led them to dig in their heels and resist. Beyer, for example, said that he chose to fight partly to protect his and his business partner's investment, and partly because he "wasn't going to allow someone to railroad me."[78] The Derys and Cristofaros fought primarily to enable their elderly parents to keep properties that they had owned or lived in for many decades.[79] Between them, the resisters owned fifteen residential properties in the Fort Trumbull area that were scheduled for inclusion in the Municipal Development Plan.[80]

Working together, the seven owners tried to stop the condemnations through political activism and organizing. They managed to attract considerable support from others in the community, including former New London Mayor Lloyd Beachy, who sympathized with them and opposed the use of eminent domain to force them out.[81] Beachy believed that redevelopment should be conducted without forcing people out and that the use of eminent domain was inconsistent with Claire Gaudiani's and the NLDC's stated commitment to "social justice."[82] He also feared that condemnation and demolition of existing homes would result in the construction of "a plastic village that nobody will want to be at."[83] But Beachy, the only member of the city council to vote against authorizing the use of eminent domain, was an exception to the local political establishment's otherwise strong support for the planned condemnations.

Despite lack of support from the city's political leaders, the Fort Trumbull property owners did manage to attract considerable local public sympathy. Their allies formed the Coalition to Save Fort Trumbull Neighborhood to try to prevent the takings.[84] The group used petitions, protests, and other activism to try to force the city and the NLDC forego the use of eminent domain.[85] One of the leaders of the group was Frederick Paxton, a history professor at Connecticut College—the very same college of which

FIGURE 1.4 The Italian Dramatic Club. (Credit: Ilya Somin.)

NLDC chair Claire Gaudiani was the president.[86] Paxton believed that Fort Trumbull could be redeveloped without using eminent domain to force out unwilling homeowners. "It just didn't make any sense," he recalled, "to go through the pain and suffering and trouble of getting people out of their homes who didn't want to leave."[87] The Coalition included other participants from a wide range of backgrounds, and "all over the political spectrum"—including some on the political left who believed it was wrong to force out people for the benefit of politically-connected business interests.[88]

Despite the efforts of the Coalition, the resisting property owners ultimately had little success in influencing the NLDC to change its plan. By contrast, the Italian Dramatic Club, a private men's club located in the redevelopment area, which was a "hot spot for politicians seeking votes and financial support," was able to use its political clout to get an exemption from the threat of eminent domain.[89] The exclusion of the Italian Dramatic Club undercuts claims that the NLDC genuinely needed to take every single property in the development area in order to carry out their development plan.

The Legal Battle

Realizing that they were up against powerful political interests stronger than themselves, the resisting owners began to consider the possibility of fighting the takings in court. They approached various local eminent domain lawyers, all of whom either refused to take the case outright or demanded extremely high fees that the owners could not pay.[90] Richard Beyer retained a local firm, only to have them withdraw later, having told him that "you don't have enough money to fight this."[91] The property owners would likely have had to give up the fight if not for the intervention of the Institute for Justice, a libertarian public interest law firm focused on strengthening judicial protection for individual freedom, with a special focus on property rights and economic liberties.[92] The Institute for Justice was initially contacted by Peter Kreckovic, a local landowner, amateur artist, and historic preservationist who had joined the Coalition.[93] Kreckovic had learned about the Institute from John Steffien, another pariticipant in the group.

IJ's top property rights litigators Dana Berliner and Scott Bullock had long been searching for cases that could promote stronger judicial enforcement of public use constraints on eminent domain. Their most notable early victory was a 1998 case in which the Institute had represented a New Jersey woman who sought to prevent the condemnation of her home for the construction of a casino owned by controversial developer Donald Trump.[94] Berliner and Bullock knew that the Supreme Court had ruled in *Berman v. Parker* (1954) that virtually any interest asserted by the government could qualify as a public use under the Fifth Amendment and reaffirmed that position in *Hawaii Housing Authority v. Midkiff* in 1984.[95] But they believed that the intellectual winds had begun to shift since then and that *Berman* and *Midkiff* were poorly reasoned precedents whose reach the Supreme Court might be willing to restrict if presented with an appropriate case.[96]

Bullock visited New London in August 2000, and met with the resisting property owners and their supporters. He concluded that the dispute was potentially a good opportunity for IJ. The Fort Trumbull case was attractive to IJ for three reasons.[97] First, the NLDC and the city did not claim that the properties they sought to condemn were "blighted." The public purpose for which the land was being condemned was purely "economic development." This potentially differentiated the case from

Berman v. Parker,[98] the key 1954 Supreme Court decision upholding the condemnation of blighted property and endorsing a broad interpretation of "public use." Although the IJ lawyers believed that the Court might be willing to cut back on *Berman's* logic, they doubted that there would be a majority for invalidating blight condemnations as well as economic development takings.

Second, the New London property owners were determined to fight to keep their land and unlikely to sell out in exchange for a higher compensation award. Berliner and Bullock were deeply impressed by their commitment and determination. They needed committed clients who would be willing to litigate the case to the point where it resulted in a published opinion that, in the event of victory, would serve as a valuable precedent protecting property rights in future cases.

Finally, the Institute's lawyers recognized that the New London property owners and their case would play well in the court of public opinion as well as the courtroom. As part of its litigation strategy, IJ had long emphasized the need to win public sympathy for its cause, an approach previously pioneered by liberal public interest groups such as the NAACP.[99] John Kramer, IJ's vice president for communications, notes that a good case should have "compelling clients, very simple facts, and outrageous acts."[100] As homeowners and small businesspeople opposing powerful governmental and corporate interests who had resorted to aggressive pressure tactics, the Fort Trumbull owners fitted that model well. For all of these reasons, IJ decided to take up the New London litigation. In Bullock's words, it was "an ideal public interest case."[101]

All of the resisting property owners are emphatic in their belief that they could never have taken the case as far as they did without IJ's intervention.[102] As Susette Kelo described it, IJ "put us on the map."[103] Bill Von Winkle emphasized that "IJ is absolutely the best at fighting for people's rights" and that "there is no comparable lawyer."[104] It is indeed true that few other lawyers have comparable expertise in litigating public use cases.

Peter Kreckovic of the Coalition to Save Fort Trumbull Neighborhood also emphasizes that the movement to oppose the takings would probably have collapsed without IJ's assistance. In the period just before the Institute became involved in the case, "we were," as he puts it "pretty much at the end of the rope" and "wouldn't have gotten anywhere without [IJ]."[105]

The Institute's lawyers provided topnotch legal representation pro bono. In addition, as a public interest firm with extensive public relations expertise, IJ helped generate extensive sympathetic media attention for the case. Ultimately, the Institute spent some $600,000 to $700,000 litigating the case even before it reached the federal Supreme Court and as much as $1 million in all.[106] It is highly unlikely that the resisting property owners could have come up with that kind of money on their own. Even if they could, they might not have been able to find a conventional law firm able to replicate IJ's performance in both the courtroom and the court of public opinion.

Even with IJ's assistance, the property owners found the long struggle with the city and the NLDC extremely burdensome. The uncertainty of not knowing whether they could keep their homes and other property was difficult to bear. In addition, the litigation was extremely stressful and time consuming. As Susette Kelo put it, "[a]ll we did for eight years, was eat and drink eminent domain . . . that's what we thought about all day long."[107] Matt Dery notes that "[s]ix years with your nuts in a vise is really a long time."[108] Bill Von Winkle recalls that "for seven or eight years, [he] was frozen financially" because he did not have control over the deeds to his property.[109]

Since neither the NLDC nor the property owners were willing to give in, the case went to trial in Connecticut Superior Court, before Judge Thomas J. Corradino. During the trial, the Institute for Justice lawyers presented evidence pointing to Pfizer's role in the takings. This material included statement by James Hicks, executive vice president of a firm that helped develop the New London development plan, indicating that Pfizer was the "10,000 pound gorilla" behind the project.[110] They also contended that the condemnations exceeded New London's powers under state law, that the taking of the seven plaintiffs' properties was not necessary to achieve the goals of the development plan, and that it violated the public use clauses of the federal and state constitutions. For their part, the NLDC and New London contended that the development plan was intended to benefit the public, not Pfizer, that the condemnations were needed to implement it, and that they were entirely constitutional.[111]

On March 13, 2002, Judge Corradino issued a complex 249 page opinion that invalidated the condemnation of eleven of the fifteen properties at issue, while upholding that of the other four.[112] Corradino began by rejecting the Institute for Justice's argument that the transfer of property to a private party for "economic development" is not a public use under the state and federal constitutions; he instead endorsed a broad interpretation of "public use" that encompassed virtually any potential public benefit.[113] Although he conceded that the record on this point was "a mixed one, if not rather confusing,"[114] Corradino ruled that he could not "conclude that the primary motivation or effect of this development plan . . . was to benefit this private entity."[115] But this conclusion was reached without complete knowledge of the full extent of Pfizer's role in shaping the development plan, which only became publicly known in 2005.[116] It is difficult to say whether the 2005 revelations would have made a difference to the judge's conclusion on this point or not.

Corradino nonetheless invalidated the condemnation of the eleven plaintiff-owned properties in the area designated as Parcel 4A on the grounds that the development plan's projected uses for the area "are so vague, shifting, and noncommittal" that the city could not prove that its condemnation was actually necessary to pursue the objectives of the development plan.[117] At various times, NLDC officials had suggested that the area might be used for a museum, for parking, or for "park support," but there was no clear plan to effectively use the property for any of those purposes.[118] The properties owned by Susette Kelo, the Derys, the Guretskys, and Bill Von Winkle were all located in Parcel 4A and therefore had escaped condemnation.[119]

The other three plaintiffs' land, however, was on Parcel 3, which the NLDC planned to transform into office space.[120] Here, Corradino concluded that the plan was specific and detailed enough to prove that condemnation was necessary to carry it out.[121] Byron Athenian, Richard Beyer, and the Cristofaro family had therefore lost.

The split decision did not completely satisfy either side. In the aftermath, the NLDC offered the property owners a settlement under which they promised not to appeal the part of the ruling invalidating the takings on Parcel 4A, if the property owners agreed not to appeal the part upholding the condemnations on Parcel 3.[122] Although NLDC leaders would have preferred to appeal the case, they yielded to pressure from the New London city council, which preferred to settle.[123]

The offer presented the plaintiffs with a difficult decision. Accepting it would mean sacrificing the three members of their group who had suffered a defeat. For the Institute for Justice, it would mean giving up the possibility of getting an appellate decision holding that economic development takings are unconstitutional. But rejecting the deal risked losing the victory that had been achieved for the owners with property on Parcel 4A.

Critics of the Institute for Justice contend that IJ persuaded the Parcel 4A property owners to sacrifice their own interests for the purpose of advancing the Institute's broader property rights agenda.[124] It is indeed true that the IJ lawyers wanted to create a favorable public use precedent and that failure to appeal would have undercut that objective. However, the owners themselves believed that they had little to lose by appealing because the NLDC refused to abjure the use of eminent domain against them in the future.[125]

In the immediate aftermath of the trial court decision, NLDC executive David Goebel stated that the agency still intended to include Parcel 4A in its redevelopment plan and would use eminent domain to acquire it if the owners refused to sell.[126] Since Judge Corradino had invalidated the takings only because the NLDC's plan for Parcel 4A was not specific enough, the possibility existed that it could resort to eminent domain again after revising the plan to make it more precise, or creating a new, more detailed plan.[127] Mayor Lloyd Beachy, who was then serving his second term in the office, urged the NLDC and the city council to "take eminent domain off the table," as did one other member of the city council, former Mayor Ernest Hewett, who had previously supported the use of eminent domain.[128] But this advice was not followed.

Matthew Dery realized that IJ "had their agenda." But he and his family ultimately decided to support the appeal because he recognized that the trial court decision may only have been "a stay of execution."[129] Moreover, after the NLDC's previous actions, he "wouldn't have trusted anything they said."[130] Bill Von Winkle expressed similar sentiments in almost exactly the same words.[131] Dery, Von Winkle, and Susette Kelo, also wanted to appeal out of solidarity with the three property owners who had lost in the trial court, with whom they had already spent years fighting in a common cause together.[132]

For these reasons, the property owners ultimately decided to reject the NLDC offer. However, they and their IJ lawyers responded with a counteroffer under which the Parcel 3 owners would agree not to appeal in exchange for city financing for moving their homes to a new location, and a guarantee that the properties on Parcel 4A would be taken out of the redevelopment plan, and eminent domain would not be used against them in the future.[133] The NLDC and the city refused this counteroffer.[134] Had they been more open to it, it is difficult to say whether the two sides could have agreed on a mutually acceptable formula for the relocation expenses for the Parcel 3 owners.

Ultimately, the two sides could not come to a mutually acceptable agreement. The plaintiffs appealed their case to the Connecticut Supreme Court. For their part, the city and the NLDC appealed their defeat over Parcel 4A.

The Supremes

On March 9, 2004, the constitutionality of the plan was upheld by the Supreme Court of Connecticut in a close 4-3 decision.[135] The majority endorsed the view that "economic development" under private ownership is a permissible public use under the federal and state constitutions.[136] It also upheld the takings on both Parcel 3 and Parcel 4A as being "reasonably necessary" to achieve the goals of the NLDC's development plan under a standard of review that is highly deferential to the decisions of the government.[137]

In a prescient dissent joined by two of his colleagues, Justice Peter Zarella agreed that economic development by private parties might be a legitimate public use. But he emphasized that such takings require "a heightened standard of judicial review . . . to ensure that the constitutional rights of private property owners are protected adequately."[138] This is because

> Economic growth is a far more indirect and nebulous benefit than the building of roads and courthouses or the elimination of urban blight. Indeed, plans for future hotels and office buildings that purportedly will add jobs and tax revenue to the economic base of a community are just as likely to be viewed as a bonanza to the developers who build them as they are a benefit to the public. Furthermore, in the absence of statutory safeguards to ensure that the public purpose will be accomplished, there are too many unknown factors, such as a weak economy, that may derail such a project in the early and intermediate stages of its implementation.[139]

If economic development qualifies as a public use, Justice Zarella believed that courts should police the political process to ensure that the economic development used to justify a taking is actually achieved by it. Otherwise, there would be too great a risk that the taking in question was merely intended to benefit a private interest at the expense of the general public: "[T]he constitutionality of condemnations undertaken for the purpose of private economic development depends not only on the professed goals of the development plan, but also on the prospect of their achievement."[140]

Zarella's dissent went on to conclude that the Fort Trumbull takings failed to meet this standard. At the time of the condemnation, he pointed out, there was no signed development agreement providing for the future exploitation of the condemned property, a circumstance that greatly reduced the chances of actually producing any economic development and made it "impossible to determine whether future development of the area primarily will benefit the public or will even benefit the public at all."[141] The NLDC had selected Corcoran Jennison as the designated development firm for the area, but had not signed any development agreement or even come close to concluding one by the time of the trial.[142] Justice Zarella also pointed out that the proposed development plan imposed few restrictions on the new private owners of the condemned property and flew in the face of market conditions that made it unlikely that the city would be able to reap significant economic benefits from the condemnations.[143] In weighing the expected economic benefits of the plan, the city failed to even consider "the loss in revenue that could result from the relocation of former residents and taxpayers out of the area" or to weigh the loss of $80 million in public funds (mostly from the state government) that had been committed to the project.[144] Zarella's fears that the condemnations would fail to produce the promised development would be amply justified by events.[145]

The majority's decision was in part dictated by its refusal to consider the possibility that the Connecticut state constitution provides stronger "public use" protections against takings than the US Supreme Court's interpretation of the federal Constitution.[146] The majority followed the court's previous practice of refusing to consider the possibility that the state constitution provides more protection for individual rights than a similar provision in the federal Constitution, unless the parties to the case explicitly raise the issue.[147]

It is true that IJ's brief in the state supreme court did not specifically state that the Connecticut constitution provides greater protection for property owners than the federal one. However, much of IJ's argument was explicitly based on state public use precedent, as was also the case with the arguments advanced in Justice Zarella's dissent.[148] In his 2008 book, *The History of the Connecticut Supreme Court*, Wesley Horton—a leading Connecticut attorney who eventually represented New London before the federal Supreme Court—criticized the state supreme court majority for refusing to even consider the possibility that the state constitution provided greater protection than the federal one.[149] As he noted, "[g]iven that the court took well over a year from oral argument to decision, and given that Zarella's dissent reads as it if were resolving a state constitutional question, the court would have avoided the subsequent national controversy if it had asked for modest supplemental briefing and if it had then found merit in the plantiffs' state constitutional claim."[150] Such supplemental briefing might not even have been necessary, given that the two sides had already extensively discussed relevant state court precedents in their original briefs.[151]

Disappointed by their narrow defeat in the state supreme court, the plaintiffs and the IJ lawyers decided to petition the federal Supreme Court to consider the case. Since the Connecticut Supreme Court had ruled that the takings were permissible under the federal Constitution as well as the state one, the federal Supreme Court had jurisdiction to hear the case, should four of the nine justices vote to grant the plaintiffs' petition for certiorari. But the Court only grants a tiny fraction of the thousands of petitions that reach it each year.

To write its brief opposing the property owners' petition for certiorari, New London brought in Wesley Horton, a highly respected appellate lawyer who had advised the city earlier in the litigation. Like his adversaries Berliner and Bullock, Horton had not previously handled a case in the U.S. Supreme Court. But he had argued over one hundred cases in Connecticut's state supreme court and was one of the state's best appellate litigators.[152] In 2001, he had represented a property owner who lost an eminent domain case in the state supreme court, in an unsuccessful effort to persuade the federal Supreme Court consider the issue.[153]

Like most experts, Horton believed it was very unlikely that the Court would agree to hear the case. For this reason, he agreed to write the opposition brief for what was, for a lawyer of his credentials, the modest fee of $10,000.[154] Should the Court take the petition, he committed to handling the case without any additional payment.

My own expectations at the time were similar to Horton's. Having followed the case from a distance, I too doubted that the Supreme Court would be willing to take it. Because the Court had long endorsed an extremely broad view of public use similar to that embraced by the Connecticut Supreme Court in *Kelo*,[155] I thought it unlikely that it would wish to reconsider it. That expectation was reinforced by the fact that

Justice Sandra Day O'Connor, a key swing voter on property rights and other issues, was also the author of the Court's ruling in *Hawaii Housing Authority v. Midkiff*, a 1984 Supreme Court decision reaffirming the broad interpretation of public use.[156] To the surprise of many, the Court nonetheless granted the petition for certiorari on September 28, 2004. IJ and its clients had a new lease on life, and Horton would have to do a lot more work to earn his $10,000.

The Supreme Court's decision to take the case attracted a new wave of media and public attention.[157] At the same time, many organizations and activists involved with eminent domain and property rights issues began to realize that the case was likely to set an important precedent. An unusually high total of thirty-seven amicus curiae ("friend of the court") briefs representing some one hundred different organizations were filed in the Supreme Court case, twenty-five of them on the side of the property owners and twelve supporting New London.[158]

The coalition of amici supporting the property owners included some surprising bedfellows. In addition to conservative and libertarian property rights advocates, there were a number of prominent left of center amici. The NAACP, the Southern Christian Leadership Conference (a historic civil rights organization of mostly African American clergy), the AARP, and the Hispanic Alliance of Atlantic County filed a joint amicus brief emphasizing the negative impact of eminent domain on the poor, minorities, and the elderly.[159] I myself authored an amicus brief on behalf of Jane Jacobs, the legendary progressive urban development theorist who had been a leading critic of blight and economic development takings since the 1960s.[160] Many of the amicus briefs on the other side were filed by organizations representing development planners and state and local governments, such as the American Planning Association, The National League of Cities, the National Council of State Legislatures, and the U.S. Conference of Mayors.[161] These groups had an obvious and understandable interest in minimizing judicial scrutiny of the exercise of their eminent domain authority.

On February 22, 2005, the Supreme Court held oral arguments in *Kelo*, in which the contending lawyers could present their positions before the justices in person. Horton conducted the argument for New London, while Scott Bullock did so on behalf of the plaintiffs. While most Supreme Court cases are decided primarily on the briefs submitted before oral argument, the arguments are closely watched by experts, because they are often an important gauge of the justices' attitudes. So it proved in this case.

The justices asked tough questions of both sides, pressing Bullock on the possibility that his position was not sufficiently deferential to the government and Horton because the economic development rationale for takings seemed to leave no room for meaningful limits on the scope of eminent domain. By far the most widely noted moment in the oral argument occurred when Justice Sandra Day O'Connor asked Horton whether the economic development rationale would allow condemnation of "a Motel 6 [if] a city thinks 'if we had a Ritz-Carlton, we'd get higher taxes.'" Horton answered that that would be "OK."[162] When Justice Antonin Scalia followed up by asking whether "[y]ou can take from A to give to B if B pays more taxes," Horton reiterated his position, stating that such a taking would be permissible if the difference in tax revenue is "a significant amount."[163]

This answer is often seen as a mistake on Horton's part and may have helped cost him Justice O'Connor's vote. O'Connor cited the Motel 6/Ritz Carlton example in her dissenting opinion as an illustration of the unbounded nature of the economic development rationale for takings.[164] Scott Bullock believed that Horton's answer played into the plaintiffs' hands.[165] Michael Cristofaro, who attended the argument, thought that Horton sounded like he "was working for us."[166]

Whether or not it was an error, Horton's answer to this question was carefully planned in advance. He had considered this exact issue in preparing for oral argument and had deliberately decided to concede the point rather than be forced to "spend ten minutes" addressing various potential hypothetical situations in what he feared might be a very difficult attempt to try to draw a line that would impose meaningful public use constraints on takings but would not lead to defeat for his clients.[167] He instead preferred to spend his limited time focusing on "the facts of my case," especially the extent to which the takings were part of a carefully produced development plan organized by a nonprofit entity accountable to the city rather than a proposal put forward by a private developer seeking to advance his or her own interests.[168]

Horton's strategy did ultimately lead to victory. In my view, it is indeed true that there are no meaningful limits to the economic development rationale, and therefore an effort to constrain it would ultimately be futile.[169] Moreover, Horton's emphasis on the extent of New London's planning process would be echoed in the Court's majority opinion.[170] Overall, Horton's approach was probably correct from the standpoint of maximizing his chances of winning. It was a risky but arguably effective "tactical decision" that enabled him to spend his oral argument time focusing on the strong points of his case rather than its main area of weakness.[171] On the other hand, however, the answer may have cost him the support of Justice O'Connor, a key swing voter who—along with Justice Anthony Kennedy—was one of the members of the Court Horton most wanted to persuade.[172] O'Connor's forceful dissent and the closely divided nature of the Court's decision would play a key role in shaking the dominance of the conventional wisdom in favor of broad judicial deference to the political process on public use issues.[173] Moreover, as Horton acknowledges, his Motel 6-Ritz Carlton answer figured prominently in media accounts of the argument,[174] exemplifying the potential for eminent domain abuse inherent in New London's position.

Conclusion

The *Kelo* oral argument was the end of an improbable path by which an initially obscure eminent domain case had reached the U.S. Supreme Court, with the potential to undercut long-standing precedent allowing government to condemn property for almost any reason. Despite the Ritz-Carlton/Motel 6 exchange, many initial reports after the oral argument suggested that the justices were unlikely to rule in favor of the property owners.[175] Wesley Horton came away from the argument believing that he had probably secured what he thought would be Justice O'Connor's decisive vote, though he also believed that the three most conservative justices—Antonin Scalia, Clarence Thomas, and Chief Justice William Rehnquist—would probably vote against him.[176]

Ultimately, the *Kelo* case turned out to be a lot closer than he and many others expected. Although New London won a nail-biting 5-4 victory, the close and controversial nature of the outcome would help undermine the long-standing conventional wisdom that public use constraints on eminent domain were a thing of the past. In the next chapter, we explore how that view became conventional wisdom in the first place.

CHAPTER TWO

From Public Use to Public Purpose

Public use has been a focus of debate for over two hundred years. During the Founding era and most of the nineteenth century, the dominant, though far from uncontested, view was that the power of eminent domain is subject to tight judicially enforceable limits. Beginning in the early twentieth century, the United States moved from a legal regime where the government was often tightly constrained in its ability to take property to one where takings like those in *Kelo* were far from unusual. Gradually, relatively narrow definitions of "public use" were displaced by the doctrine that government could condemn property for virtually any "public purpose," defined broadly to include almost any potential benefit that might be created by a taking.

This chapter traces the history of public use and its implications for modern constitutional interpretation. It starts with attitudes toward public use issues at the time of the Founding, and continues on through the nineteenth century. During those periods, relatively narrow interpretations of "public use" predominated, although opinion was far from unanimous. The mid- to late nineteenth-century view of public use is particularly important, because that was the period when the Public Use Clause of the Fifth Amendment first became applicable to the states, as a result of the adoption of the Fourteenth Amendment in 1868, which "incorporated" the Bill of Rights against state governments. While a number of scholars have surveyed nineteenth-century understandings of public use,[1] surprisingly there has not yet been a study that covers state court decisions in all the states that addressed the issue in the time frame surrounding 1868.[2] Neither has there been one that considers the implications of the 1868 understanding of public use for constitutional interpretation. This chapter helps remedy these gaps in our knowledge.

The evidence for both the Founding era and the period around 1868 is far from unequivocal. But in both cases, the more common view held that there were strict constitutional limits on takings that transfer property to private parties. The most widespread approach to public use was what I refer to as the "narrow view." That approach limits the use of eminent domain to takings for transfer to the government or to a private entity, which has a legal obligation to allow the general public to use the land in question, as in the case of a public utility.

The historical prevalence of the narrow view has important implications for judicial interpretation of public use, at least if that interpretation should be based on original meaning. While originalism is far from the only theory of constitutional interpretation, it does command widespread support. Even scholars and jurists who do not fully embrace it often recognize that original meaning is at least one factor that courts should consider in interpreting the Constitution, even if not the only one.

After considering nineteenth-century interpretations of public use, we will see how federal and state courts began to take a much more deferential approach to takings in the twentieth century, eventually creating a public use doctrine where property could be condemned for almost any reason. Both the federal Supreme Court and most state courts endorsed what I call the broad view of public use, under which eminent domain could be used for virtually any project that might create some sort of benefit to the public. By the time the *Kelo* case arose in the early 2000s, most experts believed that there was little chance that the Fifth Amendment's Public Use Clause would ever again be a meaningful constraint on takings.

Public Use in the Founding Era

The Founders and Property Rights

If there is one issue on which most of the American Founders agreed, it was the importance of protecting private property rights. John Adams emphasized that "Property must be secured or liberty cannot exist."[3] At the Constitutional Convention of 1787, Alexander Hamilton claimed that "one great obj[ect] of Gov[ernment] is the personal protection and security of property."[4] In his famous 1792 essay on "Property," James Madison, the "father of the Constitution" who also went on to author the Takings Clause of the Fifth Amendment,[5] wrote that "Government is instituted to protect property of every sort; as well that which lies in the various rights of individuals, as that which the term particularly expresses. This being the end of government, that alone is a *just* government, which *impartially* secures to every man, whatever is his *own*."[6] In *Federalist* 10, he famously wrote that "the first object of government" is the "protection of different and unequal faculties of acquiring property."[7] In addition to believing that property rights had important instrumental value in promoting prosperity and republican government, most members of the founding generation also believed that they were natural rights valuable for their own sake.[8]

Despite this emphasis on the importance of property rights, there was surprisingly little early discussion of the meaning of the Public Use Clause—or even of the Takings Clause generally—at the time it was enacted and for years thereafter.[9] Indeed, the clause was inserted into the Fifth Amendment primarily because of James Madison's personal initiative at the time the Bill of Rights was being drafted rather than because there was any great public demand for it.[10]

This seeming omission becomes understandable once we recall that the Bill of Rights originally applied only to the federal government. During the Founding era, and for many years thereafter, the dominant view was that the federal government did not have the power to condemn property by using eminent domain in the states.[11] Not until 1875 did the Supreme Court rule that Congress had the power to authorize such takings.[12] Although the federal government still had the authority to take property in the District of Columbia and in federally owned territories, there was relatively little private property in these areas at the time, particularly since federally owned western territories were at the time sparsely settled, and the capital city intended to be established in the District of Columbia had not yet been built. For that reason, nearly all early public use cases arose under the public use provisions of state constitutions, not the federal Fifth Amendment. We therefore have little direct evidence bearing on the question of whether the framers and ratifiers of the Bill of Rights endorsed a narrow or broad interpretation of "public use." But their generally strong concern about the need to protect property rights provides at least some support for the former.

Two well-known 1790's judicial opinions written by Supreme Court justices reinforce that conclusion. In *Vanhorne's Lessee v. Dorrance* (1795), a decision written by Supreme Court Justice William Paterson, while temporarily serving on a lower court (as was common in that era), referred to eminent domain as "a despotic power" that necessarily "exists in every government."[13] But he also emphasized that the power could only be exercised "in urgent cases, or cases of the first necessity" and that "a case of necessity . . . , can never occur in any nation" where the legislature seeks to "take land from one citizen, who acquired it legally, and vest it in another."[14] Paterson did not, however, attempt to definitively resolve the issue of whether government has the power to engage in private-to-private takings, even with compensation. Ultimately, he concludes that, even if the government does have that authority, it must at least pay compensation calculated by neutral arbiters or by a court.[15]

In a separate opinion in the 1798 case of *Calder v. Bull,* Justice Samuel P. Chase wrote that

> [A] law that takes property from A. and gives it to B . . . is against all reason and justice, for a people to entrust a Legislature with *such* powers; and, therefore, it cannot be presumed that they have done it. The genius, the nature, and the spirit, of our State Governments, amount to a prohibition of such acts of legislation; and the general principles of law and reason forbid them. . . . To maintain that our Federal, or State, Legislature possesses such powers, if they had not been expressly restrained; would in my opinion, be a political heresy, altogether inadmissible in our free republican governments.[16]

Calder involved a challenge to a Connecticut legislative resolution granting a new hearing in a probate trial, which the disappointed heirs challenged as a violation of the Constitution's ban on ex post facto laws. Chase raised the issue of A to B transfers as a possible alternative justification for invalidating the new hearing but rejected it on the basis that Calder's heirs had not yet actually acquired a vested property right in their inheritance and therefore could not be dispossessed by it.[17]

While Justice Chase's opinion in *Calder,* like Paterson's in *Vanhorne's Lessee,* did not address an actual eminent domain case,[18] the principles expounded in both seem clearly incompatible with a broad interpretation of public use that allows the use of eminent domain to transfer property from one private individual to another any time some public benefit might potentially be achieved thereby. Both opinions express the common Founding-era view that property rights are natural rights that legislatures are not allowed to override, and that state and federal constitutions at least implicitly incorporate those rights.

That view had its origins in prior English legal thought, such as those of the seventeenth-century political philosopher John Locke, whose views on property rights had a major influence on the American founders.[19] In a famous passage in the *Second Treatise of Civil Government*, Locke wrote that because the protection of natural property rights was one of the purposes of government, the state "cannot take from any Man part of his Property without his own consent," because "I have truly no property in that, which another can by right take from me, when he pleases, against my consent."[20] Locke also argued that exactions necessary for the "maintenance" of government could be imposed on citizens' "estates" with the consent of "the Majority" rather than of each individual.[21] This suggests that taxes and takings of property for use by the government to fulfill its essential functions need only be authorized by elected legislatures. But, although Locke was not completely clear on this point, he apparently believed that the same did not hold true for a generalized power to take property, which requires the "consent" of the property owner, "whatsoever hands" have control of the government—presumably including "hands" elected by the majority.[22]

William Blackstone's highly influential 1765 work *Commentaries on the Laws of England,* which had a major impact on American jurists, reached a similar conclusion much more explicitly and unambiguously. Blackstone emphasized that the law does not allow violations of the right of "private property . . . even for the general good of the whole community."[23] He specifically rejected the idea of takings for transfer to private parties, even if they might benefit the general public. "If," as he put it, "a new road, for instance, were to be made through the grounds of a private person, it might perhaps be extensively beneficial to the public; but the law permits no man, or set of men, to do this without the consent of the owner of the land."[24] By contrast, Blackstone was willing to allow condemnation if the property taken were kept by the state.[25]

Takings for Mill Acts and Private Roads

Despite the founding generation's generally strong commitment to property rights and the suggestive language in *Calder* and *Vanhorne's Lessee*, many scholars believe that the dominant interpretation of public use in the early republic was a broad one, which would allow condemnations for "public benefit . . . of almost any conceivable kind."[26] The main reasons why so many scholars have reached that conclusion is that state governments in the early republic often authorized the condemnation of property for privately owned mills and private roads.[27]

In the age before the rise of modern power sources, such as electricity and petroleum-based fuels, mills that harnessed waterpower were an important source of energy for various purposes. Many states adopted mill acts allowing the condemnation of property for use to build dams that would help mill owners harness the water power they needed.[28] Often, a mill could not be constructed without flooding private property located near the river or stream that was to be dammed, and eminent domain was used to force unwilling owners of such land to transfer their rights to the mill owners.[29] By the late eighteenth century, ten of the thirteen colonies had adopted mill acts allowing the use of eminent domain.[30]

But the widespread adoption of mill acts does not prove that the founding generation accepted a broad view of public use. Mill acts in the colonial era and the early republic usually authorized condemnations only for grist mills that were "generally required to be open to the public for the grinding of corn."[31] The one common feature of virtually all publicly supported mills in that era was that the owner was required to serve the community at a preset price.[32] In that respect, they were roughly analogous to modern public utilities. Even many defenders of the broad interpretation of public use have come to recognize this aspect of early mills.[33] As one of them puts it, "Mill Acts that authorized public mills more resemble the chartering of a utility to perform a public function than the condemnation of land for another citizen's benefit."[34]

In the nineteenth century, as we shall see, some states adopted laws authorizing the condemnation of property for power mills, which—unlike grist mills—were not required to serve the public as a matter of legal right.[35] But that is of much less relevance to the status of public use at the time of the Founding.[36] Moreover, at that point some state courts invalidated laws allowing condemnation for such mills, while others sought to uphold them without endorsing the broad view of public use more generally.[37]

Early laws allowing the condemnation of land for private roads are stronger evidence of the acceptance of a broad view of public use than the early mill acts were. At least apparently, these laws, which dated back to the colonial era in many states, allowed the use of eminent domain to condemn property for the purpose of building private roads to which the general public did not have a right of legal access.[38] Scholars such as Nathan Sales and Lawrence Berger point to these laws as strong evidence that the Founding generation accepted a broad interpretation of public use.[39]

But matters are far more complex than that. Many of the early private road statutes actually required the owners of roads built on condemned land to allow the general public to use them as public thoroughfares. Courts in Delaware, Massachusetts, New Jersey, North Carolina, Pennsylvania, and Vermont eventually interpreted their states' early private road statutes in this way.[40] Such roads were "open to use by the general public as completely as if they were highways, and they consequently formed a part of the general public road system of the state."[41] As an 1847 Delaware Supreme Court decision interpreting that state's long-standing private road legislation put it, "The land is taken for public use, . . . It is a part of the system of public roads; essential to the enjoyment of those which are strictly public; for many neighborhoods as well as individuals would be deprived of the benefit of the public highway, but for outlets laid out on private petition, and at private cost, and which are private roads in that sense, but branches of the public roads and open to the public for the purposes for which they were laid out."[42]

The supreme courts of Georgia and Kentucky eventually upheld the private road statutes on the grounds that they enabled landlocked private owners to perform duties of citizenship such as voting and jury service.[43] Some colonial-era state legislatures also justified private road takings on the theory that they were needed to enable individuals to assemble for mandatory militia service, as well as other civic duties.[44] Condemnation of land for the purpose of enabling individuals to perform public duties is not as fully consistent with a narrow conception of public use as requiring government ownership or use by the public. But neither does it require adoption of the broad view that any use that benefits the public in some way qualifies. If the private individual must have the condemned land to "perform all the duties which are required of him by law,"[45] that can be assimilated to a relatively narrow interpretation of public use that requires government ownership, use by the public, or use by private individuals to perform basic civic duties. Using property to perform civic duties owed could be a "public use" in the sense that the owner is using it to engage in activities specifically mandated by the state and required for the operation of government.

Some scholars contend that the founding generation was willing to let legislatures authorize takings for almost any purpose because they adhered to a "republican" ideology. As described by these writers, republicanism held that the public had a single, undifferentiated interest that would be represented by elected assemblies in such a way as to prevent takings that would benefit narrow interest groups at the expense of the general public.[46]

This is not the place to enter into the long-standing general debate about the extent to which the Founders were influenced by republicanism, with its emphasis on civic virtue, political participation, and the promotion of the common good, as opposed to liberalism, which puts a greater emphasis on individual rights.[47] But even if we concede that many of the Founders were influenced by republicanism and its ideal of a homogenous public interest, it is important to emphasize that many of them were deeply suspicious of democracy, and feared that oppressive majorities, special interests, and government officials posed a threat to property rights. This was a major theme in the political thought of James Madison, the author of the Takings Clause.[48] Many other leading Founders had similar concerns. According to legal historian and political scientist Jennifer Nedelsky, "[a]ll the Framers recognized the dangers of the 'democratic element,' its instability, and its threat to property."[49] As one leading framer, Gouverneur Morris, put it in a speech at the Constitutional Convention, "[e]very man of observation had seen in the democratic branches of the State Legislatures, . . . [and] in Congress changeableness. In every department excesses ag[ainst] personal liberty, private property, & personal safety."[50]

Some, including Morris, feared not just that the poor would threaten the property rights of the wealthy, but that the latter would use their political influence to threaten the property and other rights of the common people.[51] Moreover, even to the extent that the founding generation was generally republican in outlook and therefore prone to defer to legislatures, it is likely that the Fifth Amendment Takings Clause was an exception to this trend, representing a more liberal view of individual rights and a more skeptical view of the democratic process.[52]

In sum, we have little specific evidence about the exact definition of "public use" that predominated in the founding era. But leading members of the founding generation did place tremendous general emphasis on protecting property rights, which they regarded as a natural right as well as a beneficial institution. Founding-era views on property rights were also influenced by British political and legal theorists, such as Locke and Blackstone, both of whom explicitly linked natural property rights with opposition to takings for private parties. Many of the founders also feared that an unconstrained democratic process posed grave dangers to property rights, both because tyrannical majorities might threaten property, and because the wealthy could use the political system to promote their own narrow interests. This set of beliefs seems incompatible with an approach to public use that would allow government to condemn property for almost any purpose. Supreme Court justices' opinions in *Calder* and *Vanhorne's Lessee* strongly suggest that this general outlook indeed translated into opposition to takings that transfer property to private parties without requiring some sort of public access.

Founding-era evidence does not definitively prove that the general understanding of public use at the time endorsed the narrow interpretation rather than the broad one. But the former is far more compatible with the available evidence and the dominant understanding of property rights at the time than the latter.

Public Use in the Nineteenth Century

While there was very little litigation on public use issues during the Founding era, state courts issued numerous rulings on the subject throughout the nineteenth century. The period from the early 1800s to the late nineteenth century was a crucial one in the development of the debate over public use. Beginning in 1776, when Pennsylvania and Virginia became the first states to include public use clauses in their state constitutions,[53] almost every state eventually adopted similar clauses, usually with phraseology very close to that of the federal Fifth Amendment. Unlike the federal Public Use Clause, these state public use clauses generated a great deal of litigation during the nineteenth century.

The results of that litigation are historically important in themselves and also as a window on the understanding of public use at the time of the enactment of the Fourteenth Amendment in 1868, the event that made the Bill of Rights applicable to the states. Until that time, the Takings Clause of the Fifth Amendment did not constrain condemnations by state and local governments, because the Bill of Rights was assumed to apply only against the federal government—a conventional wisdom endorsed by the Supreme Court's well-known unanimous 1833 decision in *Barron v. City of Baltimore*.[54] The case involved an attempt to invoke the just compensation provision of the Takings Clause against a local government by John Barron, the owner of a Baltimore wharf who claimed that he was entitled to compensation for city street construction that had created mounds of sand and earth near his wharf, making it impossible for most ships to dock there.[55]

The conventional wisdom on nineteenth century state public use doctrine is that it was highly inconsistent, with great divergence between different state courts. As Lawrence Berger puts it in a much-cited article on the history of public use, "by the beginning of the twentieth century, doctrine was in a shambles and predictability of result at a minimum."[56] A well-known anonymous 1949 *Yale Law Journal* comment similarly concluded that, "[b]y the beginning of the present century, there had developed a massive body of case law, irreconcilable in its inconsistency, confusing in its detail, and defiant of all attempts at classification."[57]

The conventional wisdom is partly accurate. There was indeed considerable divergence over the interpretation of public use clauses in different states. But if we systematically consider all of the states where courts issued opinions on the issue, a different picture emerges. While a significant minority of state supreme courts dissented, a substantial majority endorsed the narrow view of public use over the broad one. The few federal Supreme Court decisions that touch on the subject also tended to support the narrow view. The narrow interpretation of public use was also endorsed by the two leading treatises on the subject, those of John Lewis,[58] and Michigan Supreme Court Justice Thomas Cooley, who was also a prominent law professor and legal scholar.[59]

Nineteenth-Century State Court Interpretations of Public Use

By the late 1870s, a period that is relevant because it includes the era when state court decisions were made by jurists from the generation that witnessed the enactment of the Fourteenth Amendment, a total of twenty-five state supreme courts had issued decisions addressing the definition of "public use" under their state constitutions. Of these, sixteen adopted the narrow view of public use or something close to it, and nine adopted the broad one. This history is summarized in table 2.1.

I count a state supreme court as having adopted the narrow or broad interpretation if it issued a decision indicating that that approach is the general rule to be followed in public use cases during the period up to 1877, unless it later adopted a different standard during the same time period, in which case the later decision predominates. One state (Alabama) adopted the narrow definition in an 1859 decision without overruling an earlier 1832 case that adopted the broad one, though it sought to reinterpret it.[60]

Many of the cases adopting the narrow definition of public use involved challenges to mill acts, which are discussed later in this chapter. Others addressed condemnations for privately owned roads,[61] or for private railroads. As the Delaware Supreme Court ruled in 1839, railroad takings could only be permitted if the railway is "designed for use by the public," which is given a right to use the railway "by all upon the same terms."[62]

Most of the decisions endorsing a broad definition upheld mill acts.[63] Broad public use decisions in western states involved condemnations for natural resource extraction industries such as mining,[64] or irrigation and drainage.[65]

Two states, Mississippi and Pennsylvania, adopted highly equivocal approaches to "public use," from which I find it virtually impossible to determine whether they endorsed the broad view or the narrow one. An 1845 Pennsylvania Supreme Court decision upheld the condemnation of property for a public landing.[66] The court noted that "The right of eminent domain does not authorize the government to take the property of the citizen for the mere purpose of transferring it to another."[67] In order to be constitutional, a taking must "must be for the use of the public, to be determined in the first place by the legislature."[68] But the court did not explain whether "for the use of the public" means a property that the public have a legal right to use, or merely one that might potentially benefit the public in some way. Surprisingly, later nineteenth-century Pennsylvania decisions failed to resolve this ambiguity until the state supreme court embraced the narrow view in 1891.[69]

Mississippi rulings from this period were similarly ambiguous. *Brown v. Beatty,* a much-cited 1857 state supreme court decision ruled that eminent domain could be used to condemn property and transfer it to a private corporation in order to build "public works, intended to promote the interests of the community" and that such public uses can be undertaken by "[a] corporation created by the legislature with a view to the construction of a work of public utility."[70] But the ruling failed to explain whether "public works" and "works of public utility" must be open to the public as a matter of right in order to qualify as public uses.[71] The taking in question in *Brown* itself was one for the benefit of a railroad corporation, and railroads are common carriers required to serve the public; thus, the taking qualified even under the narrow view of public use. What is not clear is whether the court restricted itself to the narrow view or not. Later nineteenth-century decisions failed to resolve this conundrum.

I have chosen 1877 as the cutoff date for this analysis because that was the point at which the political dominance of Reconstruction-era Republicans decisively eroded, and majority public and elite opinion moved away from the views that influenced the framing and ratification of the

TABLE 2.1 **State Court Interpretations of Public Use as of 1877**

State	Definition of Public Use	Date of Decision
Alabama	Narrow	1859[1]
California	Narrow	1857[2]
Connecticut	Broad	1866[3]
Delaware	Narrow	1839[4]
Florida	Narrow	1859[5]
Georgia	Broad	1877[6]
Illinois	Narrow	1866[7]
Indiana	Narrow	1873[8]
Iowa	Narrow	1868[9]
Kansas	Broad	1870[10]
Maine	Narrow	1855[11]
Maryland	Broad	1873[12]
Massachusetts	Broad	1860[13]
Michigan	Narrow	1877[14]
Minnesota	Narrow	1869[15]
Missouri	Narrow	1858[16]
Nevada	Broad	1876[17]
New Hampshire	Broad	1867[18]
New Jersey	Broad	1832[19]
New York	Narrow	1835[20]
Ohio	Narrow	1840[21]
Oregon	Broad	1870[22]
Tennessee	Narrow	1867[23]
Vermont	Narrow	1871[24]
Wisconsin	Narrow	1870[25]

1. *Sadler v. Langham*, 34 Ala. 311 (1859).

2. *Billings v. Hall*, 7 Cal. 1 (1857). For a detailed discussion of mid-nineteenth century California public use precedent, which concludes that it generally endorsed the narrow view, see Timothy Sandefur, "A Natural Rights Perspective on Eminent Domain in California: A Rationale for Meaningful Judicial Scrutiny of 'Public Use,'" 32 Southwestern University Law Review 569, 620–24 (2003).

3. *Olmstead v. Camp*, 33 Conn. 532 (1867).

4. *Whiteman v. Wilmington & S.R. Co.*, 2 Harr. 514 (Del. Super. 1839).

5. *Bradford v. Cole*, 8 Fla. 263 (1859).

6. *Hand Gold Mining Co. v. Parker*, 59 Ga. 419 (1877).

7. *Nesbitt v. Trumbo*, 39 Ill. 110 (1866).

8. *Wild v. Deig*, 43 Ind. 455 (1873).

9. *Bankhead v. Brown*, 25 Iowa 540 (1868).

10. *Venard v. Cross*, 8 Kan. 248 (1871).

11. *Jordan v. Woodward*, 40 Me. 317, 323 (1855).

12. *New Cent. Coal Co. V. George's Creek Coal & Iron Co.*, 37 Md. 537 (1873).

13. *Talbot v. Hudson*, 82 Mass. 417 (1860); See also, *Boston & Roxbury Mill Corp. v. Newman*, 12 Pick. 467 (Mass. 1832), which points in the same direction, but less clearly.

14. *Ryerson v. Brown*, 35 Mich. 333 (1877).

15. *Miller v. Troost*, 14 Minn. 365 (1869).

16. *Dickey v. Tennison*, 27 Mo. 373 (1858).

17. *Dayton Gold and Silver Min. Co. v. Seawell*, 11 Nev. 394 (1876).

18. *Great Falls Mfg. Co. v. Fernald*, 47 N.H. 444 (1867).

19. *Scudder v. Trenton Delaware Falls Co.*, 1 N.J. Eq. 694 (N.J. Ch. 1832); see also *Tide Water Co. v. Coster*, 18 N.J. Eq. 518 (1866).

20. *Varick v. Smith*, 5 Paige Ch. 137, 155–56 (N.Y. Ch. 1835); see also *Taylor v. Porter & Ford*, 4 Hill 140 (1843).

21. *Buckingham v. Smith*, 10 Ohio 288, 297 (1840). See also *McQuillen v. Hatton*, 42 Ohio St. 202, 204 (1884), which endorses the narrow view more clearly.

22. *Seely v. Sebastia*, 4 Ore. 25 (1870).

23. *Memphis Freight Co. v. City of Memphis*, 44 Tenn. 419 (1867). A narrow interpretation of public use is strongly implied in an earlier 1832 case, which, however, was decided on statutory grounds. See *Harding v. Goodlett*, 11 Tenn. 41 (1832).

24. *Tyler v. Beacher*, 44 Vt. 648 (1871).

25. *Whiting V. Sheboygan & F. du L.R. Co.*, 25 Wis. 167 (1870).

Fourteenth Amendment.[72] The Compromise of 1877, under which northern Republicans agreed to significantly reduce federal protection of the rights of southern African Americans, is usually considered the end of the Reconstruction era.

Judicial decisions after that point are therefore less reliable as evidence of the understanding of public use at the time the Fourteenth Amendment was drafted and ratified in the 1860s. Extending our reach beyond 1877 would, however, only further reinforce the conclusion that the narrow view was dominant. Between 1880 and 1905, an additional nine state supreme courts adopted the narrow view,[73] while only two additional states endorsed the narrow one.[74]

The Nineteenth-Century Mill Act Cases and Public Use

As in the Founding era, condemnations for mills were among the most important uses of eminent domain during the early to mid-nineteenth century. Although they were far from the only public use decisions during this era, it is important to examine these cases, both because mills had substantial political and economic significance in their own right and because they are often cited in support of the broad interpretation of public use.

While eighteenth century mill acts generally authorized condemnation only for grist mills that were open to the public as a matter of right, in the early nineteenth century, many states passed mill acts authorizing the use of eminent domain for power mills that were purely private and were not required to serve all comers who could pay their fees.[75] The widespread acceptance of such mill acts is often seen as proving "the early acceptance of the broad view that it was the great advantage to the public which justified the taking, . . . even though the public had no right to use the property."[76]

But the actual history of nineteenth-century mill act cases is much more complicated. Several state supreme courts did indeed uphold them on the basis of a broad interpretation of public use, including Connecticut, Massachusetts, New Hampshire, and New Jersey.[77] On the other hand, courts in several other states upheld their mill acts only on the basis of long-standing usage and acquiescence by state authorities, without endorsing the broad view of public use more generally. These states included Iowa, Kansas, and Nebraska.[78] The supreme courts of Maine, Minnesota, and Wisconsin upheld their states' mill acts on the basis of prolonged acquiescence while simultaneously endorsing the narrow view of public use as the general rule.[79]

An 1855 Maine Supreme court ruling concluded that "private property can only be said to have been taken for public use when . . . the public have certain well-defined rights to that use secured, as the right to use the public highway . . . But when it is so appropriated that the public have no rights to its use secured, it is difficult to perceive how such an appropriation can be denominated a public use."[80] The court only upheld the mill act because of "its great antiquity, and the long acquiescence of our citizens in its provisions," and emphasized that it was not "inclined to extend its peculiar provisions by implication."[81] An 1860 Wisconsin Supreme Court decision upheld its state's mill act only because of previous precedent and because "large amounts of capital have been invested, and most important rights acquired in mills and water powers, under the impression that [the earlier 1849 ruling] would be adhered to by the courts of this state."[82] The court made clear that, otherwise, it would only uphold mill condemnations if the public had a legal right to use the facilities.[83] An 1869 Minnesota Supreme Court opinion similarly upheld its state's mill act based on adherence to precedent, while simultaneously rejecting the broad interpretation of public use as a general rule.[84] The supreme courts of Alabama, Georgia, Michigan, New York, Vermont, and West Virginia all concluded that mill acts were actually unconstitutional.[85]

In an 1885 decision, the federal Supreme Court rejected a claim that mill act takings violate the Due Process Clause of the Fourteenth Amendment, by concluding that they do not really involve the use of eminent domain at all, due to the fact that it was a mere regulation of "the manner in which the rights of proprietors of lands adjacent to a stream may be asserted and enjoyed."[86]

Overall, the mill act decisions roughly mirror the nineteenth-century distribution of judicial opinion on public use more generally. If we combine the six states that concluded that mill acts were unconstitutional with the three that ruled they were permissible while simultaneously endorsing the narrow view of public use more generally, it turns out that the nine state supreme courts embracing the narrow view of public use in these cases significantly outnumbered those that endorse the broad one in rulings upholding them (four).[87]

It would be a mistake to conclude that the mill act cases are by themselves strong evidence that the narrow view predominated. It is still, after all, notable that more state supreme courts upheld these acts than invalidated them. But the way most of them did it at least indicates that the mill act cases do not undermine the more general conclusion that states embracing the narrow view predominated over those embracing the broad one.[88]

Nineteenth-Century Federal Public Use Decisions

Federal public use decisions in the nineteenth century were extremely limited. But the few extant cases from the early nineteenth century generally support a narrow approach to public use more than the broad one.

The Supreme Court did not rule that the federal government had the power of eminent domain until 1875.[89] And even after that time, federal takings were very rare, especially ones that might potentially run afoul of a narrow interpretation of public use. Moreover, the Court also did not recognize that the Bill of Rights—including the Public Use Clause of the Fifth Amendment—applied to the states.[90] In 1896, the Supreme Court specifically noted that "the fifth amendment, which provides, among other things, that such property shall not be taken for public use without just compensation, applies only to the federal government."[91] During the late nineteenth and early twentieth centuries, the Court did consider numerous cases challenging takings under the Due Process Clause of the Fourteenth Amendment. These decisions were often deferential to state governments; but they do not directly bear on interpretations of the Public Use Clause of the Fifth Amendment.[92]

An early nineteenth-century federal Supreme Court discussion of the public use issue leans toward the narrow view. In an 1829 opinion authored by Justice Joseph Story, who was also a leading treatise writer on constitutional law, the Court stated that "[w]e know of no case, in which a legislative act to transfer the property of A. to B. without his consent, has ever been held a constitutional exercise of legislative power in any state in the union. On the contrary, it has been constantly resisted as inconsistent with just principles, by every judicial tribunal in which it has been attempted to be enforced."[93] Such an act would be inconsistent with "[t]he fundamental maxims of a free government [which] seem to require, that the rights of personal liberty and private property should be held sacred."[94] In his influential 1833 *Commentaries on the Constitution of the United States*, Story wrote that "in a free government, almost all other rights would become utterly worthless, if the government had an uncontrollable power over the private fortune of every citizen. One of the fundamental objects of every good government must be the due administration of justice; and how vain it would be to speak of such an administration, when all property is subject to the will or caprice of the legislature, and the rulers."[95]

In 1848, the Court considered a case where the corporate owner of a franchise to operate a bridge that had been condemned in Vermont claimed that the taking violated the Contracts Clause of the Constitution by overriding the charter under which the firm previously operated the bridge.[96] The Contracts Clause bans states from adopting laws "impairing the Obligation of Contracts."[97] The Court concluded that there was no unconstitutional impairment of a contract because the property was taken through eminent domain for a public use.[98] The majority opinion did not address the issue of what qualifies as a public use, simply assuming that a public bridge does so. But, in a separate opinion, Justice Levi Woodbury endorsed the narrow view of eminent domain, writing that a condemnation for a road or a bridge would not be permissible "if the use of it be not public, but merely for particular individuals, and merely in some degree beneficial to the public. On the contrary, the user must be for the people at large,—for travelers,—or all,—must also be compulsory by them, and not optional with the owners,—must be a right by the people, not a favor."[99]

Woodbury's view was not by itself definitive. But it is notable as the most clear and specific nineteenth-century Supreme Court opinion addressing the question of what qualifies as a public use and for its specific repudiation of the broad view that any use "beneficial to the public" might qualify.

In a rare case where the late nineteenth-century Court considered a challenge to a federal condemnation—one that therefore could be attacked under the Takings Clause even without incorporation—it suggested that private-to-private condemnations should receive greater judicial scrutiny than those for purposes that fit the narrow definition of public use. In the 1896 case of *United States v. Gettysburg Electric Railway Co.*,[100] the Court considered a challenge to the federal government's condemnation of private property for the purposes of preserving the Gettysburg battlefield and building monuments to the soldiers who had fallen in the Civil War's greatest battle.[101]

The *Gettysburg* case upheld the challenged taking,[102] and this holding is usually seen as an example of the Fuller Court's deference to legislatures on public use questions.[103] Justice Clarence Thomas's *Kelo* dissent harshly criticizes as excessively deferential *Gettysburg's* statement that "when the legislature has declared the use or purpose to be a public one, its judgment will be respected by the court, unless the use be palpably without reasonable foundation."[104] However, both Justice Thomas and academic commentators ignore the fact that this language is almost immediately followed (in the very next paragraph) by the qualification that broad deference to legislative judgment is only due in cases "where the land is taken by the government itself."[105] The *Gettysburg* Court goes on to note that

> [i]t is quite a different view of the question which courts will take when this power is delegated to a private corporation. In that case the presumption that the intended use for which the corporation proposes to take the land is public is not so strong *as when the government intends to use the land itself.*[106]

This passage from *Gettysburg* does not clearly endorse the narrow view of public use. But it does suggest that private-to-private takings are treated differently from those where the government "intends to use the land itself" and deserve less deference from the courts.

Public Use and the Debate over Emancipation in the District of Columbia

One of the very rare nineteenth-century conflicts over public policy where the federal government attempted an action that might be seen as pushing the limits of public use was the recurrent debate over emancipation in the District of Columbia. In 1835–36 and again in 1862, when the measure passed during the Civil War, Congress considered legislation that would abolish slavery in the District of Columbia.[107] Unlike territory controlled by state governments, the District was under direct federal government rule. Therefore, the Fifth Amendment applied to takings in the District, much like with any other takings by the federal government.

Slave owners and their defenders considered slaves to be property no less than land or inanimate objects. Because the freed slaves would be their own owners rather than transferred to government ownership, if emancipation constituted a taking of property, it would not be permissible under the narrow definition of public use. This argument was emphasized by congressional opponents of emancipation in both 1835 and 1862. Both the criticisms and the responses of supporters shed light on nineteenth-century understandings of public use. The 1862 debate is particularly relevant, because it occurred just six years before the ratification of the Fourteenth Amendment, which incorporated the Fifth Amendment against state governments.

Because they explicitly focused on the public use question, the DC emancipation debates are far more relevant than other, more famous, nineteenth-century conflicts over slave owners' supposed property rights, such as the Supreme Court's notorious decision in *Dred Scott v. Sandford* and the debate triggered by Abraham Lincoln's September 1862 Emancipation Proclamation, which freed slaves in the rebel Confederate states. In *Dred Scott*, Chief Justice Roger Taney concluded that Congress lacked authority to abolish slavery in federal territories not because it was a violation of the Public Use Clause, but because it violated the Due Process Clause of the Fifth Amendment by supposedly depriving individuals of property without due process of law.[108] The Emancipation Proclamation was not regarded as a taking by its supporters, because it was considered an exercise of presidential war power, which is one reason why it did not include any compensation for southern slave owners.[109]

In both the 1835–36 and 1862 debates, opponents of emancipation often cited the narrow view of public use in support of their claims that emancipation is unconstitutional, even if accompanied by monetary compensation for slave owners. In the 1835–36 debate, for example, Virginia Democratic Representative John Robertson argued that "[t]o found a claim for taking private property, it must be wanted for public use . . . No attempt can be successfully made to construe these terms as conferring a right on Congress to seize upon private property, whenever they may suppose the public good, the general welfare, require it. . . . You cannot take the property of one man to bestow upon another."[110] Similarly, in the 1862 debate, Kentucky Democratic Senator Lazarus Powell—a slave state senator who had remained loyal to the Union—argued that DC emancipation violated the Public Use Clause because the property taken was not put to a public use but "turned adrift."[111]

It is not surprising that defenders of slavery would seize on any possible argument against emancipation. Both contemporaries and later scholars had every reason to view their motives with great suspicion. Still, it is telling that they placed such heavy emphasis on the narrow definition of public use. This is at least suggestive of its acceptance in the legal culture of the time.

The arguments of defenders of emancipation are perhaps even more significant. It is telling that most of them did *not* rely on the broad interpretation of public use. That theory is noticeable here precisely because of its absence, since it would have provided an easy way around public use objections to the constitutionality of emancipation. Instead of the broad view of public use, supporters of emancipation usually argued that abolition of slavery was not really a taking at all, because property in slaves was not a natural right but merely the creation of positive law. And if slavery was merely a legislative creation, it was not a true property right and could be revoked by the legislature at will.

This distinction between natural and legislatively created property rights may seem strange to modern lawyers accustomed to the notion that all property is purely the creation of positive law. But it was a commonly accepted view in the nineteenth century, particularly among opponents of slavery. The idea that property rights in slaves are not natural but purely a product of legislative creation was the dominant view in many states in the late eighteenth and early nineteenth centuries, including some in the South.[112] It underpinned the standard antebellum view that slavery could not exist in the absence of express authorization by the legislature and that a slave was presumed to become free if his or her master permanently moved the slave into a free state.[113] By the 1860s, abolitionists had long contended that the legislatively created nature of slavery meant that masters had no real property rights or at least none that could not be abolished by the legislature at will.[114]

In the 1862 debate, prominent Republican Senator Lot Morrill argued that the Takings Clause simply did not apply to slavery because "I hold that there is no private property in slaves, in the sense in which we have property in lands, or property in horses or other animals. It has a different origin; slavery is founded in force, . . . [and] never is maintained anywhere accept by statute."[115] New Hampshire Republican Senator Daniel Clarke similarly rejected the applicability of the Takings Clause by "deny[ing] entirely the property of any man in man."[116] Other defenders of emancipation in both the 1835–36 and 1862 debates made the same point, including such prominent Republican abolitionists as Massachusetts Senator Charles Sumner in 1862.[117] Similar arguments were advanced in a well-known 1831–32 debate on emancipation in the Virginia state legislature.[118]

In the 1835–36 DC debate, one proponent of emancipation, Senator Samuel Prentiss of Vermont, did endorse the broad view of public use and adopt it as a justification for emancipation, claiming that "the word use, in the constitution, is to be understood in a liberal sense, as equivalent to purpose or benefit."[119] But it is notable that he was the only one to take this position in 1835–36 and even more notable that none of the defenders of emancipation adopted it in 1862, despite repeated invocation of the narrow definition of public use by opponents.

It is possible that some supporters of emancipation avoided asserting the broad view of public use because it—unlike the argument that slave owners had no constitutional property rights at all—would require Congress to pay compensation to the slave owners.[120] However, the 1862 bill that passed Congress did in fact include considerable compensation of up to $300 per slave, a provision that was supported as politically expedient even by some staunch abolitionists, such as Senator Sumner.[121] Three hundred dollars in 1862 is very roughly equivalent to about $7,000 in today's currency, according to various inflation calculators.[122]

The debates over emancipation in the District of Columbia are not by themselves definitive evidence of the understanding of public use at the time. But the extensive reliance on the narrow definition by opponents and the near-total lack of reliance on the broad view by supporters at least reinforce other evidence suggesting that the narrow view enjoyed more widespread acceptance.

Thomas Cooley and John Lewis on Public Use

In addition to being endorsed by a majority of nineteenth-century state court rulings on the issue, the narrow interpretation of public use was also defended by Michigan Supreme Court Justice Thomas Cooley and prominent legal commentator John Lewis, authors of the leading treatise treatments of public use in the nineteenth century. Cooley was well known as perhaps the most influential late nineteenth-century authority on state constitutional law,[123] while Lewis was the author of the leading nineteenth-century treatise on eminent domain law.[124]

In his highly influential 1868 work, *A Treatise on the Constitutional Limitations Which Rest upon the Legislative Powers of the States of the American Union,* Cooley forcefully defended the narrow interpretation of public use, arguing that "*public use* implies a possession, occupation, and enjoyment of the land by the public or public agencies; and there could be no protection whatever to private property, if the right of the government to seize and appropriate it could exist for any other use."[125]

He emphasized that the alternative broad definition of public use would license takings for virtually any purpose because "there are many ways in which the property of individual owners can be better employed or occupied when the general public is considered than it actually is by the owners themselves."[126]

Cooley recognized that "[t]here is still room . . . for much difference of opinion as to what is a public use," and he admitted that many states had reached decisions contrary to the rule he preferred.[127] But he also contended that the trend of opinion was moving in his direction and that decisions like those upholding the mill acts would probably not be reached "in any State in which this question would be a new one, and where it would not be embarrassed by long acquiescence and judicial as well as legislative precedents."[128]

Writing twenty years later in 1888, Lewis reached very similar conclusions. He too contended that the narrow interpretation of public use was correct, in part because "it is the only view which gives the words any force as a limitation" on government power over private property.[129] Like Cooley, Lewis recognized that there was considerable diversity in state decisions on public use but simultaneously, argued that states were gradually moving in what he considered the right direction.[130]

Less well-well known late nineteenth-century treatises on eminent domain law, such as those of Henry Mills and Carman Fitz Randolph, also concluded that the narrow view was dominant.[131] On the other hand, it is worth noting that prominent legal scholar Christopher Tiedeman— who was not an eminent domain specialist—advocated the broad view, which he claimed had become dominant as of 1886, but without surveying relevant case law.[132]

The views of Cooley, Lewis, and other treatise writers do not by themselves prove that the narrow interpretation of public use was the dominant one at the time they wrote. But they do show support for it by writers who were the leading authorities on the subject among legal elites of the era. As we shall see, their views are relevant to the debate over the original meaning of public use at the time the Fourteenth Amendment was enacted.

The Triumph of Judicial Deference

The terms "public use" and "public purpose" were sometimes used interchangeably even in the nineteenth century. An 1894 treatise on eminent domain noted that, in the context of takings "*use* . . . is interchangeable with purpose."[133] But it was only in the twentieth century that, in the dominant view of jurists and commentators, public use was equated to public purpose in such a way as to require virtually unlimited judicial deference. This part of the history of public use can be summarized relatively quickly, as there is little dispute about the main points.

Beginning in the early twentieth century, judicial enforcement of the narrow interpretation of public use came under attack as part of the broader Progressive critique of judicial protection of property rights and economic liberties.[134] Unlike their modern liberal successors, many Progressives also abhorred judicial enforcement of individual rights more generally, including "noneconomic" ones.[135] The Progressives were hostile to judicial protection for property rights because they believed it impeded effective economic planning and was a tool that the wealthy wielded to protect their economic interests at the expense of the poor. In the 1930s, the Progressive critique of property rights was bolstered by the widespread perception that laissez-faire economic policies had caused the Great Depression and the terrible suffering that occurred in its wake.[136] The Democratic Party, which controlled the presidency for twenty years after 1932, emphasized hostility to judicial invalidation of economic legislation as one of its main litmus tests for appointees to the federal judiciary.[137]

In the early twentieth century, state courts gradually began to transition from the narrow view of public use to the broad one. A key driver of this transition was the use of eminent domain to condemn blighted and "slum" neighborhoods in urban areas and transfer them to private developers.[138] In 1940, an influential survey of public use law by leading eminent domain expert Philip Nichols, Jr., concluded that the narrow view was very much in retreat and that state decisions upholding blight condemnations were the "unkindest cuts to the narrow doctrine."[139] By 1949, a widely cited *Yale Law Journal* comment pronounced the narrow view to be on "death-watch" and celebrated its likely "permanent internment in the digests that is so long overdue."[140]

Federal decisions interpreting the Public Use Clause of the Fifth Amendment gradually moved in the same direction. Some early twentieth-century federal cases interpreting the Public Use Clause still leaned toward the narrow view.[141] In a 1916 Supreme Court decision addressing a challenge to a state taking under the Fourteenth Amendment, Justice Oliver Wendell Holmes wrote that "[t]he inadequacy of use by the general public as a universal test is established."[142] But he did not endorse the broad view of public use, and the rejection of the narrow view as "a universal test" left open the possibility that it might be the correct approach in some cases. Moreover, the ruling did not address the federal Public Use Clause.[143]

In a 1931 Supreme Court decision sometimes interpreted as an endorsement of the broad view of public use,[144] the justices ruled that a World War I government order requisitioning electric power belonging to the International Paper Company to deliver to other firms producing items deemed more useful to the war effort qualified as a taking for public use.[145] But the Court did not actually address the issue of the definition of public use. The case was an unusual situation where the federal government denied that a taking had occurred at all, so as to avoid having to pay compensation.[146] The Supreme Court rejected this theory on the grounds that the government clearly did exercise its power of eminent domain and merely indicated that the fact that the condemned power was then transferred to other private firms did not make it "any less a taking for public use."[147]

Although it hinted in the direction of a broad interpretation of public use, the case ultimately turned on the question of whether a taking had occurred at all rather than whether it was for a public use. Even so, three justices dissented without opinion, possibly because they agreed with the lower court's view that there had not been any exercise of eminent domain, due to the fact that the property in question was not put to a public use.[148]

In *United States ex rel. TVA v. Welch,* a 1946 case upholding the condemnation of property by the federal Tennessee Valley Authority, the Court edged still closer to the broad view of public use, noting that "[w]e think that it is the function of Congress to decide what type of taking is for a public use."[149] But the Court's actual holding was that "the T.V.A. took the tracts here involved for a public purpose, if, as we think is the case, Congress authorized the Authority to acquire, hold, and use the lands to carry out the purposes of the T.V.A. Act."[150] Since the TVA was clearly a government agency, this result was compatible even with a narrow interpretation of public use. In a concurring opinion, Justice Felix Frankfurter emphasized that the Court's ruling did not mean that Congress had blanket authority to decide what qualifies as a public use and that the "Court has never deviated from the view that under the Constitution a claim that a taking is not 'for public use' is open for judicial consideration, ultimately by this Court."[151] *Welch* implied the correctness of a very broad view of public use but did not fully embrace it.

Berman *and* Midkiff

In the 1954 case of *Berman v. Parker*,[152] the Supreme Court finally did decisively endorse the broad view of public use. *Berman* upheld a Washington, DC, condemnation that transferred property to private developers, justified on the grounds of alleviating urban "blight." Although there was little doubt that the area in question was indeed severely blighted,[153] a unanimous Court went beyond the narrower conclusion that government could condemn property for the purposes of alleviating blight, and emphasized the supposed need for extreme deference to all legislative determinations of public use.

Justice Douglas's opinion for the Court claimed that "[t]he role of the judiciary in determining whether [eminent domain] is being exercised for a public purpose is an extremely narrow one."[154] If the "legislature has spoken, the public interest has been declared in terms well-nigh conclusive."[155] The fact that the condemned property was to be transferred to another private owner was specifically rejected as a basis for invalidating the taking or even for subjecting it to greater scrutiny.[156] *Berman* soon became the leading Supreme Court precedent on public use issues, and remained so up to the time of *Kelo*– perhaps even to the present day.

The condemnation upheld in *Berman* was part of an urban renewal plan that forcibly displaced some five thousand African Americans and transferred the property they lived on to white real estate developers.[157] The urban renewal and blight condemnations it ultimately authorized in other states resulted in the forcible displacement of hundreds of thousands of other people, most of them also poor minorities.[158] As legal historian Wendell Pritchett points out, it was both ironic and tragic that a ruling that "enabled institutional and political elites to relocate minority populations and entrench racial segregation . . . was decided just six months after *Brown v. Board of Education*,"[159] by a Court that included nearly all the same justices. "The irony," Pritchett emphasizes, "is that, at the same time it was deciding *Berman*, the Court was deciding *Brown*, which reflects a distrust of government (particularly local government) to protect the interests of minority groups and to treat all citizens equally."[160]

In addition to establishing the dominant interpretation of the federal Public Use Clause, *Berman* also exercised enormous influence over state court interpretations of their state public use clauses. Several state courts had upheld private-to-private blight condemnations as early as the 1930s, led by the New York Court of Appeals' decision in an influential 1936 case.[161] But more did so in the aftermath of *Berman*, citing its extremely broad interpretation of public use as authority; some also endorsed *Berman's* view of public use in cases unrelated to blight.[162] Ultimately, *Berman* was used to justify the condemnation of property for "economic development," even in cases where the property in question was not blighted. In the most notorious such case, *Poletown Neighborhood Council v. City of Detroit* (1981), the Michigan Supreme Court upheld an economic development taking that forcibly displaced some four thousand Detroit residents in order to transfer their land to General Motors to build a new auto factory.[163]

Although *Poletown* was a particularly blatant example of the then-dominant approach to public use, it also witnessed early indications of dissatisfaction with that orthodoxy. Because of the large number of people displaced and the way the condemnations displaced ordinary people for the benefit of a powerful corporation, the case generated widespread national media and public attention, much of it negative.[164] Ralph Nader, the prominent left-wing political activist crusader against corporate abuses played a key role in rallying national opinion against the condemnations.[165] In the Michigan Supreme Court, there were forceful dissents by two justices, an indication that the New Deal orthodoxy on public use did not command universal allegiance among the nation's judicial elite.[166]

Despite the then-recent controversy over *Poletown,* the federal Supreme Court was perhaps even more deferential to government in its next major public use case, the 1984 decision in *Hawaii Housing Authority v. Midkiff.*[167] *Midkiff* arose from the unusual circumstances of Hawaii. For complicated historical reasons, some 47 percent of the land in Hawaii was owned by "only 72 private landowners," while another 49 percent was held by the federal or state governments.[168] The state claimed that the seventy-two landowners had established an oligopoly in the market for land and decided to establish a program to condemn the property. Although there is serious doubt as to whether there really was a landowner oligopoly setting prices above the market level,[169] the Supreme Court accepted the state's claim that one existed at face value.

While the Court could have upheld the Hawaii condemnations on the relatively narrow ground that "[r]egulating oligopoly and the evils associated with it is a classic exercise of a State's police powers,"[170] it chose—as in *Berman*—to go beyond the facts of the case and endorsed a much broader doctrine of deference to government power. In a unanimous opinion written by Justice Sandra Day O'Connor, the Court held that the scope of public use is "coterminous with the scope of a sovereign's police powers" and that takings must be upheld under the Public Use Clause so long as "the exercise of eminent domain power is rationally related to a conceivable public purpose."[171]

In light of the extremely deferential language in *Berman* and *Midkiff,* most expert observers believed that public use constraints on takings were virtually dead. In a prominent book on constitutional property rights published in 1977, Yale Law School Professor Bruce Ackerman relegated this "important peripheral issue" of public use to a footnote, because "the modern understanding of 'public use' holds that any state purpose [that is] otherwise constitutional should qualify as sufficiently public to justify a taking"—even though he himself believed that "there is at least something to be said on the other side."[172] In 1996, historian Buckner Melton wrote that "[t]oday, in *Berman's* wake, the broad view [of public use] holds the field completely."[173] As late as 2002, a treatise on takings written by two leading scholars concluded that "nearly all courts have settled on a broader understanding [of public use] that requires only that the taking yield some public benefit or advantage."[174] Even the very few scholars who defended the narrow view during this period tended to be pessimistic about the prospects that it might be effectively revived.[175]

But these postmortems for the narrow view turned out to be premature. Several state supreme courts held on to important elements of the narrow view even at its nadir between the 1950s and 1970s. The supreme courts of Arkansas, Florida, Kentucky, Maine, South Carolina, and Washington, all rejected private-to-private condemnations for economic development during that time.[176] In 1956, the Supreme Court of South Carolina even rejected the constitutionality of blight condemnations.[177]

By the late 1980s and early 1990s, a rising property rights movement had begun to challenge legal orthodoxy on Takings Clause issues, including public use.[178] Beginning in the same period, a new generation of conservative and libertarian public interest law firms—including the Institute for Justice—began to focus on property rights issues with the goal of increasing judicial protection for constitutional property rights.[179] In the ten years prior to *Kelo,* four state supreme courts—Illinois, Michigan, Montana, and South Carolina (which reaffirmed its earlier stance)—held that their state constitutions forbade economic development takings that transfer property to private parties.[180] The best known of these decisions was the Michigan Supreme Court's 2004 ruling in *County of Wayne v.*

Hathcock,[181] which overruled *Poletown*. With the exception of the Connecticut Supreme Court's closely divided ruling in *Kelo* itself, only one state supreme court—North Dakota—had created a new precedent upholding economic development rationale during that time.[182]

The late 1980s and 1990s also saw a modest revival of protection for constitutional property rights in the Supreme Court. Although the Court did not decide a significant public use case during this period, it did strengthen protection for property owners on other fronts, including requiring compensation under the Takings Clause for a wider range of "regulatory" takings.[183]

Originalism and Public Use

While the mid-twentieth Century Supreme decisively endorsed a very broad interpretation of public use, it is the history of public use in the founding era and the nineteenth century that has important implications for originalist interpretations of public use. Not all judges and legal scholars are originalists. Many support various versions of "living Constitution" theory, which hold that the meaning of the Constitution should be reinterpreted over time in order to adjust to changing conditions. But originalism has rapidly gained ground among liberal, conservative, and libertarian legal scholars over the last several decades.[184] It may even be the dominant school of thought among constitutional theorists today.[185] In addition, many scholars and jurists who reject originalism as the sole basis of constitutional interpretation believe that the original meaning is at least one of several considerations that judges should take into account.[186] During her 2010 Senate confirmation hearings, liberal Supreme Court Justice and former Harvard Law School Dean Elena Kagan declared that "we are all originalists now."[187] While that statement is an exaggeration, it does testify to the growing influence of originalism on judges and legal scholars.

Initially, most modern originalists were advocates of the "original intent" variant of the theory, which holds that the constitution should be interpreted in accordance with the intentions of the political leaders who drafted the document. Although original intent still has some adherents,[188] today the dominant school of originalism is "original meaning": the idea that constitutional interpretation should be based on the public understanding of the text at the time it was enacted.[189]

In considering the original meaning of the Bill of Rights, some originalists, such as Akhil Amar, Kurt Lash, and Michael Rappaport, have argued that we should focus on the public understanding of its meaning as of 1868, when the Fourteenth Amendment made it applicable to the states, instead of just 1791, when it was first enacted.[190] Rappaport has used 1868 evidence to shed new light on the original meaning of the Takings Clause, as applied to the question of what regulatory measures qualify as takings.[191] I seek to do the same on the question of the meaning of public use.

The 1868 understanding of public use is potentially relevant under each of the widely accepted theories of incorporation advanced by judges and legal scholars in recent decades. The Supreme Court has long pursued "selective" incorporation of the Bill of Rights under the Due Process Clause, which forbids state deprivations of life, liberty, or property without "due process of law."[192] This theory holds that provisions of the Bill of Rights are incorporated so long as they are considered "fundamental" or "essential to a fair and enlightened system of justice."[193] While a few parts of the Bill of Rights remain unincorporated by the Court under this theory,[194] the Supreme Court has recognized the incorporation of the Takings Clause, and virtually no one who supports incorporation at all denies that the Takings Clause and its public use component are among the rights included.

To the extent that the Due Process Clause approach to incorporation is an originalist one, it is certainly possible that the interpretation of "public use" understood to be "fundamental" by the framers and ratifiers of the Fourteenth Amendment was that which prevailed in 1868. Indeed, the very idea of using the concept of "due process" to protect substantive rights had undergone a long and complex evolution between 1791 and 1868, which influenced the framers of the amendment in a variety of ways.[195]

Justice Clarence Thomas and many legal scholars claim that the Bill of Rights was actually incorporated under the Privileges or Immunities Clause, which prevents states from abridging "the privileges or immunities of citizens of the United States."[196] Here too, the understanding of the Public Use Clause as of 1868 may well be the one that should be considered as incorporated against the states. As one leading advocate of incorporation under the Privileges or Immunities Clause puts it, "the meaning of the Privileges or Immunities Clause does not 'incorporate' the original understanding of the Establishment Clause [of the First Amendment]. . . . but instead represents the common understanding of the rights of American citizenship in 1868."[197] If the Establishment Clause of the First Amendment is incorporated based on the interpretation of it that prevailed in 1868, then the same is also true of the rest of the Bill of Rights, including the Public Use Clause of the Fifth Amendment.

In order to fully evaluate the implications of originalism for public use, I therefore consider both original meaning and original intent as applied to both 1791 and 1868. In each case, the evidence is equivocal but ultimately cuts in favor of the narrow interpretation of public use.

Original Intent

From an original intent point of view, the Takings Clause (including its public use component) may be easier to study than most other parts of the Constitution, because it was so clearly the personal creation of James Madison. He was its drafter and main advocate, and the clause reflects his strong personal commitment to protecting private property rights.[198]

As far as is known, Madison never directly commented on the question of whether the Public Use Clause embodies the narrow or broad interpretations of public use. But given Madison's commitment to property rights and his strong suspicion of legislatures, it seems unlikely that he intended the latter. The same goes for most of the other Founders, who, as discussed earlier, also endorsed a strong natural rights theory of property rights and also tended to be suspicious of legislative infringement on those rights.

In practice, the broad interpretation would leave the door open to "A to B" takings of exactly the kind that most members of the Founding generation considered to be unjust and beyond the legitimate scope of government power. Although not averse to some regulation of property, Madison was particularly concerned about the danger of legislation intended to redistribute property from one individual or group to others.[199] Restricting the ability of government to use eminent domain to transfer property to private individuals is clearly responsive to this concern, while allowing any possible public "benefit" to justify a taking goes against it.

It is true that the requirement of compensation might partially alleviate this danger. But, as discussed earlier in this chapter, the dominant view was that even compensated "A to B" transfers violated natural property rights. Moreover, if the compensation comes from the taxpayers rather than the new individual owners of the condemned property, the result would still be redistribution of wealth to a private interest, of the sort Madison feared, albeit in this case some of the cost would be borne by taxpayers rather than the property owner whose land is taken.

By contrast, the narrow interpretation of public use coheres well with Madison's and other Founders' desire to prevent government from undermining property rights for purposes of redistribution. By requiring that condemned property either be used by the government or made available for use by the general public, it helps ensure that eminent domain is used only to carry out some other function of government rather than for pure redistribution from one individual to another. In this way, it coheres with Madison's desire to allow regulation of property for various purposes, while at the same restricting redistribution.[200]

Moving forward to the adoption of the Fourteenth Amendment in 1868, the original intent evidence is similarly limited, but more supportive of the narrow interpretation. There was very little debate over either public use or the Takings Clause more generally. But the limited discussion that there was suggests that the main goal of incorporating the Takings Clause was to protect the property of African Americans and white supporters of the Union against the depredations of southern state governments likely to be dominated by ex-Confederates. As Representative John Bingham,[201] the leading congressional framer of the Fourteenth Amendment explained in February 1866, one of the purposes of the amendment was "to protect the thousands and tens of thousands and hundreds of thousands of loyal white citizens of the United States whose property, by State legislation, has been wrested from them under confiscation."[202]

The goal was clearly to restrict the power of state governments to threaten the property rights of African Americans and southern whites who had remained loyal during the war or supported the Republican Party afterward. This objective cannot easily be reconciled with allowing those very same state governments to condemn property for almost any purpose they wished, thereby giving them a blank check to condemn the property of both African Americans and white loyalists. The right to private property was a central component of the "civil rights" that the framers of the Fourteenth Amendment sought to protect.[203]

In both 1791 and 1868, leading framers said little about the definition of "public use" directly. But the narrow conception is a better fit with the limited available evidence and with their overall philosophy and objectives than the broad one.

Original Meaning

Today, original meaning is a far more influential mode of constitutional interpretation than original intent. For that reason, the original meaning of public use is probably more significant than its original intent. Unfortunately, the task of assessing the original meaning of the Public Use Clause is complicated by the reality that advocates of original meaning originalism disagree among themselves about what qualifies as the public meaning of the Constitution. Most importantly, they disagree on the question of *whose* understanding counts as that of the relevant public.

Some original meaning originalists focus on the actual understanding of the general public at the time.[204] Others, including Justice Antonin Scalia and leading originalist legal scholar Randy Barnett, emphasize the understanding of a "reasonable person" at the time of enactment.[205] The "reasonable person" might potentially have greater knowledge and understanding of the constitutional text than the average member of the general public.[206]

In his 2008 majority opinion for the Supreme Court in District of *Columbia v. Heller,* Justice Scalia wrote that "In interpreting [the Constitution's] text, we are guided by the principle that '[t]he Constitution was written to be understood by the voters; its words and phrases were used in their normal and ordinary as distinguished from technical meaning. . . .' Normal meaning may of course include an idiomatic meaning, but it excludes secret or technical meanings that would not have been known to ordinary citizens in the founding generation."[207] This suggests a very limited view of the knowledge and competence ascribed to the reasonable person. Others appeal to a reasonable reader with vastly greater legal sophistication. For example, Gary Lawson and Guy Seidman postulate a hypothetical "reasonable person" whom they describe as "conversant with legal traditions and conventions of the time" as well as "highly intelligent and educated and capable of making and recognizing subtle connections and inferences."[208] The Lawson-Seidman hypothetical reasonable person is, in their own words, "a formidable intellectual figure."[209]

Rather than trying to choose between these different variants of original meaning, I will try to assess the original meaning of public use based on both the likely understanding of the general public and that of a hypothetical "reasonable person" who has far greater than average knowledge.

When it comes to the understanding of the average member of the general public in either 1791 or 1868, it is difficult to reach any conclusions with certainty. We do not have systematic survey data from either period. Moreover, both modern public opinion data,[210] and the limited available evidence from the eighteenth and nineteenth centuries,[211] suggest that the public is often ignorant about a wide range of even very basic political knowledge. This suggests that many voters in 1791 or 1868 might have simply been unaware of the issue of the definition of public use or perhaps even of the very existence of the Public Use Clause.

It is probably useless to focus on the "understanding" of members of the public who simply had no idea that the Public Use Clause even existed. But those who knew little or nothing beyond the mere text of the clause would be likely to lean toward the narrow view. As even scholars who endorse the broad interpretation of "public use" recognize, the narrow interpretation is better supported by the plain text of the amendment. As a much-cited anonymous 1949 *Yale Law Journal* comment that otherwise advocates the broad view, put it, the narrow view is "consonant with the commonly understood meaning of the term 'public use'—a public use exists when the public uses something."[212] The literal meaning of "public use" seems to require some kind of actual use by the public or by their agent, the government.

Both in earlier centuries and today, the word "use" also had a metaphorical meaning. I might be said to "use" someone if I benefit from an activity he or she undertakes. But, in reading a text, especially a formal one, people lacking in specialized knowledge of the subject matter are likely to interpret words in a literal sense, unless there is some strong contextual indication that the metaphorical sense was intended by the author.[213] If I write that "Jane is using the lot across the street," most readers would interpret me as saying that she is physically occupying that property or engaging in some activity on it, as opposed to merely deriving some indirect benefit from it.

At least in a society that valued property rights as much as the eighteenth- and nineteenth-century United States, the intuitive linguistic meaning of "public use" dovetails with the average person's sense that government cannot simply condemn property for whatever reason it wants. Even today, as the negative public reaction to *Kelo* shows,[214] that view is widespread, despite the fact that the right to private property occupies a lower status in our political culture than in 1791 or 1868. Thus, it seems likely that the average "reasonable," but not very knowledgeable, member of the general public at the time of the Founding, or in 1868, would interpret "public use" in accordance with the narrow view.

What of the more sophisticated observer who is "conversant with legal traditions and conventions of the time?"[215] Such an individual would realize that there are two possible conflicting interpretations of "public use" and might have some doubts on the subject as a result. But, at the time of the Founding, he would know that the narrow view coheres better with the natural law view of property rights dominant during that era.

The sophisticated observer would also know of the long-standing canon of legal interpretation, which requires that words in a legal document should not be interpreted in such a way as to render them redundant. As the Supreme Court explained in 1840, "[i]n expounding the Constitution of the United States, every word must have its due force, and appropriate meaning" and that "[n]o word in the instrument . . . can be rejected as superfluous or unmeaning."[216] And if "public use" means any possible public benefit, then the term becomes essentially superfluous, as virtually any taking that benefits an individual could create such a benefit to some degree. The Takings Clause could then simply read "nor shall private property be taken without just compensation" without any loss of meaning. As John Lewis put it in his well-known nineteenth-century treatise on eminent domain, "[t]o give these words any effect, they must be construed as limiting the power to which they relate . . . [and] it is evident that the words *public use,* if they are to be construed as a limitation, cannot be equivalent to the general welfare or public good."[217]

In theory, it is possible to imagine some taking that transfers property in a way that creates no public benefit at all. But this is highly improbable in reality, given that almost any taking benefits some person in some way, which in turn could be said to benefit society more generally. As the Supreme Court of Ohio put it in 1884, "[t]he prosperity of each individual condues, in a certain sense, to the public welfare, but this fact is not a sufficient reason for taking other private property to increase the prosperity of individual men."[218]

The legally knowledgeable observer of 1868 would also be aware that the narrow interpretation of public use was the majority among state courts at the time.[219] In addition, these decisions are in themselves an indication of what actual legally sophisticated observers believed, and at least an approximation of the likely beliefs of the Lawson-Seidman hypothetical sophisticated reasonable reader. The views of leading late nineteenth-century treatise writers—especially Judge Thomas Cooley, whose *Constitutional Limitations* was published in 1868—might also serve as a proxy for the opinions of legally sophisticated observers.[220] The same goes for the extensive reliance on the narrow view of public use in the debates over emancipation in the District of Columbia and the relative lack of reliance on the broad view by opponents of slavery.[221] Those debates might have been especially informative for the legally knowledgeable, since they focused directly on the Public Use Clause of the federal Constitution, not just those of the states. The views of Supreme Court Justices Joseph Story and Levi Woodbury would point the sophisticated observer in the same direction.[222] Finally, the legally sophisticated observer of 1868 was likely to know that the protection of the property rights of African Americans and white Unionists in the South was one of the major goals of the Fourteenth Amendment and that the narrow interpretation of public use fits that purpose better than the broad one.

It is theoretically possible that the legally knowledgeable observer would interpret "public use" to mean something in between the narrow and broad conceptions. For example, he could interpret it to allow private-to-private condemnations only if they create a really large public benefit but not if the benefit is a small one. Something like this approach has been adopted by some state courts in the twentieth and twenty-first centuries.[223] But such an interpretation was rarely if ever actually advanced by jurists and legal commentators in the eighteenth and nineteenth centuries, perhaps in part because of a widespread assumption that such questions of degree of harm and benefit were inherently outside the scope of judicial authority and left up to the legislature.[224] It also seems unlikely that such an intermediate option would occur to legally unsophisticated readers, since it does not seem to square with the plain text of the amendment, which refers to "public use" in categorical rather than relative terms.

None of these many considerations qualifies as decisive proof of original meaning by itself. But in combination, they make a fairly strong case, especially compared to the significantly weaker evidence on the other side.

There is no single piece of "smoking gun" evidence supporting either the narrow or the broad interpretation of the original meaning of public use. But accumulated weight of imperfect evidence strongly favors the former.

The Significance of Uncertainty

Although the weight of originalist evidence supports the narrow interpretation of public use much more than the broad one, the latter does still have some support. It is possible to argue that, when the case for the constitutionality of a law is at least plausible, courts should defer to the political branches rather than strike down the statute.

Whatever the merits of this position, the originalist case for it is weak. At the time of the Founding, the dominant view was that judges should strike down unconstitutional legislation without giving special deference to the legislature, indeed that they had a special duty to engage in independent judgment on constitutional issues.[225] As Alexander Hamilton famously explained in *Federalist* 78, "the courts were designed to be an intermediate body between the people and the legislature, in order, among other things, to keep the latter within the limits assigned to their authority."[226] Hamilton envisioned the federal courts as "the bulwarks of a limited Constitution against legislative encroachments."[227] They could hardly play that role by deferring in most cases to the very legislatures whose "encroachments" they are intended to check.

An originalist could potentially conclude that deference to the legislature in the face of uncertainty is appropriate in cases where the available evidence is close to evenly balanced or when there simply is not any substantial evidence either way. But, at the very least, originalist judges have an obligation to strike down a law when there is a substantial preponderance of evidence against its constitutionality. Otherwise, it is difficult to see how judges could discharge their duty of independent judgment or serve as Hamiltonian bulwarks against legislative overreaching.

Moreover, originalists who would strike down laws only when there is no reasonably plausible argument in their defense are placed in the uncomfortable position of rejecting some of the Supreme Court's most hallowed precedents, which defenders of originalism have tried hard to find originalist justifications for, lest originalism itself be discredited by its failure to endorse them. To take two of the most obvious examples, there are serious and plausible originalist arguments against the validity of *Brown v. Board of Education*,[228] and *Loving v. Virginia,* the Court's 1967 decision striking down laws banning interracial marriage.[229] Modern originalists who seek to prove that these results are compatible with their theory recognize that there are serious opposing arguments and that long-standing conventional wisdom cuts against their position.[230] If a strong preponderance of evidence can overcome initially plausible opposing arguments in these cases, the same should apply to public use cases.

To be sure, some originalists in the 1970s and 1980s did seem to argue that the courts should defer to the political process whenever possible, most notably Judge Robert Bork, the famous originalist jurist and legal scholar. But Bork also argued for strong judicial review in cases where the historical evidence suggested that a law violates the original meaning.[231] Bork's defense of judicial restraint was based on the assumption that "[t]he makers of our Constitution . . . provided wide powers to representative assemblies and ruled only a few subjects off limits by the Constitution."[232] But in cases where this assumption proves to be invalid, Bork believed judges must enforce the original meaning of the Constitution, a view that he never fully reconciled with his simultaneous commitment to judicial deference to democracy.[233] To conclude that judicial deference to the democratic process must trump original meaning in all cases where there is a minimally plausible argument in defense of the law at issue is to sacrifice originalism to democratic majoritarianism.

Two Nonmainstream Objections

My analysis of the original meaning of public use implicitly rests on two widely but not universally accepted assumptions: that the Fourteenth Amendment "incorporates" all or most of the Bill of Rights against the states; and that the Public Use Clause imposes at least some constraint on takings, even if only a minimal one. The few originalists who reject one or both of these conclusions also have strong reason to reject the narrow interpretation of public use or its application against state governments. These two out of the box objections deserve brief consideration.

Thanks in large part to the pathbreaking work of Akhil Amar and Michael Kent Curtis, modern originalists generally accept the idea that the original meaning of the Fourteenth Amendment requires the application of the Bill of Rights to the states.[234] And virtually everyone who accepts even partial incorporation of the Bill of Rights also accepts the view that the Takings Clause and its public use component are among the rights incorporated.[235]

A minority of modern scholars still reject incorporation completely, however.[236] In this book, I do not consider their position in detail. The issue of incorporation is so large a tail that it would quickly start wagging the dog of public use if I tried to cover it here. In my view, the arguments of Amar and Curtis are very powerful. If we reject them, it is not only the Fifth Amendment that would not bind the states, but every other part of the Bill of Rights. At least so far as the federal Constitution is concerned, states would be free to censor speech and suppress religious worship protected by the First Amendment, engage in searches of homes and seizures of property forbidden by the Fourth Amendment, and inflict cruel and unusual punishment banned by the Eighth Amendment.

In a 1993 article, prominent constitutional law scholar Jed Rubenfeld argued that the Public Use Clause of the Fifth Amendment imposes no substantive restrictions on eminent domain at all. The text of the Takings Clause states that "nor shall private property be taken for public use, without just compensation."[237] Rubenfeld contends that this language means merely that, if property is taken for public use, the government must pay compensation, whereas if it is taken for other purposes, no compensation is owed at all.[238] Retired Supreme Court Justice John Paul Stevens, the author of the majority opinion in *Kelo,* has recently endorsed this view as well.[239]

As a purely textual interpretation of the Fifth Amendment, Rubenfeld's reading is plausible. However, it is at least equally plausible to interpret the text as implicitly assuming that takings for private uses are forbidden, and therefore there is no need to provide compensation for them. That assumption is compatible with the natural law understanding of property rights common at the time of the Founding, which held that government inherently lacked power to engage in naked transfers of property "from A to B."[240]

From the standpoint of originalism, as opposed to pure textualism, Rubenfeld's argument is weaker still. Without exception, eighteenth- and early nineteenth-century court decisions and statements by the Founders themselves assumed that takings required compensation regardless of whether the property was transferred to government ownership or not.[241] In an 1819 letter, for example, James Madison noted that a proposed emancipation of the slaves by the federal government would require compensation under the Constitution, even though the freed slaves would become their own owners rather than the property of the government.[242] In this letter, Madison envisions a constitutional amendment to give the federal government the power to mandate emancipation, which may explain why he was not concerned that the amendment might violate the Public Use Clause; the amendment would supersede that clause insofar as the latter would make emancipation impossible to carry out. But it might not have superseded the requirement of just compensation, which would not block emancipation completely, but merely require payment of a set price to the owners.

Allowing government unrestrained authority to transfer property from one private individual to another without even paying compensation also conflicted with the founding generation's generally strong emphasis on property rights. It seems strange, to say the least, that the Founders would have required compensation for takings needed for even the most essential public uses but no protection at all against takings for even the most blatant private ones.

Conclusion

During the Founding era and throughout much of the nineteenth century, the narrow interpretation of public use—while hardly uncontested—was generally the dominant view. It coheres with the original meaning of the Public Use Clause better than the broad alternative. This has important implications for originalist interpretations of the Clause.

During the mid-twentieth century, the narrow interpretation was routed in the federal Supreme Court and in most state courts as well. Leading jurists and legal scholars came to believe that it was largely dead. But even at the height of its dominance in the 1960s and 1970s, the broad interpretation continued to be rejected by some state supreme courts. And in the decade leading up to *Kelo*, the challenge to the reigning orthodoxy had begun to gain ground. As *Kelo* would dramatically demonstrate, that orthodoxy was more vulnerable than most experts believed. On that question, the activist lawyers of the Institute for Justice would prove to be more prescient than the dominant view among academics. Before considering the result of their efforts, we first take a look the real-world impact of the condemnations the broad view of eminent domain authorized.

CHAPTER THREE

The Perils of Public Purpose

The Supreme Court's endorsement of a broad definition of "public use" that validates takings for virtually any "public purpose" has led to serious abuses. In many cases, the takings it authorizes inflict severe harm on the poor and politically weak, while simultaneously failing to produce the economic benefits that supposedly justified the use of condemnation in the first place. In this chapter, I focus specifically on the harm caused by economic development takings like that upheld in *Kelo* and the closely related "blight" takings. Thanks to *Kelo*, the former have gotten greater public attention in recent years; but the latter have actually caused far greater harm. At least in the modern era, when they have affected hundreds of thousands of people, these are the most significant uses of eminent domain that are authorized by the courts' endorsement of an extremely broad view of public use but would not be permitted by a narrow one. Most other modern takings either affect far fewer people, fall within the narrow definition of public use, or both.[1]

The use of eminent domain for private economic development projects does have a possible economic rationale: the need to overcome holdout problems. But that admittedly genuine problem can often be overcome by market actors, without resorting to government coercion. Moreover, real-world economic development and blight condemnations usually go far beyond what might be necessary to forestall holdouts.

The harm caused by economic development and blight condemnations is of great importance for public policy. It strengthens the case for restricting or banning such takings, regardless of whether they are constitutional. But it also has significance for constitutional theory. The real-world effects of eminent domain may be irrelevant from the standpoint of originalist theories of constitutional interpretation of the sort considered in chapter 2. But they help generate a strong case against *Kelo* under several influential variants of "living Constitution" theory.

Judges and legal scholars who believe that constitutional judicial review should be used to protect poor and minority populations who lack leverage in the political process, that it should follow common law principles, or that it must reflect liberal moral values, should pay close attention to the ways in which these objectives are undermined by a broad interpretation of public use. "Popular constitutionalists" who believe that constitutional interpretation should be influenced by public opinion and popular political movements also have good reason to oppose *Kelo*.

Economic Development Takings

Authorizing the use of eminent domain for economic development takings creates the potential for serious abuses, a risk greater than with most other types of takings.

Opening the Door for Interest Group Influence

The main danger posed by "economic development" takings is the possibility that this rationale can be used to condemn virtually any property for transfer to a private commercial enterprise. As the Michigan Supreme Court explained in *County of Wayne v. Hathcock*,

> [The] "economic benefit" rationale would validate practically *any* exercise of the power of eminent domain on behalf of a private entity. After all, if one's ownership of private property is forever subject to the government's determination that another private party would put one's land to better use, then the ownership of real property is perpetually threatened by the expansion of plans of any large discount retailer, "megastore," or the like.[2]

Courts in other states that forbid economic development takings have reached the same conclusion.[3]

Those decisions may slightly overstate the case, but their basic logic is sound. Economic development can rationalize virtually any taking that benefits a private business because any such entity can claim that its success might "bolster the economy."[4] It may be possible to limit the scope of the development rationale by requiring that the economic benefit gained exceeds some preset minimum size.[5] Yet this amounts simply to saying that any taking benefiting a sufficiently large business enterprise can qualify. Moreover, this rationale actually creates perverse incentives to increase the amount of property condemned for any given project.[6]

Even some of the defenders of the economic development rationale recognize that it is nearly limitless. At the *Kelo* oral argument, as we saw in chapter 1, New London's counsel Wesley Horton admitted that the theory would allow the displacement of any property owner so long as the city believes that the taking might lead to higher tax revenue.[7] During that same argument, Justice Stephen Breyer, who ultimately voted to uphold the *Kelo* takings, stated that "there is no taking for private use that you could imagine in reality that wouldn't also have a public benefit of some kind, whether it's increasing jobs or increasing taxes, et cetera. That's a fact of the world."[8] Almost any condemnation that benefits a large business at the expense of a smaller competitor, a residential owner, or a nonprofit organization, could be rationalized on the grounds that there would be a "significant" increase in tax revenue.

In addition to the direct cost of harmful transfers to influential interest groups, opening the door to economic development takings also creates what economists call "secondary rent-seeking costs."[9] These are the expenses that interest groups and property owners incur in lobbying the government for and against the use of eminent domain, which may become substantial in situations where the availability of the economic development rationale enables an extremely wide range of groups to potentially acquire condemned land.

From a social point of view, the expenditure of resources on such lobbying is pure waste, because it does not create any productive value. Indeed, much of the resources spent on lobbying might achieve nothing but countering similar expenditures by opposing interest groups, who all covet the same land.[10] This risk is exacerbated in situations where the new owners of the condemned property are not required to compensate the previous owners themselves, because the compensation is paid for by taxpayers.[11] In such cases, interest groups have an incentive to spend even more on lobbying than they might otherwise, because a successful lobbying effort would enable them to acquire new property at far below market value.

*Lack of Binding Obligations to Deliver the Promised
Economic Benefits*

The danger of abuse created by the economic development rationale has
been exacerbated by courts' failure to require new owners of condemned
property to actually provide the economic benefits that justified condemnation in the first place. The lack of a binding obligation creates incentives for public officials to rely on exaggerated claims of economic benefit
that neither they nor the new owners have any obligation to live up to.
Courts in a number of jurisdictions have held that property cannot be
condemned without assurances that it will be employed only for public
uses that are precisely specified in advance.[12] Unfortunately, decisions
permitting economic development takings depart from this principle.

The controversial 1981 *Poletown* decision upheld the massive condemnations in Detroit primarily, if not solely, because of the "clear and
significant" economic benefits that the resulting General Motors factory
was expected to provide for the city.[13] Indeed, the majority suggested
that if the benefits were not so great, "we would hesitate to sanction approval of the project."[14] This fact renders all the more dubious the court's
failure to require either the city or GM to ensure that the expected benefits would actually materialize.

Yet, as Justice James Ryan emphasized in his dissenting opinion, the
court failed to impose even minimal requirements of this kind.[15] *City of
Detroit v. Vavro*, a 1989 Michigan Court of Appeals decision interpreting
Poletown, confirmed Ryan's view, holding that "a careful reading of the
Poletown decision reveals that . . . a binding commitment [to provide the
economic benefits used to justify condemnation] is unnecessary in order
to allow the city to make use of eminent domain."[16]

The *Poletown* condemnations dramatically illustrate the danger of
taking inflated estimates of economic benefit at face value. The City of
Detroit and GM claimed that the construction of a new plant on the expropriated property would create some 6,150 jobs.[17] The estimate of "at
least 6,000 jobs" was formally endorsed by both Detroit Mayor Coleman
Young and GM Chairman Thomas Murphy.[18] Yet neither the city nor
GM had any legal obligation to actually provide the six thousand jobs or
the other economic benefits they had promised.

The risk inherent in this arrangement was apparent even at the time.
As Justice Ryan warned in his dissent, "there are no guarantees from
General Motors about employment levels at the new assembly plant. . . .

[O]nce [the condemned property] is sold to General Motors, there will be no public control whatsoever over the management, operation, or conduct of the plant to be built there."[19] Ryan pointed out that "General Motors will be accountable not to the public, but to its stockholders"; it would therefore make decisions as to the use of the property based solely on stockholder interests, not those of the city.[20] "[O]ne thing is certain," Ryan emphasized, "[t]he level of employment at the new GM plant will be determined by private corporate managers primarily with reference, not to the rate of regional unemployment, but to profit."[21] Justice Ryan's warning was prescient. The GM plant opened two years late; and by 1988—seven years after the *Poletown* condemnations—it employed no more than 2,500 workers.[22] Even in 1998, at the height of the 1990s economic boom, the plant still had only 3,600 workers, less than 60 percent of the promised 6,150.[23]

The *Poletown* court's failure to impose any binding obligations on the new owners of property was not idiosyncratic. The same problem is evident in other states that permit economic development takings, including Connecticut with respect to the *Kelo* case.[24] Like Connecticut, other states that allow economic development condemnations also fail to require either the government or the new owners to actually provide the promised public benefits.[25] Thus, *Poletown* and *Kelo* highlight a systematic shortcoming of the economic development rationale generally. It is not an idiosyncratic problem confined to Connecticut and pre-*Hathcock* Michigan.

Why would such a systematic failure arise? There are two plausible explanations. First, requiring a binding commitment to the creation of specific economic benefits for the community might severely constrain the discretion of the new owners, thereby possibly leading to inefficient business practices. For example, if GM had been required to ensure that at least six thousand workers were employed at the Poletown plant, it might have been forced to forgo efficient labor-saving technology. Courts and public officials may well be reluctant to intrude so severely on the new owners' business judgment. The same point applies to requiring businesses to produce a set quantity of other economic benefits to the community such as some amount of investment or additional tax revenue. Requiring owners to invest X dollars or employ a specific number of workers, for example, might lead to inefficient and wasteful overinvestment, and deter cost-saving innovations.

While this is a serious problem with requiring binding commitments, it also provides a strong argument against permitting economic development takings in the first place. If there is no effective way to ensure that the promised economic benefits of condemnation are actually provided, this circumstance strengthens the argument that private economic development projects should be left to the private sector.

A second possible explanation is that many judges may have an unjustified faith in the efficacy of the political process and thus may be willing to allow the executive and legislative branches of government to control oversight of development projects. For example, the *Poletown* majority emphasized that courts should defer to legislative judgments of "public purpose."[26] Whatever the general merits of such confidence in the political process, it is misplaced in situations in which politically powerful interest groups can employ the powers of government at the expense of the relatively weak.[27]

In the absence of any binding obligations to deliver on the promised economic benefits, little prevents municipalities and private interests from using inflated estimates of economic benefits to justify condemnations and then failing to monitor or provide any such benefits once courts approve the takings, and the properties are transferred to their new owners.

Localities and businesses can sometimes circumvent the public use requirement simply by overestimating the likely economic benefits of a condemnation. Municipalities may overestimate intentionally, or they may simply take a private business' inflated estimates at face value. Both business interests and political leaders dependent on their support have tremendous incentives to overestimate the economic benefits of condemnation. Courts are in a poor position to second-guess seemingly plausible financial and employment estimates provided by officials. Even if governments and businesses do not engage in deliberate deception, there is a natural tendency to overestimate the public benefits and the likelihood of success of projects that advance one's own private interests. Such self-interested self-deception may even have a genetic basis.[28] Whether corporate and government leaders deliberately lie or honestly believe that "what is good for General Motors is good for America," the outcome is likely to be the same.

Ignoring the Costs of Condemnation

An especially striking aspect of the *Poletown* decision was the majority's failure to even mention the costs imposed by condemnation on the people of Poletown or the city of Detroit as a whole. This problem, too, is not confined to Michigan's *Poletown*-era jurisprudence; it also arises in other states that permit economic development takings.

The *Poletown* case dramatically illustrates how the promised economic benefits of condemnations often fail to materialize and are outweighed by the massive costs. Not only did the new GM plant create far fewer jobs than promised, but the limited economic benefits the plant did create were likely overwhelmed by the economic harm the project caused the city.

According to estimates prepared at the time, "public cost of preparing a site agreeable to . . . General Motors [was] over $200 million,"[29] yet GM paid the city only $8 million to acquire the property.[30] Eventually, public expenditures on the condemnation rose to some $250 million.[31] In addition, we must add to the costs borne by the city's taxpayers, the economic damage inflicted by the destruction of up to six hundred businesses and fourteen hundred residential properties.[32] Although we have no reliable statistics on the number of people employed by the businesses destroyed as a result of the *Poletown* condemnation,[33] it is quite possible that more workers lost than gained jobs as a result of the decision. If we assume, conservatively, that the 600 eliminated businesses employed an average of slightly more than four workers, the total lost work force turns out to be equal to or greater than the 2,500 jobs created at the GM plant by 1988.[34] Even if we assume that the 600 figure is too high and the true number of eliminated businesses was closer to the range of 140 to 160 estimated by some other sources,[35] it would still take only an average of 17 to 18 jobs eliminated per business to offset the gains created by the new plant. And this calculation does not consider the jobs and other economic benefits lost as a result of the destruction of numerous nonprofit institutions such as churches, schools, and hospitals. Even if we consider the *Poletown* condemnation's impact in narrowly economic terms, it is likely that it did the people of Detroit more harm than good.

The failure of the *Poletown* takings to produce any clear net economic benefit for the city has significance beyond the case itself. In *Poletown,* the magnitude of the economic crisis facing Detroit and the detailed public scrutiny given to the city's condemnation decision led the court to conclude that the economic benefit of the taking was unusually great.[36] The court even went so far as to say that, "[i]f the public benefit was not so clear and significant, we would hesitate to sanction approval of such a project."[37] If the claimed "public benefit" of even so "clear" a case as *Poletown* ultimately turned out to be a mirage, it seems unlikely that courts will do better in weighing claims of economic benefit in more typical cases where the evidence is less extensive and less closely scrutinized.

Other states that continue to permit economic development takings also give little or no consideration to the harm they cause. In *Kelo,* the Connecticut Supreme Court conceded that the plaintiff property owners in the case would suffer serious harm if forced out of their homes and businesses.[38] In addition, tens of millions of dollars in taxpayer money had been allocated to the development project, without any realistic prospect of a return that rises above a tiny fraction of that amount.[39] Yet the state supreme court refused to consider the significance of those massive costs, claiming "the balancing of the benefits and social costs of a particular project is uniquely a legislative function."[40]

Contrary to the Connecticut court, the political process often cannot be depended on to give due consideration to the "social costs" of economic development takings; such condemnations generally benefit the politically powerful, while the costs tend to fall on the poor and politically disadvantaged.

Nonmonetary Costs of Economic Development Takings

In addition to the economic costs to communities and homeowners, economic development takings also inflict major nonfinancial costs on their victims by destroying communities and forcing residents to relocate to less desired locations. As famed urban development scholar Jane Jacobs explained in her classic 1961 account,

> [P]eople who get marked with the planners' hex signs are pushed about, expropriated, and uprooted much as if they were the subjects of a conquering power. Thousands upon thousands of small businesses are destroyed. . . . Whole communities are torn apart and sown to the winds, with a reaping of cynicism, resentment and despair that must be seen to be believed.[41]

Scholars from a wide range of ideological perspectives have reinforced Jacobs's early conclusion that development condemnations inflict enormous social costs that go beyond their "economic" impact, narrowly defined.[42] They are particularly severe in the cases of people who are elderly or have lived in a given community for a long time, as witness the travails of the elderly residents of Fort Trumbull, discussed in chapter 1.[43]

Why the Danger of Interest Group "Capture" Is Unusually High

Economic development takings are not the only exercises of the eminent domain power vulnerable to capture by interest groups seeking to use the powers of government for their own benefit—"rent-seeking" as it is known in the academic literature. Indeed, interest-group capture of government agencies and rent-seeking are serious dangers for a wide range of government activities.[44] However, there are three major reasons why economic development takings are especially vulnerable to this threat: the nearly limitless applicability of the economic development rationale, severe limits on electoral accountability caused by low transparency, and time horizon problems.

As we have seen, the economic development rationale for takings can potentially justify almost any condemnation that benefits a commercial enterprise. Such a protean rationale for the use of eminent domain exacerbates the danger of interest group capture by greatly increasing the range of interest groups that can potentially use it. It also increases the range of projects that those interest groups can hope to build on condemned land that is transferred to them; any project that might increase development or produce tax revenue could be acceptable. Both factors tend to increase the attractiveness of economic development condemnations as a means of making political payoffs to powerful interest groups.

Interest group manipulation of economic development takings might be curtailed if public officials responsible for condemnations face credible threats of punishment at the polls after they approve condemnations that reward rent-seeking. Unfortunately, such punishment is highly unlikely for several important reasons.

First, the calculation of the costs and benefits of most development projects is extremely complex, and it is difficult for ordinary voters to understand whether a particular project is cost effective or not. Studies have repeatedly shown that most voters have very little knowledge of politics and public policy.[45] Most are often ignorant even of basic facts about the political system.[46] Such ignorance is not an accident or a consequence of "stupidity." It is in fact a rational response to the insignificance of any one vote to electoral outcomes; if a voter's only reason to become informed is to ensure that he or she votes for the "best" candidate in order to ensure that individual's election to office, this turns out to be almost no incentive at all because the likelihood that any one vote will be decisive is infinitesimally small.[47] Ignorance is likely to be an even more serious problem in a complex and nontransparent field such as the evaluation of economic development takings.

While the same danger may exist with some traditional narrow public use takings, they usually at least produce readily observable benefits such as a road or a bridge—public assets that can be seen and used by the average voter. Moreover, these benefits usually become apparent as soon as the project in question is completed. By contrast, the supposed public benefit of economic development takings is a generalized contribution to the local economy that the average citizen often will not even notice, much less be able to measure.

Second, even if voters were much better informed, democratic accountability for economic development takings would often still be inadequate. Unlike with most conventional takings, the success or failure of a project made possible by economic development condemnations is usually apparent only years after the condemnation takes place. Even then, it may only become clear after considerable investigation and analysis. In the *Poletown* case, the GM factory did not even open until 1985, four years after the 1981 condemnations and two years behind schedule.[48] And not until the late 1980s did it become clear that the plant would produce far less than the expected six thousand jobs.[49]

By that time, public attention had moved on to other issues, and in any event many of the politicians who had approved the original condemnations might no longer be in office. Given such limited time horizons, a rational, self-interested Detroit political leader might well have been willing to support the *Poletown* condemnations even if he or she anticipated that the expected benefits would eventually fail to materialize. By the time that became evident to the public, he could be out of office in any event. In the meantime, he could benefit from an immediate increase in political support from General Motors and other private interests benefiting from the taking.

Third, the victims of economic development and blight condemnations tend to be poor and politically weak, which sharply curtails their ability to resist. In many cases, they are low-income, racial minorities, or both.[50] In areas where private-to-private condemnations are common, racial minorities constitute 58 percent of the population (compared to 30 percent in the United States as a whole), and adults with a less than a high school level of education are 34 percent (compared to 19 percent nationally).[51] In other cases, as in *Kelo*, they are not poor but still have far less political influence than the developers and other well-organized interest groups who benefit from takings. As a general rule, local governments are unlikely to target the property of the wealthy and influential for these kinds of takings, because they wish to avoid a difficult political struggle. But they rightly believe they can more easily overcome the resistance of the poor or politically weak. Such would have been the result in the *Kelo* case itself but for the unusual intervention of the Institute for Justice.[52]

Some claim that abusive condemnations will be constrained by the power of property owners over local governments. Because property owners are the dominant interest in many localities,[53] they may be able to use their political power to prevent abusive economic development condemnations. However valid with respect to other functions of local government, this argument is flawed when applied to economic development takings. Because of their nontransparent nature and the general problem of political ignorance, property owners are unlikely to be able to determine which development condemnations serve their interests and which do not. Moreover, even in situations where voters do understand the trade-offs involved, the relevant variable is not the political power of property owners generally, but the power of those who are targeted for condemnation. As in *Poletown,* these are likely to be poor, politically unorganized, or both.

The political weakness of most of the property owners targeted by economic development and other private-to-private takings undercuts claims that lack of resistance to many such takings proves that they are justified or at least do not inflict substantial harm.[54] Many owners capitulate simply because they believe—often correctly—that resistance is futile. As we saw in chapter 1, many of the Fort Trumbull owners chose not to fight the condemnation of their land for precisely that reason. Even those who did persist might well have given up much earlier, if not for the unexpected involvement of the Institute for Justice.[55] Resistance may also be uncommon because condemning authorities target people who are unlikely to have the influence to fight back effectively, while avoiding initiating condemnations against those who do. The NLDC's decision to exempt the influential Italian Dramatic Club while proceeding against less powerful landowners is an example of this phenomenon.

Public reaction against abuses of eminent domain has at some points in history led to the imposition of tighter political constraints on takings, including the use of eminent domain by railroads and mining interests in the nineteenth century.[56] But the persistence of harmful economic development and blight takings on large numbers of people for many decades on end suggests that such political checks work far too slowly, when they work at all.

Blight Takings

Although the *Kelo* case focused public attention on the dangers of pure "economic development" takings, far more people have been harmed by blight condemnations, takings ostensibly intended to alleviate dangerous conditions and social pathologies that plague urban neighbhorhoods. Since the beginning of large-scale blight removal programs in the 1930s and 1940s, hundreds of thousands of people have been forcibly displaced by such takings. Blight condemnations pose two dangers. First, over the years the concept of "blight" has been expanded so far that, in many states, almost any area can be declared blighted and thereby open to condemnation. Second, even condemnations in genuinely "blighted" areas often cause far more harm than good, inflicting tremendous suffering on the poor and politically weak.

Expansion of the Definition of Blight

The concept of "blight" has turned out to be highly susceptible to creative expansion. Early blight cases upheld condemnations in areas that closely fit the layperson's intuitive notion of "blight": dilapidated, dangerous, disease-ridden neighborhoods. In *Berman v. Parker*, the 1954 case where the Supreme Court upheld the constitutionality of blight takings, the neighborhood in question was characterized by "[m]iserable and disreputable housing conditions."[57] According to studies cited by the court, "64.3% of the dwellings [in the area] were beyond repair, 18.4% needed major repairs, only 17.3% were satisfactory; 57.8% of the dwellings had outside toilets, 60.3% had no baths, 29.3% lacked electricity, 82.2% had no wash basins or laundry tubs, [and] 83.8% lacked central heating."[58]

In more recent decades, many states expanded the concept of blight to encompass almost any area where economic development could potentially be increased. In the 2001 *West 41st Street Realty* case, a New York appellate court held that the Times Square area of downtown Manhattan was sufficiently "blighted" to justify the condemnation of land needed to build a new headquarters for the *New York Times*![59]

In the 2003 case of *City of Las Vegas Downtown Redevelopment Agency v. Pappas*, the Nevada Supreme Court held that downtown Las Vegas is blighted, thereby permitting condemnation of property for the purpose of building a parking lot servicing a consortium of Las Vegas casinos.[60] The court concluded that an area suffers from "economic blight" if there are "downward trends in the business community, relocation of existing businesses outside of the community, business failures, and loss of sales or visitor volumes."[61] In two recent controversial decisions, the New York Court of Appeals—that state's highest court—ruled that a neighborhood can be declared blighted and subject to condemnation if there is "room for reasonable difference of opinion as to whether an area is blighted" in the sense of suffering from "economic underdevelopment" or "stagnation."[62] It reached this conclusion despite the fact that the clause of the New York state constitution authorizing blight condemnations applies only to "substandard and unsanitary areas."[63] The two rulings upheld the condemnation of substantial amounts of property based on extremely dubious evidence of blight, for takings that benefited a firm controlled by powerful developer Bruce Ratner in one case, and Columbia University in the other.[64]

Virtually any neighborhood, no matter how prosperous, occasionally suffers "downward trends in the business community, . . . business failures, and loss of sales or visitor volumes."[65] Similarly, it is hard to find any area in the country where there is no room for "reasonable disagreement" about whether it is underdeveloped. If Times Square and downtown Las Vegas qualify as "blighted," it is difficult to think of any place that would not. A sufficiently expansive definition of blight is essentially equivalent to authorizing economic development takings. Almost any large commercial enterprise can argue that condemning land for its benefit might help improve "trends in the business community."[66]

While these cases may seem extreme, they are not aberrations but the culmination of a widespread trend toward expansion of the definition of blight. In 1997, a St. Louis suburb declared a "thriving shopping mall" blighted because it was "too small" and especially because it lacked a Nordstrom's.[67] Officials in the affluent city of Coronado, California, went even further and declared the entire jurisdiction blighted in 1985.[68] Similarly broad blight designations have been adopted in many other urban and suburban communities.[69] Overall, as one study concludes, the concept of "'blight' has lost any substantive meaning" and has become a mere "legal pretext" enabling local governments to attract funding and dispose of property as they see fit.[70]

In the aftermath of *Kelo*, some states have enacted tighter definitions of blight, and five have completely abolished blight takings that transfer property to private parties.[71] But, as we shall see in chapter 5, broad definitions of blight still persist in many parts of the country.

Condemnations in Genuinely Blighted Neighborhoods

The second danger posed by the blight exception is perhaps even more serious. Even in cases where the condemned property really is blighted under a narrow definition of the term, condemnation of property often serves the interests of developers while actually causing harm to the area's residents. Indeed, condemnations in truly blighted neighborhoods have probably caused far more harm than either *Poletown*-style economic development condemnations in nonblighted areas or condemnations driven by dubious expansions of the definition of blight.

Large-scale condemnations to alleviate blight began in the 1920s and 1930s, and greatly expanded with the "urban renewal" programs of the 1940s and 1950s. Early and mid-twentieth-century urban planners believed that they were essential to the promotion of economic growth and the alleviation of urban pathologies, such as poverty, crime and threats to public health.[72]

Some leading early planning advocates also viewed poor minorities who moved to urban areas in large numbers in the early twentieth century as "invaders" who helped spread social pathology.[73] Many analogized blighted neighborhoods to diseases that could be excised by expert-led government intervention in much the same way as expert doctors perform operations to excise diseases.[74] Such medical analogies were used to justify eliminating poor neighborhoods entirely through the use of eminent domain rather than improving them through piecemeal reforms. As New York City Comptroller Joseph McGoldrick put it in 1944, "[w]e must cut out the whole cancer and not leave any diseased tissue."[75]

The Supreme Court embraced such analogies in its landmark decision in *Berman v. Parker,* which approvingly cites "experts [who] concluded that if the community were to be healthy, if it were not to revert again to a blighted or slum area, as though possessed of a congenital disease, the area must be planned as a whole."[76]

The results produced by these supposedly enlightened applications of planning expertise were far from healthy themselves. Blight takings displaced hundreds of thousands of people and inflicted enormous social and economic costs, with comparatively few offsetting benefits.[77] Legal historian Wendell Pritchett concludes that the use of eminent domain in "urban renewal programs uprooted hundreds of thousands of people, disrupted fragile urban neighborhoods and helped entrench racial segregation in the inner city."[78] By 1963, over 600,000 people had lost their homes as a result of urban renewal takings.[79] The vast majority ended up living in worse conditions than they had experienced before their homes were condemned,[80] and many suffered serious nonpecuniary losses as well.[81] More recent blight condemnations have inflicted similar harms on communities and poor property owners.[82]

The sheer scale of forced relocations driven by "urban renewal" condemnations dwarfs the harms inflicted by economic development condemnations in nonblighted areas. While *Poletown's* displacement of some 4,200 people was regarded as extreme compared to other economic development takings,[83] it is worth noting that the blight condemnation upheld in *Berman* was part of a redevelopment plan that forcibly displaced over 5,000 people,[84] and this fact evoked little outrage or surprise among contemporary observers. Wendell Pritchett points out that "none of the briefs in *Berman* even mentioned the fact that the project would uproot thousands of poor blacks."[85] Sociologist Herbert Gans estimates that, altogether, some one million households were displaced by federally sponsored urban renewal condemnations between 1950 and 1980.[86] Assuming that the average household size was equal to the 1962 national average of 3.65 persons,[87] that means that federally sponsored urban renewal condemnations forcibly relocated over three million people. New York City forcibly displaced some 250,000 people between 1946 and 1953 alone.[88]

This history points to a serious flaw in the logic endorsed by the Michigan Supreme Court in *Hathcock*: that in blight cases the disposition of condemned property is irrelevant because "the act of condemnation . . . *itself* . . . was a public use,"[89] a claim later also endorsed by Justice Sandra Day O'Connor in her dissent in *Kelo*.[90] As Herbert Gans pointed out, the key flaw in urban renewal condemnations is precisely the fact that "redevelopment proceeded from beginning to end on the assumption that the needs of the site residents were of far less importance than the clearing and rebuilding of the site itself."[91] As a result, the residents of blighted neighborhoods suffered massive harm, while their former homes were converted to commercial or residential uses that primarily benefited developers and middle-class city residents.[92] In the *Berman* case, for example, only about 300 of the 5,900 new homes built on the site were affordable to the neighborhood's former residents.[93]

Gans and other reformers recommend that redevelopment programs be redesigned so as to create "benefit" for "the community as a whole and for the people who live in the slum area; not for the redeveloper or his eventual tenants."[94] But such recommendations are flawed because they assume that benefiting local residents and "the community as a whole" is the real purpose of blight takings in the first place. In reality, such condemnations often deliberately target poor and minority property owners for the purpose of benefiting politically powerful development interests and middle-class homeowners who are expected to move in after the redevelopment process is completed.

So many poor African Americans were dispossessed by urban renewal condemnations in the 1950s and 1960s that urban renewal came to be known as "Negro removal" in many places.[95] Famous African American writer and political activist James Baldwin stated that "urban renewal . . . means moving the Negroes out. It means Negro removal, that is what it means."[96] Urban elites sometimes deliberately focused urban renewal condemnations on the poor and African Americans.[97] Between 1949 and 1963, 63 percent of all families displaced by urban renewal condemnations were nonwhite.[98] Between 1949 and 1973, some two-thirds of the people displaced under takings sponsored by the Urban Renewal Act of 1949 were African American.[99] Hispanic groups, such as Puerto Ricans, were also commonly targeted.[100]

Today, blight takings are nowhere near as common as in the era of large-scale urban renewal projects in the 1950s and 1960s. Events such as the urban riots of the late 1960s led to a curtailment of urban renewal programs.[101] Some defenders of *Kelo* therefore claim that abusive condemnations have largely been eliminated.[102] But blight takings are still relatively frequent and still tend to target the poor and racial minorities.[103] In the late 1990s and early 2000s, the era immediately preceding *Kelo*, urban development projects involving residential displacement had become more common than at any time since the 1960s.[104]

These patterns led the NAACP and the Southern Christian Leadership Conference to file an amicus brief urging the Supreme Court to forbid economic development takings in *Kelo*.[105] The brief emphasized that economic development takings disproportionately target the minority poor, and cited various recent examples.[106]

There may still be an economic rationale for using condemnation as a means of alleviating blight. It may sometimes be the case that the elimination of blight involves a collective action problem, since no one property owner in a blighted neighborhood will have a strong incentive to make major improvements on his or her own property unless others in the area do the same. If a single owner is the only one to make improvements, he is unlikely to recoup their full value because the value of the property will still be dragged down by virtue of its location in a generally dilapidated area. On the other hand, if all or most of the other owners make improvements on their holdings, the first owner can reap the benefits of increased land values in the area even if she does nothing to improve her own tract. Yet even in these situations, the fact that some centralized coercion may be desirable does not mean that the use of condemnation is the proper solution to the problem. Local governments have numerous other tools to deal with these sorts of problems, including the application of nuisance law, enforcement of housing codes, and the use of tax abatements or subsidies to incentivize improvement of dilapidated properties.[107]

The use of eminent domain is likely to be inferior to less coercive policies because it requires dispossession of the current residents of "blighted" neighborhoods, and it carries a much more severe risk of interest group "capture." Even if condemnation may be theoretically justified in some cases of blight, the interest group dynamics involved suggest that real-world blight condemnations are more likely to be driven by the needs and interests of politically powerful developers and middle-class residents than those of the politically weak citizens of blighted neighborhoods.

Many of the same flaws undermine claims that the use of eminent domain for transfer to private parties is needed to address the dangers posed by vacant and abandoned property in deteriorating urban neighborhoods, an issue emphasized in an important recent work by sociologist Debbie Becher.[108] She estimates that some 92% of the lots taken by eminent domain in Philadelphia between 1992 and 2007 were vacant, and mostly located in "distressed" or "devastated" neighborhoods (though she still found hundreds of takings targeting occupied lots as well).[109]

When private developers need to acquire vacant lots for their projects, it should not be difficult for them to do so through voluntary transactions. If the current owners have no plans to use the lots themselves, but are saddled with expenses for property taxes or maintenance, they may actually be eager to sell for any reasonable price, if only to get rid of a tax liability.[110]

If the owners are delinquent on their taxes, or endangering public health and safety, local governments have many other tools for acquiring the delinquent property or forcing the owner to repair dangerous conditions.[111] In addition to imposing penalties on owners of delinquent property, local governments can also foreclose on them; while foreclosure procedures in some states are difficult and cumbersome, there are a variety of ways to improve them.[112] Such reform is surely preferable to trying to combat tax delinquency by giving government broad power to condemn property in "blighted" areas regardless of whether it is delinquent or poses a health risk or not. Moreover, eminent domain processes are also procedurally complex, and many defenders of economic development and blight condemnations argue that vulnerable property owners should be protected by making the procedures even more elaborate.[113]

Finally, it should also be emphasized that vacant lots are not necessarily either abandoned or harmful. In some cases, owners of vacant lots are holding on to them as an investment or waiting until it becomes more clear what the best use of the particular lot is.[114] Premature construction of facilities that turn out not to be economically viable is wasteful, and may impede neighborhood development rather than further it.

The ultimate long-term solution to blight is economic growth. As neighborhoods become wealthier, their residents can more easily afford to improve dilapidated buildings and repair infrastructure. Fewer lots will be left vacant, as there are more economically viable uses for them. Recent research in development economics shows that the security of property rights is crucial to long-term development because insecurity deters investment for fear that the owners will lose the fruits of their efforts.[115]

In sum, even in areas where there is "real" blight—perhaps especially there—the condemnation process is likely to cause more harm than benefit and to be abused for the benefit of private interests at the expense of the poor and politically weak.

The Holdout Problem

The most common argument for economic development and blight takings is that they are necessary to facilitate economic development in situations where large-scale projects require assembling a large number of lots owned by numerous individuals. If the coercive mechanisms of eminent domain cannot be employed, it is claimed a small number of "holdout" owners could either block an important development project or extract a prohibitively high price for acquiescence.[116] As renowned property scholar Michael Heller puts it, without eminent domain, "[t]he United States lacks a good, fast way to assemble land for needed economic development."[117]

For example, let us assume that a group of fifty contiguous properties with separate owners are each worth $100 if dedicated to their current uses ($5,000 in all), but they would be worth a total of $50,000 (an average of $1,000 each) if combined into a single large development project in order to build a factory. There would thus be a net social gain of $45,000 ($50,000 – $5000) from combining the properties into a single tract.

But if the owners of the separate properties know that a developer is trying to buy them all up in order to build the factory worth $45,000 more than the current use of their lands, any one of them could try to hold out and refuse to sell unless the developer gives them, say, $5000. It would be rational for the developer to accede to this demand if it were made by only one owner; in such an eventuality the developer still makes a net gain of about $40,100.[118]

But if all fifty current owners (or even just ten of them) resort to the same strategic gambit, the project will be blocked. In that scenario, payments to the owners will equal or exceed the project's expected profit. In theory, then, holdouts could block many socially valuable assembly projects.

Some defenders of economic development takings contend that holdouts exacerbate the problem of sprawl.[119] Since there are more potential holdouts in densely populated urban areas, if developers are not allowed to use eminent domain to overcome them, they will have incentives to build in suburban and rural areas, thereby increasing sprawl.

In analyzing holdouts, it is important to distinguish between "strategic holdouts"—those who refuse to sell because they hope to obtain a higher price—and "sincere dissenters" who genuinely value their land more than the would-be developer does.[120] The former are attempting to take advantage of the developers' assembly problem in order to raise the price, as the above example illustrates.

The latter, by contrast, are not attempting to get a better price but are instead unwilling to sell because they genuinely place a high enough value on their property that they prefer to keep it rather than accept any payment that the buyer is willing to offer. For example, the resisting property owners in *Kelo* and *Poletown* repeatedly indicated that their objective was to keep their homes rather than to obtain a higher price from the condemning authority.[121] As New London lawyer Wesley Horton noted at the *Kelo* oral argument, "there are some plaintiffs who are not going to sell at any price. They want to stay there."[122]

In a situation where there are sincere dissenters, transferring their property to a developer would actually lower the overall social value of the land because, by definition, the dissenters value it more than the developer does. An ideally efficient policy would, therefore, enable developers to prevent strategic holdouts but not allow them to override the wishes of sincere dissenters.

This is true even if the dissenters are motivated by unusual "idiosyncratic" preferences, which are sometimes described as distinct from more common types of sincere dissenters.[123] If a sincere dissenter refuses to sell at the price offered by would-be developers because she attaches some unusual idiosyncratic value to the property in question, leaving the land in her hands is still the most efficient result. From an economic standpoint, it does not matter why the current user values the land more than a potential purchaser does, only that the former does in fact value it more. Indeed, one of the main benefits of private property is precisely that it enables owners to pursue their own personal values, even if those values are different from those of most other members of the community.

As is suggested by the existence of numerous large development projects that did not rely on eminent domain, much development can proceed without fear of holdouts either because local property owners are unlikely to attempt the strategy or because developers can build around them if they do, without undermining their overall project. Even large and complex development projects can usually go forward despite having to build around a small number of dissenters.[124] Cases where a proposed project is genuinely impossible without forcibly removing every preexisting owner are extremely rare.[125] In many cases, "the 'holdout argument' is often used as a bargaining tactic for invoking eminent domain rather than the result of a true assessment of the strategic importance of the parcel of property" – a reality dramatically demonstrated by the willingness of developers to proceed with projects where the use of eminent domain was prevented by judicial or political resistance, despite claims that a holdout problem existed.[126]

It is highly likely that there was no genuine holdout problem blocking the Fort Trumbull development plan at issue in the *Kelo* case, as illustrated by the New London Development Corporation's willingness to build around the politically connected Italian Dramatic Club.[127] In an amicus brief focusing on this issue, prominent University of Chicago Law School property scholar Richard Epstein pointed out that "holdouts were a complete nonproblem" in Fort Trumbull because property already owned by the government in the area was more than large enough to contain all the new facilities expected to be built under the NLDC's plan.[128]

Some defenders of eminent domain point to "architectural holdouts"—people who refuse to sell properties that ultimately become surrounded by a development project—as a justification for the need to expel such recalcitrants by force.[129] But these cases actually prove the opposite point. Rather than showing that eminent domain is needed to prevent holdouts from blocking valuable projects, such stories demonstrate that many such projects can proceed even if a few sincere dissenters refuse to sell. These stories thereby weaken the rationale for using eminent domain to clear away property owners who refuse to sell to developers. It turns out that these projects actually did *not* need to acquire 100 percent of the land demanded by their developers in order to succeed.

And if the project can proceed without acquiring the land of every single owner in the area, there is little risk, if any, that a small number of strategic holdouts can scuttle the project by refusing to sell unless they get an exorbitant share of the project's expected profits. Indeed, the fact that the holdouts refuse to sell even after it became clear that the development project would proceed despite their refusal, is a strong indication that they were not strategic holdouts at all. They were, in fact, sincere dissenters. If so, allowing them to stay in place not only respects their property rights, but is actually the economically efficient course of action. By refusing to sell even though there is no prospect of becoming a strategic holdout, sincere dissenters show that they genuinely value the land in question more than the developer does.[130]

Sincere dissenters could potentially block economically efficient assembly projects in situations where the would-be purchaser must offer the same price to every existing owner in an area and is thereby unable to pay a premium to buy out the sincere dissenters, even though the purchaser genuinely values the land more than they do.[131] But this problem can be overcome if the purchaser is willing and able to offer different prices to different owners.

Some development projects do require acquisition of 100 percent of the land in a given area. In such situations, where holdouts could be a genuine problem, private developers have tools for dealing with holdout problems without recourse to government coercion. For reasons Lloyd Cohen points out, holding out is not a simple strategy: "The successful holdout requires accurate information and a high degree of negotiating, bargaining, and bluffing skills."[132] The would-be strategic holdout needs to first know that there is an assembly project going on and then be able to bargain effectively with those undertaking the project. Developers seeking to prevent holdout problems must therefore either deprive potential holdouts of the "accurate information they need" or take away their ability to "negotiate, bargain, and bluff."[133]

Fortunately, there are at least two common strategies that can help achieve these objectives. The first—secret assembly—stymies potential holdouts by depriving them of information. The second—precommitment— undercuts the would-be holdout's ability to bargain. In both cases, developers are able to prevent strategic holdouts but cannot victimize sincere dissenters.

Secret Assembly

In many cases, developers can negotiate with individual owners in secret or use specialized "straw man" agents to assemble the properties they need without alerting potential holdouts to the possibility of making a windfall profit by holding the project hostage.[134] Secret assembly prevents holdouts by denying them knowledge of the existence of a large assembly project. It also allows the developer to buy out potential sincere dissenters who value their property more than other landowners in the area, because the assembler can pay different prices to different owners.

The major drawback of secret assembly is the possibility of detection. As soon as potential holdouts learn that the land in the area is being bought up as part of a large assembly project, they have the information that they need to engage in strategic bargaining. However, empirical evidence suggests that this is not as serious a problem as might be thought.

Even high-profile property owners undertaking major projects have routinely used secret assembly successfully. For example, the Disney Corporation resorted to it to assemble the land needed to build Disney World in Orlando, Florida, in the 1960s.[135] Disney has also made effective use of the same strategy to acquire land for a major new theme park in Virginia.[136] Others who have successfully used secret assembly include

Harvard University, which has repeatedly used it to acquire property for major projects in the Boston area,[137] and locally prominent developers in Las Vegas, Providence, and West Palm Beach, among others.[138] If even high-profile developers such as Disney and Harvard can successfully utilize secrecy without their plans being discovered in time for holdouts to take advantage of the information, then lesser-known developers—who are less apt to be closely watched by the public and the press—should be able to do so with at least equal prospects of success.

As Daniel Kelly points out in an important article, the use of secrecy to prevent holdouts has a major advantage over eminent domain. Condemnation "may force a transfer where the existing owners actually value the land more than the private assembler."[139] By contrast, secrecy "eliminates the risk of erroneous condemnations" because it relies on "voluntary transactions, which ensure that every transfer is mutually beneficial (and thus socially desirable)."[140] Many property owners attach "subjective value" to their land over and above its fair market value, for example those with strong social ties in a particular neighborhood. Secret assembly allows such people to refuse to sell unless and until they are offered enough compensation to fully offset their losses. It thereby enables developers to prevent strategic holdouts but does not allow them to ignore the wishes of sincere dissenters.

The limitations of the secret assembly strategy help explain why eminent domain should, in at least some cases, be available for traditional public uses such as government-owned facilities and private common carriers, even though it should not be used to transfer land to private developers. Unlike a private developer, government often cannot operate in secrecy because of the need for open deliberation and transparency in public administration.[141] Private developers also have an advantage in keeping their purposes secret, because they can usually act more quickly than governments, thus leaving less time during which their plans might be discovered by potential holdouts.[142] Moreover, secrecy in government, even if feasible, might pose a heightened risk of corruption.[143] These points are important because many commentators have long assumed that the "holdout rationale applies equally to both takings for the government and takings for private parties."[144]

A slightly different rationale can justify the use of eminent domain for private common carriers such as railroads and public utilities. In order to build a railroad or power line that connects Point A to Point B, the developer must acquire properties that connect with each other in a narrow, relatively straight line between the two points. Moreover, he or she cannot leave out even a small stretch of the distance, lest there be a break in the resulting railway or power line, rendering the whole useless. Other things equal, it is reasonable to assume that it is much more difficult to conceal the true purposes of such an unusual pattern of acquisition than those of the acquisitions for projects such as Disney's or Harvard's. The logic is similar to that which justifies the use of eminent domain to acquire land to build publicly owned roads.[145] Furthermore, because of the highly regulated nature of public utilities, their acquisition processes may often require public openness for some of the same reasons as those of government. Therefore, common carriers and public utilities may need to utilize eminent domain, while ordinary developers probably will not.

Even in the case of roads and other infrastructure facilities that require the acquisition of rights of way along a predetermined route, it is possible that private developers can effectively use secret assembly and other noncoercive means to overcome assembly problems in at least some cases, as economist Bruce Benson showed in a 2005 article.[146] Even in this classic scenario, which is particularly conducive to potential holdouts, the need for condemnation may be overstated. If so, that fact strengthens the case for secret assembly as a superior alternative to condemnation in cases where private parties seek to acquire property for economic development.

Precommitment Strategies

A second mechanism by which developers can prevent holdout problems without recourse to eminent domain is by means of "precommitment" strategies or "most favored nation" contract clauses. The developers can sign contracts with all the owners in an area where they hope to build, under which they commit themselves to paying the same price to all, with, perhaps, variations stemming from differences in the size or market value of particular properties. By this means, the developer successfully "ties his hands" in a way that precludes him from paying inordinately high prices to the last few holdouts.[147] Precommitment strategies work because they prevent the would-be holdout from being able to "negotiate, bargain, and bluff."[148] Any such attempt at bargaining or bluffing can be met with the response that the buyer is unable to accept the holdout's terms because doing so would render the entire project unprofitable by requiring an equally hefty payout to all the other sellers.

In some respects, a precommitment approach is even better than secrecy, because it can potentially be utilized even by assemblers that must operate openly such as government agencies and public utilities. But precommitment may be a more difficult strategy to implement effectively because it requires that the buyer predetermine a set price for each lot to be purchased in advance of beginning the assembly process. This increases the likelihood of making a mistake such as offering too low a price as a result of underestimating the value the seller attaches to the land. Furthermore, empirical evidence on the use of precommitment strategies is much sparser than that for secrecy. The literature on them has not so far revealed real-world examples of successful use of this strategy for major development projects comparable to the effective use of secrecy by Disney, Harvard, and others.

Implications

Between them, secrecy and precommitment provide alternatives to eminent domain that render it largely unnecessary for use in private economic development projects. They also help explain why private assembly projects can and should be distinguished from the assembly of land for government use or for common carriers and utilities.

In addition to overcoming the holdout problem, secret assembly and precommitment strategies also undercut other, less well-known justifications for using eminent domain for private development. For example, it is theoretically possible that eminent domain is needed to overcome high transaction costs of contacting individual owners and negotiating with them.[149] In practice, however, the transaction costs of eminent domain are likely to be just as high as those of negotiation. The use of eminent domain still requires the government to contact the present owners, and often also to go through various procedural requirements—some of them potentially time-consuming—before the land can be taken.[150]

Eminent domain for private projects has also been defended on the ground that it is necessary to promote projects that create benefits for the community that might not be taken account of by private developers acting on their own. For example, some development projects might provide public goods for the community that no individual developer has an incentive to produce on their own, because once they are created, area residents can enjoy them even without paying to defray the costs of production.[151]

But negotiation, secret assembly, and precommitment strategies can be used to acquire land for such projects just as readily as for other types of private development. If the government concludes that private developers are not undertaking enough of these projects because they are failing to internalize some of their benefits to the community, it can simply offer to subsidize them. The government can most efficiently provide public goods by subsidizing their production, rather than by using eminent domain.[152] Subsidization from general tax revenue avoids the risk of inefficient transfers inherent in the use of condemnation, and also insures that the cost of producing the good is borne by the entire community that benefits from it, rather than arbitrarily concentrated on the preexisting owners of condemned property.

The availability of these alternatives to eminent domain also undercuts claims that condemnation for economic development is needed to combat sprawl.[153] Developers who have an assembly project in an urban area can use secret assembly to forestall strategic holdouts. In cases where greater population density is correlated with a greater number of sincere dissenters who genuinely value their land more than the developer does, this suggests that it would be more efficient for developers to build in less dense areas, where there are fewer competing uses of property, and fewer people will be displaced.

As Robert Bruegmann shows in an important book, sprawl has beneficial as well as negative aspects. It enables people to enjoy greater privacy and autonomy, and diminishes housing costs.[154] Low-density living also helps mitigate some environmental problems associated with high-density areas such as local air pollution and damage to coastal environments.[155] Another advantage is channeling new development toward locations where it destroys less subjective value and displaces fewer existing land uses.

To the extent that some areas still suffer from excessive sprawl, governments have numerous other tools for mitigating the issue, such as offering subsidies or tax breaks for development in denser areas. If diminishing sprawl truly benefits the community as a whole, as advocates claim, it makes sense to impose the costs on the entire community rather than arbitrarily concentrate them among victims of eminent domain. Spreading costs is also likely to be more efficient than eminent domain, because it is less likely to destroy subjective value concentrated in particular properties that might be condemned. Cities can also greatly reduce sprawl by cutting back on the rigid zoning restrictions that massively inflate housing and real estate prices in many northeastern and West Coast urban areas.[156]

It is impossible to categorically rule out the possibility that there might be socially beneficial economic development projects that can only succeed through the use of eminent domain. We can, however, conclude that such projects are likely to be extremely rare, in light of the fact that even major projects undertaken by prominent corporations and universities successfully rely on secret assembly.

In theory, we should still allow the use of eminent domain for those rare efficient development projects that cannot utilize secrecy or precommitment to prevent strategic holdouts.[157] Unfortunately, however, there is no way of confining the use of the economic development rationale to those rare circumstances. Once the prospect of economic development or blight alleviation is allowed to justify takings, it can and will be used by powerful interest groups to facilitate projects that fail to provide economic benefits that justify their costs, could have been undertaken without resorting to coercion, or both.[158] The political power of the beneficiaries of condemnations is likely to be a far more potent determinant of the decision to condemn than any objective economic analysis of holdout problems.

Public Use and the Living Constitution

The evidence on the real-world effects of a broad interpretation of public use has important implications for the status of Public Use Clause under "living Constitution" theories of constitutional interpretation. Although constitutional theorists who adhere to the living Constitution school of thought tend to also endorse the Court's decisions in *Berman* and *Kelo,* there is in fact a strong living Constitution case against these outcomes.

There are many different variants of living Constitution theory. Not all of them are at odds with a broad interpretation of public use. But several of the most influential versions of living Constitution theory do cut against it. These include John Hart Ely's "representation-reinforcement" theory,[159] theories that claim that judges should use common law and other flexible interpretative methods to adapt the Constitution to take account of modern conditions,[160] and Ronald Dworkin's theory that the Constitution should be interpreted in accordance with liberal principles "so as to make its history, all things considered, the best it can be."[161] The same is true of "popular constitutionalism," the idea that constitutional interpretation should be influenced by popular political movements.[162]

Representation-Reinforcement

Representation-reinforcement theory suggests that the judiciary should usually be deferential to the democratic process, except in cases where judicial intervention might actually strengthen democratic control of government. Obvious examples of such representation-reinforcing judicial intervention are decisions protecting freedom of speech or the right to vote, without which democracy cannot work. But representation-reinforcement theorists also argue that courts can intervene to protect groups that are unable to effectively protect themselves in the political system.[163] Representation-reinforcement theory builds on the famous footnote 4 of *United States v. Carolene Products* (1938), where the Supreme Court suggested that stronger judicial intervention is warranted in cases where it is needed to protect "discrete and insular minorities" whose political weakness "tends to seriously curtail the operation of those political processes ordinarily to be relied upon to protect minorities."[164] The classic example is that of unpopular racial or religious minorities, or groups such as gays and lesbians.[165] But, in principle, the same point applies to judicial review of laws targeting other politically weak or unpopular groups. As Ely pointed out, it extends to all of "society's habitual unequals, notably racial minorities, but also aliens, 'illegitimates,' and poor people."[166]

As we have seen, blight and economic development takings disproportionately target the poor and racial minorities, and other politically weak groups.[167] Even those victims who are not poor or racial minorities are, at the very least, usually people with little influence over local and state government, a point missed by critics who argue that the people like the *Kelo* plaintiffs do not deserve judicial protection under representation-reinforcement theory, because they were neither poor nor members of historically oppressed minority groups.[168] Judge Richard Posner, for example, argues that judicial intervention to enforce public use limitations on takings is unnecessary because "[p]roperty owners and the advocates of property rights are not a helpless, marginalized minority."[169] While this may be true of property owners *in general*, it is not true of most of those who are targeted for condemnations that transfer property to private interests.[170]

Wealthy and politically connected property owners rarely suffer from economic development and blight takings, because politicians and developers are usually savvy enough to avoid targeting them. Similarly, the political power of the press as a whole will not prevent government from violating free speech rights if such violations usually target segments of the press that are politically unpopular or have little lobbying power. Just as the power of the press does not obviate the need for judicial enforcement of the First Amendment, the political power of property owners cannot substitute for judicial review of economic development and blight condemnations.

Moreover, in at least one important respect, victims of eminent domain are actually less able to use the political process to protect themselves than are other politically weak minorities. If they have the right to vote, the latter can at least try to form new political coalitions at the next election and seek to elect candidates more favorable to their interests. By contrast, victims of eminent domain are often forced to leave the communities where they live, if their homes are taken. The same is often true of small business owners, whose loss of their businesses often forces them to move as well.

People who are forced to leave the jurisdiction that condemned their property cannot continue to vote in local elections and thereby forfeit most of their power to use the political process to protect themselves. By the time the next election happens, they are no longer around to try to "vote the bastards out." They can still potentially seek intervention by the federal or state government from their new location. But, for politically weak groups, trying to influence a higher-level government is likely to be even more difficult than influencing a lower-level one.

In addition, the ability of victims of eminent domain to use the political process is further undermined by the economic and psychological trauma of forced displacement.[171] People who have suffered these effects often have little time, resources, and energy to devote to political activity, since they are understandably focused on trying to recover from their ordeal and start news lives elsewhere. As Justice Clarence Thomas put it in his *Kelo* dissent "[i]f ever there were justification for intrusive judicial review of constitutional provisions that protect 'discrete and insular minorities,' . . . surely that principle would apply with great force to the powerless groups and individuals the Public Use Clause protects."[172]

Even strong advocates of representation-reinforcement theory would not necessarily want courts to intervene any time that a politically weak group has suffered a defeat in the political process. In that event, judges might have nearly unlimited power to reverse legislative decisions they do not approve of. But the situation is different when a weak minority is targeted in a way that might plausibly be connected to an enumerated constitutional right.

John Hart Ely's influential work emphasized the need for courts to aggressively enforce provisions of the Constitution that can plausibly be interpreted as representation-reinforcing.[173] He even specifically described the compensation requirement of the Fifth Amendment as one of them, because it is a "protection of the few against the many."[174] The Public Use Clause contained in the same amendment can be described in much the same way. It too protects the politically weak few against the predations of both "the many" and narrow interest groups more powerful than themselves.

Representation-reinforcement theory does not necessarily require judicial protection for *all* politically weak minorities. Violent criminals, for example are a small, politically weak minority group. But few would advocate strong judicial scrutiny of laws that disadvantage them, because nearly everyone assumes that their political weakness is in some sense deserved.

Perhaps courts should only show special solicitude for underrepresented minorities if their weakness is *undeserved*.[175] In the case of politically weak victims of eminent domain, it is hard to see any good justification for their powerlessness relative to developers, government planners, and others who promote blight and economic development takings. This is especially true in light of the fact that their weakness is often in part the result of poverty or racial minority status.

If we assume that the correct interpretation of "public use" is at least somewhat ambiguous, representation-reinforcement theory therefore counsels in favor of interpreting it in a way that would give greater protection for property rights.

Common Law Constitutionalism

Common law constitutionalism is a strain of living Constitution theory that has attained greater prominence in recent years, thanks in large part to the important work of David Strauss.[176] The core idea of common law constitutionalism is that judges should treat constitutional law much as they have traditionally approached the common law: making decisions by paying close attention to precedent, while also adjusting that precedent to take account of new information and changing social conditions. Numerous judges who do not fully endorse common law constitutionalism still use this methodology in many of their rulings.

Common law constitutionalism's general deference to precedent initially strengthens the case for adhering to the broad interpretation of "public use." After all, the Supreme Court has followed that approach since 1954, when it decided *Berman v. Parker.*[177] But common law constitutionalism also allows courts to reverse or narrow precedents, in some circumstances, just as judges often do in ordinary common law cases.[178] David Strauss, the leading academic advocate of the theory, argues that precedent can be overruled in cases where an old rule has become "unworkable" (in the sense of creating internal contradictions in the rule) and in cases where courts purporting to apply the old rule have over time deviated from it.[179]

The ultra-broad definition of public use adopted in *Kelo* and other similar cases fits at least one of these two criteria. It is unworkable in the sense of being internally contradictory. Between *Berman* and *Kelo*, the Supreme Court adopted a deferential approach to public use issues but also repeatedly reiterated the idea that condemnations, which do not serve a genuine public purpose, are unconstitutional. As the Court put it in *Hawaii Housing Authority v. Midkiff*, its "cases have repeatedly stated that 'one person's property may not be taken for the benefit of another private person without a justifying public purpose.' "[180] Justice John Paul Stevens's majority opinion in *Kelo* similarly noted that "the City [of New London] would no doubt be forbidden from taking petitioners' land for the purpose of conferring a private benefit on a particular private party."[181]

Unfortunately, the Court's adoption of the broad definition of "public use," combined with broad deference to the government's claims that a public benefit will actually be achieved by a particular taking, renders this constraint on condemnations unworkable. As we have seen, virtually any taking transferring property to a private party can be justified as promoting "economic development," especially if the government is not even required to prove that the promised development will actually occur. Therefore, the rule adopted in cases, such as *Berman, Midkiff,* and *Kelo,* is self-defeating. It makes it virtually impossible for courts to enforce the requirement that takings cannot be constitutional "without a justifying public purpose."[182]

Recognizing this problem would not necessarily require the Supreme Court to jettison the broad definition of public use entirely. It could instead adopt the approach advocated by Justice Sandra Day O'Connor in her *Kelo* dissent, which rejects private-to-private economic development takings but permits blight condemnations in areas that are genuinely blighted. From the standpoint of maintaining precedent, this would enable the Court to narrow the scope of *Berman* and *Midkiff* without overruling them entirely.[183] But the economic development rationale for takings would, at the very least, have to be rejected, since it permits almost any taking that transfers property to a private business and thus makes it impossible to enforce any meaningful limits on the range of purposes for which property may be condemned.

The Court could, of course, have attempted to solve this problem by ruling that the Public Use Clause imposes no substantive constraints on takings at all, as advocated by Justice Stevens after his retirement from the Court.[184] But that would be a radical break with centuries of precedent and therefore inimical to the common law approach so long as there is a reasonably viable alternative.[185]

Common law courts also often overrule precedent when they conclude that experience shows that a rule is pernicious or has harmful effects. As Strauss puts it, the "common law process" can take account of "the lessons of the past."[186] When it comes to economic development and blight condemnations, the courts can look to decades of experience in which such takings have inflicted great harm on the poor and politically weak, while producing little of the prosperity that supposedly justified them in the first place.

Finally, common law constitutionalist courts can consider the growing number of state supreme court decisions that had invalidated economic development takings under their state constitutions.[187] State supreme court decisions are not binding precedent for federal courts. But common law courts often take account of relevantly similar decisions in other common law jurisdictions. American common law courts routinely cite relevant precedents from Britain, Australia, and other common law countries. The U.S. Supreme Court has even sometimes cited foreign decisions in constitutional cases, and common law constitutionalism supports this practice.[188] The strong trend of state decisions striking down economic development takings and repudiating *Kelo* as a guide to the interpretation of state public use clauses is at least relevant for federal judges seeking to apply common law constitutionalism.

Ronald Dworkin's Moral Theory of Constitutional Interpretation

The late Ronald Dworkin's moral theory of constitutional interpretation is one of the most influential versions of living Constitution theory. Dworkin argued that constitutional interpretation should be influenced by moral considerations, though not completely determined by them. Where the constitutional text and history are relatively ambiguous, the Dworkinian judge will be guided by "the best available interpretation of American constitutional text and practice as a whole," taking into consideration "justice and fairness and the right relation between then."[189] He or she relies on a "moral reading" of the Constitution that "brings political morality into the heart of constitutional law."[190]

The Dworkinian jurist would rely less on such moral considerations in cases where the text and history of the Constitution is clear and unambiguous.[191] But, as we saw in chapter 2, the broad interpretation of "public use" adopted by the Supreme Court in *Kelo* is, at the very least, far from clearly correct. Dworkin argued that judges should use moral reasoning to interpret constitutional rights that are broadly worded in "abstract moral language," among which he specifically included those rights protected by the Bill of Rights.[192] The term "public use" occurs in the Bill of Rights and certainly uses "abstract moral language." A Dworkinian judge would therefore give consideration to moral theory in determining its meaning. He or she seeks to interpret the Constitution "so as to make its history, all things considered, the best it can be."[193]

There are many different conceptions of justice that a Dworkinian judge could potentially rely on in addressing ambiguous elements of the Constitution. Dworkin himself discussed libertarian, utilitarian, egalitarian, and equal opportunity conceptions of justice with respect to property rights.[194]

Given the empirical record of economic development and blight condemnations, there is a strong case for overruling *Kelo* and *Berman v. Parker* under any of the four. This is fairly obviously true under a libertarian conception, which urges strong protection for property rights regardless of the wealth of the owner. A utilitarian conception of justice, which requires government to maximize the happiness and welfare of its citizens, would also condemn such takings, since they usually inflict far more harm than they create benefit. Moreover, much of the harm is inflicted on the poor, who can less easily bear the loss of property than the affluent. Egalitarian and equal opportunity conceptions of justice require the government to either seek to equalize the material wealth of their citizens or provide them with relatively equal starting points for pursuing economic opportunities.[195] Blight and economic development takings are inimical to either of these approaches, because of their tendency to victimize the poor and racial minorities, thereby reducing their chances of either attaining the same standard of wealth as the average middle-class white American, or attaining equal opportunity.

Dworkin cautioned readers that a jurist applying his theory should "refuse to substitute his judgment for that of the legislature when he believes the issue in play is primarily one of policy rather than principle, when the argument is about the best strategies for achieving the overall collective interest through goals like prosperity or the eradication of poverty."[196] Such policy considerations relating to "overall collective interests" are *part* of the issue at stake in the debate over public use. But they are only a part. These kinds of takings also impinge on the rights of poor and politically weak minority groups.

As Dworkin recognized, some parts of the Constitution were adopted in part to ensure "the protection of individuals and minorities against the will of the majority."[197] The Public Use Clause and the Takings Clause are clearly examples of this type of provision. Moreover, in practice, enforcement of public use limitations on takings is likely to primarily benefit poor and politically weak minority groups. In some of his work, Dworkin emphasized the need to protect the poor against government policies that reduce the resources available to them, even in some cases where such redistribution promotes overall societal welfare.[198]

There is a strong Dworkinian case for interpreting the Public Use Clause to ban blight and economic development takings. The Dworkinian judge might, however, be open to other kinds of takings that transfer property to private parties, especially if the latter can somehow be distinguished from economic development takings in a way consistent with the text and history of the Public Use Clause.

Popular Constitutionalism

Popular constitutionalism is a relatively new theory that has attracted considerable attention over the last decade. It holds that constitutional interpretation is, and often should be, influenced by public opinion and popular political movements, such as the civil rights movement, the women's rights movement, the gay and lesbian rights movement, and the gun rights movement.[199] Some scholars discuss popular influence over constitutional interpretation as a purely empirical matter, holding that constitutional interpretation in the courts has been influenced by political movements, regardless of whether that influence is beneficial or not.[200] But others contend that such influence is normatively desirable for a variety of reasons, including ensuring the legitimacy of the Constitution, adjusting its meaning to changing circumstances, and others.[201] Such normative popular constitutionalists are not always clear on how strong a popular movement must be before it can legitimately influence constitutional interpretation. And few if any of them would argue that popular opinion should be the *only* factor that courts take into account in deciding constitutional questions.

If popular opinion should be given any significant weight in judicial decision-making at all, there is a strong popular constitutionalist case for reversing *Kelo.* It is difficult to find *any* modern Supreme Court decision that attracted popular opposition as broad as that aroused by *Kelo,* which has been consistently opposed by over 80 percent of the public.

Compared to other popular constitutional movements, the anti-*Kelo* movement stands out for the breadth of its support. Most popular constitutionalist movements draw primarily on one side of the political spectrum and stimulate bitter opposition on the other. For example, the feminist and gay rights movements drew primarily on the political left and were opposed by most conservatives, while the gun rights movement has the opposite valence.[202] Most recently, the Tea Party movement has emerged as a popular constitutionalist movement on the political right, which has drawn skepticism from moderates and forceful opposition from the left.[203]

By contrast with these examples, opposition to *Kelo* cuts across conventional political lines, with groups as varied as the libertarian Institute for Justice, the popular conservative talk-show host Rush Limbaugh, left-wing presidential candidate Ralph Nader, and the NAACP all uniting in opposition to it.[204] Public opinion polls show overwhelming opposition to economic development takings among liberals and conservatives, Democrats and Republicans, blacks and whites, women and men, and nearly every other significant demographic or political subset of the population.[205] Moreover, the breadth of opposition has held steady even years after *Kelo,* so it cannot be considered merely a knee-jerk reaction in the immediate aftermath of the case.[206] If there was ever a case where popular constitutionalist movements can legitimately influence the outcome, this should be it.

It is possible that public opposition to *Kelo* was in part the result of ignorance. For example, as we shall see in chapter 5, voters may well have been ignorant of the fact that *Kelo* was largely consistent with previous Supreme Court precedent. But if ignorance vitiates the force of public opinion on constitutional issues, that is not so much a defense of *Kelo* as a critique of popular constitutionalism more generally. Political ignorance on numerous political issues—both constitutional and otherwise—is ubiquitous.[207]

A popular constitutionalist could still defend *Kelo* based on the theory that popular opinion can sometimes be outweighed by other considerations. It is also fair to observe that public opinion on blight takings is far less clear than that on pure economic development takings; though the opposition to the latter surely also implies opposition to blight takings based on extremely broad definitions of "blight" that make the blight rationale just as expansive as the economic development one. But whatever weight popular movements should have in constitutional deliberation, in this case it comes down firmly in favor of overruling *Kelo.*

Other Variants of Living Constitutionalism

Not every version of living constitutionalism cuts against *Kelo.* For example, some living constitutionalists would prefer to abjure judicial review entirely and leave constitutional interpretation entirely to the political process.[208] A less-sweeping version of this approach is the "Thayerian" idea that judges should defer to the legislature in constitutional cases except in cases where the unconstitutionality of the challenged law is so clear that it is "not open to rational question."[209] Others counsel extraordinary deference to precedent, including even extremely dubious precedent.[210] But such sweeping theories have consequences that go well beyond *Kelo,* many of which are unwelcome to most living constitutionalists. For example, Thayerian deference would have required the Supreme Court to defer to the legislature in such canonical cases as *Brown v. Board of Education,*[211] since the unconstitutionality of racial segregation in public education was far from unequivocally certain in 1954. In the years immediately after it was decided, *Brown* was seriously questioned not only by segregationists, but even by such leading liberal jurists and legal commentators as Judge Learned Hand and Columbia Law School Professor Herbert Wechsler.[212] Similarly, broad deference to precedent would cut against a wide range of Supreme Court decisions endorsed by most living constitutionalists, including the Warren Court's decisions promoting racial equality and protecting the rights of criminal defendants, and more recent decisions protecting gays and lesbians against government repression and discrimination.[213]

Bruce Ackerman's theory of "constitutional moments" might also support the result in *Kelo*.[214] Ackerman contends that the meaning of the Constitution can legitimately be modified by the action of strong popular supermajorities validated by congressional legislation and presidential support as well as by the formal amendment process of Article V of the Constitution. He argues that such a constitutional moment occurred during the New Deal era of the 1930s, as well as at the time of the enactment of the Reconstruction Amendments in the years immediately after the Civil War (which he contends should be understood as being outside the standard formal amendment framework, because the procedures mandated by Article V were not fully followed).[215]

Because of the central role that Ackerman's theory assigns to the New Deal period, it might well validate the broad view of public use endorsed by the Supreme Court in *Berman v. Parker*. Most of the justices who decided *Berman* were New Deal Democratic appointees, and there is little doubt that their position reflected the dominant view among New Deal jurists.[216] Under Ackerman's approach, changes in constitutional meaning that enjoyed sufficient broad support during the New Deal period must be adhered to, even if they go against the preexisting meaning of the Constitution. It is more than plausible to argue that the transformation in the meaning of public use was just one of the many changes validated by the New Deal revolution in constitutional doctrine. This is probably the most intuitive and straightforward application of Ackerman's theory to public use.

But the implications of constitutional moment theory for public use are not completely unequivocal. While there is no doubt that judges and other legal elites moved toward a broad interpretation of public use during the New Deal period, it is not clear that the change enjoyed supermajority support from public opinion or even that most of the public was aware of it. And Ackerman's theory requires broad, supermajority popular support to legitimate constitutional change outside the Article V process, not just elite support.[217] There must be "mobilized popular deliberation."[218]

Unlike some of the other changes in constitutional doctrine that occurred during the New Deal period, public use was not a major issue in national political campaigns at the time, nor was it a major focus of nationwide public debate.[219] Thus, it is possible that New Deal–era changes in public use doctrine do not fit the criteria of Ackerman's theory.

One could argue that the public understood the New Deal as sweeping away all judicial enforcement of "economic" rights and that public use was implicitly included, even if not much explicitly discussed. But that assertion would require proof that the public really did understand New Deal constitutional change in such an expansive way.

It is also possible that Ackerman's theory leaves room for judicial enforcement of at least a relatively narrow definition of public use because of the harmful impact of the broad definition on racial minorities and the poor. In his most recent book, Ackerman argues that the New Deal transformation in constitutional law should be understood in conjunction with the civil rights revolution of the 1950s and 1960s, which led to a new understanding that policies that undermine the dignity and equality of vulnerable minorities are unconstitutional or at least constitutionally suspect.[220] On this interpretation of Ackerman's theory, judicial enforcement of public use constraints on takings can be viewed as part of what Ackerman considers the civil rights era's "intergenerational synthesis" of the New Deal era's removal of judicial constraints on government economic regulation with the preexisting Constitution's emphasis on protecting individual rights against government intrusion and the Fourteenth Amendment's antidiscrimination provisions.[221] That synthesis involves protection of vulnerable minority groups against government oppression, and also of privacy rights and dignitary interests.

Economic development and blight takings often both target politically weak minorities, and undermine the dignity and privacy of those forcibly expelled from their homes and small businesses. To adapt a point made by Justice Clarence Thomas in his *Kelo* dissent, if searching a home can infringe constitutionally protected privacy rights, the same is surely true when the government decides to destroy the home and force its residents to move elsewhere.[222]

This interpretation of Ackerman's theory might not justify invalidation of all broad-public use takings, only those that expel people from their homes, target vulnerable minorities, or both. Takings aimed at churches and small businesses might also be covered, since such properties are often integral to the dignity of their owners and have high "subjective value" that goes beyond their market value.[223] But this approach would lead to the invalidation of most blight and economic development takings of the kind at issue in *Berman* and *Kelo*.

Ultimately, the implications of Ackerman's theory for public use are ambiguous. They depend crucially on whether the New Deal approach to public use accumulated broad enough public support, and whether intergenerational synthesis might justify enforcing a narrower definition of public use, assuming that the broad one really was properly adopted during the 1930s.

Because there are so many different variants of living Constitution theory, it is certainly possible to find some that can justify *Kelo*. Thayerian deference clearly would, and Ackerman's theory might potentially do so, depending on how it is interpreted. But it is still noteworthy that some of the most influential variants of living constitutionalism cut against it, including several that have had a major influence on both judicial and academic opinion.

Conclusion

Blight and economic development takings authorized by a broad interpretation of public use have inflicted great harm on vulnerable poor, minority, and politically weak groups. They also often undermine economic development more than promote it.

These aspects of blight and economic development takings contribute to a strong living Constitution case for overruling *Kelo*. That case encompasses several of the most influential variants of living constitutionalism, and deserves serious consideration from scholars and judges who either reject originalism or at least believe that it should not be the only basis of constitutional interpretation.

Having considered the problem of public use from both originalist and living Constitution points of view, we are now ready to examine the *Kelo* decision itself. The ruling has many shortcomings that should trouble originalists and living constitutionalists alike.

CHAPTER FOUR

The *Kelo* Decision

*K*elo was the first major U.S. Supreme Court public use case since *Hawaii Housing Authority v. Midkiff*, over twenty years before. It came at a time when most experts believed that public use was largely dead as a meaningful constraint on takings. *Kelo* was a painful defeat for property owners in that it upheld the "economic development" rationale for condemnation and advocated broad judicial deference on public use issues.[1] On the other hand, *Kelo* did signal a slight tightening of judicial scrutiny of public use relative to the previously dominant rule that the public use requirement is satisfied so long as "the exercise of the eminent domain power is rationally related to a conceivable public purpose."[2] Far more importantly, the fact that four justices not only dissented but actually concluded that the economic development rationale should be categorically forbidden shows that the judicial landscape on public use has changed.[3] Support for a virtually limitless definition of public use can no longer be portrayed as the consensus view of the federal judiciary.

Justice Stevens's Majority Opinion

The opinion of the Court written by Justice John Paul Stevens was in many ways unsurprising in light of *Berman v. Parker* (1954) and *Hawaii Housing Authority v. Midkiff*.[4] Like those earlier precedents it emphasized the need to maintain the Court's "policy of deference to legislative judgment in this field."[5] The majority rejected the property owners' argument that the transfer of their property to private developers rather than to a public body required any heightened degree of judicial scrutiny.[6] It also refused to require the city to provide any evidence that the takings were likely to actually achieve the claimed economic benefits that provided their justification in the first place.[7] On all these points, the *Kelo* majority chose not to "second-guess the City's considered judgments about the efficacy of the development plan."[8]

Though the majority position on these issues was doctrinally consistent with previous Supreme Court decisions, the factual circumstances of *Kelo* were considerably different from those of the earlier cases. For the first time, the Supreme Court upheld the condemnation of nonblighted residential property for transfer to private interests solely on the ground that the resulting transfer might increase economic development. While this result was consistent with preexisting doctrine, it nonetheless made explicit a threat to ordinary middle- and working-class homeowners that in the earlier cases seemed merely latent.

The majority also justified its emphasis on deference by relying on cases from "the late nineteenth" and early twentieth centuries that supposedly "embraced the broader and more natural interpretation of public use as 'public purpose.' "[9] As we shall see, these Progressive-era precedents did not purport to apply the Public Use Clause but instead addressed challenges to takings based on nineteenth- and early twentieth-century doctrines of economic substantive due process under the Due Process Clause of the Fourteenth Amendment.[10]

Despite the broad theme of deference and the extensive reliance on *Berman* and *Midkiff*,[11] Stevens's majority opinion nonetheless departs from near-total deference in three ways. First, references to *Midkiff's* ultradeferential statement that takings will be upheld if they are "rationally related to a conceivable public purpose"[12] are conspicuous by their absence. Nor did the *Kelo* majority rely on the almost equally broad *Midkiff* claim that the scope of public use is "coterminous with the scope of a sovereign's police powers."[13]

Second, Stevens's opinion emphasizes the importance of the fact that the New London takings were part of a "comprehensive" development plan.[14] Stevens distinguished between such condemnations and a "one-to-one transfer of property, executed outside the confines of an integrated development plan."[15] The latter scenario, Stevens notes, "raise[s] the suspicion that a private purpose was afoot" and might potentially be unconstitutional.[16]

Even if we interpret the majority opinion as requiring that economic development condemnations be part of a "comprehensive" development plan, this rule fails to impose any meaningful constraints on the condemnation powers of local governments. Since Stevens also emphasized that courts should not "second-guess" either "the efficacy" of development plans or condemning authorities' "determinations as to what lands [they] need to acquire," it will almost always be possible for officials to concoct a plan to justify almost any condemnations they might wish to undertake.[17] As Scott Bullock, one of the attorneys for the *Kelo* plaintiffs, notes, "nearly all condemnations for transfer to private parties occur pursuant to development plans and within designated redevelopment areas."[18] Indeed, *99 Cents Only Stores v. Lancaster Redevelopment Agency*, the case cited by Stevens as an example of a pure "one-to-one transfer,"[19] actually struck down a taking that the government justified as necessary to implement a redevelopment plan.[20]

Finally, Stevens held out some small hope for property owners in noting that pretextual takings, where the official rationale for the taking is a pretext "for the purpose of conferring a private benefit on a particular private party" are unconstitutional.[21] This could potentially be interpreted as a meaningful constraint on takings, though its exact meaning is far from clear. The question of what qualifies as a pretextual taking has bedeviled lower courts in the wake of *Kelo,* with many being willing to give at least some teeth to this restriction on eminent domain.[22]

The *Kelo* majority's limited withdrawal from the ultradeferential approach adopted in *Berman* and *Midkiff* represents at least a small concession to increasing skepticism about the use of eminent domain. A future Court could potentially give some real teeth to this element of *Kelo* by imposing substantive standards on the quality of development plans, by requiring cities to present at least some real evidence that condemnation is indeed necessary to achieve the claimed public benefits of the plan, or by adopting a robust pretextual takings doctrine. Even in combination, these steps would fall well short of eliminating abusive economic development takings. But it is nonetheless significant that *Kelo* leaves the door to meaningful judicial scrutiny of public use slightly ajar, whereas *Berman* and *Midkiff* had virtually slammed it shut.

Justice Kennedy's Concurrence

Justice Kennedy's concurring opinion echoes the majority in emphasizing that public use issues should generally be considered under a "deferential standard of review."[23] Unlike the majority opinion, Kennedy seemingly reiterated *Midkiff's* highly deferential "rational-basis test."[24] But he also held out the prospect of more stringent judicial review of public use in two different ways. First, he suggested that rational basis review should not be interpreted as requiring virtually complete deference to government determinations of public use. Second, and perhaps more radically, he left open the possibility that some takings should actually be presumed invalid.

Kennedy emphasizes that "[t]he determination that a rational-basis standard of review is appropriate does not . . . alter the fact that transfers intended to confer benefits on particular, favored, private entities, and with only incidental or pretextual public benefits, are forbidden by the Public Use Clause."[25] He contends that deference to condemning authorities might be relaxed if there is "a plausible accusation of impermissible favoritism to private parties."[26] In such cases, courts must "treat the objection as a serious one and review the record to see if it has merit."[27]

Under Kennedy's approach, a court should "strike down a taking that, by a clear showing, is intended to favor a particular private party, with only incidental or pretextual public benefits."[28] This is intended to be rational basis review with at least some real bite, a point that Kennedy drives home by analogizing his approach to cases that use the Equal Protection Clause of the Fourteenth Amendment to strike down "classification[s] that [are] clearly intended to injure a particular class of private parties."[29] These cases struck down classifications that would have been upheld under a straightforward application of the standard ultradeferential rational basis test.

Furthermore, Kennedy holds open "the possibility that a more stringent standard of review than that announced in *Berman* and *Midkiff* might be appropriate for a more narrowly drawn category of takings . . . in which the risk of undetected impermissible favoritism to private parties is so acute that a presumption (rebuttable or otherwise) of invalidity is warranted under the Public Use Clause."[30] Kennedy is careful to note that such a presumption of invalidity will not be triggered merely by the fact that the condemnation is justified on the basis of promoting "economic development," and he refuses to engage in "conjecture as to what sort of cases might justify a more demanding standard."[31] Even so, Kennedy's approach holds out the possibility of more stringent judicial review of public use in some types of cases.

The true meaning of Kennedy's opinion is extremely difficult to judge. Although he was the swing voter in a 5-4 decision, he signed on to the

majority opinion and did not merely concur in judgment. This makes it
difficult to tell to what extent there really is a difference between his view
and that of the other four justices in the majority.[32] Furthermore, Kennedy is vague in his explanation of what would count as "a clear showing
[that a condemnation] is intended to favor a particular private party, with
only incidental or pretextual public benefits."[33] And, as already noted, he
refused to explain what circumstances, if any, would trigger a "presumption of invalidity."[34] Finally, as we shall see, it is far from clear that even
the most careful inquiries into government motives can succeed in curbing eminent domain abuse.[35]

The long-term significance of Kennedy's opinion is highly conjectural.
This is particularly true in light of the fact that two of the four *Kelo* dissenters (Chief Justice Rehnquist and Justice O'Connor) have departed
the Court, replaced by Justice Samuel Alito and Chief Justice John Roberts. Two members of the *Kelo* majority—Stevens and David Souter—
have also retired and been replaced. We can no longer be certain if Justice Kennedy is still the Court's median voter on public use issues. These
essential caveats notwithstanding, Justice Kennedy's opinion, perhaps
more so than the majority, leaves open the door for a retreat from judicial
deference on public use issues. Whether a future Court will choose to
enter that door remains to be seen.

Assessing the *Kelo* Majority

While *Kelo* represents a modest advance over the extreme deference to
government power established in *Berman* and *Midkiff,* it still has significant flaws. These include failure to take into account defects in the political
process underlying takings, misinterpretation of relevant precedents, and
an excessive confidence in judicial ability to ferret out on a case-by-case
basis takings characterized by impermissible "favoritism" to private parties. These flaws are, to a large extent, also shared by Justice Kennedy's
concurring opinion.

Deferring to a Flawed Political Process

Deference to the political process is the central theme of *Kelo,* as of *Berman* and *Midkiff* before it. This stance has several major shortcomings.
Perhaps most important, it fails to come to grips with the many defects of

the political processes underlying economic development takings. These flaws make it likely that the condemnation process will be captured by interest groups, with the result that numerous takings might be undertaken whose costs greatly outweigh their benefits.[36] Perhaps the most striking aspect of the Court's stance is not that it came down on the side of deference, but that it failed to even consider the possibility that flaws in the political process might justify a stronger judicial role.

The Court's advocacy of deference might be more defensible if it had concluded, as do a few scholars, that the text and original meaning of the Public Use Clause simply do not place any substantive limits on the scope of eminent domain.[37] Justice Stevens, as we have seen, ultimately adopted this view after his retirement.[38] Yet the *Kelo* majority, like the *Berman* and *Midkiff* courts before it, still endorsed the long-standing view that the Public Use Clause does impose constraints on takings. It emphasized that "the City would no doubt be forbidden from taking petitioners' land for the purpose of conferring a private benefit on a particular private party."[39] At the same time, it also concluded that the judgment as to whether a particular taking is purely private is almost completely left up to the government, in order to "afford legislatures broad latitude in determining what public needs justify the use of the takings power."[40] The Court's position gives state and local governments the power to determine the scope of an individual right guaranteed by the Bill of Rights, with little or no judicial scrutiny.

This approach would be understandable if there were little or no reason to expect government to overreach or to be "captured" by private interests seeking to benefit from the use of the eminent domain power. In fact, however, there is good reason to expect problems of this type.[41]

At the very least, there is no reason to expect government to be able to police itself in the public use field better than it does with respect to most other individual constitutional rights. As James Ely notes, "among all the guarantees of the Bill of Rights, only the public use limitation is singled out for heavy [judicial] deference."[42] In his dissent, Justice Thomas rightly emphasized that the Court's approach is in serious tension with its much more aggressive stance in enforcing other constitutional rights such as the Fourth Amendment right to be free from "unreasonable" searches and seizures.[43] As Thomas put it, the Court is willing to second-guess legislative judgments "when the issue is only whether government may search a home," yet is unwilling to question "the infinitely more intrusive step of tearing down . . . homes."[44]

The Court's deferential approach on public use also directly conflicts "with its handling of the other major constitutional check on eminent domain, the just compensation requirement."[45] In this field, the Court has consistently refused to defer to legislative judgment and has forced government to pay "fair market value."[46] Yet it is difficult to understand why a government that can be trusted to determine when property should be condemned cannot also be trusted to determine what constitutes "just compensation" under the Fifth Amendment. The difference cannot simply be a matter of deference to legislative expertise. The question of determining how much compensation should be paid is often no less complex than that of public use. Neither is a field where the judiciary is likely to have greater technical competence than the legislature.[47]

The *Kelo* Court's ultradeferential approach to public use issues has been defended on two interrelated grounds: the need to give latitude to superior legislative expertise, and respect for federalism and the diversity of local conditions. Thomas Merrill, a leading academic defender of the *Kelo* decision, contends that "lawyers and judges are not particularly good at anticipating the ways in which reconfigurations of ownership rights may produce significant public benefits," and argues that "politically accountable actors" are likely to perform this role better.[48] Justice Stevens's majority opinion claims that "the needs of society have varied between different parts of the Nation," thereby justifying "a strong theme of federalism, emphasizing the 'great respect' that we owe to state legislatures and state courts in discerning local public needs."[49] Neither legislative expertise nor federalism, however, can justify the extreme divergence between the Court's treatment of the Public Use Clause and its approach to other constitutional rights.

There is no doubt that economic development takings and other condemnations sometimes involve complex policy issues on which judges have little expertise. It is likely that legislative and executive officials also have greater expertise than judges on such traditional constitutional questions as whether or not a given search is "reasonable," as required by the Fourth Amendment; whether or not a particular type of speech should be restricted because that is the only way to promote a compelling state interest; and whether and to what extent racial or gender classifications are necessary to advance important public values. All of these involve complex issues hotly disputed by both experts and members of the general public. On all of them, legislatures and executive officials are likely to have greater expertise than judges. Yet that does not prevent federal courts from strongly enforcing the First, Fourth, and Fourteenth Amendments. It is difficult to see why superior legislative expertise justifies differential treatment of the Public Use Clause.

The federalism rationale for deference has similar weaknesses. It is certainly true that land use and eminent domain policies often depend in part on diverse local conditions that are better understood by state and local officials than federal judges. But the federal judiciary enforces numerous other constitutional rights that similarly constrain government policies that vary on the basis of local conditions on which state officials might have superior expertise. For example, the Supreme Court has recognized that the reasonableness of a search under the Fourth Amendment often depends on "the facts of a particular case in light of the distinctive features and events of the community" on which local judges and "law enforcement officers" may have specialized "expertise."[50]

Often, local officials and police have far greater knowledge about "the distinctive features and events of the community" relevant to the constitutionality of a particular search than federal judges. Indeed, the "reasonableness" of a search may depend on local conditions to an even greater degree than public use decisions do. Whether a search is reasonable may depend on conditions that vary from day to day and house to house. Yet federal judges routinely address these issues and do not simply defer to the views of local law enforcement authorities. Similar variations in local conditions are relevant to a wide range of constitutional rights, including freedom of speech, and freedom of religion, among others.[51]

In each of these cases, the courts exercise nondeferential judicial review in the face of the admittedly superior expertise of the legislature because that expertise may be used in ways that violate constitutional rights. Legislative expertise has little value if it is used to benefit the politically powerful at the expense of the poor and weak rather than to advance the public interest, as often happens with blight and economic development takings.

By barring certain categories of takings, judicial enforcement of the Public Use Clause can also give greater scope to a form of expertise that often outstrips that of the legislature: the local knowledge of property owners themselves, who often understand their land and its potential uses better than government policy makers do. Where courts strike down takings for violating the Public Use Clause, it is not judges but property owners who determine the ultimate disposition of the land in question. Even if judges know less about the relevant issues than government officials do, property owners are likely to know more, both because they are more familiar with their land and because they have stronger incentives to acquire relevant information and use it effectively.[52]

These points apply just as readily to the idea that federal courts should defer to state courts on public use questions, as to deference to state and local legislatures. Federal courts do not defer to state courts with respect to other constitutional rights that relate to complex local issues, including Fourth Amendment rights against searches and seizures. State courts, like state legislatures, will sometimes fail to effectively protect federal constitutional rights. In such cases, federal courts must intervene. Moreover, it is far from clear that state judges necessarily have significantly greater expertise on constitutional property rights issues than federal judges.[53]

In addition, nondeferential judicial enforcement of the Public Use Clause need not require much specialized expertise on the part of judges. If judges either enforce a ban on economic development takings or adopt the narrow view of public use more generally, they need not opine on the question of whether a particular taking will result in long-term economic benefits or not. They need only determine whether the taking in question is an economic development condemnation or whether it is a transfer of property to a private party that does not have a legal obligation to serve the public. The answers to these questions will not always be completely obvious.[54] But there is no reason to believe that these rules are more difficult to apply than many other legal rules and standards routinely administered by federal courts.

Finally, the federalism rationale for *Kelo* rings hollow as a defense of the deferential approach to public use more generally. If taken seriously, it implies a higher level of scrutiny for condemnations undertaken by the federal government. Yet few if any defenders of *Kelo* have ever advocated such a two-tier approach to the Public Use Clause. Indeed, *Berman v. Parker,* the leading prodeference Supreme Court precedent—upheld a taking by the District of Columbia, which is under federal jurisdiction.

Ferreting out Favoritism?

Both the *Kelo* majority and Justice Kennedy's concurring opinion exhibit excessive confidence that courts can ferret out "improper" favoritism to private interests, while still maintaining a highly deferential posture. Justice Stevens's majority opinion claims that the risk of favoritism in economic development takings can be eliminated or at least minimized so long as the taking in question is part of an "integrated development plan."[55] Justice Kennedy asserts that undue favoritism can prevented so long as "[a] court confronted with a plausible accusation of impermissible favoritism to private parties . . . treat[s] the objection as a serious one and review[s] the record to see if it has merit, though with the presumption that the government's actions were reasonable and intended to serve a public purpose."[56]

Neither approach is likely to work well. The requirement of having an "integrated development plan" is especially unlikely to fulfill its purpose, as nearly all economic development takings are initiated as part of some sort of plan; this was even true of the case that Stevens's opinion cites as a paradigmatic example of impermissible favoritism.[57] Even if the jurisdiction in question did not initially intend to adopt a plan, after *Kelo* it would surely choose to do so in order to insulate itself from legal challenge. Since the *Kelo* majority specifically indicates that courts should not "second-guess" the plan's quality or likelihood of it actually achieving its goals,[58] even a very poorly designed plan is likely to pass muster.

The requirement of an integrated development may potentially stymie an extremely poor local government that cannot afford to put together even a rudimentary plan or an extremely incompetent one that does not think to do so even after *Kelo*. But it is unlikely that any significant number of dubious condemnations will be prevented.

Justice Kennedy's approach at first glance seems more promising. Since he would require courts to investigate the possibility of favoritism in a relatively nondeferential way, there is at least some chance that courts acting as he recommends might uncover abuses in cases where they have occurred. Yet Kennedy's model suffers from two important shortcomings: the possibility that favoritism is much more difficult to detect than he seems to suppose and the difficulty of dealing with cases where motives are mixed. In the real world, the pursuit of public and private benefit is often much more closely intertwined than Kennedy assumes.

The history of the *Kelo* case itself casts serious doubt on Kennedy's assumption that courts can effectively ferret out illegitimate motives. The Connecticut trial court, all seven justices of the state supreme court, and both the majority and dissenting justices in the U.S. Supreme Court all concluded that the takings arose from the New London authorities' desire to promote economic development, not from interest group lobbying by Pfizer or other private interests.[59]

Unfortunately, this assumption turned out to be flawed. While New London Development Corporation officials really did believe that the takings would benefit the city, it is also the case that they were undertaken in large part because of lobbying by Pfizer. As we saw in chapter 1, Pfizer played a major role in planning the taking, and the condemnation of the properties owned by the *Kelo* plaintiffs was undertaken in response to its demands. The full extent of Pfizer's role was only revealed by an investigative reporter after the case was over.[60] The significance of these revelations about Pfizer's influence over the New London condemnation decision extends well beyond their implications for the *Kelo* case itself. Despite almost five years of litigation, massive coverage by both national and local media, and detailed judicial review by both state and federal courts, the extent of Pfizer's role was not fully appreciated until it was too late.

This history strongly suggests that timely exposure of favoritism toward private interests will be even less likely in ordinary economic development takings cases. Such cases are likely to receive little or no public scrutiny, and, of course, few will be reviewed by state or federal supreme courts. Moreover, most property owners are likely to be represented by counsel with considerably less commitment, skill, resources, and experience than the Institute for Justice lawyers who provided pro bono representation for Susette Kelo and the other New London owners. Although the Institute for Justice lawyers were able to uncover a great deal of the evidence pointing to Pfizer's role in the New London condemnations, it is likely that the less skilled and experienced lawyers who litigate most eminent domain cases will be less successful.

Justice Kennedy's framework might trip up an occasional foolish or incompetent local government that makes the mistake of admitting improper motives. But it is far less likely to foil more skillful officials and developers.

Even more fundamentally, Justice Kennedy's approach is unlikely to be effective because it assumes an unrealistically clear separation between public and private interests. Almost any new commercial development will provide at least *some* benefit to the local economy in the form of increased employment or additional tax revenue for local government. Local officials can always cite such benefits as their "true" motivation and label any benefit to private parties incidental. Such assertions will not always be disingenuous. Like most people, local government officials and the private interest groups they promote are likely to genuinely believe that policies that serve their political and economic self-interest also advance the public good.

Kennedy's opinion is vague as to how much favoritism for private interests has to be found before a court can declare the resulting condemnations unconstitutional or even what kind of evidence is necessary to trigger a less deferential form of judicial scrutiny than that applied by the majority.[61] Some passages suggest that the sort of evidence eventually revealed by *The Day* might have been sufficient to at least trigger "a more demanding standard" of scrutiny.[62] For example, Kennedy states that his endorsement of the majority opinion was in part based on the purported fact that "[t]he identity of most of the private beneficiaries [of the condemnations] were unknown at the time the city formulated its plans,"[63] an assertion undermined by the revelations about Pfizer's crucial role in the initiation of the project. But it is not clear whether this factor alone would be enough to cast doubt on a taking in Kennedy's eyes. Be that as it may, it is likely that even very detailed judicial scrutiny of the motivations behind economic development takings will fail to ferret out numerous instances of favoritism.

We may not know the precise nature of Justice Kennedy's "as-yet-undisclosed" thinking, as Justice O'Connor called it,[64] unless and until the Supreme Court takes another public use case. Because Kennedy chose to endorse the majority opinion rather than concur in judgment only, his concurring opinion technically has no legally binding effect.[65] But his view might turn out to be crucial if he continues to be the Court's swing voter on public use issues. It has also already had some influence on lower courts attempting to apply the *Kelo* pretext standard.[66] New London's counsel Wesley Horton may be right to believe that Kennedy's concurrence is "the important opinion to follow."[67] For these reasons, it is vital that we understand the Kennedy opinion's significant shortcomings.

Conflation of "Substantive Due Process" Precedents and Public Use

The majority opinion in *Kelo* is in large part based on a claim of adherence to precedent. "For more than a century," the Court asserts, "our public use jurisprudence has wisely eschewed rigid formulas and intrusive scrutiny in favor of affording legislatures broad latitude in determining what public needs justify the use of the takings power."[68] Justice Stevens's majority opinion repeatedly cites late nineteenth and early twentieth century cases to support the proposition that "when this Court began applying the Fifth Amendment to the states at the close of the nineteenth century, it embraced the broader and more natural interpretation of public use as 'public purpose.'"[69] Academic defenders of *Kelo* have echoed the claim that it is required by a century of precedent.[70] An influential amicus brief in support of New London written by prominent legal scholars Thomas Merrill and John Echeverria on behalf of the American Planning Association also emphasized this point.[71]

Unfortunately, the majority's claim that the Court "began applying the Fifth Amendment to the states at the close of the nineteenth century" is simply wrong.[72] The nineteenth and early twentieth century cases cited by Justice Stevens and others as support for extreme judicial deference under the Public Use Clause in fact addressed public use challenges under the "*Lochner*-era" doctrine of "substantive" due process stemming from the Due Process Clause of the Fourteenth Amendment.[73] The period takes its name from the Court's much-reviled 1905 decision in *Lochner v. New York*, which used the Due Process Clause to strike down a New York law restricting the hours that bakers could work;[74] though it is important to recognize that the idea of using the Due Process Clause to protect economic rights long predated *Lochner* and that *Lochner* was not considered an especially important or novel ruling when it was decided.[75]

The *Kelo* majority cites the 1896 case of *Fallbrook Irrigation District v. Bradley* as the first instance where the Court expansively defined public use as "public purpose."[76] But the *Fallbrook* decision itself unequivocally states that the constitutional issue raised in the case "is based upon that part of the fourteenth amendment of the constitution which reads as follows: 'Nor shall any state deprive any person of life, liberty, or property without due process of law, nor deny to any person within its jurisdiction the equal protection of the laws.'"[77] The opinion specifically indicates that the Fifth Amendment "applies only to the federal government."[78]

The other early cases cited by Stevens are exactly the same.[79] Without exception, they address Fourteenth Amendment substantive due process challenges to takings and do not so much as mention the Fifth Amendment Public Use Clause.[80] And even in regards to the Due Process Clause, the cases did not reflect so complete a deference as the *Kelo* majority claims. In *Clark v. Nash* (1905), the Court specifically noted that "we do not desire to be understood by this decision as approving of the broad proposition that private property may be taken in all case[s] where the taking may promote the public interest."[81] In a 1901 decision involving the application of the Takings Clause in the District of Columbia, the Court emphasized that taking cases involving the application of the Due Process Clause to state governments were governed by a different set of doctrinal rules from those that apply in Fifth Amendment takings cases.[82]

Although not as deferential as *Berman, Midkiff,* and *Kelo,* the early twentieth century Due Process Clause takings cases did leave broad discretion to state governments. This should not be surprising. It was consistent with the Court's approach to other Due Process Clause cases during the same period. This included economic liberties cases, in which the Court upheld most forms of labor and regulatory legislation, and was even praised by some Progressives for what they considered to be its generally positive record, until it became somewhat more aggressive in the 1920s.[83]

Justice Stevens's misinterpretation of nineteenth and early twentieth century precedents was perhaps understandable in light of the fact that Justice Thomas committed the same mistake in his dissenting opinion. Thomas accepted the majority's claim that *Fallbrook* and its progeny adopted a broad interpretation of public use and merely argued that such a broad interpretation was not needed to address the facts of those cases, which actually involved traditional public uses where the condemned property was either owned by the government or open to use by the public as a matter of right.[84] Both Stevens's majority opinion and Thomas's dissent simply ignore the fact that these cases were brought on the basis of substantive due process because the Supreme Court of that era rejected the idea of incorporation of the Bill of Rights against the states.[85]

Stevens's and Thomas's mistake may have been due to the modern tendency to read our acceptance of incorporation back into precedents that date from an era when the idea of incorporation was rejected by the Supreme Court majority.[86] Nonetheless, both the text of these early opinions and more recent historical scholarship show that they were part of the early twentieth-century doctrine of Fourteenth Amendment economic due process.[87]

To his great credit, Justice Stevens later admitted what he calls this "embarrassing to acknowledge" error in a November 2011 speech, the year after he retired from the Supreme Court in 2010.[88] Justice Stevens came to recognize that the early twentieth-century cases cited as precedents in his opinion "were Fourteenth Amendment substantive due process cases."[89] He still continues to believe that the Court got the result in *Kelo* correct, because he now endorses the theory that the Public Use Clause does not impose any substantive constraints on takings at all.[90] That theory, however, really does go against centuries of precedent and has other weaknesses as well.[91]

The *Kelo* majority's mistaken reliance on early substantive due process precedent does not by itself prove that the ruling was wrong, or even that it lacked a basis in precedent. After all, the Court still derives precedential support for its decision from the sweeping language of *Berman* and *Midkiff,* which could be used to uphold almost any condemnation.[92]

Even so, the Court's error is significant for several reasons. First, the majority justices themselves thought the early cases important enough to devote a considerable amount of space to analyzing them and to emphasize the resulting claim that *Kelo* rests on "more than a century" of Supreme Court precedent.[93] Second, precedent-minded jurists and commentators might be less willing to endorse the result in *Kelo,* if they recognize that its true precedential basis relies mainly on broad, largely unsupported statements in two comparatively more recent decisions.

Third, Stevens's reliance on *Lochner*-era precedents undercuts possible concerns that a reversal of *Kelo* would somehow lead to a revival of *Lochner*-era economic "substantive due process" jurisprudence.[94] Exactly the opposite is true. It was the *Kelo* majority that extended the reach of *Lochner*-era due process precedents by mistakenly applying them to the Public Use Clause of the Fifth Amendment. A decision reversing *Kelo* could help establish a clearer distinction between public use and due process cases, and thereby prevent the latter from exercising any undue influence on the former. In recent decades, the Supreme Court has aggressively enforced many other parts of the Bill of Rights against state governments—including the just compensation requirement of the Takings Clause—without thereby somehow reviving *Lochner.* Repudiating *Kelo* and its reliance on *Lochner*-era decisions poses even less danger in this regard than judicial enforcement of other parts of the Bill of Rights. Finally, the serious flaws in the Court's application of precedent are significant in their own right, given that we rely on the Court to properly apply precedent in a wide range of constitutional and statutory fields.

The Dissents

The dissenting opinions by Justice Sandra Day O'Connor and Justice Clarence Thomas ultimately reached the correct conclusion: that economic development takings are unconstitutional. Both made some good points. But both also had notable weaknesses. Overall, however, they are valuable challenges to the previously dominant conventional wisdom on public use.

Justice O'Connor's Lead Dissent

The principal dissent in *Kelo* was written by Justice O'Connor, a striking development in light of her earlier authorship of the Court's opinion in *Midkiff,* possibly the most deferential of all the Court's public use decisions.[95] Even more striking is the fact that O'Connor and the other dissenters not only would have invalidated the New London takings, but would categorically forbid all private-to-private condemnations undertaken for the purpose of "economic development."[96] It was somewhat surprising that four justices were willing to take such a position despite the availability of narrower grounds for striking the New London takings, such as the lack of proof that the claimed benefits of the condemnations would ever be realized, the rationale embraced by the dissenting justices in the Connecticut Supreme Court.[97]

O'Connor's main argument is the claim that allowing economic development condemnations forecloses the possibility of any meaningful limits on the scope of condemnation. Because it is always possible to claim that transferring property from one owner to another would increase economic production, "[t]he specter of condemnation hangs over all property. Nothing is to prevent the State from replacing any Motel 6 with a Ritz–Carlton, any home with a shopping mall, or any farm with a factory."[98] Wesley Horton's oral argument concession had clearly made an impression on O'Connor, and not the one he wanted to create.[99]

O'Connor went on to conclude that "[u]nder the banner of economic development, all private property is now vulnerable to being taken and transferred to another private owner, so long as it might be upgraded— i.e., given to an owner who will use it in a way that the legislature deems more beneficial to the public—in the process."[100] This concern is well founded. It is indeed possible to use the prospect of economic development to justify virtually any taking that transfers property to a private business.[101]

Unlike the majority, O'Connor emphasized that the political processes that control condemnation are often defective and she expressed concern that "the fallout from this decision will not be random" but will instead sanction takings that victimize "those with fewer resources" for the benefit of "those with more."[102] This was a valid concern, amply supported by the sad history of blight and economic development takings.[103]

The most difficult challenge Justice O'Connor faced was the need to distinguish the Court's earlier highly deferential public use decisions, including her own opinion in *Midkiff*, which she did not wish to overrule. Despite her admission that the Court's decision was in part based on *Midkiff* and *Berman*, O'Connor contends that the *Kelo* majority "significantly expands the meaning of public use."[104] This argument is difficult to credit in light of the fact that the majority's definition of public use is actually slightly narrower than O'Connor's own expansive statement of the concept in *Midkiff*.[105]

O'Connor acknowledged that the *Kelo* majority opinion in "a sense . . . follows from errant language in *Berman* and *Midkiff*."[106] She therefore explicitly repudiated *Midkiff*'s statement that the scope of public use is "coterminous with the scope of a sovereign's police powers" and *Berman*'s holding that legislatures could use eminent domain to accomplish any "object" otherwise within their authority.[107] Strangely, she did not also reject—or even refer to—the *Midkiff* "rational basis" standard, despite the discussion of it in Justice Kennedy's concurring opinion. Instead O'Connor sought to distinguish *Berman* and *Midkiff* because

> In both these cases, the extraordinary, precondemnation use of the targeted property inflicted affirmative harm on society—in *Berman* through blight resulting from extreme poverty and in *Midkiff* through oligopoly resulting from extreme wealth. And in both cases, the relevant legislative body had found that eliminating the existing property use was necessary to remedy the harm . . . Thus a public purpose was realized when the harmful use was eliminated. Because each taking *directly* achieved a public benefit, it did not matter that the property was turned over to private use.[108]

This emphasis on eliminating harmful preexisting uses may have been borrowed from Michigan Supreme Court's effort to distinguish permissible blight condemnations from impermissible "economic development" takings in *County of Wayne v. Hathcock,* the then-recent 2004 case that overruled the notorious 1981 *Poletown* decision.[109]

Unfortunately, O'Connor's effort to distinguish *Berman* and *Midkiff* in this way runs into significant problems. The most obvious is that *Ber-*

man and *Midkiff* were decided on the basis of reasoning that went well beyond simply allowing the government to use private-to-private takings to eliminate "affirmative harms." Both also endorsed a general policy of judicial deference on public use issues. Moreover, this was not just "errant" language, as O'Connor claimed in her *Kelo* dissent. Evidence from the justices' conference notes strongly suggests that the justices who decided *Berman* and *Midkiff*, including O'Connor herself, were well aware that these decisions would have the effect of almost completely eliminating federal judicial review of public use issues.[110] O'Connor's thinking on public use issues had clearly changed between 1984 and 2005 to a greater extent than she was prepared to admit, perhaps even to a greater extent than she herself realized.[111]

O'Connor's difficulty in distinguishing *Berman* and *Midkiff* is not necessarily fatal. O'Connor could have justified the same result while acknowledging that *Berman* and *Midkiff* really did endorse judicial deference even in cases that do not involve remediation of "affirmative" harm. She could have argued that the Court should repudiate the reasoning of *Berman* and *Midkiff* without also overruling the results of the two cases.

A more serious flaw in Justice O'Connor's position is that the distinction between remediation of affirmative harm and promoting economic development may not be logically coherent. It is not true that the objectives of a blight taking or a taking intended to remedy a supposed oligopoly in the housing market are achieved merely by eliminating the preexisting "harmful use" of the property, thereby rendering the later ownership of the land by a private owner "irrelevant."

Blight can only truly be eliminated if the new owner uses the condemned land in a way that promotes beneficial development. The history of blight condemnations shows that this often fails to occur.[112] Similarly, the housing shortage supposedly caused by an oligopoly in *Midkiff* could only be eliminated if the new owners of the land used it to increase the housing stock available to potential homebuyers. In reality, the main beneficiaries of the *Midkiff* condemnations turned out to be affluent real estate speculators and tenants, and the price of housing did not fall.[113] Moreover, in distinguishing blight takings, Justice O'Connor did not make clear how dilapidated an area must be before it qualifies for *Berman*-style judicial deference. If it need only meet the extremely broad definitions of blight enshrined in the laws of many of the states,[114] there is virtually no meaningful difference between blight takings and economic development takings. In my view, the most plausible interpretation of O'Connor's reasoning is that takings based on an expansive definition of blight are also unconstitutional.[115] But the opinion is somewhat ambiguous on this point.

Ultimately, *Berman, Midkiff,* and *Kelo* all involved situations where the use of eminent domain was rationalized by claims that the transfer of property to a new private owner would benefit the community more than preexisting uses did. Distinguishing between them is more difficult than Justice O'Connor's opinion lets on.

This is not to say that O'Connor's position is completely untenable. Many state supreme court rulings (including *Hathcock*) and state laws effectively distinguish between blight condemnations under a relatively restrictive definition of blight and economic development takings.[116] The Supreme Court could certainly have adopted the same approach in its interpretation of the federal Public Use Clause. Doing so would have required limiting *Berman* to cases where the condemned area is indeed "blighted" in the narrow sense of the term indicating a serious threat to public health and safety.

There remains the problem of explaining why courts should interpret the Public Use Clause to distinguish between the benefits of blight alleviation and those of economic development. The simplest solution would be to cut the Gordian knot and overrule *Berman* completely, an approach that would be consistent with originalism and several versions of living constitution theory.[117] But if O'Connor and the other dissenters were unwilling to completely overrule a long-established precedent, such as *Berman,* they could instead have recognized that it was unsound to begin with, but then suggested that it was too well-established to completely reverse. *Midkiff* might be treated similarly, though the more recent date of the decision and the fact that it dealt with a highly unusual situation would make it easier to overrule outright without trampling on settled expectations.

If *Berman* were treated as a mistaken decision that nonetheless cannot be overruled completely because of respect for precedent, then the blight-economic development distinction might be defended as a reasonable compromise between the need to avoid overruling *Berman* and the need to give the Public Use Clause at least some meaningful teeth.

This compromise would leave some difficult questions unanswered. Most notably, what if any other "affirmative harms" are great enough to justify the kind of extreme judicial deference that is given to blight takings under *Berman*? But that issue could have been left to case-by-case determination by future decisions, as often happens when a Supreme Court decision resuscitates protection for a constitutional right that was previously neglected. For example, *Brown v. Board of Education* famously invalidated state-mandated segregation in public education, but without making clear whether state-mandated racial segregation in other contexts was also unconstitutional.[118]

Because the Supreme Court had virtually abdicated enforcement of the Public Use Clause for so many years, it is unrealistic to expect that any one decision would fully resolve all the issues raised by an effort to revitalize the clause. The revival of judicial review in this area would necessarily have to proceed incrementally. It is difficult to say whether Justice O'Connor's particular approach is the best way of proceeding. But, as state experience shows, it is at least reasonably plausible.

Justice Thomas's Solo Dissent

Justice Thomas's dissent was a much more thoroughgoing attack on the majority than O'Connor's. Like O'Connor, whose dissent he also joined, Thomas emphasized the danger that economic development takings could target virtually any property and expresses concern that areas inhabited by the poor and minorities are likely to be disproportionately affected.[119] "Allowing the government to take property solely for public purposes is bad enough," he wrote, "but extending the concept of public purpose to encompass any economically beneficial goal guarantees that these losses will fall disproportionately on poor communities. Those communities are not only systematically less likely to put their lands to the highest and best social use, but are also the least politically powerful."[120]

Yet, Thomas was prepared to go much farther than O'Connor in reconsidering precedent, including overruling *Midkiff, Berman,* and other cases endorsing a broad definition of public use. He "would revisit our Public Use Clause cases and consider returning to the original meaning of the Public Use Clause: that the government may take property only if it actually uses or gives the public a legal right to use the property."[121]

Much of Thomas's argument is based on a detailed analysis attempting to show that the original meaning of "public use" encompassed only condemnations that resulted in actual ownership by the state or a legal right of the public to use the condemned property.[122] Far from being the aberration described by O'Connor, in Thomas's more accurate account *Kelo* "is simply the latest in a string of our cases construing the Public

Use Clause to be a virtual nullity, without the slightest nod to its original meaning."[123]

In my view, Thomas reached the correct conclusion to a greater extent than either the majority opinion or O'Connor.[124] Unlike the majority, Thomas gave serious consideration to the text and original meaning of the Public Use Clause. He also refused to apply the clause in a highly deferential way that is radically divergent from the way other constitutional rights are treated.

"Something has gone seriously awry with this Court's interpretation of the Constitution," he emphasized, if judges need not defer to government in scrutinizing decisions to search a home but must be ultradeferential in considering decisions to tear down the home and evict its residents.[125] Unlike O'Connor, he fully recognized the problematic nature of *Berman* and *Midkiff,* and the continuity between those decisions and *Kelo.* His opinion is impressive in its willingness to return to first principles and consider the possibility that the Supreme Court's public use jurisprudence went badly wrong long before *Kelo.* As Wesley Horton puts it, Thomas's opinion "holds together much better than O'Connor's dissent."[126] But Thomas also relies on a relatively narrow range of sources and sometimes fails to adequately address opposing views.[127]

Thomas appropriately begins with the text of the Public Use Clause and endorses the narrow interpretation of public use, stating that "[t]he most natural reading of the Clause is that it allows the government to take property only if the government owns, or the public has a legal right to use, the property."[128] But he recognizes that the broader view of public use is also linguistically plausible and that, at the time of the Founding, the word "use" was sometimes employed in the broader sense of "convenience" or "help."[129] In preferring the narrow interpretation, Thomas notes that Article I of the Constitution twice utilizes the word "use" in the narrow sense in outlining Congress's powers to impose duties and imposts, and raise and support armies.[130] But it is possible that the Constitution could use the same word in different senses in different contexts, especially since the Bill of Rights was drafted years after the original Constitution.

Similarly plausible but not definitive is Thomas's point that "the phrase 'public use' contrasts with the very different phrase 'general Welfare' used elsewhere in the Constitution. . . . ("Congress shall have Power To . . . provide for the common Defence and general Welfare of the United States"); preamble (Constitution established 'to promote the general

Welfare'). The Framers would have used some such broader term if they had meant the Public Use Clause to have a similarly sweeping scope."[131] If the framers of the Fifth Amendment had the broad interpretation of "use" in mind, they may not have felt the need to use a "broader term," such as general welfare, which itself was understood more narrowly at the time of the Founding than today.[132]

Thomas's textual analysis is therefore plausible but far from conclusive. He might have done better to point out that a literal meaning is more likely to fit public understanding than a metaphorical one.[133]

In addressing the history and original meaning of public use, Thomas recognized that practice was not always consistent with a narrow interpretation of the term, noting the examples of takings for private roads and mill acts.[134] But he gives only a brief and cursory discussion of these practices, before concluding that they were aberrations.[135] He gives almost no consideration to the various nineteenth-century state supreme court decisions that endorsed a broad conception of public use. He also cited only a few of the many state court decisions that endorsed a narrow one.[136] In fairness, at the time *Kelo* was decided, scholars had not yet done a comprehensive survey of the positions of all the nineteenth-century state supreme courts on public use questions.[137]

Perhaps Thomas's most important omission is the lack of any systematic discussion of the understanding of public use at the time the Fourteenth Amendment was enacted in 1868, the point at which the Public Use Clause presumably first became applicable against state governments. As discussed in chapter 2, this history is important to understanding the original meaning of public use as applied against the states.

In addition, Thomas uncritically follows Justice Stevens's majority opinion in accepting the idea that deferential early twentieth-century Supreme Court opinions applying "substantive due process" analysis to takings by state governments were genuine public use opinions.[138] In some instances, he even interprets those cases as being more deferential than they actually were. For example, Thomas describes the Court's 1905 decision in *Clark v. Nash* as endorsing the view that any "public purpose" qualifies as a "public use."[139] While *Clark* did indeed interpret the Due Process Clause to allow a wider range of takings than the narrow view of public use, it also emphasized that it was *not* endorsing the view that eminent domain can be used to pursue any "public interest."[140]

Overall, Thomas's opinion gets several important points right. But in some instances he undercut the force of his argument by failing to give sufficient consideration to opposing views. In others, he did so by making unnecessary concessions.

Conclusion

Although the decision was an important defeat for property rights advocates, *Kelo* nevertheless represented progress relative to the Court's previous ultradeferential public use jurisprudence. Even Justice Stevens's majority opinion was less deferential than *Berman* and *Midkiff* had been. Justice Kennedy's key swing-vote concurring opinion holds out the promise that economic development takings might yet be constrained in the future, albeit with little clarity as to the circumstances where this might occur. The dissents by O'Connor and Thomas represent major challenges to post–New Deal public use orthodoxy, even if both also have notable analytical drawbacks. As Julia Mahoney put it in an early assessment of the decision, "[w]hen confronted with *Kelo,* with its obvious implications for the property rights of millions of Americans, all the Justices retreated from the near total deference model."[141]

The majority's retreat was modest and grudging. Nonetheless, the extreme closeness of the decision severely undercut the previously dominant view of the Public Use Clause, under which most jurists simply assumed that the ultradeferential *Berman-Midkiff* approach was unquestionably correct. Informed observers now had to admit that there was a serious debate over the proper interpretation of public use, one in which the validity of post–New Deal orthodoxy could no longer be taken for granted. As we shall see in chapter 7, many state court judges greeted *Kelo* with skepticism and refused to use it as a guide to the interpretation of their state public use clauses. Some instead endorsed a position resembling that of the *Kelo* dissenters.

Most Supreme Court decisions affect society primarily in their role as legal precedents that must be followed by lower courts. Few pay attention to them other than legal professionals. As the next chapter describes, *Kelo* turned out to be a dramatic exception, generating a broader public backlash than any other recent Supreme Court ruling.

CHAPTER FIVE

The Political Backlash

M ost Supreme Court decisions get little public attention. Even many of the more significant ones are soon forgotten by all but experts in the relevant fields of law. *Kelo* was a rare exception. It generated more public attention than all but a handful of other Supreme Court rulings.[1] And the overwhelming majority of that attention was hostile. This massive political reaction resulted in important gains for property rights advocates. But their success was not as great as it at first seemed.

The negative public reaction to *Kelo* does not in itself prove that the Court got the decision wrong. Neither does it necessarily indicate that economic development takings are bad policy. But the reaction is an important part of the story of *Kelo* and its impact on property rights. It also exemplifies both the power and limits of public outrage.

The *Kelo* backlash led to more new state legislation than that generated by any other Supreme Court decision in history. Forty-five states have enacted post-*Kelo eminent domain* reform laws. The closest competitor is *Furman v. Georgia*,[2] a 1972 decision that struck down all then-existing state death penalty laws. In response, some thirty-five states and the federal government enacted new death penalty statutes intended to conform to *Furman*'s requirements between 1972 and 1976.[3] But the response to *Kelo* is even more striking than that generated by *Furman*, because the former did not deprive the states of any power they previously enjoyed. Whereas the legislative response to *Furman* was largely an effort to restore the preexisting status quo, the reaction to *Kelo* sought to change it.

Although not a federal court decision, the Massachusetts Supreme Judicial Court's 2003 ruling in *Goodridge v. Department of Public Health* mandating same-sex marriage under its state constitution deserves mention because it led some thirty other states to enact constitutional amendments banning gay marriage between 2003 and 2008.[4] Yet neither *Furman* nor *Goodridge* generated a legislative backlash that extended to as many states as *Kelo*. Moreover, the anti-gay marriage amendments cannot be solely attributed to the backlash against *Goodridge*. They were also spurred by litigation that eventually led to pro-gay marriage state court decisions in Connecticut and California.[5]

A strong case can be made that *Kelo* has drawn a more extensive legislative reaction than any other single court decision in American history. The *Kelo* majority "emphasize[d] that nothing in our opinion precludes any State from placing further restrictions on its exercise of the takings power."[6] Numerous states took up that implicit invitation.

In light of the massive backlash *Kelo* generated, prominent scholars and jurists such as Judge Richard A. Posner and future Supreme Court Chief Justice John Roberts (when questioned about *Kelo* at his Senate confirmation), have suggested that the political response demonstrates that legislative initiatives can protect property owners and that judicial intervention may be unnecessary.[7] In an article published soon after the decision came down, Posner claimed that the political reaction to *Kelo* is "evidence of [the decision's] pragmatic soundness."[8] He reiterated that view in a 2008 book in which he added that opponents of eminent domain have "plenty of political muscle, which they are free to use."[9] Justice John Paul Stevens, author of the *Kelo* majority opinion, also cited the political backlash as proof of the correctness of his decision. Although he recognized that economic development takings are harmful, he claimed that "the public outcry that greeted *Kelo* is some evidence that the political process is up to the task of addressing such policy concerns," thereby obviating the need for judicial intervention.[10]

Such arguments dovetail with the traditional view that rights supported by majority public opinion will be protected by democratic political processes and do not require additional protection through judicial review.[11] As James Madison famously wrote in *Federalist* 10, "[i]f a faction consists of less than a majority, relief is supplied by the republican principle, which enables the majority to defeat its sinister views by regular vote."[12] Only "[w]hen a majority is included in a faction," he argued, does "the form of popular government" enable it to threaten "the rights of other citizens."[13]

Unfortunately, the political backlash to *Kelo* did not provide the same level of protection for property owners as would a judicial ban on economic development takings. The majority of the newly enacted post-*Kelo* reform laws are likely to be ineffective.

At the same time, however, it is important to recognize that many states have enacted strong post-*Kelo* reform laws. In earlier work, I emphasized the extent to which the results of the *Kelo* backlash fell short of optimistic expectations, and of the predictions of conventional wisdom in political and legal theory.[14] But it is equally important to recognize that it led to substantially greater protection for property rights against takings than had existed before 2005.

The Public Reaction

Kelo was greeted by immediate and widespread outrage. Both state-level and national polls showed overwhelming public opposition to economic development takings—a consensus that cut across gender, racial, ethnic, and partisan lines.

The decision was also condemned by politicians and activists across the political spectrum ranging from anti-corporate activist Ralph Nader on the left to controversial talk show host Rush Limbaugh on the right.[15] The U.S. House of Representatives immediately passed a resolution denouncing *Kelo* by a lopsided 365–33 vote.[16] In addition to denunciations from conservatives and libertarians, *Kelo* was also assailed by numerous liberal political leaders including former President Bill Clinton,[17] then-Democratic National Committee Chair Howard Dean, and prominent African American California Democratic Representative Maxine Waters.

Ignoring the fact that all four of the dissenting justices were Republican appointees, Dean denounced a "a [R]epublican-appointed Supreme Court that decided they can take your house and put a Sheraton Hotel in there."[18] Waters called it "the most un-American thing that can be done."[19] Even socialist Bernard Sanders, an independent Representative from Vermont, supported property rights in this instance, stating that he "disagree[d] with the Supreme Court's decision in *Kelo v. New London,* "because he "believe[d] that the result of this decision will be that working families and poor people will see their property turned over to corporate interests and wealthy developers."[20]

The NAACP—the nation's leading African-American civil rights organization, the AARP, the liberal Southern Christian Leadership Conference, and others had filed a joint amicus brief in *Kelo* urging the Court to rule in favor of the property owners.[21] At a September 2005 United States Senate Judiciary Committee hearing on the ruling, Hilary Shelton, director of the NAACP's Washington Bureau, testified that "the NAACP was very disappointed by the *Kelo* decision," in part because "allowing municipalities to pursue eminent domain for private economic development . . . will clearly have a disparate impact on African Americans and other minorities."[22]

Many right of center organizations also opposed the ruling.[23] Conservatives and libertarians denounced it as a threat to property rights, while liberal opponents of the decision often emphasized the danger to the poor and racial minorities. In Weare, New Hampshire, home of Supreme Court Justice David Souter, one of the justices in the majority, activists sought to have the local government use eminent domain to take the justice's house and build a "Lost Liberty Hotel" on the site.[24]

Public opinion mirrored the widespread condemnation of *Kelo* by political elites and activists. In two national surveys conducted in the fall of 2005, 81 percent and 95 percent of respondents were opposed to *Kelo*.[25] As table 5.1 demonstrates, opposition to the decision cut across racial, ethnic, partisan, and gender lines. The data in the table comes from two 2005 polls on *Kelo*, one conducted by the Saint Index and one by Zogby, and a 2009 survey by Stephen Ansolabehere and Nathaniel Persily for Knowledge Networks. In the Saint Index survey, which has the better-worded question of the two 2005 polls,[26] *Kelo* was opposed by 77 percent of men, 84 percent of women, 82 percent of whites, 72 percent of African Americans, and 80 percent of Hispanics. The decision was also opposed by 79 percent of Democrats, 85 percent of Republicans, and 83 percent of Independents. Public opposition to *Kelo* was deep as well as broad. In the Saint Index survey, 63 percent of respondents not only disagreed with the decision, but said that they did so "strongly."[27] A 2006 Saint Index survey found that 71 percent of respondents supported reform laws intended to ban "the taking of private property for private development" projects, and 43 percent supported such laws "strongly."[28]

The 2009 survey results closely mimic those of the 2005 polls and show that public hostility to economic development takings was not simply the result of an immediate emotional reaction to the *Kelo* decision. As in the 2005 Saint Index poll, the 2009 survey shows over 80 percent opposition to economic development takings; once again, the overwhelming opposition cuts across racial, gender, ideological, and partisan lines. The 2009 data is not completely comparable to the 2005 polls, because the question asked respondents whether "local government" should have the power to

TABLE 5.1 **National Public Opinion on *Kelo* and Economic Development Takings**

		Zogby 2005[1]		Saint Index 2005[2]		Knowledge Networks 2009[3]	
		% Agree	% Disagree	% Agree	% Disagree	% Agree	% Disagree
	Total	2	95	18	81	17	83
Gender	Male	2	94	22	77	18	82
	Female	2	95	14	84	15	85
Racial/ Ethnic Group[4]	White	2	94	17	82	14	86
	African-American	0	97	28	72	23	77
	Asian	0	100	26	68	–	–
	Hispanic/Latino	2	98	18	80	26	74
	Native American	–	–	7	93	–	–
Party[5] Affiliation	Democrat	3	94	20	79	19	81
	Independent	<1	99	17	83	4	96
	Republican	3	92	14	85	14	86
Ideology	Liberal	–	–	22	77	19	81
	Moderate	–	–	18	81	19	81
	Conservative	–	–	17	82	12	88

1. Zogby International, American Farm Bureau Federation Survey 27, question 28 (Nov. 2, 2005). Question wording: "Do you strongly agree, somewhat agree, somewhat disagree, or strongly disagree with the recent Supreme Court ruling that allowed a city in Connecticut to take the private property of one citizen and give it to another citizen to use for private development?" Ibid. The totals given here differ slightly from those published by Zogby because they correct a minor clerical error in Zogby's tabulation.

2. Saint Index 2005, question 10. Question wording: "The U.S. Supreme Court recently ruled that local governments can take homes, business and private property to make way for private economic development if officials believe it would benefit the public. How do you feel about this ruling?" Ibid.

3. Data based on Stephen Ansolabahere and Nathaniel Persily, Field Report: Constitutional Attitudes Survey 61 (Knowledge Networks, July 2010), Question 215 (breakdown provided by the authors). Question wording: "Governments sometimes use the power of eminent domain to acquire a person's property at a fair market price for other uses. Recently, a local government transferred someone's property to private developers whose commercial projects could benefit the local economy. Do you think the local government should be able to use eminent domain for this purpose or not?" The data for this question excludes a small number of respondents (about 2.6 percent) who refused to answer the question or for whom data is missing. Ibid., 61.

4. The figures for Asians, Hispanics, and Native Americans in the Zogby and Saint Index surveys may be unreliable because of small sample sizes.

5. The Figure for independents in the 2009 Knowledge Networks poll is likely unreliable, because I have assigned respondents who said they "lean" Democrat or Republican to those respective parties rather than labeling them as independents. As a result, respondents considered as "independent" represent only about 4 percent of the total sample.

engage in economic development takings rather than whether they agreed with the Supreme Court decision upholding their constitutionality. Even so, it is fairly strong evidence of public hostility to such condemnations, both because it came four years after *Kelo* and because the question wording was favorable to the pro-*Kelo* side.[29]

Table 5.2 presents results for eight individual state surveys, all of which are similar to the national data, with opposition to *Kelo* ranging from 86 to 93 percent of respondents. The state surveys each use different question wording and therefore are not completely comparable to the

TABLE 5.2 **State-by-State Public Opinion on** *Kelo*

State	% Agree with Kelo	% Disagree
Connecticut[1]	8	88
Florida[2]	12	88
Kansas[3]	7	92
New Hampshire[4]	4	93
Minnesota[5]	5	91
North Carolina[6]	7	91
Pennsylvania[7]	9	90
Tennessee[8]	8	86

1. Quinnipiac University Polling Institute Poll, "Quinnipiac University Poll: Connecticut Voters say 11-1 Stop Eminent Domain, Quinnipiac University Poll Finds; Saving Groton Sub Base is High Priority," question 33 (2005), http://www.quinnipiac.edu/x1296.xml?ReleaseID=821. Question wording: "As you may know, the Court ruled that government can use eminent domain to buy a person's property and transfer it to private developers whose commercial projects could benefit the local economy. Do you agree or disagree with this ruling? Do you agree/disagree strongly or somewhat?" Ibid.

2. Mason Dixon Polling & Research Inc., "Florida Voters Oppose Court Decision on Eminent Domain, Strongly Support State Law To Protect Property Rights" 5 (2005), http://www.rg4rb.org/surveyEmDom.html. Question wording:

> In that Connecticut case, the U.S. Supreme Court ruled government can use the power of eminent domain to acquire a person's property and transfer it to private developers whose commercial projects could benefit the local economy. Do you agree or disagree with this ruling? (Is that strongly agree/disagree or somewhat agree/disagree?).

Ibid.

3. Cole Hargrave Snodgrass & Associates, "A Survey of 400 Registered Voters in Kansas with a 200-Sample Subset," (2006), http://www.castlecoalition.org/pdf/polls/amcns-prosp-poll-KS.pdf. Question wording:

> For years, governments have used the power of eminent domain to take control of private property and then use that property for schools, hospitals, roads, parks and other public services. Recently, the Kansas Supreme Court has expanded the government's ability to use eminent domain to include taking control of private property and transferring it not for public services, but to other private interests such as shopping centers or car lots. Do you favor or oppose the increased use of eminent domain to include taking private property and transferring ownership to other private interests? (After response, ask:) Would you say you strongly (favor/oppose) or only somewhat (favor/oppose)? Ibid. Survey question wording on file with author.

4. University of New Hampshire Survey Center Granite State Poll (2005), http://www.unh.edu/survey-center /news/pdf/gsp2005_summer_sc072005.pdf. Question wording:

> Recently, the Supreme Court ruled that towns and cities may take private land from people and make it available to businesses to develop under the principle of eminent domain. Some people favor this use of eminent domain because it allows for increased tax revenues from the new businesses and are an important part of economic redevelopment. Other people oppose this use of eminent domain because it reduces the value of private property and makes it easier for big businesses to take land. What about you? Do you think that towns and cities should be allowed to take private land from the owners and make it available to developers to develop or do you oppose this use of eminent domain?

Ibid.

5. Decision Resources Ltd., Minnesota Auto Dealers Association Survey (2006), http://www.castlecoalition .org/pdf/polls/Survey-for-Strib.pdf. Question wording: "What is your opinion—do you support allowing local governments to use eminent domain to take private property for another private development project? Do you feel strongly this way?" Ibid.

6. John William Pope Civitas Institution, John William Pope Civitas Institute Survey (2005), http://www .jwpcivitasinstitute.org/keylinks/pollaugust.html. Question wording: "The Supreme Court recently expanded the power of government to take private property for non-public use. Do you agree or disagree with this expansion of government's right to take private property?" Ibid.

7. Lincoln Institute of Public Opinion Research, Inc., Keystone Business Climate Survey (2006), http://www .lincolninstitute.org/polls.php. Question wording: "A recent U.S. Supreme Court decision upheld the taking of private residential property by local municipalities to enable private developers to build higher tax-yielding structures on that land. Do you agree or disagree with this ruling?" Ibid.

8. Social Science Research Institute at the University of Tennessee, Knoxville, Tennessee Poll 6 (2006), http:// web.utk.edu/~ssriweb/National_Issues.pdf. Question wording: "Sometimes the property taken through eminent domain is given to other private citizens for commercial development, rather than for public uses, such as road or schools. Would you say you favor or oppose this use of eminent domain?" Ibid.

national surveys or to each other. Nevertheless, the national and state-by-state survey results collectively paint a picture of widespread and overwhelming opposition to *Kelo* and economic development takings.

The near consensus on *Kelo* among political leaders, activists, and the general public leads one to expect that the ruling would be followed by the enactment of legislation abolishing, or at least strictly limiting, economic-development takings. Yet, in many states, that did not occur.

The Legislative Response

Much of the legislative response to *Kelo* has fallen short of expectations. At both the state and federal level, the majority of the newly enacted laws are likely to impose few, if any, meaningful restrictions on economic-development takings. Thirty-seven state legislatures have adopted post-*Kelo* reform laws. But twenty-two of these are largely symbolic in nature, providing little or no protection for property owners. The limited reforms enacted by the federal government are likely to be no more effective than most of the state laws. The major exceptions to the pattern of ineffective post-*Kelo* reforms are the fourteen states that enacted reforms by popular referendum. Eight or nine of these provide meaningful, new protection for property owners. Strikingly, citizen-initiated referendum initiatives have led to the passage of much stronger laws than those enacted through referenda initiated by state legislatures. While there is overwhelming public support for measures banning economic development takings, some twenty-nine of the forty-nine states that had not adopted reforms before *Kelo* have enacted either ineffective reforms or none at all.[30] The same is true of the federal government.

Legislative reforms are classified as "effective" so long as they provide property owners with at least some significant protection against economic-development condemnations beyond that available under preexisting law. Thus, even if the new law does not categorically ban economic-development takings, it is still considered "effective" if it forbids them in some substantial range of cases.

My analysis mainly focuses on state reforms that restrict the range of purposes for which states can condemn private property, and does not consider reforms that change eminent domain procedure or increase compensation for property owners. For reasons discussed in chapter 8, the latter types of reforms do not meaningfully address the dangers posed by economic development takings.

State Reforms

A total of forty-five states have enacted post-*Kelo* eminent domain reform laws. The aggregate results are summarized in table 5.3. Table 5.4 describes the effectiveness and type of reform enacted in each state. My coding of all but a few states is very similar to that adopted by previous scholars and that of the Institute for Justice in its report on post-*Kelo* reform.[31]

Table 5.5 shows that the enactment of effective post-*Kelo* reform seems unrelated to the degree to which the state in question had previously engaged in private-to-private condemnation. Only seven of the twenty states with the greatest number of private-to-private takings between 1998 and 2002 have enacted effective post-*Kelo* reforms. The table is based on a study by the Institute for Justice, the libertarian public interest law firm that represented the property owners in *Kelo*.[32] The IJ figures have their limitations. They likely underestimate the prevalence of condemnations for the benefit of private parties because they were compiled from news reports and court filings.[33] Many cases are unpublished, and many other condemnations go unreported in the press. Some of the condemnations in the study involved the taking of multiple properties, sometimes hundreds at a time, while others only applied to a small amount of land.[34] Finally, the figures unfortunately do not separate economic-development takings from other private-to-private condemnations. Nonetheless, they do give a rough indication of which states engage in private-to-private condemnations more than others.

A similar picture emerges if we compare states with large numbers of threatened private-to-private condemnations to those with few, or if we analyze the data with respect to the frequency of actual or threatened condemnations relative to the size of the state's population.[35] In each case, states with relatively large numbers of actual or threatened condemnations were not more likely to enact effective reforms than those with few or none. Only seven of the twenty states with the most threatened condemnations have enacted effective reforms.[36] The same is true of just seven of the twenty states with the most private-to-private condemnations relative to population size.[37]

On the other hand, it is noteworthy that three of the four states with the largest number of takings—Pennsylvania, Kansas, and Michigan—have enacted effective reforms. But the IJ figures are only approximate, and

TABLE 5.3 **State Post-*Kelo* Reform Laws**[1]

Mode of Enactment		Number of States	
		Effective Law	Ineffective Law
Legislature		15	22
Referendum			
	Citizen-initiated	5	1
	Legislature-initiated	3 or 4	4 or 5
No Post-*Kelo* Reforms Enacted		5	

1. The total number of states listed adds up to more than forty-five because a few states had effective legislative reforms followed by ineffective legislative-referendum initiatives; such states are thus counted in both of those categories. The state of Florida enacted legislative and referendum initiative reforms that were both effective and is counted in both "effective" categories. Nevada had an effective referendum initiative followed by an ineffective legislative reform.

TABLE 5.4 **Effectiveness of Reform by State**

State	Effectiveness of Reform[1]	State	Effectiveness of Reform[1]
Alabama	Effective (L)	Montana	Ineffective (L)
Alaska	Ineffective (L)	Nebraska	Ineffective (L)
Arizona	Effective (CR)	Nevada	Effective (L & CR)
Arkansas	No Reform	New Hampshire	Effective (L & LR)
California	Ineffective (L & CR)	New Jersey	Ineffective (L)
Colorado	Ineffective (L)	New Mexico	Effective (L)
Connecticut	Ineffective (L)	New York	No Reform
Delaware	Effective (L)	North Carolina	Ineffective (L)
Florida	Effective (L & LR)	North Dakota	Effective (CR)
Georgia	Effective (L & LR)	Ohio	Ineffective (L)
Hawaii	No Reform	Oklahoma	No Reform
Idaho	Ineffective (L)	Oregon	Effective (CR)
Illinois	Ineffective (L)	Pennsylvania	Effective (L)
Indiana	Effective (L)	Rhode Island	Ineffective (L)
Iowa	Ineffective (L)	South Carolina	Ineffective (LR)
Kansas	Effective (L)	South Dakota	Effective (L)
Kentucky	Ineffective (L)	Tennessee	Ineffective (L)
Louisiana	Effective (LR)	Texas	Ineffective (L & LR)
Maine	Ineffective (L)	Utah	Enacted Prior to *Kelo*
Maryland	Ineffective (L)	Vermont	Ineffective (L)
Massachusetts	No Reform	Virginia	Effective (L & LR)
Michigan	Effective (L & LR)	Washington	No Reform
Minnesota	Effective (L)	West Virginia	Ineffective (L)
Mississippi	Effective (CR)	Wisconsin	Effective (L)
Missouri	Ineffective (L)	Wyoming	Effective (L)

1. As of early 2014. "L" refers to passed state legislation; "CR" refers to passed citizen-initiated referenda; "LR" refers to passed legislature-initiated referenda.

TABLE 5.5 **Post-*Kelo* Reform in States Ranked by Number of Private-to-Private Condemnations, 1998–2002**

State	No. of Takings	Effectiveness of Reform
Pennsylvania	2,517	Effective (L)
California	223	Ineffective (L & CR)
Kansas	155	Effective (L)
Michigan	138	Effective (L & LR)
Maryland	127	Ineffective (L)
Ohio	90	Ineffective (L)
Florida	67	Effective (L & LR)
Virginia	58	Effective (L & LR)
New York	57	No Reform
New Jersey	51	Ineffective (L)
Connecticut	31	Ineffective (L)
Tennessee	29	Ineffective (L)
Colorado	23	Ineffective (L)
Oklahoma	23	No Reform
Missouri	18	Ineffective (L)
Rhode Island	12	Ineffective (L)
Arizona	11	Effective (CR)
Texas	11	Ineffective (L & LR)
Washington	11	No Reform
Minnesota	9	Effective (L)
Alabama	8	Effective (L)
Illinois	8	Ineffective (L)
West Virginia	8	Ineffective (L)
Kentucky	7	Ineffective (L)
Louisiana	5	Effective (LR)
Massachusetts	5	No Reform
Indiana	4	Effective (L)
Iowa	4	Ineffective (L)
Mississippi	3	Effective (CR)
Nevada	3	Effective (L & CR)
Maine	2	Ineffective (L)
Arkansas	1	No Reform
Nebraska	1	Ineffective (L)
North Carolina	1	Ineffective (L)
North Dakota	1	Effective (CR)
Alaska	0	Ineffective (L)
Delaware	0	Effective (L)
Georgia	0	Effective (L & LR)
Idaho	0	Ineffective (L)
South Dakota	0	Effective (L)
Wyoming	0	Effective (L)
Hawaii	0	No Reform
Montana	0	Ineffective (L)
New Hampshire	0	Effective (L & LR)
New Mexico	0	Effective (L)
Oregon	0	Effective (CR)
South Carolina	0	Ineffective (LR)
Utah	0	Enacted Prior to *Kelo*
Vermont	0	Ineffective (L)
Wisconsin	0	Effective (L)

it is likely that they underestimate the number of economic-development condemnations in some states. It is therefore difficult to know whether Pennsylvania, Kansas, and Michigan really were three of the top four states in this category. It would also be unwise to draw broad conclusions from just three cases, especially in light of the fact that nearly all the other states with large numbers of private-to-private takings in the Institute for Justice study either enacted ineffective reforms or none at all.

Reforms Enacted by State Legislatures

As of 2014, thirty-seven state legislatures have enacted post-*Kelo* reforms. In addition, the state of Utah effectively banned economic development takings in a statute enacted several months before *Kelo* was decided by the Supreme Court.[38] However, twenty-two of the thirty-seven new state laws provide little or no protection for property owners against economic development takings. Only fifteen state legislatures have enacted laws that either ban economic development takings or significantly restrict them. The ineffective state laws are of several types. By far the most common are laws that forbid takings for economic development but in fact allow them to continue under another name such as "blight" or "community development" condemnations.

Laws with Broad Exemptions for Blight Condemnations

Nineteen states have enacted post-*Kelo* reform laws whose effect is largely negated by exemptions for blight condemnations under definitions of blight that make it possible to include almost any property in that category. This is by far the most common factor undermining the potential effectiveness of post-*Kelo* reform laws.[39]

All but five states permit condemnation for blight and most of these define the concept broadly.[40] For decades, courts have interpreted broad definitions of blight in ways that allow the condemnation of almost any property. If virtually any area can be condemned as blighted, a ban on economic development takings would be essentially irrelevant.[41]

Nineteen post-*Kelo* reform laws continue this pattern, using definitions of blight that are either identical to those enshrined in preexisting law or relevantly similar to them. These reform laws thereby undermine the effectiveness of their bans on private-to-private condemnations for economic development. Ten of these followed a common standard pattern. The rest have somewhat more idiosyncratic but comparably broad definitions of blight.

Ten state post-*Kelo* laws leave in place definitions of blight that include any area where there are obstacles to "sound growth" or conditions that constitute an "economic or social liability." These include reform laws in Alaska, Colorado, Missouri, Montana, Nebraska, North Carolina, Ohio, Texas, Vermont, and West Virginia.[42]

Any obstacle to economic development can easily be defined as impairing "sound growth," making this definition of blight broad enough to justify virtually any condemnation under an economic development rationale. Similarly, an impediment to economic development can be considered an "economic or social liability." Several of the state laws listed above require that, in order to be blighted, an area that is an "economic or social liability" must also be "a menace to the public health, safety, morals, or welfare."[43] This additional condition is unlikely to be a significant constraint because almost any condition that impedes economic development could be considered a "menace to the public . . . welfare."

Under Florida's prereform blight statute, which used this exact wording, the Florida Supreme Court found that even undeveloped land could be considered "blighted" if its current state impedes future development.[44] The Supreme Court of Arizona has similarly described this language as an "extremely broad definition of . . . 'blighted area' " that gives condemning authorities "wide discretion in deciding what constitutes blight."[45] With the partial exception of two recent Missouri decisions that impose only modest restrictions, it is almost impossible to find published state court opinions that interpret this language as a meaningful constraint on the scope of blight condemnations.[46]

Nine other states have similarly broad blight exemptions, albeit with different wording. Illinois's new law exempts blight condemnations from its ban on economic development takings and retains its preexisting definition of blight,[47] which defined a blighted area as one where "industrial, commercial, and residential buildings or improvements are detrimental to the public safety, health, or welfare because of a combination of 5 or more of the following factors."[48] The list of factors include dilapidation; obsolescence; deterioration; below minimum code standards; illegal use of structures; excessive vacancies; lack of ventilation, light, or sanitary facilities; inadequate utilities; excessive land coverage and overcrowding of structures and community facilities; deleterious land use or layout; environmental clean-up; lack of community planning; or an assessed value that has declined in three of the last five years.[49] The concept of "detriment" to "public welfare" is extremely broad and surely includes detriment to local economic welfare and development. The list of factors includes numerous conditions, such as deterioration, "deleterious land use or layout," lack of community planning, a declining assessed value, "excessive" land coverage, and obsolescence—that exist to some degree in most communities.[50]

The Idaho law is a close case. It enacts a seemingly narrow definition of blight.[51] But this restriction is less significant than it would otherwise be, because the law allows a blight designation when the property in question poses an "actual risk of harm" to public "morals" or "welfare," concepts that could potentially be defined broadly enough to include most economic development takings.[52] It also contains an exemption for "those public and private uses for which eminent domain is expressly provided in the constitution of the state of Idaho,"[53] which in Idaho includes condemnations "necessary to the complete development of the material resources of the state."[54] This loophole does not completely vitiate the state's ban on economic development takings, because the Idaho Supreme Court has interpreted takings for development of "material resources" to include only those necessary "to develop valuable resources, such as timber, minerals, or other products of natural resources."[55] But in a state with extensive natural resource deposits, it further weakens an already shaky reform law.

The new Nevada law bans all private-to-private condemnations, other than an exception for blight takings.[56] Nevada statutory law defines blight very broadly, allowing an area to be declared blighted so long as it meets at least four of eleven factors.[57] The list of factors included at least six that are extremely broad and could apply to almost any area.[58] However, Nevada voters have since approved a state constitutional amendment that provides much stronger protection for property owners than that available under the statute enacted by the legislature.[59]

Kentucky's post-*Kelo* reform law likewise retains a very broad preexisting definition of blight.[60] The law allows condemnation of property for "urban renewal and community development" in "blighted" or "slum" areas.[61] An area can be considered "blighted" or a "slum" if there are flaws in the "size" or "usefulness" of property lots in the area, or if there are conditions "constitut[ing] a menace to the public health, safety and welfare."[62]

Maine's reform statute also incorporates a broad definition of blight from prior legislation.[63] Prior Maine law defined blight as including areas in which properties suffer from "[d]ilapidation, deterioration, age or obsolescence."[64] Condemnations that further "urban renewal" projects, are authorized in areas which are designated as blighted because conditions there are detrimental to "public health, safety, morals or welfare."[65] Condemnation for "community development" can occur in areas that are considered blighted under the same definition, except that threats to "morals" are not included.[66]

The new Tennessee law attempts to tighten the definition of "blight" but ultimately leaves it very broad. Under the new statute,

> "Blighted areas" are areas (including slum areas) with buildings or improvements which, by reason of dilapidation, obsolescence, overcrowding, lack of ventilation, light and sanitary facilities, deleterious land use, or any combination of these or other factors, are detrimental to the safety, health, morals, or welfare of the community. Welfare of the community does not include solely a loss of property value to surrounding properties nor does it include the need for increased tax revenues.[67]

The inclusion of the term "welfare of the community" seems to leave the door open to most economic development takings. Economic development is generally considered a component of community "welfare." This conclusion is not much affected by the stipulation that " '[w]elfare of the community' . . . does not include solely a loss of property value to surrounding properties nor does it include the need for increased tax revenues."[68] Condemnations that promote "development" by increasing property values are still permitted so long as there is some other claim of even a small economic benefit, such as an increase in employment, savings, or investment.

Rhode Island's reform law mandates that "[n]o entity subject to the provisions of the chapter shall exercise eminent powers to acquire any property for economic development purposes unless it has explicit authority to do so and unless it conforms to the provisions of this section."[69] The requirement of having "explicit authority" is not a meaningful constraint because state law already gives virtually all local government the power to condemn property in "arrested blighted areas," "deteriorated blighted areas," and "slum blighted areas."[70] All three of these concepts are defined extremely broadly.[71] The new law may actually increase the power of redevelopment agencies to condemn property, because it allows them to take any property for the purposes of "correcting conditions ad-

versely affecting public health, safety, morals, or welfare," and this authorization is "not limited to" areas that have been declared blighted.[72]

New Jersey's eminent domain reform law, enacted in September 2013,
is the most recent post-*Kelo* law to date.[73] It reinstates a definition of
blight that covers any conditions "detrimental to the safety, health, morals, or welfare of the community," even though the New Jersey Supreme
Court had, in 2007, invalidated condemnations under such a broad definition as incompatible with the state constitution.[74] The new law also
makes it procedurally more difficult for property owners to challenge
blight designations by allowing such challenges only within forty-five days
after a blight designation is declared, which could be years before it is actually used to authorize a taking.[75] Finally, the law facilitates the creation
of "development areas" where localities can offer subsidies to developers
and then makes it easy to transform development areas where eminent
domain cannot be used to transfer property to private developers into
ones where it can.[76]

Iowa's post-*Kelo* law is a somewhat ambiguous case. The Iowa statute includes a less broad blight exemption but one that might still be extensive enough to allow a wide range of economic development takings.
The Iowa statute permits condemnation of blighted areas and defines
blight as:

> [T]he presence of a substantial number of slum or deteriorated structures; in-
> sanitary or unsafe conditions; excessive and uncorrected deterioration of site
> or other improvements; tax or special assessment delinquency exceeding the
> fair value of the land; defective or unusual conditions of title; or the existence of
> conditions which endanger life or property by fire and other causes; or the ex-
> istence of conditions which retard the provision of housing accommodations
> for low or moderate income families, or is a menace to the public health and
> safety in its present condition and use.[77]

Whether or not this is a broad definition of blight depends on the
definition of such terms as "deteriorated structures" and "excessive and
uncorrected deterioration of site." If the concept of "deterioration" is defined broadly, virtually any area could be considered blighted because
all structures gradually deteriorate over time. Since one of the conditions
justifying a blight designation is "the presence of a substantial number of
slum *or* deteriorated structures,"[78] we might presume that the term "deteriorated" can be applied to structures that are not dilapidated enough

to be considered "slum[s]." Otherwise, the inclusion of the term "deterio-rated" would be superfluous.

In addition, it is possible that a wide range of areas could be considered blighted by applying the statute's provision that an area is blighted if there are "conditions which retard the provision of housing accommodations for low or moderate income families."[79] Since the law does not state that the "retardation" must be of significant magnitude, the existence of conditions that impair the provision of low and moderate income housing even slightly might be enough to justify a blight designation.

State Reform Laws that are Ineffective for Other Reasons

While broad blight exemptions are by far the most common type of loophole in post-*Kelo* laws, several post-*Kelo* statutes are ineffective for other reasons. The most notable of these are those of California, Connecticut, and Maryland. The Texas and Ohio laws, already briefly discussed above, also have major loopholes besides those created by their blight exemptions. I also briefly consider Washington's new eminent domain law, even though the latter is not truly a response to *Kelo*.

In September 2006, the California state legislature enacted a package of five post-*Kelo* eminent domain reform bills.[80] None of the five came close to actually forbidding condemnations for economic development. Four of the five laws created minor new procedural hurdles for local governments seeking to condemn property.[81] As Timothy Sandefur of the Pacific Legal Foundation showed in a detailed analysis, none of the laws impose restrictions that significantly impede the exercise of eminent domain in California.[82]

Senate Bill 1206 attempts to narrow the definition of blight but still leaves it broad enough to permit the condemnation of almost any property that local governments might want to take for economic development purposes. The bill requires that a blighted area have both at least one "physical condition" that causes blight and one "economic" condition.[83] Both lists of qualifying conditions include vague criteria that could apply to almost any neighborhood.[84] Moreover, a blight condemnation requires just one of several conditions from each list. It should, however, be noted that in 2011, California abolished the state's redevelopment agencies, which had been responsible for many economic development and blight condemnations, for fiscal reasons unrelated to the *Kelo* backlash;

the law was later largely upheld against legal challenges by the California Supreme Court.[85] This law does not, however, prevent other state and local agencies from carrying out similar takings.

The new Connecticut law merely forbids the condemnation of property "for the primary purpose of increasing local tax revenue."[86] This restriction does not prevent condemnations for either economic development or blight alleviation. Connecticut law allows local governments to condemn property for both purposes.[87] Even the goal of increasing tax revenue can still be pursued so long as it is part of a more general plan for local "redevelopment."[88] In practice, it is likely impossible to prove that a given property is being condemned primarily for the purpose of "increasing local tax revenue" as distinct from the goal of promoting economic development more generally. It is ironic that the state in which the *Kelo* case originated has enacted one of the nation's weakest post-*Kelo* reform laws, one that would not have prevented the condemnations challenged by Susette Kelo and her fellow New London property owners.

Maryland's new law does not forbid condemnations for either economic development *or* blight. Instead, it merely requires a condemnation to occur within four years of its authorization.[89] This restriction is unlikely to impede economic development takings. Not only is the four-year period quite long, but reauthorization is likely to be easily obtained under the state's extremely broad definition of "blighted" and "slum" areas, both of which are eligible for condemnation under Maryland law.[90]

The main shortcoming of the Ohio law restricting economic development takings was its temporary nature. The new law mandated that

[U]ntil December 31, 2006, no public body shall use eminent domain to take . . . private property that is not within a blighted area, as determined by the public body, when the primary purpose for the taking is economic development that will ultimately result in ownership of that property being vested in another private person.[91]

Even within the short period of its effect, the law probably only had a very limited impact. While it forbade condemnations where economic development was the "primary purpose," nothing prevented such takings if the community could cite some other objective to which the development objective was an adjunct or complement.[92] Creative local governments could easily come up with such proposals. Furthermore, the Ohio law explicitly exempted blighted areas from its scope;[93] the definition of blight under Ohio law is broad enough to cover almost any area.[94]

The Ohio legislation also established a "Legislative Task Force to Study Eminent Domain and its Use and Application in the State."[95] However, the twenty-five member commission was largely dominated by pro-eminent domain interests. Fourteen of the twenty-five members were required to be representatives of groups that tend to be supportive of broad eminent domain power. Only four were required to be members of groups likely to support strict limits on condemnation authority, and seven represented groups with mixed incentives.[96] As was perhaps to be expected, the commission's final report recommended only minor reforms in state law. For example, it suggested tightening the state's broad definition of blight, but its proposed new definition is almost as broad as the old one.[97] In July 2007, the Ohio state legislature enacted a new reform law that adopted the definition of blight recommended by the commission.[98]

Texas's post-*Kelo* legislation is likely to be almost completely ineffectual because of its major loopholes. It forbids condemnations if the taking

> (1) confers a private benefit on a particular private party through the use of the property; (2) is for a public use that is merely a pretext to confer a private benefit on a particular private party; or (3) is for economic development purposes, unless the economic development is a secondary purpose resulting from municipal community development or municipal urban renewal activities to eliminate an existing affirmative harm on society from slum or blighted areas . . . .[99]

Taken literally, the first criterion in the act might be used to forbid almost all condemnations, since even traditional public uses often "confer a private benefit on a particular private party through the use of the property."[100] Presumably, however, this prohibition is intended merely to forbid condemnations that create such a private benefit without also serving a public use. Otherwise, the state legislature would not be able to protect "community development" and "urban renewal" takings, which surely confer "private benefits" for "particular" persons.[101]

The legislation's ban on pretextual takings merely reiterated preexisting law. *Kelo* itself forbids pretextual takings.[102] The ban on takings for economic development purposes is largely vitiated by exemption for condemnations where "economic development is a secondary purpose resulting from municipal community development."[103] Virtually any project that promotes economic development can also be plausibly characterized as advancing "community development." It is difficult to see how the two concepts can be meaningfully distinguished in real-world situations. Indeed, Texas law defines "community development" to permit condemnation of any property that is "inappropriately developed from the standpoint of sound community development and growth."[104] It is surely reasonable to suppose that "sound community development and growth" includes economic "development and growth."[105]

The Texas legislation does contain two potentially effective elements. First, it eliminates judicial deference to governmental determinations that a challenged condemnation is for a legitimate public use.[106] This shifts the burden of proof in public use cases to the condemning authority. Second, it seems to forbid private-to-private condemnations under laws other than those allowing the use of eminent domain for blight alleviation and "community development."[107] However, as noted above, Texas's definition of "community development" is so broad that it can be used to justify almost any condemnation, even under a nondeferential approach to judicial review. Judges are unlikely to find that very many takings run afoul of the community development statute's authorization of condemnation of property that is "inappropriately developed from the standpoint of sound community development and growth."[108] Ultimately, the potentially effective elements of the Texas law are swallowed up by the "community development" exception.[109]

The state of Washington's 2007 eminent domain law probably is not a true response to *Kelo*.[110] It does not even pretend to restrict economic development takings or cut back on the definition of public use in any other way. Instead, the new statute seems to be a reaction to a 2006 Washington Supreme Court decision, which held that property owners are not entitled to personal notice of public meetings called to consider the necessity of initiating eminent domain proceedings against them.[111]

Because the new law was neither a response to *Kelo* nor an attempt to narrow the definition of public use, I do not classify it as a post-*Kelo* reform. But if it were to be viewed as a post-*Kelo* reform, it would be classified as adding little or nothing to the protections Washington property owners already enjoyed before *Kelo*. The state supreme court banned economic development takings in 1959,[112] and Washington already had a narrow definition of blight.[113]

Effective Reforms Enacted by State Legislatures

Fifteen state legislatures have enacted laws that either abolish or significantly constrain economic development takings. The most sweeping of these reforms are Florida's and New Mexico's, which not only abolish condemnations for economic development, but also ban all blight condemnations, even those that occur in areas that would meet a strict definition of the term.[114] Florida and New Mexico therefore became the second and third states to abolish blight condemnations, following in the footsteps of Utah, which did so prior to *Kelo,* but later partly reversed itself.[115] Unlike Utah and New Mexico, which made little use of economic development and blight takings even before the enactment of their new laws,[116] Florida has an extensive record of dubious economic development and blight condemnations.[117] Due to its broad scope and enactment in a large state that previously made extensive use of private-to-private takings, the new Florida law is probably the most important post-*Kelo* legislative victory for property rights activists.

South Dakota's new law is only slightly less sweeping than Florida's. It continues to permit blight condemnations, but does not allow *any* takings—including those in blighted areas—that "transfer property to any private person, nongovernmental entity, or other public-private business entity."[118] This forbids economic development takings and also greatly reduces the political incentive to engage in blight condemnations, since local governments can no longer use such takings to transfer property to politically influential interests.

Kansas's reform law is similar to South Dakota's insofar as it bans nearly all private-to-private condemnations.[119] It also forbids condemnations "for the purpose of selling, leasing or otherwise transferring such property to any private entity" except in cases where they are needed for public utilities or where there is defective title.[120] Blight condemnations are limited to cases where the property in question is "unsafe for occupation by humans under the building codes."[121]

Nine state reform laws couple a ban on economic development condemnations with restrictions on the definition of blight that, roughly speaking, restrict blight condemnations to areas that fit the intuitive definition of the term. This formula was successfully used in the Alabama, Delaware, Georgia, Indiana, Michigan, New Hampshire, Virginia, and Wyoming reform laws.[122]

Alabama partially reversed its post-*Kelo* reform in 2013,[123] though it is not yet clear whether the new reform completely negates the earlier reform. The Republican state legislators who sponsored the recent revision claim that it does not. But I am skeptical, because the new law seems to permit the use of eminent domain for a wide range of "private uses and purposes imbued with a public interest," including privately owned "automotive, automotive-industry related, aviation, aviation-industry related, medical, pharmaceutical, semiconductor, computer, electronics, energy conservation, cyber technology, and biomedical industry manufacturing facilities."[124] I have chosen to continue to classify Alabama as a state with an effective reform law, because the new law arguably does not reverse all of the gains made by the previous one. But that characterization is now open to serious question.

In the case of Nevada, the new legislation was enacted only in the aftermath of a referendum initiative that would ban both economic development and blight condemnations entirely.

A recent Virginia Supreme Court decision interpreting the Virginia post-*Kelo* law confirms that its limitations on blight condemnations have teeth, holding that the condemnation of nonblighted property is forbidden, even if it is located in a generally blighted area.[125]

Two state laws—Pennsylvania and Minnesota—forbade economic development takings and restrict the definition of blight but temporarily undermined their effectiveness by exempting large parts of the state from the law's coverage. The Pennsylvania law forbids "the exercise by any condemnor of the power of eminent domain to take private property in order to use it for private commercial enterprise"[126] and imposes a restrictive definition of blight. But it also temporarily exempted Philadelphia and Pittsburgh, as well as some other areas, from its coverage.[127] These two cities, by far the state's largest urban areas, were also the sites of many of the state's most extensive private-to-private takings.[128] The provision exempting the two cities expired on schedule on December 31, 2012, but not before Philadelphia took advantage of the delay by condemning a large number of properties for transfer to private developers, including the taking of a successful artists' studio for the purpose of building a parking lot and a supermarket, just four days before the deadline expired.[129] During the course of 2012, the Philadelphia Redevelopment Authority seized some twelve times as many properties as the year before, probably in an effort to beat the deadline.[130]

Minnesota's 2006 law was similar. It too banned economic development takings and restricted the definition of blight,[131] while creating
some major geographic exemptions. In this case, the exemptions included
land located in some 2000 Tax Increment Financing Districts, including
much of the territory of the Twin Cities of Minneapolis and St. Paul,
where a high proportion of the state's condemnations take place.[132] Like
Pennsylvania's exemptions, Minnesota's were time-limited, scheduled to
expire in five years.[133] But the Minnesota exemptions were superseded
by a new law enacted in early 2009.[134]

Wisconsin's post-*Kelo* law is perhaps the weakest that I have chosen
to classify as effective. It exempts blight condemnations from its ban on
economic development takings and defines blight relatively broadly. The
definition includes

> [A]ny property that, by reason of abandonment, dilapidation, deterioration,
> age or obsolescence, inadequate provisions for ventilation, light, air, or
> sanitation, high density of population and overcrowding, faulty lot layout
> in relation to size, adequacy, accessibility, or usefulness, unsanitary or un-
> safe conditions, deterioration of site or other improvements, or the existence
> of conditions that endanger life or property by fire or other causes, or any
> combination of such factors, is detrimental to the public health, safety, or
> welfare.[135]

However, the statute also exempts residential property consisting of
a single dwelling unit from condemnation for blight alleviation unless it
has "been abandoned," the people residing on the property are not relatives of the owner, or "the crime rate in [or near] the property is at least
3 times the crime rate in the remainder of the municipality."[136] Thus, the
Wisconsin law provides important new protection for some types of family homes and therefore is at least marginally effective.

Like the Wisconsin reform, some of the other effective state laws may
not have more than a modest impact. The reforms enacted by Alabama,
Georgia, and South Dakota were adopted by states that had little or no
recent history of resorting to private-to-private condemnations.[137] Thus,
they forbid practices in which their state and local governments rarely
engaged, though there is some value in forestalling potential future
abuses. Overall, only seven states that had recently engaged in significant
amounts of economic development and blight condemnations adopted
legislative post-*Kelo* reform measures with real teeth.[138]

Reforms Enacted by Referendum

In sharp contrast to legislatively enacted post-*Kelo* reforms, those adopted by popular referendum are generally much stronger. In 2006, ten states adopted post-*Kelo* reforms by popular referendum.[139] All ten passed by large margins ranging from 55 percent to 86 percent of the vote.[140] Three more states—Mississippi, Texas, and Virginia—enacted reforms by referendum in later years. Of these, at least eight and possibly nine provided significantly stronger protection for property owners than was available under existing law. Two states—Georgia and New Hampshire—passed initiatives that added little or nothing to post-*Kelo* reforms already enacted by the state legislature.[141] South Carolina and Texas voters adopted largely ineffective reform laws.[142] Referenda initiated by citizen groups were far more likely to lead to effective laws than those enacted by state legislatures. Indeed, only one state—Louisiana—passed a legislature-initiated referendum that provided significantly greater protection for property owners than that available under preexisting statutory law enacted through the ordinary legislative process.[143]

Four states—Arizona, Louisiana, Mississippi, and Oregon[144]—enacted referendum initiatives that essentially followed the standard formula of combining a ban on economic development takings with a restrictive definition of blight. A 2009 Louisiana appellate court decision ruled that the blight exception, although generally fairly narrow, was broad enough to justify condemnation of property devastated by Hurricane Katrina in 2005.[145]

In addition to adopting a narrow definition of blight, the Mississippi initiative also forbids most transfers of condemned land to a private property until at least ten years have elapsed since the taking.[146] Nevada and North Dakota's initiatives went one step beyond this and amended their respective state constitutions to ban nearly all condemnations that transfer property to a private owner.[147]

Florida's referendum initiative could not add much in the way of substantive protections to the state's legislatively enacted post-*Kelo* law, already the strongest in the country.[148] However, Constitutional Amendment 8 did alter the state constitution to provide an important procedural protection: no new law allowing "the transfer of private property taken by eminent domain to a natural person or private entity" can be passed without a three-fifths supermajority in the state legislature.[149] This might be an important safeguard for property owners against the erosion of public use protections by future state legislatures.

Like its Florida counterpart, Virginia's Question 1—the most recently enacted post-*Kelo* referendum initiative—came in the wake of a strong legislative reform.[150] Question 1 bans takings where the "the primary use is for private gain, private benefit, private enterprise, increasing jobs, increasing tax revenue, or economic development, except for the elimination of a public nuisance existing on the property."[151] These provisions largely mirror the requirements of Virginia's 2007 legislative reform.[152] But because Question 1 is a constitutional amendment, it does entrench these protections for property owners against future legislative erosion. The amendment also has some valuable provisions forbidding the condemnation of more property than is necessary for the "public use" justifying the taking, increasing compensation for owners of condemned property, and specifying that the right to private property is "fundamental," which usually triggers a higher degree of judicial protection when the right is threatened.[153]

Georgia's referendum law added little to that state's strong legislatively enacted post-*Kelo* statute, requiring only that any new private-to-private takings be approved by local elected officials.[154] New Hampshire's referendum initiative also came in the wake of a strong legislative proposal and adds nothing to it.[155] Absent the earlier legislation, it would provide no real protection at all, since it only forbids condemnations "for the purpose of private development or other private use of the property."[156] This wording is largely useless because it does not foreclose the standard argument that the transfer of property to a private party will promote "public" development that benefits the community as a whole, not just specific private interests.

South Carolina's referendum seems to forbid takings for economic development. However, the wording may actually permit such takings, since it states that "[p]rivate property must not be condemned by eminent domain for any purpose or benefit, including, but not limited to, the purpose or benefit of economic development, unless the condemnation is for public use."[157] This, however, leaves open the question of whether economic development is in fact a public use—the very issue addressed by *Kelo* with respect to the federal Constitution. Current South Carolina Supreme Court case law already holds that economic development is not a public use under the state constitution.[158] The new constitutional amendment adds nothing to that ruling and leaves open the possibility that future court decisions will be able to reverse it in the absence of a clear textual statement in the state constitution to the contrary.

The South Carolina amendment also narrows the definition of blight to "property constituting a danger to the safety and health of the community by reason of lack of ventilation, light, and sanitary facilities, dilapidation, deleterious land use, or any combination of these factors."[159] However, this provision also has a potential loophole, since "deleterious land use" and "health of the community" could both be interpreted broadly to cover "deleterious" land uses that weaken the community's "economic health."

The state of California enacted an ineffective referendum initiative, Proposition 99, in June 2008.[160] This initiative was put on the ballot by the California League of Cities and other pro-condemnation groups for the purpose of forestalling the more restrictive Proposition 98 (sponsored by property rights advocates).[161] Proposition 99 protects only owner-occupied residences against condemnations with the purpose of transferring property to "private persons" if the owner has lived in the home for at least one year.[162] Renters, who make up 42 percent of California households, are left unprotected.[163] The same is true of businesses and homeowners who have lived in their residences for less than one year.[164]

Even the new protection for homeowners is likely to be ineffective, because the measure allows the condemnation of owner-occupied homes if they are "incidental" to a "public work or improvement" project.[165] This means that homes could still be taken for transfer to private developers if the proposed project allocated some space for a "public" facility such as a community center or library. Proposition 99 also allows government officials to claim that their true purpose is promoting economic or community development rather than conveyance of the property to a private person, which is only a means to an end. This, of course, is precisely the argument accepted by the Supreme Court in *Kelo*, when it held that the transfer of the condemned property to a private party was constitutionally permissible because it was undertaken for the "public purpose" of promoting development.

The new Michigan amendment is an ambiguous case. The amendment forbids condemnation of property "for transfer to a private entity for the purpose of economic development or enhancement of tax revenues."[166] However, it did not change the state's previously broad definition of "blight." Despite the passage of almost ten years, it is not yet clear whether the landmark 2004 state supreme court decision in *County of Wayne v. Hathcock* will be interpreted to constrain condemnation of property under very broad blight designations.[167] If *Hathcock* is held to limit broad blight designations, then the new constitutional amendment would have the modest but real advantage of providing explicit textual foundations for *Hathcock*'s holding and reducing the chance of its reversal or erosion by future courts.

If, on the other hand, *Hathcock* is interpreted to permit broad definitions of blight, then the Michigan referendum initiative will be largely ineffective in its own right. At this point, however, the status of the Michigan referendum initiative is largely moot because Michigan's legislative reform has already narrowed the definition of blight.[168] Thus, the Michigan constitutional amendment enacted by referendum reinforces the accomplishments of the previous statutory reform but might not have been effective as a stand-alone law.

In analyzing the post-*Kelo* referendum initiatives, it is important to note that five of the eight clearly effective laws were enacted by means of initiative processes that allow activists to place a measure on the ballot without prior approval by the state legislature.[169] Two of the other three (Florida and Virginia) were sent to the voters by a legislature that had already enacted strong post-*Kelo* reform laws. Only the Louisiana state legislature forwarded to the voters a referendum initiative without first enacting a strong legislative reform of its own. By contrast, four of the five largely ineffective initiatives required preapproval by state legislatures,[170] and the same was true of the ambiguous Michigan case.[171] In sum, the key contrast is not so much between legislative reform and referendum initiatives, but between referenda enacted without the need for approval by the state legislature and every other type of reform law, which did require legislative backing.

Federal Reforms

By comparison with the far more extensive state-level reforms, federal post-*Kelo* reform efforts are notable primarily for their minimalistic nature. The most significant federal reform effort—the Private Property Rights Protection Act—failed to pass the Senate, despite repeatedly getting through the House of Representatives. And its effects would likely have been quite modest, even if it did pass. Other federal reform efforts have also had little or no effect.

The Private Property Rights Protection Act

On November 3, 2005, the U.S. House of Representatives passed the Private Property Rights Protection Act of 2005 (PRPA) by an overwhelming 376 to 38 margin.[172] But the bill died in the Senate Judiciary Committee, and the 109th Congress ended without the Act being passed into law.[173] In May 2007, under the new Democratic Congress, the bill was reported out of the Agriculture Committee, but failed to come to a vote of the full House of Representatives.[174]

The PRPA was resuscitated in 2012 and passed the House of Representatives on a voice vote in February of that year.[175] Yet again the PRPA came before the Senate Judiciary Committee, and yet again it stalled there until the end of the congressional term.[176] In February 2014, the bill passed the House of Representatives a third time, this time by a 353-65 vote.[177] As of August 2014 the PRPA is once more before the Senate Judiciary Committee, and it is not clear whether it will finally pass before the end of the congressional term. Despite its failure to achieve passage so far, I consider it here because it is the most important federal effort to provide increased protection for property owners in the aftermath of *Kelo*.

The PRPA would block state and local governments from "exercis[ing] [their] power of eminent domain, or allow[ing] the exercise of such power by any person or entity to which such power has been delegated, over property to be used for economic development or over property that is subsequently used for economic development, if that State or political subdivision receives Federal economic development funds during any fiscal year in which it does so."[178] Violators are punished by the loss of all "[f]ederal economic development funds for a period of two fiscal years."[179] Condemnation for economic development is broadly defined to include any taking that transfers property "from one private person or entity to another private person or entity for commercial enterprise carried on for profit, or to increase tax revenue, tax base, employment, or general economic health."[180] The bill might appear to create significant incentives to deter state and local governments from pursuing economic development takings. But any such appearance is deceptive because of the small amount of federal funds that offending state and local governments stand to lose.

States and localities that run afoul of the PRPA would risk losing only "federal economic development funds,"[181] defined as "any Federal funds distributed to or through States or political subdivisions of States under

Federal laws designed to improve or increase the size of economies of States or political subdivisions of States."[182] The precise definition of "economic development funds" remains unclear, as it is difficult to tell precisely which federal programs are "designed to improve or increase the size of the economies of States or political subdivisions of States."[183] A Congressional Research Service analysis concluded that the PRPA ultimately would delegate the task of identifying the relevant programs to the attorney general.[184] But it is likely that the Act would only apply to at most about 1.8 percent of federal funds granted to states and localities, and therefore probably be only a modest deterrent to economic development takings, except in perhaps some areas where economic development grants might constitute an atypically large share of the local budget.[185] While the PRPA may have some beneficial effects at the margin, its impact if enacted is likely to be quite limited.

The Bond Amendment

The Bond Amendment, named after its sponsor Senator Christopher Bond, was enacted on November 30, 2005, as an amendment to the 2006 appropriation bill for the Transportation, Treasury, and Housing and Urban Development departments, the Judiciary, the District of Columbia, and various independent agencies.[186] It forbade the use of funds allocated in the Act to "support" the use of eminent domain for "economic development that primarily benefits private entities."[187]

The Bond Amendment did not have more than minimal impact on the use of eminent domain by state and local governments. First, it only forbade those economic development takings that "primarily benefit . . . private entities."[188] This restriction made it possible for the condemning jurisdiction to argue that the primary benefit of the development will go to the public. Under *Kelo*'s lenient standards for evaluating government claims that takings create public benefits, it is unlikely that such an argument would ever fail in federal court.[189]

Second, the Bond Amendment categorically exempted condemnations for, among many other things, "utility projects which benefit or serve the general public," an exception that opened the door to at least some private economic development projects.[190]

The Bond Amendment's impact was also small because very few projects that did not fall within one of its broad exceptions are likely to be funded by federal transportation and housing grants in any event. The law completely excludes from coverage "mass transit" and "highway projects."[191] There are few, if any, eminent domain projects previously funded by federal transportation or housing grants that the bill actually forbade. Finally, the amendment only applied to the 2006 fiscal year and was not renewed in later years.

President George W. Bush's 2006 Executive Order

On June 23, 2006, the one-year anniversary of the *Kelo* decision, President George W. Bush issued an executive order that purported to bar federal involvement in *Kelo*-style takings.[192] On the surface, the order seems to forbid federal agencies from undertaking economic development condemnations, but its wording undercuts this goal. The key part of the order reads as follows:

> It is the policy of the United States to protect the rights of Americans to their private property, including by limiting the taking of private property by the Federal Government to situations in which the taking is for public use, with just compensation, and for the purpose of benefiting the general public and not merely for the purpose of advancing the economic interest of private parties to be given ownership or use of the property taken.[193]

Read carefully, the order does not in fact bar condemnations that transfer property to other private parties for economic development. Instead, it permits them to continue so long as they are "for the purpose of benefiting the general public and not merely for the purpose of advancing the economic interest of private parties to be given ownership or use of the property taken."

Unfortunately, this language validates virtually any economic development condemnation that the federal government might want to pursue. Officials can (and usually do) claim that the goal of a taking is to benefit "the general public" and not "merely" the new owners.[194] Even had President Bush's order been worded more strongly, its impact would have been limited. The vast majority of economic development condemnations are undertaken by state and local governments, not by federal agencies. Nonetheless, it is noteworthy that the Bush administration apparently chose to issue an executive order that was almost certain to have no effect even in the rare instances where the federal government does involve itself in *Kelo*-like takings.

Conclusion

The *Kelo* backlash has led to important gains for property rights. In many states, there are much stronger constraints on blight and economic development takings than existed before *Kelo*. But the backlash has also yielded far less effective reform than many expected. This result is striking in light of the overwhelming public opposition to the decision.

The next chapter considers the question of why the backlash often fell short of expectations. In many cases, the same political ignorance that often facilitated dubious takings before *Kelo* also helped undermine efforts to achieve reform through the political process.

CHAPTER SIX

Why the Backlash Often Fell Short

Why, in the face of the massive public backlash against *Kelo,* has there been so much ineffective legislation? Multiple factors are likely at work. But the weakness of much post-*Kelo* legislation is at least in large part due to widespread public ignorance. Survey data show that the overwhelming majority of citizens know little or nothing about post-*Kelo* reform laws in their states. The vast majority do not know whether their states have passed post-*Kelo* reform legislation and even fewer know whether that legislation is likely to be effective.[1]

This widespread ignorance may well account for the ineffectiveness of many of the new laws. It also helps account for several other aspects of the *Kelo* backlash, including its timing and the greater effectiveness of laws enacted by referenda relative to those adopted through the legislative process.[2] The political ignorance theory accounts for the pattern of reform laws better than the main alternative explanation, which holds that the relative paucity of effective reform laws is primarily the result of interest group lobbying.[3]

As discussed in chapter 3, voters are "rationally ignorant" of public policy, having little incentive to acquire any substantial knowledge about the details of government actions.[4] The publicity surrounding *Kelo* made the public at least somewhat aware of the problem of economic development takings. But it did not lead most voters to closely scrutinize the details of proposed reform legislation. Few citizens have the time or inclination to delve into such matters, and many are often ignorant of the very existence of even the most important legislative measures. Survey data shows that the vast majority of Americans were indeed ignorant of the content of post-*Kelo* reform legislation in their states. In an August 2007 Saint Index survey, only 21 percent of respondents could correctly answer whether or not their states had passed eminent domain reform legislation since *Kelo,* and only 13 percent both knew whether their states had passed legislation and correctly indicated whether that legislation was likely to be effective.[5]

The political ignorance hypothesis cannot explain every aspect of the *Kelo* backlash. But it correctly predicts three important events: the sudden emergence of the *Kelo* backlash, in spite of the fact that economic development takings were already permitted under existing precedent; the passage of "position-taking" laws by both state and federal legislators; and the fact that that post-*Kelo* laws enacted by popular referendum tended to be much stronger than those enacted by state legislatures. No other theory can easily account for all three of these seeming anomalies.

Public Ignorance of Post-*Kelo* Reform Laws

As we saw in chapter 3, most citizens are "rationally ignorant" about most aspects of public policy because there is so little chance that an increase in any one voter's knowledge would have a significant impact on policy outcomes. Survey data compiled at my request by the Saint Consulting Group, a firm that sponsors surveys on land use policy, confirm that most Americans have little or no knowledge of post-*Kelo* reform. The data compiled in table 6.1 are based on an August 2007 Saint Index national survey.[6] It therefore counts as having enacted post-*Kelo* reform only in those states that had passed their laws before the poll was conducted.

The Saint Index results demonstrate that political ignorance about post-*Kelo* reform is widespread. Only 13 percent of respondents could both correctly answer whether or not their states had enacted eminent domain reform laws between 2005 and the date of the survey, and correctly answer a follow-up question about whether or not those laws were likely to be effective in preventing condemnations for economic development.[7] Only 21 percent could even correctly answer the first question in the sequence: whether or not their states had enacted eminent domain reform since *Kelo* was decided in 2005.[8] These figures do not change significantly if we drop the very close cases of Idaho and Wisconsin from the sample or classify both effective and ineffective answers as correct for survey respondents in these two states.[9]

It is also important to recognize that 6 percent of respondents believed that their states had enacted post-*Kelo* reforms that were likely to be "effective" in reducing economic development takings even though the state in fact had not. This is not a large number in absolute terms, but it still represents more than one-third of the 17 percent of respondents who expressed any opinion at all about the effectiveness of their states' reforms.[10] An additional 2 percent wrongly believed that their states' reform laws were ineffective even though the opposite was in fact true. Even among the small minority of Americans who paid close enough attention to post-*Kelo* reform legislation to have an opinion about its effectiveness, there was a high degree of ignorance.[11]

Table 6.1 indicates that ignorance about state post-*Kelo* reform cuts across gender, racial, and political lines. Some 85 percent of men and 90 percent of women were ignorant about the condition of post-*Kelo* reform, as were 82 percent of African Americans, 89 percent of whites, and similar overwhelming majorities of liberals and conservatives, Democrats and Republicans, and other groups. It is difficult to avoid the conclusion that most Americans are ignorant about the existence, or lack thereof, of post-*Kelo* reform in their states, and even fewer can tell whether the reform was effective or not.

The Saint Index data may even understate the amount of ignorance about post-*Kelo* reform. Some respondents may have gotten the right answers by guessing. In order to get a correct answer, respondents living in the eight states that had not passed any post-*Kelo* reform by 2007 needed only to get one binary question correct and had a 50 percent chance of getting the right answer through random guessing. Residents of the forty-two states that have passed reform laws needed to get two such questions correct and thus had a 25 percent chance of doing so through random guessing.[12] Past research shows that many survey respondents will guess in order to avoid admitting ignorance about the subject matter of a poll question, and that may have happened in this case as well.[13] An additional factor biasing the knowledge levels found in the Saint Index survey upward is the fact that the pollsters only surveyed Americans over the age of twenty-one. Political knowledge is generally correlated with age,[14] and young adults (people aged eighteen to twenty-nine) have the highest incidence of ignorance of any age group.[15] The exclusion of eighteen to twenty year olds from the sample reduces the representation of this group in the aggregate data.

The fact that most citizens are ignorant about post-*Kelo* reform is not surprising. Large majorities know little or nothing about far more important policies. For example, polls conducted around the time of the

TABLE 6.1 **Public Knowledge of State Post-*Kelo* Reform[1]**

	Group	% Unaware of the Condition of Post-*Kelo* Reform in Their State
	Total	87
Gender	Male	85
	Female	90
Racial/Ethnic Group[2]	White	89
	African American	82
	Asian	75
	Hispanic/Latino	100
	Native American	75
Party Affiliation	Democrat	89
	Independent	83
	Republican	89
Ideology	Liberal	88
	Moderate	90
	Conservative	87

1. Saint Index 2007, questions 9, 10. I counted as "correct" those respondents who both (1) knew whether or not their states had passed post-*Kelo* eminent domain reform laws and (2) correctly answered the question about whether or not those laws were effective. Respondents from the eight states that had not enacted any post-*Kelo* laws were counted as giving correct answers to both questions, if they correctly answered the first question by stating that their states had not adopted any reforms. Totals have been rounded off to the nearest whole number. The State of Utah presented a difficult methodological dilemma because it had banned economic development takings prior to *Kelo*. Respondents who stated that it had an effective reform were credited with a "correct" response. Coding the Utah results the other way does not significantly alter the overall results because of the extremely low number of Utah respondents in the sample.

2. The results for Hispanics, Asians, and Native Americans may be unreliable because they are based on very small sample sizes of twenty-four, twelve, and twelve respondents, respectively. Saint Index 2007.

2010 election found that only 34 percent realized that the controversial Troubled Asset Relief Program bank bailout policy had been enacted under President George W. Bush rather than under Barack Obama, and only 33 percent realized that the economy had grown during the previous year, even though the vast majority of voters told pollsters that the economy was the most important issue in the election.[16] What may be somewhat surprising—especially to nonexperts—is that public ignorance is so widespread despite the immense outcry that the issue has generated.

Possible Alternative Explanations of the Saint Index Data

There are several possible objections to my theory that the Saint Index data prove the existence of widespread ignorance about post-*Kelo* reform that undermines the ability of voters to force through the sorts of policies favored by overwhelming majorities. I consider four such potential objections here and tentatively conclude that none of them withstand close scrutiny.

Because post-*Kelo* reforms were enacted over a two-year period between the time *Kelo* was decided in June 2005 and the time the Saint Index data was collected in August 2007, it is conceivable that voters were well informed of the contents of their states' legislation at the time but later forgot that knowledge. To test that theory, I checked whether the respondents from Connecticut, Maryland, Montana, Nevada, New Mexico, Ohio, Virginia, and Wyoming—the eight states whose post-*Kelo* laws were enacted in 2007—had greater knowledge than respondents in states where reform legislation passed in 2005 and 2006.[17] Two of these states—Nevada and Ohio—passed their second post-*Kelo* reform laws during this time period. The eight states in question all enacted eminent domain reform laws between February 28 and July 10, 2007, just a few months or weeks before the Saint Index survey was conducted, from August 1 to August 10, 2007.

The data show that the 122 respondents from those eight states had almost exactly the same knowledge levels as those in the rest of the country.[18] Twenty-six percent of respondents in the eight 2007 states knew whether or not their states had passed post-*Kelo* reform laws, a figure only slightly higher than the 20 percent rate compiled by respondents from the other forty-two states.[19] Similarly, 12 percent of respondents in these eight states could correctly answer both the question about the existence of reform laws and the question about their effectiveness; the figure for the other forty-two states was 13 percent.[20] While some forgetting could have taken place even in the few weeks between the passage of the 2007 laws and the time of the Saint Index survey, one would still expect that respondents in the eight states would be less likely to forget than those in states that had enacted their reforms earlier. The lack of any statistical difference between the two sets of respondents suggests that forgetting is not a major factor in accounting for the widespread ignorance revealed in the 2007 Saint Index data.

Public ignorance about post-*Kelo* reform might also be less bleak than the data suggests if those who cared about the issue strongly were mostly well informed about it. This scenario would be consistent with the "issue public" hypothesis advanced by some political scientists, which holds that citizens are likely to be well informed about a small number of issues that they care about intensely, even if they remain ignorant about most others.[21] However, survey data show that the percentage of the public who care intensely about eminent domain reform is much greater than the mere 13 percent who know enough about it to be able to determine whether their states have passed effective post-*Kelo* laws or not.[22] As discussed earlier, 63 percent of respondents in a 2005 Saint Index survey said that they "strongly" opposed the *Kelo* decision.[23] A 2006 Saint Index poll question showed that 43 percent "strongly" support reforms intended to ban economic development takings.[24] Even the smaller of these two figures is still more than three times greater than the percentage of respondents who knew whether or not their states had passed effective reforms as of the time of the August 2007 Saint Index survey.[25]

Political ignorance greatly reduces the number of voters who could potentially use the level of post-*Kelo* reform in their states as a basis for electoral decisions. In other words, it greatly diminishes the size of the potential "issue public." Even if the 13 percent who gave accurate answers on the survey all feel strongly about the issue and make effective use of that knowledge in deciding which candidates to support in state and local elections, that still leaves several times that number of citizens who also feel strongly about banning economic development takings but lack the necessary knowledge to reward political leaders who support effective reform and punish those who oppose it.

A third potentially benign interpretation of widespread ignorance of post-*Kelo* reform is the "miracle of aggregation."[26] Even if many or most voters are ignorant about a particular issue, that may be irrelevant to political outcomes if their errors are randomly distributed. In that situation, ignorance-driven votes for candidate or policy A would be offset by a similar number of "mistaken" votes for alternative B, and electoral outcomes would be determined by the (potentially very small) minority of well-informed citizens. With respect to post-*Kelo* reform, there are two serious problems with this scenario. First, even random error is likely to have an important impact on policy. Second, the errors are not in fact randomly distributed but are skewed toward overestimation of the effectiveness of post-*Kelo* reform laws.[27]

Even if errors really are randomly distributed, the existence of widespread ignorance still greatly diminishes the number of voters who can take account of post-*Kelo* reform in choosing candidates. It likely eliminates at least 70 percent of those voters who "strongly" support a ban on economic development takings.[28] This greatly reduces the potential pressure on officeholders to comply with overwhelming popular sentiment.

If, for example, 10 percent of the 43 percent of Americans who say they strongly support effective post-*Kelo* reform would be willing to vote on the issue if they were informed about it, ignorance will have reduced the number willing to change their vote based on the issue from 4.3 percent of the adult population to a maximum of 1.3 percent.[29] And even that figure unrealistically assumes that the 13 percent with accurate knowledge of post-*Kelo* reform in their states were all drawn from among the 43 percent who care "strongly" about banning economic development takings. It also assumes that none of them got the correct answers on the survey through random guessing.

The miracle of aggregation theory also fails in this case because respondent mistakes about post-*Kelo* reform are not randomly distributed. It was far more common for voters to believe that their state had passed effective reform, even if it had not, than for them to believe that it had not done so in cases where it actually had. As discussed earlier, some 6 percent of the 2007 Saint Index survey respondents wrongly believed that their states passed effective reform, whereas only 2 percent mistakenly believed that their state had failed to enact effective reform, even though it had. The 6 percent figure constitutes more than one-third of all those respondents (17 percent) who had any opinion on the effectiveness of post-*Kelo* reform in their states at all.

Unfortunately, it is impossible to use the 2007 Saint Index data to determine whether these 17 percent were disproportionately drawn from the subset of respondents most interested in post-*Kelo* reform issues. But it is plausible that they were. If so, it is possible that the 6 percent of respondents who mistakenly believed that their states has passed effective post-*Kelo* reform constitute a substantial percentage of those who would otherwise use the issue as a criterion for voting.

Finally, it is possible that voters could learn about the effectiveness of post-*Kelo* laws by relying on the statements of interest groups and other "opinion leaders" who have incentives to be better informed than ordinary citizens.[30] However, as I have discussed at greater length elsewhere, reliance on opinion leaders itself requires considerable knowledge, including the knowledge needed to select opinion leaders to follow who are both well-informed and trustworthy.[31] Moreover, the ways in which the *Kelo* issue cuts across traditional party and ideological lines makes it more difficult for voters to identify opinion leaders to follow based on traditional political cues such as partisan or ideological affiliation.[32] Most important of all, the widespread ignorance revealed in the Saint

Index survey shows that most citizens either did not acquire relevant information from opinion leaders or obtained information that turned out to be misleading.

Political Ignorance as an Explanation for the Anomalies of the Backlash

The political ignorance hypothesis gains traction from the fact that it can account for three otherwise anomalous aspects of the *Kelo* controversy: the massive backlash against a decision that largely reaffirmed existing case law that had previously excited little public controversy, the paucity of effective reform measures despite widespread public opposition to economic development takings, and the striking divergence between citizen-initiated referendum initiatives and all other types of post-*Kelo* reform measures.

Explaining the Timing of the Backlash

Some *Kelo* defenders complain that the backlash against the decision was excessive in light of the fact that the case made little change in existing law. After all, eminent domain was not a prominent national issue before *Kelo*, even though existing constitutional doctrine permitted economic development takings under the federal Constitution. A spokesman for California redevelopment agencies lamented that *Kelo* led to "a hue and cry about how bad things are in California, yet *Kelo* changed nothing."[33] But the reaction is understandable once we recognize that—for most people—*Kelo* was the first inkling they ever had that private property could be condemned merely to promote economic development by other private parties. This sudden realization led to outrage and a desire for change.

Public ignorance helps explain why economic development takings became common despite the fact that the vast majority of citizens oppose condemnation of private property for such purposes. Before *Kelo*, most of the public probably did not even realize that economic development condemnations existed. This ignorance accounts for the suddenness of the *Kelo* backlash. It also helps explain why there was relatively little public pressure to reform eminent domain law before *Kelo*.

Explaining the Paucity of Effective Reform Laws

Public ignorance is also the best available explanation for the seeming scarcity of effective post-*Kelo* reform laws. The highly publicized Supreme Court decision apparently increased awareness of eminent domain abuse, perhaps as a result of extensive press coverage. But while the publicity surrounding *Kelo* made much of the public at least somewhat aware of the issue of economic development takings, it probably did not lead voters to scrutinize the details of proposed reform legislation. The Saint Index survey showed that almost 80 percent of Americans do not even know whether their states had passed a reform law at all.[34]

Few citizens have the time or inclination to delve into such matters, and many are often ignorant of the very existence of even the most important government policies. Thus, it would not be difficult for state legislators to seek to satisfy voter demands by supporting "position-taking" legislation that purported to curb eminent domain,[35] while in reality having little effect. In this way, they can simultaneously cater to public outrage over *Kelo* and mollify developers and other interest groups that benefit from economic development condemnations.

This strategy seems to have been at the root of the failure of post-*Kelo* reform efforts in California. In that state, legislative reform efforts were initially sidetracked by the introduction of weak proposals that gave lawmakers "a chance . . . to side with the anti-eminent domain sentiment without doing any real damage to redevelopment agencies."[36] At a later stage in the political battle, the Democratic majority in the state legislature tabled even these modest reforms by claiming that they were being blocked by the Republican minority, despite the fact that "the stalled bills required only simple majority votes and thus needed no Republicans to go along."[37] As one Sacramento reporter put it, the entire process may have been "just a feint to pretend to do something about eminent domain without actually doing anything to upset the apple cart."[38] Eventually, California did enact some reforms but only ones that are almost completely ineffective.[39] A leading advocate for eminent domain reform in Nevada believes that, in his state as well, legislators sought to "look good while not upsetting anyone."[40]

The California League of Cities, an organization composed of local governments with an interest in preserving their eminent domain authority, also sought to exploit political ignorance about post-*Kelo* reform. The CLC succeeded in placing an essentially meaningless eminent domain reform referendum initiative—Proposition 99—on the state's 2008 ballot as a way of preempting a stronger referendum initiative sponsored by property rights advocates.[41] Proposition 99 cleverly included a provision stating that it would supersede any other eminent domain referendum enacted on the same day, so long as the latter got fewer votes than the CLC proposal.[42]

Such maneuvers would be difficult to pull off if the public paid close attention to pending legislation. But they can be quite effective in the presence of widespread political ignorance.

Explaining the Relative Success of Citizen-Initiated Referendum Initiatives

As we saw in chapter 5, there is a great difference between the effectiveness of citizen-initiated referendum initiatives and all other types of post-*Kelo* reforms. Five of the six citizen-initiated referenda passed since *Kelo* provide strong protection for property owners against economic development takings.[43] By contrast, only fifteen of thirty-seven state legislative initiatives are comparably effective, as are only three or four of eight legislature-initiated referenda.[44] Reforms initiated by Congress and the president at the federal level are also largely cosmetic in nature.[45]

The likely explanation for this striking pattern is consistent with the political ignorance hypothesis. Citizen-initiated referendum proposals are usually drafted by activists rather than by elected officials and their staffs. This was the case with all four of the post-*Kelo* citizen-initiated referenda enacted in 2006.[46] Unlike state legislators, the property rights activists who wrote the citizen-initiated anti-*Kelo* ballot initiatives had no need to appease powerful procondemnation interest groups in order to improve reelection chances. They also had little reason to promote reforms that fail to produce real changes in policy. Unlike ordinary citizens, committed activists in a position to draft referendum proposals and get them on the ballot have strong incentives to acquire detailed information about eminent domain law; they have a real chance of influencing policy outcomes through their actions. Property rights activists can and do influence legislatively enacted reforms as well. But anything they propose in that setting must be filtered through the legislative process, where organized interest groups will have a significant say.

California's Proposition 99, the one citizen-initiated referendum measure that does not provide meaningful protection to property owners, is the exception that proves the rule. Proposition 99 was not drafted by property rights activists, but by local governments seeking to protect broad eminent domain authority by forestalling a rival ballot measure that would have provided stronger protection for property owners.[47] Proposition 99 passed easily, getting some 63 percent of the vote.[48] Although we do not have any definitive data, it is likely that California voters could not tell the difference between a referendum measure that provided meaningful new protection for property owners and one that did not. The sponsors of Proposition 99 achieved their goal of defeating the rival Proposition 98, though the defeat of the latter was at least in large part the result of its inclusion of a phase out of rent control.[49]

The Proposition 99 experience supports my conjecture that citizen-initiated referenda provide effective protection because of the identity and purposes of their drafters. When the drafters are property rights activists seeking to ban *Kelo*-style takings, citizen-initiated referenda result in strong limitations on eminent domain. When initiatives are drafted by procondemnation interest groups, such as the CLC, they will most likely provide only cosmetic reforms. Either way, rationally ignorant voters are likely to support them.

Interest Group Power as an Alternative Explanation

The most obvious alternative explanation for the scarcity of effective reform laws is the political power of developers and other organized interest groups that benefit from the transfer of property condemned as a result of economic development and blight condemnations.[50] As a Virginia advocate of eminent domain reform put it, "[o]ne of the biggest obstacles to effectuating eminent domain reform is the disparity in power, funding, and political clout between the well organized, well funded, politically connected takers lobby that opposes reform and the individual owners seeking reform."[51] There is no question that this factor does play a role. Developers, local government planning officials, and other interest groups have indeed spearheaded opposition to post-*Kelo* reform.[52] In Texas, for example, advocates of strong eminent domain reform concluded that lobbying by developers and local governments played a key role in ensuring that that state passed an essentially toothless reform law.[53]

Quantitative studies of post-*Kelo* legislation find that strength of reforms was influenced by the relative power of interest groups, with strong reforms more likely to be enacted in states with more valuable home construction and less likely to be enacted in more urbanized states and slow-growing states.[54] Increased home construction implies a state where homebuilders have greater influence, and they have an interest in preventing uses of eminent domain that target homes and thereby diminish the value of residential property.[55] In slow-growing states, developers and other organized interest groups have fewer alternative investment opportunities and thus greater interest in using eminent domain to acquire property. In more urbanized and densely populated areas, developers and other similar interest groups find it more costly to purchase land through the market and therefore have stronger incentives to lobby for the use of eminent domain to help acquire it.

Still, the interest group explanation has three crucial shortcomings relative to the political ignorance hypothesis. It cannot explain why the *Kelo* backlash arose when it did; it cannot fully explain how a small coalition of interest groups could overcome overwhelming and strongly felt majority public opinion. Finally, it also cannot explain why states would pass ineffective reform laws, as opposed to simply doing nothing.

The *Kelo* backlash arose in 2005 despite the fact that *Kelo* made little change in existing Supreme Court takings doctrine.[56] Interest group theory cannot explain this fact. After all, pro-property rights interest groups sought to restrain takings even before *Kelo*. Supporters of broad eminent domain power were satisfied with the status quo both before and afterward. By contrast, political ignorance can readily account for the timing of the backlash.

Second, the mere existence of interest group opposition does not explain why state legislators would choose to satisfy a few small interest groups while going against the preferences of the vast majority of the electorate.[57] It is possible that the procondemnation interest groups simply have more intense preferences about the issue than most of the opponents in the general public and are therefore more likely to cast their votes based on politicians' stances on the issue. But 63 percent of the respondents in the 2005 Saint Index survey said that they not only opposed *Kelo,* but felt "strongly" about it; more recent survey data shows that 43 percent of Americans "strongly support" reform legislation banning economic development takings.[58] If just a fraction of the 63 percent, or even the 43 percent, were willing to let post-*Kelo* reform influence their voting decisions, they would probably constitute a much larger voting bloc than all the pro-*Kelo* developers and government officials put together. For example, if 10 percent of those who felt "strongly" about the issue were willing to switch their votes as a result, they would constitute a voting bloc of about 4 to 6 percent of the electorate—more than enough to change the outcome of a close election. Presumably, that would give candidates strong incentives to support effective bans on economic development takings.

For this reason, it is likely that, to the extent that interest group opposition was able to stymie effective post-*Kelo* reform and force the passage of merely cosmetic legislation, this occurred only because most voters were unaware of what is happening. Political ignorance is the handmaiden of interest group power in the political process. Interest groups did play a role in the enactment of ineffective post-*Kelo* reforms. Without them, legislators would have little to lose from the enactment of stronger reform measures. But the legislators were able to satisfy interest group demands only because of public ignorance. Absent widespread ignorance, interest groups at odds with the majority of the general public would find it far more difficult to block eminent domain reform.

Finally, interest group power cannot explain why numerous states passed ineffective post-*Kelo* reform laws instead of simply doing nothing. After all, procondemnation interest groups would have been satisfied with the continuation of the pre-*Kelo* status quo, which in these states already allowed the condemnation of property for almost any reason. Why waste valuable legislative time and attention on new laws that merely perpetuate the status quo? Interest group power alone cannot account for this. By contrast, political ignorance theory has a simple and compelling explanation for the enactment of ineffective reform laws: they can be used to persuade rationally ignorant voters that something had been done to solve the problem of economic development takings, even if the new legislation would have little or no real impact.

The political ignorance theory is reinforced by studies finding that the strength of a state's post-*Kelo* reform has little or no relationship to the ideology or partisan loyalty of the voters in that state, even though conservative and Republican voters were, on average, more likely to oppose *Kelo* than liberals and Democrats were.[59] This suggests that the strength of public opposition to *Kelo* had little influence on the effectiveness of the reforms adopted in a given state.

The significance of such quantitative studies should not be overstated, as many of the variables used are necessarily imprecise,[60] and the availability of only fifty cases leaves a large margin for statistical error. But the available evidence does provide some additional support to for the political ignorance explanation. Voter ignorance enabled political leaders to significantly discount majority public opinion—despite its great intensity and one-sidedness. This freed them to instead cater to the needs of organized interests. Interest groups did have an impact. But they succeeded in achieving their goals only because legislators were often willing to go against majority public opinion.

The political ignorance theory does not completely explain the pattern of post-*Kelo* legislation. For example, it does not account for the fact that a few state legislatures that had previously engaged in extensive economic development takings still enacted strong reforms. But it is more consistent with the available evidence than any alternative theory proposed so far.

Conclusion

The *Kelo* backlash led to important progress for property rights. Many states enacted significantly stronger protections for property rights against takings than existed before. But widespread political ignorance played a major role in reducing the effectiveness of reform efforts. This hypothesis is the only one proposed so far that can account for the conjunction of three anomalies: the sudden and massive public outrage against *Kelo,* despite the fact that the decision made few changes in existing law; the scarcity of effective reforms, despite deep and broad public opposition to economic development takings; and the striking divergence between citizen-initiated referenda and all post-*Kelo* laws enacted by other means. It is also supported by survey data documenting widespread public ignorance of post-*Kelo* reform.

The partial failure of the *Kelo* backlash also indicates an important limitation of the long-standing conventional wisdom that judicial review is not needed to protect individual rights that enjoy the backing of majority public opinion. As James Madison famously wrote in *Federalist* 10, "[i]f a faction consists of less than a majority, relief is supplied by the republican principle, which enables the majority to defeat its sinister views by regular vote."[61] Only "[w]hen a majority is included in a faction," he argued, does "the form of popular government" enable it to threaten "the rights of other citizens."[62] The *Kelo* experience suggests that Madison was overly optimistic. The majority cannot defeat the "sinister views" of a well-organized minority, if the majority does not know what is going on. Despite broad and strongly felt public opposition to *Kelo* and economic development takings, both the federal government and the majority of states failed to enact effective reform legislation banning them.

Such effective legislation as was enacted was in large part the result of the publicity generated by the *Kelo* litigation and the resulting Supreme Court decision. If not for efforts to secure judicial intervention, there would likely have been little if any effective political action at all. As in the case of previous reform efforts, such as the civil rights movement and the gay rights movement, litigation and political activism have been complements, not substitutes.[63] Each enhances the likely effectiveness of the other.

The likelihood of effective political action to curb eminent domain abuse may well diminish over time as public attention drifts to other issues. A July 2009 survey conducted by scholars at Columbia and Harvard University found that some 81 percent of Americans still oppose the use of eminent domain to transfer property to private parties for economic development.[64] This result is similar to that found by polls conducted in the immediate aftermath of *Kelo* four years earlier.[65] But the 2009 study also found that only 42 percent recalled that the Supreme Court had upheld the constitutionality of such takings, while 14 percent believed that it had struck them down, and the rest said they did not know.[66]

This suggests that public attention to eminent domain issues is beginning to tail off. The public's focus has understandably moved on to other issues, such as the Affordable Care Act health care legislation, the failing economy, the financial crisis that helped cause it, and the persistent problems of the War on Terror. The political backlash against *Kelo* has gradually faded. It is probably no accident that the vast majority of post-*Kelo* reform legislation occurred in the first three years after *Kelo,* with only five states enacting new reform laws after 2008.[67] While praising the public reaction to *Kelo*, Fort Trumbull plaintiff Richard Beyer laments that "[t]he attention span of the public lasts maybe seven days"—a figure he probably did not mean to be taken literally.[68] Beyer is surely right to worry that the public's necessarily limited attention often wanes quickly.

As eminent domain recedes from the political spotlight, interest groups will once again be able to promote dubious economic development and blight condemnations without fear of the kind of unusual public scrutiny generated by *Kelo* and its aftermath. As Beyer put it, "[t]he government knows . . . They know that the [public's] attention span is minimal."[69]

For this reason, the need for judicial intervention to restrict takings may well increase over time rather than diminish. In Alabama, Illinois, and Minnesota, post-*Kelo* eminent domain reforms have already been partially rolled back by state legislatures, as public attention has moved on to other issues and political leaders and interest groups feel able to return to something closer to pre-*Kelo* business as usual.[70] Minnesota has adopted a law allowing the use of condemnation to build privately owned sports stadiums.[71] State legislators and interest groups that benefit from broad eminent domain authority have begun to take advantage of the waning of public focus on the issue.

Eminent domain abuse could potentially again become a prominent political issue, particularly if another public use cases reaches the Supreme Court or some particularly dramatic abuse attracts widespread media and public attention. But such events may only occur rarely. For example, over twenty years passed between the 1981 *Poletown* case, the last eminent domain case to become a national sensation before *Kelo*,[72] and *Kelo* itself.

Overall, the *Kelo* story demonstrates that political action can sometimes protect individual rights but also that it has significant limits. If public ignorance can often prevent the political process from providing effective protection for individual rights in such a high-profile case, it might also fall short in other cases where rights supported by majority opinion are at stake. Judicial review is not just a check on the tyranny of the majority. Sometimes, it may also be needed to protect us against the consequences of the majority's political ignorance.

The political reaction to *Kelo* was accompanied by a less visible, but almost equally important, judicial reaction, as state and lower federal courts struggled to make sense the Supreme Court's decision and considered whether its interpretation of the federal Public Use Clause should serve as a model for the interpretation of similar provisions in state constitutions. As we shall see in chapter 7, the judicial reaction to *Kelo* was far from uniformly supportive. Many state courts greeted *Kelo* with skepticism and refused to adopt it as a guide to the interpretation of their state constitutions.

CHAPTER SEVEN

The Judicial Reaction

In addition to the better-known legislative reaction, *Kelo* also had an impact on public use litigation in both federal and state courts. In the aftermath of the federal Supreme Court decision, several state supreme courts addressed the question of whether its deferential approach to economic development takings also applied under their state constitutional public use clauses. Both federal and state courts have sought to interpret *Kelo*'s statement that "pretextual" takings are an exception to the decision's generally ultra-deferential approach.[1] Finally, several important recent state court decisions considered the implications of *Kelo* for condemnations of "blighted" property.

Unlike the legislative reaction, which has been extensively studied,[2] there has been much less analysis of the judicial reaction to *Kelo*.[3] This is unfortunate because state and federal judges are likely to continue to play an important role in addressing public use issues. Although numerous states have enacted post-*Kelo* reform laws, many of them leave much to be desired as we saw in chapter 5.

This chapter helps fill the gap. With some important exceptions, it shows that state courts have not reacted to *Kelo* by adopting similarly permissive approaches to public use issues. Three state supreme courts have explicitly repudiated *Kelo* as a guide to their state constitutions.[4] Other recent state supreme court decisions have imposed constraints on takings that go beyond *Kelo*, even if they have not completely rejected the *Kelo* approach. Two state supreme courts—Rhode Island and Maryland—have also restricted so-called quick take condemnations, which governments use to condemn property under streamlined procedures that give owners few procedural rights.[5]

Two decisions by the New York Court of Appeals are significant exceptions to this trend. New York's highest court has continued to give wide scope for even the most questionable condemnations, where there are strong indications that property was taken at the behest of influential private interests.[6] But overall, the trend of post-*Kelo* state public use decisions seems to be in the direction of tighter restrictions on the use of eminent domain.

By contrast, federal and state courts have been all over the map in their efforts to apply *Kelo*'s strictures against "pretextual" takings. There is no consensus in sight on this crucial issue. None seems likely to develop unless and until the Supreme Court decides another case on this issue.

State Public Use Clauses and *Kelo*

In the wake of *Kelo*, several state supreme courts considered the issue of whether economic development takings were permissible under their own state constitutions. Other courts considered closely related public use takings involving "blight" and "quick take" condemnations.

Decisions Rejecting Kelo *as a Guide to the Interpretation of State Public Use Clauses*

Two state supreme courts—Ohio and Oklahoma—have directly addressed the question of whether their state constitutions permit *Kelo*-style economic development takings. Both explicitly rejected *Kelo* and ruled that their state constitutions forbid economic development takings.[7] The Ohio Supreme Court's opinion in *Norwood v. Horney*—a case striking down a taking of property under a definition of "blight" broad enough to encompass almost any area—explicitly criticized *Kelo* and other decisions upholding economic development takings for adopting "an artificial judicial deference to the state's determination that there was sufficient public use."[8] The Ohio court favorably cited a passage in Justice Sandra Day O'Connor's *Kelo* dissent that rebuked the majority for reducing the public use requirement to "hortatory fluff."[9] It ruled that the views of the "dissenting justices of the United States Supreme Court in *Kelo* are better models for interpreting Section 19, Article I of Ohio's Constitution" than those of the majority.[10] The Oklahoma Supreme Court similarly rejected *Kelo* as a guide to its state constitution's Public Use Clause.[11]

In *Benson v. State*, the Supreme Court of South Dakota also refused to adopt *Kelo*'s interpretation of public use, albeit in a case that did not address the specific issue of economic development takings.[12] The court concluded that the view that "public use" requires actual use of the condemned property by the government or the general public "accords" better with the text and original meaning of the phrase than *Kelo*'s equation of "public use" with "public purpose" or public benefit.[13]

State decisions adopting stricter public use standards than *Kelo* are not inherently inconsistent with *Kelo* itself. Justice Stevens's majority opinion explicitly "emphasize[d] that nothing in our opinion precludes any State from placing further restrictions on its exercise of the takings power."[14] Nonetheless, state courts' refusal to apply the *Kelo* standard represents at least a partial repudiation of the federal Supreme Court's approach, insofar as they reject the latter's view that courts should broadly defer to the government's determination of what counts as a public use. The *Kelo* majority's advocacy of deference was based not just on federalism, but also on the claim that judges should defer to the political process on public use issues more generally.[15]

Moreover, at least two of these three state court decisions repudiating *Kelo* did not rely on variations in local conditions or other factors peculiar to their states as justifications for rejecting its approach. The state supreme court justices in these cases repudiated the *Kelo* approach on general rather than state-specific principles. As discussed above, the Ohio court repudiated *Kelo* on the general ground that it gives too much deference to the government, specifically endorsing Justice O'Connor's dissent on this point. South Dakota's rejected it as a textually implausible reading of the term "public use."[16]

The Oklahoma decision did not repudiate *Kelo* as clearly as the others, because it relied in large part on differences between the wording of the Oklahoma and federal public use clauses: "While the Takings Clause of the U.S. Constitution provides 'nor shall private property be taken for public use without just compensation,' the Oklahoma Constitution places further restrictions by expressly stating '[n]o private property shall be taken or damaged *for private use,* with or without compensation.' "[17]

State Supreme Court Cases Invalidating
"Quick Take" Condemnations

Two state supreme courts—Maryland and Rhode Island—have substantially constrained "quick take" condemnations in the aftermath of *Kelo*.[18] These cases do not directly address the issue raised in *Kelo* itself. But all three decisions (including two by the Maryland court) discuss *Kelo* and place important constraints on the scope of their state public uses clauses that go beyond those imposed in *Kelo* itself.[19]

Quick take condemnation laws allow local governments to take property under streamlined procedures that give landowners little time and opportunity to contest the taking of their land, other than to seek compensation after the fact. Under the Rhode Island statute, "the condemning authority obtains title and may take possession of property merely by filing a declaration of condemnation and satisfying the court that its estimate of compensation is just."[20] The Maryland procedure is similar.[21]

In *Rhode Island Economic Development Corp. v. The Parking Co.*, the Rhode Island Supreme Court ruled that a quick take condemnation was unconstitutional in a case where the condemning authority sought to use the procedure to "gain control of [a garage] at a discounted price" rather than achieve the stated public purpose of increasing parking for the public.[22] The court ruled that the claimed public purpose could not be achieved by the taking because it would not actually create any additional parking spaces; nor would it achieve the additional goal of promoting the local economy.[23]

The Rhode Island court asserted that its decision was consistent with *Kelo* because the *Kelo* takings involved a "comprehensive and thorough economic development plan," while its own case did not.[24] But the Rhode Island taking arose as part of an effort to develop and expand parking near a public airport.[25] It was therefore also adopted as part of a planning process. Moreover, *Kelo* emphasized that judges should not "second-guess" condemning authorities' "considered judgments about the efficacy of [a] development plan" or about whether or not condemnation was needed to achieve the plan's goals.[26] The Rhode Island court's willingness to question the efficacy of the quick take condemnation is at the very least in tension with the *Kelo* approach. Finally, *Parking Co.* emphasized that "[i]f a legislature should say that a certain taking was for a public use, that would not make it so; for such a rule would enable a legislature to conclude the question of constitutionality by its own declaration."[27] In the court's view, "a legislative declaration of public use is instructive, and entitled to deference, but not conclusive."[28] This contrasts with the U.S. Supreme Court's statement in *Berman v. Parker* indicating that the legislature has "well-nigh conclusive" discretion in defining what counts as a public use.[29] *Kelo* relied heavily on the *Berman* precedent,[30] though admittedly it did not explicitly reiterate this particular point.

Although it addressed a "quick take" condemnation, *Parking Co.* ultimately relied on reasoning that applies more broadly to any takings where the claimed public use is unlikely to be achieved and may be a pretext for other motives.[31] These sorts of problems, however, are likely to be especially common with quick take condemnations, where there is less time for careful planning.

The Maryland decision in *Mayor of Baltimore v. Valsamaki*, also constrains quick take condemnations in a way that is less deferential than *Kelo*. It invalidated the quick take condemnation in question because "the City failed to provide sufficient reasons for its *immediate* possession of and title to the subject Property."[32] Proof of the need for "immediate" possession of the land in question was, the court concluded, required under Maryland's state constitution and statutory law.[33] The Maryland Court of Appeals reiterated this requirement in a very similar case decided one year later.[34] Like the Rhode Island decision, the Maryland court claimed that its ruling was consistent with *Kelo* because the taking in question was not the result of "comprehensive" planning.[35]

However, the *Valsamaki* condemnation, like that in *Kelo,* was in fact part of a redevelopment plan, even if the connection between the taking and the plan was somewhat vague given that the City of Baltimore claimed only that the taking would advance the goals of the plan by facilitating "business expansion."[36] And, as we have seen,[37] *Kelo* forbade courts from second-guessing the efficacy of the proposed plan or the need for the condemnation of individual properties to achieve its goals. The Maryland court's willingness to closely scrutinize the necessity for the quick take condemnation under the plan represents a degree of "second-guessing" that *Kelo* would not permit.

State Decisions Constraining the Scope of Blight Condemnations

State court decisions on blight takings are a significant part of the judicial reaction to *Kelo*. Blight condemnations are a particularly prevalent type of private-to-private condemnation, more common than pure economic development takings. As discussed in chapter 3, blight takings are problematic in two ways. Many states define blight so broadly as to allow almost any property to be declared blighted and condemned. In addition, even blight takings in genuinely dilapidated areas often cause great harm by forcibly displacing poor and politically weak people who are left worse off than they were before.

Since *Kelo*, little, if anything, has been done by state courts to constrain takings in areas that are genuinely "blighted." But several post-*Kelo* state blight decisions addressed the issue of overbroad definitions of what counts as blight. In the *Norwood* case, discussed earlier, the Supreme Court of Ohio made clear that its ban on economic development takings also applies to overbroad blight condemnations.[38] *Norwood* invalidated an effort to condemn property that had been declared blighted because it was located in a "deteriorating area," a standard that the Ohio court rejected because it would enable virtually any area to be declared blighted: "[t]o permit a taking of private property based solely on a finding that the property is deteriorating or in danger of deteriorating would grant an impermissible, unfettered power to the government to appropriate."[39]

In *Gallenthin Realty Development, Inc. v. Borough of Paulsboro*, the New Jersey Supreme Court invalidated a taking where open land had been defined as "blighted" because it was not "fully productive."[40] The court ruled that, under New Jersey's state constitution, a blight taking required evidence of "deterioration or stagnation that has a decadent effect on surrounding property."[41] *Gallenthin* is significant because it curtails one of the less appreciated dangers of allowing economic development takings: the possibility that developers and other interest groups might use them to take over property devoted to natural amenities such as parks or privately managed wildlife refuges.[42]

A Pennsylvania appellate court likewise interpreted its state's blight law, which at the time allowed condemnation of "economically undesirable" land uses as "blighted," to permit only condemnation of property that had been put to "an actual, objectively negative use . . . rather than merely a use relatively less profitable than another."[43] It repudiated the idea that Pennsylvania law allows the use of "blight" designations to authorize takings that are "purely [for] 'economic development.' "[44] Unlike *Norwood* and *Gallenthin*, the Pennsylvania decision was purely statutory in nature and did not hold that overbroad blight takings violate the state constitution. At the same time, it does use the takings upheld in *Kelo* as an example of the kind that are not permitted under Pennsylvania state law.[45]

New York Decisions Upholding a Virtually Unlimited Definition of Blight

The two most high-profile post-*Kelo* blight cases are *Kaur v. New York State Urban Development Corp.* and *Goldstein v. New York State Urban Development Corp.*,[46] both decided by the New York Court of Appeals, that state's highest court. Both decisions upheld the constitutional validity of extremely broad definitions of blight and also endorsed *Kelo*'s highly deferential approach to public use issues. More problematically, both also upheld blight condemnations despite considerable evidence of political corruption in the blight designation process.[47]

In *Goldstein*, the court upheld a major condemnation as part of the Atlantic Yards development project. The Empire State Development Corporation, a state government agency, took a large area for the purpose of transferring it to a firm controlled by politically influential developer Bruce Ratner, who sought to use it primarily to build high-income housing and a new stadium for the New Jersey Nets professional basketball team, which he at the time owned.[48] The court concluded that the property in question could be condemned as "blighted" and that blight alleviation is a "public use" recognized by the New York Constitution, thanks to a constitutional amendment allowing the condemnation of slum areas.[49] The property, however, was very far from being a slum, and much of it was in good shape.[50]

The property owners conceded that some property in the area was blighted but not any that was to be condemned.[51] The court itself noted that the Atlantic Yards area "do[es] not begin to approach in severity the dire circumstances of urban slum dwelling" that led to the enactment of the blight amendment in 1938.[52] To get around this problem, the court held that "blight" alleviation is "not limited to 'slums' as that term was formerly applied, and that, among other things, economic underdevelopment and stagnation are also threats to the public sufficient to make their removal cognizable as a public purpose."[53]

Virtually any area occasionally suffers from "economic underdevelopment" or "stagnation" and therefore could potentially be condemned under this rationale. Moreover, even under this expansive definition of blight, the decision states that courts can only strike down a condemnation if "there is no room for reasonable difference of opinion as to whether an area is blighted."[54] With respect to any neighborhood, there is nearly always "room for reasonable difference of opinion" as to whether the area is "underdeveloped" relative to some possible alternative uses of the land in question.

Defining blight this broadly and then deferring to the government's determination of whether such "blight" actually exists comes close to reading the public use restriction out of the state constitution. It is unlikely that the New York State constitutional amendment allowing condemnation of "substandard and insanitary areas" was originally understood to mean that virtually any area could be declared blighted and condemned.[55]

Goldstein went beyond merely adopting an extremely broad definition of blight. It also chose to overlook extensive evidence indicating that the blight study commissioned by the ESDC was heavily biased and deliberately rigged to reach a predetermined conclusion. As Judge Robert Smith pointed out in his dissenting opinion, the original rationale for the condemnation was "economic development—job creation and the bringing of a professional basketball team to Brooklyn."[56] Apparently, "nothing was said about 'blight' by the sponsors of the project until 2005" when the ESDC realized that a blight determination might be needed for legal reasons.[57]

Moreover, the decision to condemn the property had already been made, and the firm conducting the blight study knew what outcome the condemning authorities sought. The firm was also hired and paid by Ratner himself.[58] Perhaps for that reason, the firm's report strained to find evidence of blight, counting minor flaws such as "weeds," "graffiti," and "underutilization."[59]

The majority also failed to consider the relevance of evidence showing that Ratner himself had created much of the "blight" used to justify the condemnation.[60] By the time the study was conducted in 2005, "Ratner had already acquired many of the properties he wanted (thanks to eminent domain) and left them empty, thus *creating* much of the unsightly neglect he now cites in support of his project."[61] Other parts of the area may have fallen into disrepair in part because "Ratner's plan to acquire the properties and demolish the buildings had been public knowledge for years when the blight study was conducted," and owners therefore had no reason to invest in their upkeep.[62]

Ratner and the ESDC disputed some of these claims.[63] The key point, however, is that the majority refused to even consider their possible rele-

vance and concluded that the takings were permissible even if the allega-
tions against the developer and the condemning authority were correct,
so long as there was room for "reasonable difference of opinion" over the
presence or absence of blight.[64] As the majority explained,

> It may be that the bar has now been set too low—that what will now pass as
> "blight," as that expression has come to be understood and used by political
> appointees to public corporations relying upon studies paid for by developers,
> should not be permitted to constitute a predicate for the invasion of property
> rights and the razing of homes and businesses. But any such limitation upon
> the sovereign power of eminent domain as it has come to be defined in the
> urban renewal context is a matter for the Legislature, not the courts.[65]

Kaur featured a combination of the same three elements as *Goldstein*:
a broad definition of blight, a possibly rigged blight study, and the likelihood that much of the "blight" used to justify the condemnations in
question was actually caused by the beneficiaries of the proposed taking. The *Kaur* takings arose from an effort by Columbia University to
acquire property for expansion in the Manhattanville neighborhood in
Harlem in New York City.[66]

Unusually, the *Kaur* taking had been invalidated in a close 3-2 decision by one of New York's intermediate appellate courts, the Appellate
Division, First Department.[67] In *Kaur,* as in *Goldstein,* there was little
evidence of actual blight. Indeed, the Appellate Division concluded that
there was "no evidence whatsoever that Manhattanville was blighted prior
to Columbia gaining control over the vast majority of property therein."[68]

The ESDC only ordered a blight study after Columbia had already
acquired most of the property in the area and therefore "gained control
over the very properties that would form the basis for a subsequent blight
study."[69] When Columbia presented the agency with a plan to use eminent domain to acquire the remaining property and use it for Columbia's
"sole benefit," a blight study was commissioned from Allee King Rosen
& Fleming, Inc., a firm employed by Columbia on an earlier phase of
the same project.[70] AKRF was also the firm employed by Ratner in the
Atlantic Yards case.[71]

AKRF was instructed by the ESDC to use a methodology "biased in
Columbia's favor," that allowed blight to be proven by the presence of mi-
nor defects such as "unpainted block walls or loose awning supports."[72]
As the Appellate Division concluded, "[v]irtually every neighborhood

in the five boroughs will yield similar instances of disrepair that can be captured in close-up technicolor."[73] Moreover, most of the alleged blight that was found by AKRF was located on property owned by Columbia itself and possibly allowed to develop in order to justify a blight finding.[74]

The Appellate Division thereby concluded that the area could not be considered blighted and also ruled that the blight findings were an unconstitutional "pretextual" taking, since the allegedly rigged blight study showed that the blight rationale was a mere pretext for a scheme to benefit Columbia.[75]

The New York Court of Appeals unanimously reversed the Appellate Division's decision, relying primarily on the extremely broad definition of blight upheld in *Goldstein* just a few months earlier.[76] It refused to consider most of the evidence that the AKRF study deliberately used biased methodology, noting only that AKRF's objectivity was not compromised merely "because Columbia had previously engaged AKRF" to produce its development plan for the area.[77] The court also noted that AKRF's findings were confirmed by a study conducted by a different firm, Earth Tech,[78] but did not consider the relevance of the fact that that firm was also required to use the same biased methodology as AKRF.

The court further emphasized that a third firm, Urbitran, had conducted a study finding blight in the area prior to AKRF's, thereby calling into question the Appellate Division's finding that there was no evidence of blight prior to the acquisition of most of the area by Columbia.[79] However, the court did not dispute the Appellate Division's finding that the ESDC had not in fact relied on the Urbitran study in making its decision to condemn the property and had commissioned the AKRF study because ESDC staff doubted the adequacy of the Urbitran findings.[80]

Both *Goldstein* and *Kaur* upheld takings under an extremely broad definition of blight. More unusually, both decisions refused to give more than perfunctory consideration to the strong evidence that the new private owners of the condemned property had rigged "blight" studies in their favor and were themselves responsible for a substantial proportion of the alleged blight those studies found.

Taken together, *Goldstein* and *Kelo* make it virtually impossible to challenge blight condemnations in New York. As Justice Catterson of the Appellate Division explained, "Unfortunately for the rights of citizens . . . the recent rulings of the Court of Appeals . . . have made plain that there is no longer any judicial oversight of eminent domain proceedings."[81] This may be a slight exaggeration,[82] but not by much. The two cases are striking exceptions to the general post-*Kelo* pattern of stronger judicial scrutiny of public use issues.

Was the Judicial Reaction Caused by the Political Backlash Against Kelo?

The generally negative nature of the state judicial reaction to *Kelo* leads one to ask whether state courts acted as they did because of the strong political backlash against *Kelo*. Historically, court decisions have often been influenced by public opinion and the political climate.[83] Some leading scholars believe that state courts may have been "chastened by the backlash against *Kelo*" and therefore "become more vigilant in policing proposed takings."[84] It may well be, however, that the post-*Kelo* state court decisions were largely continuations of a preexisting trend toward stronger judicial scrutiny of public use issues. In the decade before *Kelo*, four state supreme courts ruled that economic development takings violate their state constitutions, while only one created a new precedent going the other way.[85]

It is difficult to say whether the *Kelo* backlash accelerated the preexisting judicial trend or merely continued it. Because we only have a small sample size of cases (four state supreme court decisions striking down economic development takings in the decade prior to *Kelo* and three since then), it is impossible to tell the difference between a flat trend line and a slight acceleration. What can reasonably be said is that state judicial decisions have not seen the same sudden upsurge of restrictions on takings that occurred in the political arena. There, over forty states passed new laws in less than five years, after a decade in which most saw few or no comparable reforms. By contrast, recent judicial developments seem to be a continuation or, at most, a modest acceleration of a preexisting trend.

There are two key factors in the difference between the legislative and judicial reactions. Unlike state legislatures and public opinion, state courts had been on a path toward gradually stronger enforcement of public use restrictions on takings for years prior to *Kelo*. They therefore did not need to make a radical change of course in order to move in a more restrictive direction. On the other hand, the greater insulation of state courts from public opinion also reduced their incentive to make major symbolic gestures toward appeasing public opinion. Even in states where judges are chosen by electoral processes, judicial elections are less competitive and less visible to voters than those for the state legislature and the governorship.[86]

While the judicial reaction to *Kelo* was less dramatic and sweeping than the political reaction, it may turn out to have greater long-term staying power. The political backlash against *Kelo* has gradually diminished in intensity, as public attention moves on to other issues.[87] By contrast, the trend toward greater judicial skepticism of eminent domain may well continue.

The Problem of Pretext

The one area where *Kelo* leaves room for potentially significant judicial scrutiny of public use issues is that of "pretextual takings" where the official rationale for the taking is a pretext "for the purpose of conferring a private benefit on a particular private party."[88] Unfortunately, *Kelo* says very little about the question of how to determine whether or not a taking that transfer property to a private party is in fact pretextual. As one federal district court decision notes, "[a]lthough *Kelo* held that merely pretextual purposes do not satisfy the public use requirement, the *Kelo* majority did not define the term 'mere pretext.' "[89]

To add to the confusion, the *Kelo* majority noted that one possible indication of a pretextual taking is the presence of a "one-to-one transfer of property, executed outside the confines of an integrated development plan."[90] But the case Justice Stevens cited as an example actually involved a redevelopment plan.[91] Justice Kennedy's concurring opinion also suggested that a taking may be invalidated if it showed "impermissible favoritism" to a private party.[92] But like the majority opinion, which Kennedy joined, he was extremely unclear as to how to determine what counts as a taking "intended to favor a particular private party."[93]

In what is probably the most thorough analysis of *Kelo*'s pretext standard, Notre Dame law professor Daniel Kelly identifies four criteria that courts use to determine whether a private-to-private taking is pretextual:

1. The magnitude of the public benefit created by the condemnation. If the benefits are large, it seems less likely that they are merely pretextual.
2. The extent of the planning process that led to the taking.
3. Whether or not the identity of the private beneficiary of the taking was known in advance. If the new owner's identity was unknown to officials at the time

they decided to use eminent domain, it is hard to conclude that government undertook the condemnation in order to advance his or her interests.

4. The subjective intent of the condemning authorities. Under this approach, courts would investigate the motives of government decision makers to determine what the true purpose of a taking was.[94]

Since *Kelo*, many state and federal courts have struggled with the problem of how to decide whether a taking is pretextual. All four factors identified by Kelly have played a role.

The Government's Intentions

In *Middletown Township v. Lands of Stone*, the Pennsylvania Supreme Court emphasized the subjective intent standard, concluding that courts must look for "the real or fundamental purpose behind a taking . . . the true purpose must primarily benefit the public."[95] A more recent decision by the same court reiterated this standard but also noted that the crucial factor in determining purpose is that "the public must be the primary and paramount beneficiary of the taking."[96]

Similarly, the Hawaii Supreme Court's decision in *County of Hawai'i v. C&J Coupe Family Ltd. Partnership* states that *Kelo* and Hawaii state constitutional law require courts to look for "the actual purpose" of a taking to determine whether the official rationale was a "mere pretext."[97] A later follow-up decision in the same litigation reiterated the purpose-based approach but also ruled that "the burden of proof" in establishing pretext falls on the property owner; the court refused to adopt a categorical rule forbidding pretextual condemnations where the power of eminent domain is delegated to a private organization.[98] Although it ultimately concluded that the challenged taking was not pretextual, the court did engage in detailed scrutiny of the condemning authorities' purpose and planning.[99] The Hawaii and Pennsylvania courts differ somewhat insofar as Hawaii does not share Pennsylvania's emphasis on using the distribution of benefits from the taking as an indication of intent.

In a 2010 case, the Connecticut Supreme Court also suggested that a focus on motive may be appropriate under *Kelo*, noting that the case does not authorize "bad faith" takings.[100] It thereby became the third state supreme court to stress the relevance of this factor.

Subjective motive was also emphasized by the New York Appellate Division in the *Kaur* case, which held that condemnations benefiting

Columbia University were pretextual under *Kelo* in large part because of evidence that the condemning authority had deliberately rigged a blight study in Columbia's favor.[101] Strangely, the New York Court of Appeals failed to consider the Appellate Division's application of *Kelo* when it overruled the lower court and upheld the taking.

The Appellate Division adopted a similar approach in an earlier 2007 case where it struck down as pretextual a taking for the supposed purpose of creating office space and affordable housing. The court concluded that the taking was impermissible because the government's "true purpose for condemnation" was to assist a private developer, a conclusion it reached based on the timing of the decision to condemn and the fact that the taking would not actually result in a net increase in affordable housing in the area.[102] The precedential status of this decision may be in question after *Kaur*.[103]

Legal scholars Lior Strahilevitz and Eduardo Penalver have similarly interpreted *Kelo* as focusing on subjective intentions, concluding that the majority opinion imposes a requirement that "the condemnor's actual intent must be to foster a "public use."[104] Intent was also the focus of several pre-*Kelo* federal cases that invalidated takings on pretext grounds, including the *99 Cents* case favorably cited by the *Kelo* Court itself.[105]

The Magnitude of Expected Public Benefits

The Court of Appeals of the District of Columbia emphasized the magnitude of the public benefits of the taking relative to the private ones that "[i]f the property is being transferred to another private party, and the benefits to the public are only 'incidental' or 'pretextual,' a 'pretext' defense may well succeed."[106] This court is the highest court of the District of Columbia and is the equivalent of a state supreme court.[107]

The court remanded a takings case to the trial court and instructed lower courts to "focus primarily on [the] benefits the public hopes to realize from the proposed taking."[108] This approach mirrors an element of Justice Anthony Kennedy's concurring opinion in *Kelo* itself, where Kennedy suggested that a taking might be invalidated if it has "only incidental or pretextual public benefits."[109] Somewhat inconsistently, the Court of Appeals later ruled—in an appeal arising from the same case— that "the District need only show that the D.C. Council approved the Skyland legislation for the purpose of economic development in order to defeat the allegation of pretext."[110]

In *MHC Financing Ltd. Partnership v. City of San Rafael*, the federal district for the Northern District of California interpreted *Kelo* as requiring ' "careful and extensive inquiry into whether, in fact, the development plan is of primary benefit to the developer . . . [and] only incidental benefit to the City.' "[111] This language is taken from Justice Kennedy's description of the trial court's efforts in *Kelo* itself. But Kennedy did not make clear whether such a "careful and extensive inquiry" is actually required. The district court may also have erred in relying on Kennedy's opinion rather than that of the majority, since Kennedy also signed on to the latter, thereby ensuring that it had five votes.[112] The *MHC* district court opinion was later reversed by the Ninth Circuit Court of Appeals, in a decision that gives extremely broad deference to the political process.[113]

The Planning Process

The Maryland, Pennsylvania, and Rhode Island courts have also relied on the absence of extensive planning as an indication of a pretextual taking.[114] This builds on *Kelo*'s emphasis on the presence of an "integrated development plan" in New London.[115]

Whether the Identity of the Main Beneficiary of the Taking Was Known in Advance

Only one post-*Kelo* pretext decision seems to have turned on the fact that the identity of the new private owner was not known in advance by condemning authorities. In *Carole Media v. New Jersey Transit Corp.*, the United States Court of Appeals for the Third Circuit upheld a taking of a firm's license to post advertisements on public billboards owned by the New Jersey Transit Corporation.[116] The New Jersey state legislature adopted a policy under which the billboard licenses would be allocated by a competitive bidding process.[117] Although there was some evidence that the new policy was adopted in part because it was likely to favor the interests of a rival firm, All Vision, the court upheld the condemnations because "there is no allegation that NJ Transit, at the time it terminated Carole Media's existing licenses, knew the identity of the successful bidder for the long-term licenses at those locations."[118] As a result of this ignorance, the court ruled that "this case cannot be the textbook private taking involving a naked transfer of property from private party *A* to *B* solely for *B's* private use."[119]

This analysis sidestepped the problem that a taking can be intended to benefit a known private party even if the benefit to that party comes in a form other than receiving ownership of the condemned property. In this case, the benefit to All Vision was that it would receive extensive management fees for organizing the bidding process and managing the billboards until the rights to them were sold to new bidders.[120]

This problem highlights an important shortcoming of focusing solely on the benefits to the new private owner in determining whether a taking is pretextual. Other narrow private interests might also benefit and play a decisive role in pushing through the condemnations. This is an important part of the story in the *Kelo* case itself, where Pfizer expected to benefit from the condemnation, even though it was not slated to become the owner of the condemned property.[121]

In all of the federal and state post-*Kelo* pretext cases discussed so far except for *Carole Media*, the court either invalidated a taking as pretextual or remanded the case for detailed inquiry into that possibility by the trial court. This suggests an effort to give the pretext standard some real bite. Most courts applying *Kelo* have left open at least some substantial possibility that a taking could be ruled pretextual.

The major exceptions to this pattern are several decisions that mandate such extreme deference as to make it virtually impossible to prove pretext.

Extreme Deference

In two of its decisions, the Second Circuit Court of Appeals has taken an extremely deferential approach to pretext issues, falling just short of defining the pretext cause of action out of existence. A recent Ninth Circuit decision adopted a similar approach, as did a 2011 ruling by the Supreme Court of Guam.

In *Goldstein v. Pataki*, the Second Circuit considered a challenge to the same Atlantic Yards takings that were later upheld in state court by the New York Court of Appeals.[122] Despite the considerable evidence that the taking was intended to benefit developer Bruce Ratner, who had initiated the project and lobbied for its adoption by the government, the Second Circuit refused to consider either evidence of improper motive or evidence concerning the distribution of benefits from the condemnation.[123] So long as a taking is "rationally related to a classic public use," the court ruled that it is impermissible to "give close scrutiny to the mechanics of a taking . . . as a means to gauge the purity of the motives of various government officials who approved it."[124] The Second Circuit also rejected claims that the takings should be invalidated because most of the benefits would flow to Ratner or because any benefits to the community might be "dwarf[ed]" by the project's costs.[125] Similarly, the court rejected the idea that any significant scrutiny was required because they "acknowledged [the] fact that Ratner was the impetus behind the project, i.e., that he, not a state agency, first conceived of developing Atlantic Yards . . . and that it was his plan for the Project that the Empire State Development Corporation eventually adopted without significant modification."[126]

The court did note that their decision "preserve[es] the possibility that a fact pattern may one day arise in which the circumstances of the approval process so greatly undermine the basic legitimacy of the outcome reached that a closer objective scrutiny of the justification being offered is required."[127] But it is difficult to see what those circumstances might be if neither subjective intent, nor the distribution of the projects costs and benefits, nor the presence of an identifiable private beneficiary who played a key role in initiating the taking are enough to trigger such "objective scrutiny." One possible answer is that heightened scrutiny might be required by the absence of a sufficiently rigorous planning process. But the Second Circuit seems to reject that option by suggesting that inquiry into "the mechanics of a taking rationally related to a classic public use" is inappropriate.[128]

Even more deferential to the government than *Goldstein v. Pataki* was the Second Circuit's 2006 decision in *Didden v. Village of Port Chester*,[129] decided two years before *Goldstein*. In 1999, the village of Port Chester, New York, established a "redevelopment area," giving designated developer Gregg Wasser a virtual blank check to condemn property within it.[130] When local property owners Bart Didden and Dominick Bologna sought a permit to build a CVS pharmacy in the area, Wasser demanded that they must either pay him $800,000 or give him a 50 percent partnership interest in the store, threatening to have their land condemned if they refused.[131] They, indeed, refused, and a day later the village condemned their property.

In an unsigned opinion joined and probably written by future Supreme Court Justice Sonia Sotomayor,[132] the Second Circuit panel upheld this taking:

[T]o the extent that [the property owners] assert that the Takings Clause prevents the State from condemning their property for a private use within a redevelopment district, regardless of whether they have been provided with just compensation, the recent Supreme Court decision in *Kelo v. City of New London,* obliges us to conclude that they have articulated no basis upon which relief can be granted.[133]

The opinion does not even consider the possibility that a pretextual taking might have occurred, despite the fact that the taking likely would not have happened at all but for Didden and Bologna's refusal to give in to Wasser's financial demands. It is difficult to find a more blatant example of pretextual intent.

Even if the relevant standard is the distribution of benefits from the taking rather than subjective intent, *Didden* is still an extremely dubious ruling. There was little if any plausible public benefit in this case because Wasser's plan for the condemned land was to build a Walgreens pharmacy—virtually identical to Didden and Bologna's plan to build a CVS pharmacy.[134] Even if the Walgreens pharmacy was in some way better for the community than a CVS would have been, the lion's share of the benefits clearly went to Wasser.

The other potentially relevant factors also cut in favor of a finding of pretext. The taking only occurred due to the property owners' rejection of Wasser's financial demands. It is difficult to argue that it was the result of any "comprehensive" or systematic planning process. And an identifiable private beneficiary was clearly present before the decision to use eminent domain was taken; indeed, he instigated that decision.

In sum, all four conceivably relevant factors militated in favor of a ruling that a pretextual taking had occurred. Yet, the court completely dismissed that possibility in a short, cursory opinion. The *Didden* case also involved some complex factual and procedural issues. But none of them ultimately diminish its highly deferential nature.[135]

In the post-*Kelo* jurisprudence on pretextual takings, *Didden* is an extreme outlier because it seems to define the possibility of a pretextual taking out of existence. It ruled that a pretextual taking did not occur despite the fact that almost every relevant fact cuts the other way. Because it was an unpublished opinion, *Didden* has no precedential value. Second Circuit rules forbid citation of unpublished summary orders filed before 2007.[136] It is nonetheless noteworthy as the most extreme post-*Kelo* example of judicial endorsement of a blatantly pretextual taking. It is also significant as a possible window into the thinking of Justice Sotomayor, who now has more influence over constitutional property rights jurisprudence since her appointment to the Supreme Court in 2009.

In the *Goldstein* and *Kaur* cases discussed earlier, the New York Court of Appeals treated pretext claims much the same way as the Second Circuit did in *Goldstein* and *Didden*. In both cases, the court ignored strong evidence that all four pretext factors cut against the government. Both featured considerable evidence of improper intent, a distribution of benefits strongly favoring the new private owner of the condemned area, a private beneficiary whose identity was known in advance, and a planning process that was often perfunctory and biased in favor of a preconceived decision in favor of condemnation.[137]

The *Goldstein* majority ignored *Kelo*'s pretext standard and the lower court cases interpreting it, probably because the property owners' federal constitutional claims had already been rejected in federal court in *Goldstein v. Pataki*. Less defensibly, the New York Court of Appeals also completely ignored *Kelo* and related pretext cases in *Kaur*, despite the fact that the lower court decision striking down the Columbia takings relied heavily on *Kelo*'s pretext analysis.[138] Unlike in *Goldstein*, no federal court had already decided the property owners' Fifth Amendment pretext claims, and the property owners continued to press those arguments in the Court of Appeals. Thus, it is difficult to understand why the *Kaur* court failed to even cite *Kelo*, much less discuss the relevant federal precedents interpreting pretextual takings. At the same time, the state court would likely have had to follow the Second Circuit's extremely deferential approach to *Kelo*'s pretext standard, since New York falls within the jurisdiction of that federal court of appeals, and state courts must follow federal court interpretations of Supreme Court opinions interpreting the federal constitution.

A similarly ultradeferential approach was adopted by the Ninth Circuit in a decision in 2013, overruling a district court ruling that had focused on the distribution of benefits as an indication of pretext.[139] The Ninth Circuit ruled that "extreme deference is due to the legislature" and indicated that a taking must be upheld under the Public Use Clause so long as it is " 'rationally related to a conceivable public purpose.' "[140] It did not even consider the possibility that tighter judicial scrutiny is warranted in cases where there is evidence that the official rationale for a condemnation is pretextual.

Finally, mention should be made of *Ilagan v. Ungacta*, a 2011 decision by the Supreme Court of Guam that adopted a highly deferential

approach similar to that of the Ninth Circuit.[141] The *Ilagan* decision—
issued by the highest court of a U.S. island territory in the Pacific—also
ignored multiple indications of pretext in a case where the city of Agana
used a largely moribund "economic development" plan to condemn a
parking lot and transfer it to relatives of the then-mayor of Agana.[142]

The Future of Pretextual Takings Claims

As should by now be clear, there is no consensus among either state or
federal judges on the criteria for determining what counts as a pretextual
takings claim after *Kelo*. Some decisions emphasize the subjective intentions of condemning authorities, some focus on the magnitude of the
expected public benefits of a taking, some on the extent of the planning
process, and some on a combination of factors. Each of these approaches
to pretextual takings has potential flaws. Focusing on the projected benefits seems to conflict with *Kelo*'s insistence that courts must not "second-
guess" the government's weighing of the costs and benefits of a project.[143]
Requiring the government to prove that the claimed benefits will actually materialize could undercut *Kelo* even further. If courts instead focus
only on projected benefits without considering the likelihood of achieving them, then officials can justify pretextual takings simply by presenting exaggerated claims of public benefit that they know they will not be
required to live up to.[144]

Inquiry into subjective intentions runs into the well-known difficulties
of ascertaining motivations. It is often hard to discern another person's
true motives, or even one's own. Moreover, it is difficult to decide what
to do when the governments' motives are mixed, as is often the case. In
practice, public officials can usually persuade themselves that any taking
that advances their political interests and helps an influential constitu-
ency that benefits from a taking also advances the public interest.[145]

Finally, relying on a detailed planning process to prevent pretextual
takings ignores the possibility that politically influential private interests
can "capture" the planning process and bend it to their own purposes. A
more extensive planning process is not necessarily less prone to favoritism than one that is less elaborate.[146]

For these reasons, even a relatively robust effort to enforce *Kelo*'s pretext doctrine by state and lower federal courts is likely to result in only
modest protection for property owners. It does not follow, however, that
courts should simply adopt the ultradeferential approach to pretext ques-

tions favored by the Second and Ninth Circuits. At least three of the four factors identified by lower courts that have avoided the path of extreme deference are all potential indications of pretext even if imperfect ones.

A taking is more likely to be pretextual if there is extensive evidence that key government decision makers were motivated by a desire to advance the interests of influential private parties. While official motives are often difficult to assess, courts routinely do address such issues in other cases such as seeking to determine whether an ostensibly neutral government policy was actually motivated by racial or religious discrimination.[147]

Heightened judicial suspicion is also warranted if a single private party captures the lion's share of the gains from a taking. That is at least some indication that the true purpose the taking was not to benefit the general public, even if not completely definitive proof.

In assessing both motives and benefits, it is important for judges to recognize that the pretextual beneficiary need not always be the new owner of the condemned property. Sometimes, it could be a politically influential third party such as Pfizer in the *Kelo* case itself.

Justice Kennedy, in his *Kelo* concurring opinion, was probably right to suppose that a pretextual taking is less likely in cases where the "identities of most of the private beneficiaries were unknown at the time that the [government] formulated its plans" for condemnation.[148] It is reasonable to apply a higher degree of judicial scrutiny in cases where beneficiaries' identities are known in advance. As discussed earlier, such beneficiaries might include third parties, such as Pfizer, as well as the projected new owners of the condemned property.

None of these three factors is definitive proof of pretext by itself. Each can sometimes be explained away as ultimately innocent. But the presence of any of them—and especially the presence of more than one—should lead courts to adopt a less deferential approach, shifting at least some of the burden of proof to the government.[149]

Whether the presence or absence of extensive planning is relevant to pretext claims is more debatable. Extensive planning does not necessarily indicate the absence of a scheme to benefit a private party at the expense of the public; the planning could itself be part of an effort to benefit the private interest. Similarly, a condemnation undertaken with little or no planning might have no untoward motive. Courts might, however, investigate the planning process as part of an inquiry into government motives. If the record shows that planners primarily sought to benefit a specific private party, that would be additional evidence of an illicit motive. If, conversely, it looks like they sought to benefit the public more generally, that would be evidence in support of the government.

Ultimately, it is difficult for courts to establish the presence or absence of illicit favoritism in the many cases where government officials simultaneously seek to benefit an influential private interest *and* also sincerely believe that they are acting in the public interest. Few people see themselves as cackling villains deliberately sacrificing the public good out of narrow self-interest. Even when that is indeed what they are doing, they are often able to convince themselves that what is good for them is also good for the public.[150] For this and other reasons, it is unlikely that even an aggressively applied pretextual takings doctrine will impose more than minor constraints on harmful uses of eminent domain.

So far, nonetheless, most courts that have addressed the matter have at least attempted to enforce a meaningful pretext constraint on takings. Their efforts to do so have utilized a variety of contradictory approaches to defining pretext. It seems unlikely that any consensus will emerge in this area any time soon, unless the Supreme Court decides to review a case that settles the dispute. Sooner or later, the Court is likely to do just that, rather than allow a five-way split to continue in the lower courts indefinitely.

When and if a pretext case does reach the Supreme Court, it could potentially serve as a vehicle not only for clarifying the pretext doctrine, but for reconsidering *Kelo* more generally. *Kelo* remains one of the Supreme Court's most controversial decisions, and many have called for it to be overruled.[151] A pretext case, perhaps one with unusually egregious facts, could give the Court an opportunity to either narrow *Kelo* or overrule it entirely.

Conclusion

In the aftermath of *Kelo,* several important state court decisions have considered whether *Kelo*'s deferential approach to public use will also be the rule under their state constitutions. With the notable exception of the New York Court of Appeals, the courts have generally given property owners greater protection than would be allowed under *Kelo*, and several state supreme courts have explicitly repudiated it as a guide to the interpretation of their state constitutions.

Both state and federal courts have tried to interpret the meaning of *Kelo's* statement that pretextual takings are still forbidden by the Constitution. No clear consensus on the meaning of pretext has emerged. It is quite possible that the pretext question will be the next public use issue that comes before the Supreme Court. It could even lead the Court to reconsider *Kelo* itself.

Whatever else can be said about the judicial reaction to *Kelo*, its fragmented and often skeptical nature underscores the extent to which the Supreme Court's decision remains controversial. There is no longer anything resembling a consensus on public use issues among the nation's judicial elite. The situation is in sharp contrast to the reaction to *Berman v. Parker,* the 1954 decision where the Supreme Court ruled that blight condemnations are permissible and first endorsed a highly deferential approach to the Public Use Clause. *Berman* was quickly adopted by many state supreme courts as a guide to the interpretation of their state constitutions.[152] Where an earlier generation of jurists largely embraced the post–New Deal orthodoxy on public use, today's judiciary is deeply divided.

Just as *Kelo* and its legacy continue to divide judges, it is also the focus of widespread disagreement about strategies for limiting the abuse of eminent domain. Many argue that those abuses can be constrained by reforming blight and economic development takings rather than banning them. The next chapter assesses several proposals along these lines.

CHAPTER EIGHT

Should Blight and Economic Development Takings Be Reformed or Banned?

The dangers of abusive economic development and blight takings are now widely recognized. But some believe that they can be effectively minimized through safeguards that fall short of a categorical ban on the economic development rationale. While not without merit, such strategies are unlikely to be as effective as a ban. In some cases, they may even make the situation worse.

This chapter examines several alternatives to a categorical ban on blight and economic development takings: increased compensation payments to owners of condemned property, increased procedural protections for property owners, special protection for homes, heightened scrutiny of private-to-private condemnations, giving local communities greater say over takings decisions, and reliance on interjurisdictional mobility and competition to restrain abusive local governments. Some of these options could be implemented by state legislatures, some by courts (either federal or state), and some by a combination of both.

Other critics of a ban on economic development takings have, by contrast, argued that it is likely to be ineffective because it does not go far enough. They predict that banning private-to-private condemnations will only promote equally harmful condemnations that transfer property to government ownership. If a ban is limited to economic development takings, while still permitting at least some blight takings, opponents fear that it will lead to a concentration of takings in areas inhabited by the poor.[1] Such concerns have a measure of validity. Even a complete ban on economic development and blight condemnations will not eliminate all eminent domain abuse. But it is likely to make the situation significantly better than it would be otherwise.

A complete ban can potentially be instituted by either a federal Supreme Court decision, state judicial decisions interpreting state constitutional public use clauses, state legislation, federal legislation, or some combination of the above. For reasons discussed in chapters 5 and 6, I am skeptical that a nationwide ban on economic development takings can be achieved without a federal Supreme Court decision overruling *Kelo*. Both Congress and a majority of state legislatures were unable or unwilling to enact such a ban even under the immediate impact of the massive *Kelo* backlash. It seems unlikely that most will do so in the foreseeable future. History also suggests that, while some state courts may enforce strong public use constraints on takings, there is likely to be at least a substantial minority that will not. Even at the height of the influence of the narrow view of public use in the nineteenth century, a significant number of state Supreme Courts endorsed the broad view.[2] In this chapter, however, we compare the relative merits of a categorical ban and other possible reforms without regard to the means by which the former might be achieved.

Increased Compensation for Property Owners

The injustices inflicted by economic development takings are exacerbated by the fact that the owners of condemned property generally receive compensation far below the true value of what they lose.[3] Scholars with a variety of political viewpoints have argued that current compensation levels are inadequate and have urged an increase.[4] During the *Kelo* oral argument, several justices, including Stephen Breyer, Anthony Kennedy, and David Souter—all of whom ultimately voted to uphold the *Kelo* takings—suggested that the traditional "fair market value" compensation standard was inadequate and seemed inclined to favor a more generous formula.[5] Justice Breyer asked whether "there is some way of assuring that the just compensation actually puts the [owner of a condemned home] in the position he would be in if he didn't have to sell his house."[6] Justice Kennedy, in turn, wondered whether "when you have property being taken from one private person ultimately to go to another private person, that what we ought to do is to adjust the measure of compensation, so that the owner . . . can receive some sort of a premium for the development."[7] Leading property scholars, such as James Krier and Christopher Serkin, and Thomas Merrill, have also argued for increasing compensation as a tool for alleviating eminent domain abuse.[8]

Unfortunately, there are two serious problems with this approach: one well known in the takings literature and the other often ignored.[9] The well-known difficulty is the challenge of estimating the "subjective value" that owners assign to their property.[10] In most cases, it is reasonable to assume that property owners value their holdings at more than the market price; otherwise, they would presumably have sold the property already.[11] Many owners attach sentimental value to their property, have valuable connections with friends and neighbors in the area, derive unusually great value from a given location, or simply have a particularly high distaste for the prospect of moving. In addition to such individual subjective value, large-scale takings may also destroy subjective value attached to entire communities, by undermining social ties of various kinds.[12] Unfortunately, it is often impossible to determine *how much* particular owners value their land above the properties' fair market prices. Simply asking the owners will not solve the problem, since they would have a strong incentive to overstate the value of the land in order to receive greater compensation.

It might be possible to incentivize owners to reveal the true value they attach to their property by allowing them to choose the compensation level paid for condemned land, but then require them to use the new assessed value as the baseline for future property taxes if the government chooses not to pay the price and instead forego condemnation, an idea proposed by property scholars Abraham Bell and Gideon Parchomovsky.[13] But their approach is likely to be impractical, because owners would be stuck with the assessed value in the future, despite major potential changes in their life circumstances and real estate markets.[14] When self-assessment was used to estimate property values for both takings and taxation in Taiwan between 1954 and 1977, owners tended to systematically underestimate the value of their property relative even to market prices, possibly for this very reason.[15] However, the Taiwanese system relied on self-assessments conducted before owners knew whether or not their land might be targeted for condemnation in the near future.[16] The Bell-Parchomovsky proposal, which calls for assessments conducted after owners know the government seeks to condemn their land, might be less subject to this bias. But owners faced with the prospect of being stuck with the same tax assessment base indefinitely might still be prone to understating their true valuations.

Bell and Parchomovsky would also forbid the owners from selling their property for less than the indicated amount at any time after the government refuses to pay it and thereby foregoes condemnation.[17] This constraint might deter owners from overstating their subjective value, but it is likely to introduce errors in the opposite direction, since owners would otherwise risk being stuck with a property they no longer want after their personal or professional circumstances have changed.

Attempting to establish a formula that pays owners a set rate above market value runs into the same types of problems as the fair market value approach. Whatever the rate set, some owners' subjective valuation of their land will still be higher than the formula provides, while others might actually be overcompensated. Moreover, setting too high a compensation level might give owners an incentive to actually lobby *in favor* of condemnation of their property, as may have happened in the 1984 *Midkiff* case, where some of the seventy-two large landowners who dominated Hawaii's real estate market may have preferred to have their land condemned rather than purchased on the market because the former turned out to be advantageous for tax reasons.[18] Therefore, it is difficult to imagine a compensation formula that can, in Justice Breyer's formulation, put the property owner "in the position he would be in if he didn't have to sell"[19] without simultaneously creating a serious risk of overcompensation that would create perverse incentives to lobby for condemnation.[20] None of this refutes the widespread - and generally accurate - perception that current law undercompensates the owners of condemned property. But it does highlight a danger that could arise if the law is changed to increase compensation to levels far above fair market value.

The second shortcoming of a compensation-based approach is often ignored but is perhaps even more telling.[21] As the *Poletown* case dramatically demonstrated,[22] property owners are not the only victims of ill-conceived economic development takings. The taxpayers who have to pay for the taking, as well as absorb some of the economic damage caused by the expropriation of existing businesses, nonprofit institutions, and public buildings, are also among the victims. As experienced eminent domain real estate appraiser Wallace Kaufman points out, "Property owners . . . are not the only ones put at risk" in an eminent domain case. "The other principal party to a takings case is not, as many people presume, the government. It is the taxpayer."[23]

In *Poletown*, taxpayers eventually had to pay some $250 million to acquire the property in question and prepare it for General Motors' use, a figure that does not include various indirect costs to the community such as the loss of expropriated businesses, churches, and schools.[24] In *Kelo,* tens of millions of dollars in taxpayer money was spent on New London's redevelopment project, with little prospect of anything approaching a commensurate return on the public's investment.[25] Ironically, raising compensation levels actually exacerbates the taxpayer costs of economic development takings.

The political process could potentially screen out and prevent takings that cost the taxpayers more than they are worth. But this is unlikely, because economic development takings are extremely difficult for citizens to assess. As discussed in chapter 3, widespread political ignorance, lack of transparency, and time horizon problems combine to ensure that many economic development condemnations will be undertaken despite the fact that their costs to the public greatly outweigh the benefits.[26] These problems are exacerbated in situations where a large part of the cost is borne by taxpayers in jurisdictions other than the one that decides to proceed with condemnation and expects to reap the benefits of the development project.[27] Such a situation often arises when development condemnations undertaken by local governments are subsidized by state and federal grants.[28]

If even such highly publicized and much debated condemnations as *Poletown* and *Kelo* are vulnerable to these dangers, the risk is likely to be even more severe in more typical cases. These considerations substantially reduce the likelihood that even greatly increased compensation levels will significantly reduce the incidence of economically inefficient takings for development purposes.[29]

The danger of taxpayer exploitation can arise even with conventional takings. But economic development takings are particularly susceptible to this problem because of the great difficulty of assessing their benefits, the long period of time that is likely to elapse before any benefits are realized, and the strong incentives of developers and condemning authorities to overstate their benefits in ways that are difficult for the public to penetrate.[30]

A final problem with the strategy of increasing compensation is that empirical evidences suggests that lower-income property owners with less valuable properties are often undercompensated even by the fair market value standard, whereas wealthier owners of higher-valued properties are far more likely to get more compensation than current law requires.[31] The causes of this bias are not completely clear. It could be due to a variety of distortions inherent in the eminent domain real estate assessment process that work against the interests of poor, inexperienced, or legally unsophisticated property owners.[32] But if the greater political influence and legal sophistication of wealthier owners is an important part of the explanation, this suggests it may be difficult to reform the legal and political system to increase compensation for the sorts of poor and politically weak owners who tend to be targets of economic development and blight condemnations.

None of this suggests that increasing compensation levels is useless. To the contrary, the problem of subjective value suggests that there is a strong case for increasing compensation for takings at least somewhat above market value.[33] Indeed, that case goes beyond economic development and blight takings and is applicable to other types of condemnations as well. But there is good reason to believe that increased compensation is not, by itself, an adequate solution to the abuses caused by economic development and blight takings. In some situations, it may even exacerbate them by increasing taxpayer costs and creating incentives for "overcompensated" property owners to lobby for condemnation of their property.

Procedural Safeguards

An alternative to judicial review urged by many *Kelo* critics is that of procedural safeguards for eminent domain defendants.[34] Possible protections include requiring extra advance notice of condemnation proceedings, mandating a detailed report laying out the purpose for which eminent domain is to be used, extensive public hearings to justify the planned taking, and an opportunity for opponents of the project to "voice their objections to being uprooted."[35] In theory, "strict enforcement of these procedural protections makes eminent domain largely self-regulating" because "[r]equiring the condemning authority to jump through enough procedural hoops will cause the costs of eminent domain to rise relative to the costs of voluntary exchange," thereby ensuring that "[e]minent domain will be used only when the transaction costs of voluntary exchange are truly prohibitive."[36]

Procedural protections for eminent domain defendants certainly have some value, and it is true that their cost could sometimes deter abusive condemnations. Advocates are right to believe that the "delay" created by "procedural hoops" can in some instances increase the costs of condemnation and thereby "increase . . . the bargaining leverage of property owners faced by condemnation."[37] But there are several major reasons why procedural protections are unlikely to be an adequate substitute for a judicial ban on economic development takings.

Perhaps the most fundamental limitation of the argument that the cost of "jumping through procedural hoops"[38] will deter abuses of the eminent domain power is that it implicitly assumes that the public officials who decide on condemnation and the private interests they seek to benefit will be the ones who bear those costs. In reality, most of the procedural costs are likely to be borne by taxpayers, not by condemning authorities or by the new owners of the condemned property. It is taxpayers who would bear the costs of additional hearings, preparation of reports justifying condemnation, and any extra compensation paid to property owners to persuade them not to exercise their procedural rights to the hilt.

This distinction would be unimportant if taxpayers closely monitored the costs of eminent domain. In reality, however, the complex and nontransparent nature of the condemnation process combine with generally widespread political ignorance to ensure that this will rarely be the case.[39] Thus, condemning authorities might often choose to accept even very substantial procedural costs, so long as those costs are borne by taxpayers who are unlikely to be aware of them and therefore unlikely to punish the offending officials at the polls.

A second problem with purely procedural remedies for eminent domain abuse is the possibility that increased costs might deter relatively small-scale condemnations but not large ones. Many of the procedural costs, such as preparing a plan, holding hearings, and so forth, are likely to be relatively fixed, regardless of the size and scope of the planned condemnation. Thus, the procedural cost of condemning one thousand properties is likely to be far less than one thousand times greater than the cost of condemning one. In cases where the planned project and its associated condemnations are expected to be on a very large scale, any procedural costs are likely to be only a small fraction of the total cost. More importantly, they will be only a small fraction of the benefits expected by the new private beneficiaries of the takings, such as Pfizer in *Kelo* or General Motors in the *Poletown* case. Procedural remedies are likely to be least effective in those cases where very large numbers of people are likely to be displaced. And such large-scale condemnations are also the ones that have the greatest potential for abuse.

A third major shortcoming of procedural remedies is the seeming impossibility of properly calibrating the level of protection. If procedural protections are to be "self-regulating" in the way that advocates hope,[40] they must be based on a reasonably accurate calculation of the level of cost that will deter socially harmful takings while still permitting beneficial ones to go forward. Unfortunately, there is no way for legislatures or courts to judge what level of procedural protection to provide other than by trying to estimate the likely costs and benefits of the condemnations themselves.

A major reason why supporters of procedural protection advocate them as an alternative to substantive scrutiny under the Public Use Clause is that they believe that "courts are not very good at policing the uses to which eminent domain is put."[41] Attempting to calibrate levels of procedural protection in order to achieve the "right" amount of deterrence merely reintroduces substantive judicial review of takings by the back door. Moreover, it actually forces courts to make a more complicated calculation than does traditional substantive review of public use issues. The latter requires that courts judge only the substantive nature of the taking. On the other hand, calibrating procedural protections to achieve optimal deterrence requires courts to both calculate the costs and benefits of condemnation and *also* determine what level of procedural protection is necessary to achieve the right level of deterrence.

To be sure, advocates of procedural remedies might argue that the relevant calculations should be made not by judges but by legislatures or by administrative officials. This could enable the use of greater technical expertise in setting protection levels. But it does so at the cost of relying on the political process to solve the problem of eminent domain abuse, despite the fact that it is the defects of that process which largely caused the problem in the first place.

If victims of economic development takings had sufficient political power to force legislatures to enact procedural protections strong enough to deter abuses, they would presumably also have had sufficient clout to prevent such condemnations from being initiated in the first place. Unfortunately, the political economy of economic development takings ensures that most property owners targeted for condemnation are likely to have relatively weak political influence, while their opponents are likely

to be powerful interest groups who are "repeat players" in the condemnation process.[42] Thus, the political process is unlikely to enact sufficient
procedural protections to prevent socially harmful takings for precisely
the same reasons that it often allows them to go forward in the first place.

Even if legislators do make a good-faith effort to enact effective procedural protections, they face many of the same information problems as
courts do. Like judges, legislators have no good metric for determining
how much procedural constraint on eminent domain is optimal.

Finally, it is important to recognize that, to the extent that procedural
protections make the eminent domain process longer and more complex,
they also increase the costs borne by property owners who choose to
contest a taking. These burdens include both the direct costs of the time
and money devoted to the fight, and the indirect costs of months or years
of uncertainty, during which time the owners will not know whether they
will get to keep their property or not. As described in chapter 1, the *Kelo*
property owners could not have afforded to contest their takings for
years on end without the intervention of the Institute for Justice, which
provided topnotch legal representation for free. Few property owners
targeted by blight or economic development condemnations have the resources necessary to wage such a prolonged fight on their own.

Procedural protections for property owners caught up in the eminent domain process are not wholly worthless. They can serve a useful
purpose in providing notice to affected property owners and allowing
them to raise objections. The cost of procedural protections might also
serve to deter some relatively small-scale and marginal condemnations.
But this remedy is unlikely to be sufficient to prevent most of the worst
abuses.

Special Protection for Homes

A number of prominent scholars have suggested that homes should get
special protection against eminent domain beyond that extended to other
types of property. Advocates of this approach include leading constitutional law and property scholars such as Akhil Amar, Daniel Farber,
Margaret Radin, Benjamin Barros, and Eduardo Penalver.[43]

The strongest argument for giving homes extra protection is the relatively high subjective value that many people attach to them.[44] More than
with most other types of property, owners are likely to attach greater

value to their homes than the fair market price compensation normally given to owners of condemned property. This is particularly true in the case of homes owned by longtime residents, people who live in unusually close-knit communities, or the elderly. Even scholars skeptical of the more general case for giving homes special status concede that forcible displacement inflicts disproportionately great harm on some categories of homeowners.[45] The suffering of the elderly residents of Fort Trumbull whose homes were condemned in the *Kelo* case is a good example of this kind of harm.[46]

There is little doubt that the condemnation of homes often inflicts great suffering. But that is not a good justification for denying protection to other kinds of property. Homes are not the only properties often targeted for condemnation that have high subjective value. The same can also be said for houses of worship and various other nonprofit institutions, for example.[47] Small businesses are also often targeted for condemnation and often suffer losses that go beyond the market value of the condemned land.[48] In many cases, small businesses are dependent on the advantages inherent in a particular location in ways that cannot easily be replicated at a new site. For example, involuntary relocation can disrupt relationships with long-time customers or force a business to abandon a site that is strategically located for the convenience of patrons.

On the other hand, it is far from invariably the case that homes always have high subjective value. Many people attach only modest additional value to their homes, and adjust to relocation without great difficulty, or at least no more than is experienced by commercial enterprises when they are forced to move.[49]

Furthermore, the harms of dubious economic development and blight condemnations are not limited to the property owners directly displaced. Such takings also victimize taxpayers who are forced to pay compensation and other associated costs, and the community as a whole, which suffers when the use of eminent domain undermines long-term prospects for economic growth and development.[50]

There is therefore little justification for requiring greater protection against eminent domain for homes than for properties devoted to other uses. None of this proves that homes are somehow undeserving of protection. A law forbidding or significantly restricting blight and economic development takings that target homes is far preferable to a regime under which all property is vulnerable to such condemnations.[51] But it is inferior to one that protects all property equally.

Heightened Scrutiny

Unlike economic development takings decisions in some other states,[52] the *Poletown* opinion was careful to avoid giving a blank check for all condemnations that might be said to promote development, emphasizing that "[o]ur determination that this project falls within the public purpose . . . does not mean that every condemnation proposed by an economic development corporation will meet with similar acceptance simply because it may provide some jobs or add to the industrial base."[53] Instead, the court held that "[w]here, as here, the condemnation power is exercised in a way that benefits specific and identifiable private interests, a court inspects with heightened scrutiny the claim that the public interest is the predominant interest being advanced."[54] The Delaware Supreme Court followed Michigan's example in adopting the heightened scrutiny test.[55] A similar approach was advocated by the three dissenting justices in the Connecticut Supreme Court's decision in *Kelo*.[56]

Unfortunately, the heightened scrutiny test failed to provide adequate protection against eminent domain abuse and in one crucial respect actually made the situation worse. Similar problems undercut academic proposals to control eminent domain abuse through "means-ends" scrutiny of condemnations, or by limiting economic development takings to cases where genuine holdout problems exist.

Shortcomings of the Poletown *Heightened Scrutiny Test*

The purpose of the heightened scrutiny test was to ensure that there is a "clear and significant" public benefit resulting from condemnation. Unfortunately, the test creates a perverse incentive to increase the amount of property condemned rather than reduce it. Since the public benefit involved is strengthening the local economy, the larger the commercial project served by a condemnation—and the more property owners expropriated as a result—the greater the chance that courts will find that the resulting economic growth is "clear and significant" enough to pass the test.

In fact, Michigan cases applying the heightened scrutiny test displayed precisely this kind of bias in favor of major projects dispossessing large numbers of property owners. Courts applying the test sometimes invalidated condemnations of small amounts of property intended to benefit individuals and small- to medium-size businesses.[57] But in the main,

Michigan courts applying *Poletown* felt themselves compelled to uphold condemnations of large amounts of property for the benefit of major commercial enterprises. Thus, in 1989 the Michigan Court of Appeals reluctantly held that *Poletown* required it to uphold the condemnation of 380 acres of land in order to "transfer the property to [the] Chrysler Corporation for the construction of a new automobile assembly plant."[58] Ironically, the court of appeals believed that both the Chrysler condemnation and *Poletown* itself constituted "abuse[s] of the power of eminent domain."[59] Nonetheless, it was forced to follow *Poletown* and endorse the validity of the condemnation of large amounts of property for the benefit of Chrysler.[60] And, of course, in *Poletown* itself, the construction of a large GM plant was held sufficient to justify the displacement of some 4,200 people.[61]

The *Poletown* heightened scrutiny test protected property owners least precisely when protection was most needed: in cases where substantial numbers of people are displaced for the benefit of large, politically powerful interest groups. Indeed, interest groups seeking to ensure approval of condemnations under *Poletown* were well-advised to plan large construction projects utilizing as much property as possible.

The failure of the heightened scrutiny test to curtail the danger to private property created by the *Poletown* decision is also evidenced by the prevalence of private-to-private condemnations in Michigan during the period when the test applied. According to a 2003 study by the Institute for Justice, which represented the *Kelo* plaintiffs, from 1998 to 2002 alone, at least 138 condemnation proceedings had been filed in Michigan for the purpose of transferring property to private parties; 173 more were threatened.[62]

Michigan's record in this respect compared poorly with that of other states. In the five-year period from 1998 to 2002, only two other states had more reported condemnation filings for the purpose of transferring property to private interests.[63] The city of Detroit—the jurisdiction involved in *Poletown itself*—achieved the dubious distinction of filing more condemnations for private ownership than any other city in the nation in the same time period.[64] Detroit's aggressive use of eminent domain failed to stem the economic decline that eventually led the city to bankruptcy in 2013. Indeed, it likely made the city's problems even more severe by destroying neighborhoods and rendering property rights insecure.[65]

Admittedly, we cannot know for certain the degree to which Michigan really was worse than other states in this regard, due to limitations in the Institute for Justice data.[66] We can be reasonably confident, however, that Michigan's heightened scrutiny requirement failed to reduce such condemnations to levels significantly below those observed elsewhere, including in states that lack heightened scrutiny.

Means-Ends Scrutiny

Academic proposals to increase scrutiny of economic development takings by imposing "means-ends" scrutiny of condemnation decisions are similar to the heightened scrutiny test and suffer from some of the same weaknesses.[67] Supporters of means-ends scrutiny argue that it will constrain eminent domain abuse by ensuring that the "redevelopment project to be enabled by eminent domain is reasonably necessary to stem the tide of suburban sprawl, to renew a lifeless downtown, or to advance whatever goal the government uses to justify the exercise of eminent domain."[68] The Institute for Justice advanced a similar idea as a fallback position in the federal Supreme Court in *Kelo*, arguing that even if economic development takings are constitutionally permissible, courts should carefully scrutinize them to ensure that the promised development is likely to materialize.[69]

Means-ends scrutiny is vulnerable to the same types of perverse incentives as the *Poletown* heightened scrutiny test. The larger the development project in question, the easier it will be for condemning authority to claim that condemnation is "reasonably necessary" to ensure its completion and that noncoercive alternatives will not suffice. Thus, like *Poletown* heightened scrutiny, means-ends analysis is likely to create a perverse incentive to actually increase the scale of economic development condemnations.

A related problem is that, so long as economic development is regarded as a legitimate public use, means-ends scrutiny could probably be used to justify virtually any condemnation that dispossessed homeowners or nonprofit institutions for the benefit of for-profit business interests. Almost by definition, the latter are likely to produce more development and tax revenue than the former.[70] And so long as the current owners are unwilling to sell voluntarily at the price offered by developers, there is a strong argument that the "development" in question cannot be achieved by noncoercive means.

Depending on how stringent it is, means-ends scrutiny could potentially curb at least some dubious economic development takings. For example, it could prevent condemnations where the government has no

clear plan how it intends to use the property, or where the expected economic benefits seem extremely small compared to the costs. But it is unlikely to prevent some of the most serious abuses, and could potentially
even create perverse incentives to increase their scale.

Limiting Economic Development Takings to Cases with Genuine Holdout Problems

Leading takings scholar Richard Epstein has argued that courts should
limit private-to-private economic development takings to situations where
there are genuine holdout problems, carefully scrutinizing the facts of
each case to determine whether such a problem exists.[71] Epstein urges
courts to permit the use of eminent domain for private development projects where it is needed to "overcome serious holdout problems" that block
valuable projects that would make a net contribution to the economy. At
the same time, he would have them "keep a tight rein on public uses" in
order to prevent abuses like those that occurred in *Kelo* and *Poletown*.[72]
Epstein's view is similar to that of economist Thomas Miceli, a prominent expert on eminent domain who also argues that private-to-private
condemnations that go beyond the narrow definition of public use should
mostly be limited to cases where there are holdout problems.[73]

Epstein's approach is appealing because it potentially allows us to
both have our cake and eat it. If properly applied, it would block the numerous blight and economic development takings that needlessly victimize property owners without actually promoting economic growth. But it
would also permit the few genuinely productive economic development
takings to go forward.

Unfortunately, it is unlikely that real-world judges could implement
Epstein's approach effectively. In order to make the system work, judges
would have to determine whether a proposed taking really is needed
to overcome holdout problems and whether the resulting project really
would make a substantial contribution to the economy. In one of his
books, Epstein also suggests that such condemnations should be confined
to properties "where the loss of subjective value is small."[74] That might
require courts to make determinations about the extent of subjective
value at risk.

As the Michigan experience with heightened scrutiny suggests, judges
are unlikely to do a very good job of determining whether a given project
would to result in substantial economic value or not.[75] Moreover, judges

who are ideologically or politically sympathetic to government planning are understandably likely to give some leeway to planning officials in cases where the economic projections are uncertain.[76] In an ideologically diverse judiciary where most judges are not as libertarian as Epstein, such cases are likely to be common and would probably undermine his goal of using judicial scrutiny to limit economic development takings to cases where "the locational necessities are great."[77]

Careful analysis of takings to determine whether or not there is a genuine holdout problem is likely to require considerable economic sophistication and leave plenty of room for judicial discretion. The same goes for determinations of subjective value, which is, by its very nature, often difficult to measure.[78] Even judges with extensive knowledge of economics and land use policy and a complete absence of ideological bias, will often find it difficult to make good decisions on these issues. And most judges are neither economists nor land-use experts nor free of ideological preconceptions.

In addition, Epstein's fear that a bright-line rule against economic development takings would block valuable development projects is partly mitigated by the existence of secret assembly and other market mechanisms for getting around holdout problems in cases where they really do exist.[79] These mechanisms are not foolproof, and it is likely that a categorical ban on economic development takings would forestall at least a few genuinely valuable development projects. No bright-line rule is likely to be as efficient as the exercise of case-by-case discretion by unbiased and omniscient judges. But a categorical ban on economic development takings is likely to prove superior to the exercise of discretion by the kinds of judges that typically populate real-world courts.

Effective enforcement of public use limits on takings is likely to cause some inefficiency by preventing at least a few development projects that should be permitted in an ideal world. But there are similar costs to the enforcement of virtually any other constitutional right. Enforcement of criminal defendants' rights will sometimes allow the guilty to go free and commit additional crimes. Protecting freedom of speech can facilitate the spread of dangerous ideas, such as racism, Nazism, or communism, which might ultimately lead to the adoption of harmful and unjust government policies. Protecting the rights of suspected terrorists might enable some genuine terrorists to escape and kill more innocent civilians. None of these rights are perfect. And perhaps none would be needed in a world where we could trust judges or other government officials to exercise well-informed and unbiased case-by-case discretion. But we accept them, nonetheless, because their net impact is superior to realistically feasible alternatives. The same reasoning justifies judicial enforcement of public use limitations on takings.

Epsteinian judicial scrutiny would likely result in greater protection for property rights than the highly deferential approach adopted by the Court in *Kelo*. But it is unlikely to be as effective as a categorical ban on economic development takings where the result does not often turn on difficult issues left up to judicial discretion.

Giving Communities a Greater Say in Condemnation Decisions

One possible way to limit eminent domain abuse without banning economic development takings is to create mechanisms to give area residents greater control over condemnation decisions. Legal scholars Michael Heller and Roderick Hills have put forward a particularly interesting institutional reform along these lines, which they call the "land assembly district" (LAD).[80] Heller and Hills' approach would allow the formation of an LAD in any area where a developer, a local resident, or other interested party might propose it, subject to the approval of government land-use planning agencies.[81] If the government sought to condemn property in such an area on the grounds that a beneficial development or infrastructure project would otherwise be blocked by holdouts, the taking would only go forward if a majority of voters in the area support it in a referendum.[82] Residents who own more land in the area might have greater voting rights than those who own less.[83]

The virtue of this approach is that takings would only go forward if a majority of local voters believed them to be beneficial to their interests. This would eliminate or at least alleviate the problem of inadequate compensation of victims of eminent domain.[84] Heller and Hills are aware that the LAD system could potentially lead to a local "tyranny of the majority," with majority preferences overriding those of individual landowners who assign unusually high value to their property. But they believe that this danger is likely to be mitigated by the relatively homogenous nature of most neighborhoods and by their idea that the LADs be required to obey a preset formula for dividing up the compensation payments for the sale of their land to a developer.[85]

The Heller-Hills LAD system might indeed give landowners greater protection against dubious takings than they now enjoy in jurisdictions where there are few constraints on blight and economic development condemnations. But it has a number of significant limitations relative to a categorical ban on such takings. The biggest constraint is that a majoritarian voting process involving more than a very small number of people creates significant incentives for rational ignorance. Because the chance of casting a decisive vote is likely to be low, participants in the referendum will have little incentive to carefully assess the developer or government's compensation offer and determine whether it really will be preferable to holding on to their land.[86] This is a significant disadvantage relative to market mechanisms for land acquisition such as secret assembly. In the latter case, individual owners have much stronger incentives to become well informed.

Furthermore, as Daniel Kelly has pointed out, Heller and Hills may significantly underestimate the risk of majoritarian tyranny in such situations. Even in otherwise homogenous neighborhoods, some landowners could easily attach much greater subjective value to their property than others.[87] If the size of such a minority is large enough or the subjective value even a small minority assigns to its land sufficiently high, this could easily result in takings that destroy more value than they create.

Perhaps most important of all, if LADs really do impede abusive condemnations to any great degree, it seems likely that developers and organized interest groups would lobby to alter the legislation governing the creation and functioning of LADs to their advantage. For example, they could skew the distribution of voting rights to the advantage of owners willing to sell for a relatively low price or manipulate the process by which the LAD boundaries are drawn. If these groups are powerful enough to push through dubious condemnations in the first place, they are likely also powerful enough to influence the details of the LAD governance structure.

This problem also bedevils other proposed mechanisms for giving local communities a greater say in takings decisions. For example, sociologist Debbie Becher suggests that the government should protect communities targeted for condemnation by appointing state-funded "community organizers" to help residents mobilize to defend their interests.[88] But, as she acknowledges, this reform would be extremely difficult to implement in an effective way, because "[p]oliticians will be reluctant to provide such a resource, and will be very tempted to cut the lifeline to any professionals explicitly organizing against official plans."[89] An alert and well-informed electorate could probably block such maneuvers. But if the electorate were that motivated and knowledgeable, abusive condemnations probably would not be a serious problem in the first place.[90]

Federalism and Interjurisdictional Mobility

For many economists and legal scholars, interjurisdictional competition is a seemingly obvious alternative to judicial intervention as a means of protecting property owners against abusive takings. If a local government engages in repeated abusive condemnations, owners and investors are likely to choose to relocate elsewhere or not move to that community in the first place.

Some who deploy the federalism argument against judicial enforcement of property rights argue that such intervention is unnecessary because competitive federalism will constrain abuses.[91] Advocates claim that state and local governments that abuse the power of eminent domain or engage in excessive regulatory takings will lose business and taxpayers to other jurisdictions, thereby suffering financial losses as a result.[92] Robert Ellickson contends that this factor helps account for what he considers to be the relatively strong political reaction to *Kelo,* under which various states and localities have enacted strong reform laws intended to curb economic development takings.[93] Vicki Been has argued that courts need not closely police local government land use regulations because "a developer dissatisfied with a community's exactions policy can take the project to another jurisdiction that offers better terms."[94] Her point could be applied to economic development takings as well.

Been's and Ellickson's arguments are an extension of standard economic theories arguing that the combination of decentralization and mobility will constrain subnational government abuses and force them to adopt efficient economic policies that benefit citizens.[95] On this view, exit rights could potentially be an adequate protection for aggrieved property owners even absent judicial protection.

The Impact of Immobility

The main difficulty with such competitive federalism justifications for *Kelo* is that they fail to take adequate account of the immobility of property rights in land. Property owners are unlikely to "vote with their feet" against eminent domain because, if they move out, they cannot take their land with them. Exit rights are little help in protecting assets that you cannot take with you when you leave.[96]

This crucial point suggests that competitive federalism is particularly unlikely to protect property rights in land. In some instances, limits on state and local governments' ability to tax mobile assets, such as income, might actually incentivize them to target immobile ones, such as land, in order to find ways to transfer resources to favored interest groups.[97] In this way, competitive federalism might actually exacerbate rather than alleviate the exploitation of immobile resources. For example, state and local governments are limited in their ability to raise income taxes because of tax competition between jurisdictions. Migration patterns tend to favor low-tax jurisdictions.[98] This factor increases state and local government incentives to target immobile resources such as land instead. Other evidence suggests that local governments generally tend to overexploit immobile capital, while oversubsidizing mobile resources.[99]

Limitations of Exit and Voice

Even if competitive federalism does not exacerbate state and local government tendencies to exploit immobile resources, it at least is unlikely to protect them from state predation. Individuals might choose to leave a given jurisdiction. But they will have to leave their land behind, still available for the state to take. For this very reason, it is unlikely that individuals who fear threats to their immobile property will choose to migrate for that purpose in the first place. After all, doing so incurs moving costs but does not actually accomplish the goal of protecting the threatened property.[100]

The problem is not simply that exit rights "cost money," which is lost as a result of regulatory impositions.[101] It is that moving fails to accomplish the purpose of freeing the owner from the very burden he or she seeks to avoid. If the owner move without selling the property, he is no better off than before, since the land remains subject to the same danger of condemnation as before. If the owner does sell, the price he or she gets will be proportionately lower as a result of the risk of condemnation, and the resulting loss will simply take the form of a lower sale value. Either way, the immobility of property prevents the owner from using exit rights as a means of escaping regulatory burdens imposed on land. For this reason, targeting immobile property is unlikely to cost the state by incentivizing the owners to flee and take their mobile assets and income with them.

Landowners who believe that their land is threatened could potentially avoid the danger, if they sell the land and move before the threat
materializes. For example, if they suspect their land is likely to be condemned by local government, they could try to sell the property before
the condemnation actually happens. But this strategy is only likely to
work if the real estate market fails to take account of the risk of condemnation and incorporate it into the price of the land. In reality, the threat
of eminent domain tends to drive down land prices in a given area, a phenomenon known as "condemnation blight."[102] As Ellickson recognizes,
"if the abuse [of property rights] were widely known, exiting in this fash-
ion would not enable the landowner to avoid financial loss because most,
if not all, of the cost of the abuse would be negatively capitalized in the
sale price."[103]

Regulatory and tax burdens that affect mobile assets also sometimes
impact immobile ones as well. For example, high state income taxes or
a weak economy caused by poor regulatory policies might reduce land
values. However, there is an important distinction between a regulatory
burden that primarily affects a mobile asset and one whose impact falls
mostly on an immobile one. In the former case, affected individuals still
have a significant incentive to move to avoid the burden, since doing so
can relieve them of most of it, even if not all.

Consider, for example, a flawed economic policy 80 percent of whose
costs come in the form of reduced incomes and 20 percent in the form of
reduced home values. Exit rights can still be used to avoid 80 percent of
the associated harm. In this scenario, many of the losers from the policy
will have an incentive to exit from the jurisdiction in order to avoid it.

By contrast, the costs of eminent domain mostly fall on immobile
assets, and exit therefore cannot be used to avoid most of them. The key
point is not so much whether a policy targets immobile assets in a formal
legal sense, but whether its effects can be escaped by moving. With most
uses of eminent domain, the answer is largely "no."

Despite recognizing that "[t]he immobility of land reduces political
pressures on states and cities to treat landowners fairly,"[104] Ellickson
nonetheless claims that competitive pressures will reduce such abuses because their presence is likely to drive down land prices. This in turn gives
voters incentives to mobilize against them and local governments reason
to cut back on abuse in order to maintain their tax bases.[105] As a class,
homeowners wield great influence over local governments, and keeping
up the value of their property is usually one of their main objectives.[106]

Ellickson's point would be an important constraint on local government abuse of property rights if all or most property was equally threatened by such abuses, thereby driving down prices across the board. In fact, however, the use of eminent domain for transfer to private parties generally targets the poor and politically weak.[107]

Politically vulnerable groups do indeed suffer declines in the value of their property in jurisdictions that make extensive use of eminent domain and other restrictions on property rights. But there is likely to be little or no impact on the value of other land in the area. For this reason, many jurisdictions can abuse property rights extensively without risking more than a modest erosion of their property tax base. The fact that politically vulnerable groups are the ones targeted also makes it unlikely that they can effectively use their "voice" in the political process to make up for the ineffectiveness of exit rights.[108]

The perverse incentives of local governments are often exacerbated by "time horizon" problems. Even if ill-advised takings and other restrictions on property rights do erode the tax base or otherwise weaken the local economy, the effects usually do not become evident for several years, by which time the political leaders who adopted these policies might well be out of office, and public attention will, in any event, have moved on to other matters.[109] By contrast, transferring land to politically favored interests at the expense of the poor or politically weak creates immediate political benefits for politicians.

The relatively short time horizons facing politicians further reduce the impact of competitive federalism in restraining abuses of property rights. Given the immobility of land, any negative competitive effects from such abuses are likely to be modest in size and emerge only slowly. When they finally do, enough time may have passed that the political leaders responsible will escape any political retaliation.

Historical evidence on the use of eminent domain also undercuts claims that it can be successfully constrained by competitive federalism. If the theory were true, then takings that inflict great harm on property owners for little or no social gain should be extremely rare, if not nonexistent. In reality, large-scale abuse of eminent domain authority by state and local governments is far from uncommon in American history. As we saw in chapter 3, millions of people have been forcibly displaced by dubious blight and economic development takings since the 1940s. This suggests that competitive federalism is far from a foolproof constraint on such abuses.

The significance of immobility does suggest that state and local governments should be less likely to threaten the rights of owners of mobile assets. For example, the California Supreme Court has ruled that local governments can use eminent domain to condemn sports teams in order to prevent them from moving, thereby authorizing the City of Oakland to use eminent domain against the Oakland Raiders in order to prevent their planned move to Los Angeles.[110] Such condemnations are also probably legal in the many other states that define "public use" very broadly and under broad federal public use standards.[111] Yet condemnations of sports teams and other mobile assets are extremely rare, probably because the owners of such assets can move them out of state before any condemnation is completed.[112] In 1985, an effort by the City of Baltimore to condemn the NFL's Baltimore Colts franchise in order to keep it from moving to Indianapolis failed because the Colts were able to depart before the city paid compensation for the taking.[113] The federal district court agreed that "it is now beyond dispute that intangible property is properly the subject of condemnation proceedings" but refused to uphold the condemnation because the Colts were able to leave the jurisdiction before compensation was paid.[114]

It is certainly likely that eminent domain abuse would be more common in a world without exit rights and interjurisdictional competition. But it is also likely that the power of exit is at its weakest in protecting rights to real property and other immobile assets. It is not an adequate substitute for judicial review or for laws banning economic development and blight condemnations.

Will Bans Fail Because They Do Not Go Far Enough?

While most critics of bans on economic development and blight condemnations contend that they are unnecessary because they go too far, some claim that they are likely to fail because they do not go far enough. Such arguments take several different forms.

The most obvious is the possibility that eminent domain abuse could simply continue in the form of takings that transfer property to government ownership or to common carriers and public utilities, as is permissible even under the traditional narrow interpretation of public use.[115] This is not a new line of argument. An 1876 Nevada Supreme Court decision that rejected the narrow definition in favor of the broad view did so in part on the ground that the narrow view does not actually provide meaningful protection for property owners:

> [I]t is argued, that in sustaining this act upon the principles we have announced, there is no limitation to the exercise of legislative will in the appropriation of private property . . . I am of opinion that this argument is more specious than sound . . . [T]he danger of an improper invasion of private rights is not, in my judgment, as great by following the construction we have given to the constitution as by a strict adherence to the [the narrow interpretation of public use]. If public occupation and enjoyment of the object for which land is to be condemned furnishes the only and true test for the right of eminent domain, then the legislature would certainly have the constitutional authority to condemn the lands of any private citizen for the purpose of building hotels and theaters. Why not? . . . The public have the same right, upon payment of a fixed compensation, to seek rest and refreshment at a public inn as they have to travel upon a railroad. One purpose is, so far as the legal rights of the citizen are concerned, as public as the other. The same principle is applicable to theaters. . . . It is certain that this view, if literally carried out to the utmost extent, would lead to very absurd results, if it did not entirely destroy the security of the private rights of individuals.[116]

Some modern scholars have adopted a similar line of argument, though without necessarily endorsing the 1876 Nevada Supreme Court's conclusion that courts should therefore endorse the broad view of public use.[117] Critics fear that governments could even potentially condemn private property for transfer to ostensible government ownership that is, in reality, just a smokescreen for control by a private corporation.[118]

The objection is not without some force. There is little doubt that takings that transfer property to government ownership or to a common carrier or public utility *can* sometimes have some of the same harmful effects as blight and economic development takings. They can victimize the poor and politically weak, and also transfer property to uses that are less valuable to the community than those of the preexisting owners. On the other hand, as discussed in chapter 3, the case for allowing the use of eminent domain for government-owned facilities and some public utilities and common carriers is much stronger than the case for using it for private economic development or to eliminate blight.[119]

In any event, the relevant question is not whether takings for narrow public uses can be harmful or unjust, but whether the continued existence of a power to engage in such takings negates the benefits of a ban on blight and economic development takings. It would only do so if governments can readily substitute narrow public use takings in all or most situations where they would have used blight or economic development takings.

It seems improbable that such a substitution is actually feasible in most cases. A private firm or developer is unlikely to want to invest in a new property if the land is going to remain under the government's control rather than its own, since it would then risk losing that investment any time the government might wish to put the property to a different use. Similarly, businesses that are not conventionally public utilities or common carriers will often find it burdensome to have a legal obligation to serve all members of the public at all times.

Private interests could potentially lobby the government to condemn property and then effectively turn it over to private control, with government ownership reduced to a mere fig leaf.[120] For example, the government could condemn a property and then turn it over to a private firm under a ninety-nine–year lease with minimal rent, and without any restrictions on what the firm could use the land for.

But such private control under the guise of "public" ownership should be invalidated by courts applying the narrow interpretation of public use. A public use requires genuine use by either the government or the general public, not merely a paper statement that such use exists. For any constitutional right to be a meaningful protection against government abuse, it must have substantive bite, not just form. For example, facially neutral laws will be invalidated under the Equal Protection Clause Fourteenth Amendment, if it turns out that their true purpose is to discriminate against a racial or ethnic minority.[121] Similarly, a law that on its face authorizes the condemnation of property for public use runs afoul of the Public Use Clause, if in reality the land will be under the total or near-total control of a private entity.

State courts applying relatively restrictive definitions of public use have, on the basis of such reasoning, struck down takings for private roads that, although theoretically open to the public, will in fact be completely controlled by a single private party.[122] In 2000, a Massachusetts state court invalidated a taking for a publicly owned baseball stadium because the taking was "done primarily to benefit" the private owner of the sports team, which would have nearly complete control of the stadium and reap most of the benefits.[123] In 2011, the Texas Supreme Court ruled that a private firm cannot use eminent domain to build a pipeline as a "common carrier" if the pipeline, although theoretically open to the general public, in reality only connects two facilities owned by the firm itself.[124]

These types of cases do not provide a perfect test that can definitely separate out genuine public uses from shams. But they are helpful and illustrative. As with many other constitutional rights, the rights protected by the Public Use Clause do not always have absolutely clear boundaries. There will inevitably be some difficult borderline cases. But effective judicial enforcement of public use restrictions should, at the very least, make circumvention difficult.

Even genuine public use takings can still sometimes be unwise, wasteful, or create injustices that inflict severe harm on vulnerable property owners in exchange for little or no public benefit.[125] As legal scholar Alexandra Klass has shown in a series of important articles, many states—especially in the West—have extremely lax standards for the use of eminent domain for transmission lines, natural resource extraction, and pipelines.[126] Although takings for such purposes often meet the narrow definition of public use, they still sometimes enable interest groups to use eminent domain to promote projects that enrich themselves, but create very little benefit for the general public.

The same is true of takings for publicly owned universities. Although universities provide important educational benefits and also sponsor socially valuable research, the use of eminent domain to transfer property to them rarely if ever benefits the general public, as opposed to interest groups within the university system. The educational and research benefits of universities can be realized more efficiently without resorting to eminent domain.[127]

Even worse, many states allow the use of eminent domain to build publicly owned sports stadiums.[128] In 1994, a federal appellate court upheld a condemnation intended to acquire property to build a publicly owned parking lot for the Texas Rangers' stadium, for which the franchise—then owned by future president George W. Bush—would pay a nominal one dollar annual rent to use.[129] Such projects continue despite the fact that government-supported stadiums make virtually no net contribution to local economies.[130] Urban development scholars Alan Altshuler and David Luberoff note that it is "virtually impossible to find an independent economist who view[s] sports facility subsidies as good investments in local economic growth."[131]

The ideal constitution would likely impose tighter constraints on narrow public use takings than the Fifth Amendment does. Among other things, it might require the condemning authority to present substantial evidence that the taking will produce extensive public benefits that accrue to the general public. Since a constitutional amendment along such lines is unlikely, state governments and state courts should consider imposing some tighter constraints on their own initiative,[132] though such efforts are likely to be bedeviled by the public's rational ignorance about the subject, as compared to the superior knowledge and organization of narrow interest groups.[133]

Effective enforcement of public use constraints on takings cannot and will not put an end to all eminent domain abuse. But it can eliminate some of its more pernicious manifestations.

A closely related critique of the narrow approach to public use is that its restrictions on eminent domain will simply incentivize the government to pursue the same ends by using other powers such as taxation and regulation.[134] In such a scenario, property owners might be even worse off than if the government had resorted to the use of eminent domain, since the latter at least entitles the owners to compensation, whereas taxation and regulation usually do not.[135]

Taxation and regulation *can* potentially be substitutes for the use of eminent domain. Instead of condemning property in order to give it to General Motors to build a factory, the government could enact a regulation requiring the present owners to allow GM to operate a factory on the site (perhaps in exchange for nominal rent).

But such substitution cannot evade public use restrictions on eminent domain in cases where the regulation in question either requires owners to grant others permanent physical occupation of their land or deprives them of virtually all economic value. The Supreme Court has held that regulations with such requirements qualify as takings and therefore must be subject to the constraints of the Public Use Clause.[136] Most blight and economic development takings that transfer property to private parties do in fact aim at permanent physical occupation of the condemned land, a complete transfer of its economic value, or both.

Another variant of this argument is that banning private-to-private economic development and blight takings will simply lead governments to condemn more property for publicly owned development projects. As Judge Richard Posner puts it, "[t]he more limitations the Court place[s] on the private development of condemned land, the more active the government itself would become in development."[137] Such a trend, critics argue, might even lead takings to be less efficient, because government management of condemned property could be less effective than private.[138]

This might potentially happen in some instances. But Posner's critique overlooks the key point that the desire to transfer land to politically influential interest groups is often a key factor in incentivizing governments to engage in condemnation in the first place.[139] If judicial enforcement of public use limitations on takings eliminates that option, much of the impetus for economic development condemnations will disappear. In this context, it is worth noting that there is no evidence indicating that condemnations for publicly owned development are unusually frequent in states where courts have enforced state constitutional bans on economic development takings.

Finally, we should briefly consider claims that laws or judicial decisions banning economic development takings without banning blight condemnations in genuinely blighted areas are likely to harm the poor by diverting the use of eminent domain to blighted areas.[140] As discussed in chapters 2 and 3, I believe that the Public Use Clause should be interpreted to ban blight takings as well as economic development takings. Post-*Kelo* reform laws should also ban both types, as has indeed been done in a few states, such as Florida and Nevada.[141] But it does not follow that reform laws and judicial decisions that only ban economic development takings are worse than no restrictions at all.

Given the vast differences between neighborhoods that are blighted, in the narrow sense of that term, and most other areas, it seems highly unlikely that eminent domain–driven development projects that might have occurred in the latter will migrate to the former as a result of laws banning economic development takings in nonblighted areas. An area that is severely dilapidated is unlikely to be attractive to the same types of businesses and developers as would prefer to build in a nonblighted area. Even given that a few such displacements may occur, it is important to recognize that economic development takings in nonblighted areas also disproportionately victimize the poor and politically weak. On net, a restriction on economic development takings that applies only to nonblighted areas is likely to benefit the poor significantly, even if not as much as one that also eliminates blight condemnations.[142]

Even if such limited bans provide tangible benefits to the poor, it is possible that these benefits are outweighed by the "expressive" harm of enacting laws that "privilege . . . the stability of middle-class households relative to the stability of poor house-holds" and "express . . . the view that the interests and needs of poor house-holds are relatively unimportant."[143] But it seems unlikely that limited reforms inflict great enough psychological harm on the poor to outweigh their tangible benefits for poor and nonpoor alike.

The poor themselves, at least, do not seem to think so. Survey evidence shows that members of poor households oppose the *Kelo* decision and support reform laws banning takings for "private development" by roughly the same lopsided majorities as more affluent households do.[144] Given widespread voter ignorance, such survey data may have little relevance to debates over the tangible costs and benefits of banning economic development takings. Both poor voters and wealthy ones might be ignorant on these points. But surveys *are* a more useful indication of the intangible expressive effects on the poor, since these are mostly psychological effects in their own minds.

A ban on economic development takings that does not also ban blight condemnations is far from ideal. But here, as elsewhere, the best should not be the enemy of the good.

Conclusion

There is a great deal of merit in many proposals that seek to limit eminent domain abuse without banning blight and economic development takings outright. If it turns out that a categorical ban cannot be achieved, these ideas deserve serious consideration. Some, particularly increasing compensation, should probably be adopted even if a ban is possible. Increased compensation is often desirable even in cases where property is condemned for narrowly defined public uses.

Yet piecemeal reforms are not an adequate substitute for a comprehensive solution. Each such proposal has important shortcomings. They all leave some large percentage of property owners unprotected, perpetuate the victimization of taxpayers and the community at large, or both.

Conclusion

The *Kelo* case was an important setback for property rights advocates, but also a significant step forward. The close 5-4 nature of the decision rekindled a debate that most experts had thought was definitively resolved: whether the Public Use Clause imposes any meaningful constraints on eminent domain. The case also brought enormous public attention to the issue of eminent domain abuse, which in turn led to the enactment of an unprecedented number of reforms—more than followed in the aftermath of any other Supreme Court decision.

Although many of the new laws were largely ineffective, a substantial minority did significantly increase protection for property rights. In addition, *Kelo* was repudiated as a guide to the interpretation of state public use clauses by most of the state supreme courts that considered the issue since 2005. It would be an overstatement to conclude that the cause of property rights gained more by losing *Kelo* than it would have by winning it.[1] But defeat certainly turned out to be more productive for the losers than most would have expected.

Property rights advocates may in time succeed in persuading the Supreme Court to overrule *Kelo* or narrow it. Even if they do not, it is a safe bet that the meaning of the Public Use Clause and the appropriate uses of eminent domain will remain hotly contested issues for a long time to come.

The Aftermath in New London

After their painfully close defeat in the Supreme Court, the seven *Kelo* plaintiffs all eventually settled with the New London Development

Corporation and the city, and were forced to finally give up their land. Because of the enormous nationwide sympathy generated by the Supreme Court decision, the property owners were able to get much better compensation arrangements than would have been possible otherwise. Connecticut officials wanted to settle with the plaintiffs in order to avoid further adverse publicity.[2] Susette Kelo agreed to surrender her land only after the city and state increased the compensation offer, and a private donor, Avner Gregory, agreed to pay the expense of lifting her house off of its foundations and moving it to a new site elsewhere in New London.[3] Gregory purchased the house from Kelo for the nominal sum of $1 and still owns it today.[4]

The Cristofaro family secured the right to transplant some treasured shrubs that Pasquale Cristofaro had moved to the property many years earlier, after the family's previous home was condemned as part of an urban renewal project.[5] Unfortunately, the shrubs were still destroyed during the demolition of the house, despite Michael Cristofaro's vehement protests.[6] The Cristofaros also persuaded the city to agree to erect a plaque near the site of their home in honor of Margherita Cristofaro, who had passed away during the long struggle, in 2003. Michael Cristofaro believes that her life was likely shortened by stress caused by the harassment the family endured.[7]

The Dery family members were able to stay in their homes until eighty-eight year old Wilhelmina Dery passed away in 2006. Their lengthy battle had at least achieved the goal of enabling her to live out her remaining days in the house where she was born and lived her whole life.[8] But, as in the case of Mrs. Cristofaro, the family was convinced that the stress caused by the litigation and the NLDC's efforts to force them to capitulate had shaved some years off of her life.[9] Ultimately, the last six remaining property owners received some $4.1 million in compensation payments for their land, far more than had been offered by the NLDC earlier.[10] The negative publicity created by the case led the city and state to be far more generous than they would have been otherwise. But it is questionable whether even this amount was sufficient to offset the material and psychological pain of the lengthy struggle they endured. The *Kelo* plaintiffs themselves believe that it was not.

Even years later, all of the *Kelo* plaintiffs I spoke with remain understandably bitter about their treatment by the city authorities and the NLDC. Michael Cristofaro describes the NLDC leadership as "heartless" people who would have "thrown us out on the street" if they could.[11]

The *Kelo* struggle and its aftermath was also an unhappy time for some of the participants on the other side. In 2001, NLDC chair Claire Gaudiani was forced to resign from her position as president of Connecticut College.[12] While the main cause was conflict with faculty over internal college issues, some of Gaudiani's opponents in the faculty and student body also cited her role in the New London condemnations.[13] More generally, the controversy over the New London takings damaged her previously positive reputation and public image.[14]

Peter Ellef, the influential adviser to Governor Rowland who played a key role in obtaining state government support for the NLDC project,[15] pled guilty to bribery charges in October 2005, part of a corruption scandal that brought down multiple high officials in the Rowland administration, including the governor himself, who was forced to resign in 2004.[16] Ellef had taken bribes in exchange for favorable treatment for a state contractor.[17] Although the scandal was unrelated to the *Kelo* takings, critics wondered whether Ellef's and Pfizer's role in the condemnations was part of the same pattern of collusion between state government and politically influential business interests.[18]

In 2010, Justice Richard Palmer, one of the members of the 4-3 majority that upheld the condemnations in the Connecticut Supreme Court, apologized to Susette Kelo for the ruling.[19] He later suggested that he would have voted differently had he known at the time that "the city's development plan had never materialized and, as a result, years later, the land at issue remains barren and wholly undeveloped."[20]

But Palmer also insisted that the Connecticut court "ultimately made the right decision in so far as it followed governing Supreme Court precedent."[21] This statement is correct in so far as it goes. But it elides the fact that Justice Palmer could have voted to strike down the law under the Connecticut state constitution, as the three dissenting justices did. Moreover, many of the shortcomings of the NLDC's development plan were already well known at the time and were extensively discussed by Justice Peter Zarella in his state supreme court dissent.[22] Had Palmer joined with Zarella and the other dissenters back in 2004, the condemnations could have been averted, and the case would likely never have reached the federal Supreme Court.

Palmer's apology did not impress the New London plaintiffs. Richard Beyer told me that he was "not interested" in Palmer's apology because "no apology in the world" could make up for what was done to the families displaced by the takings.[23] Susette Kelo herself said that "[i]t was nice he did it" but still "too little too late."[24] Bill Von Winkle commented that Palmer was "100 percent right, just a couple years late."[25] Frederick Paxton of the Coalition to Save Fort Trumbull Neighborhood was more forgiving, calling Palmer's apology "a wonderful thing [for the justice] to do."[26]

In early 2012, New London Mayor Daryl Justin Finizio also issued an apology to the displaced property owners, admitting "that mistakes were made," and that "our development strategy was flawed."[27] He has called the *Kelo* condemnations a "black stain" on the city and denounced the Supreme Court decision upholding them as a "corruption of the constitutional interpretation of public use."[28]

In the fall of 2013, Mayor Finizio proposed that the condemned property should be put to a true "public use," such as a publicly owned garage powered by environmentally conscious solar panels.[29] Whether this idea will turn out to be more viable than previous plans to use the property remains to be seen.

As of early 2015, almost ten years after the Supreme Court upheld the *Kelo* condemnations, the properties that were the focus of an epic legal battle remain empty and undeveloped.[30] Several plans to redevelop these lots have fallen through.[31] The only creatures making regular use of them in the intervening years have been a colony of feral cats.[32]

These failures were not simply caused by adverse publicity resulting from the public backlash against the Supreme Court ruling or by the recession and financial crisis that began in 2008. As a 2005 *New York Times* article noted, the failure was a result of "contract disputes and financial uncertainty" and the unwillingness of investors to commit to a flawed project.[33] As early as 2002, Pfizer had begun to lose interest in utilizing the new facilities expected to be built in the development area.[34] In 2009, the firm announced plans to close down its New London facility and began to transfer the employees working there elsewhere.[35] With Pfizer's departure, the city lost 1,400 jobs that state officials had attracted to the area by committing to redevelop Fort Trumbull in a way that suited the firm's needs.[36]

The city has managed to successfully redevelop the portion of the Fort Trumbull land that was previously part of the Naval Undersea Warfare Center closed in 1995. It is now a leased research and development center.[37] But that property already belonged to the city after the center had closed, and there was no need to use eminent domain to redevelop it.

Eventually, the condemned land will almost certainly be used for some productive purpose or other. In the meantime, however, it will have

FIGURE 9.1 Former site of Susette Kelo's house—May 2014. (Credit: Ilya Somin.)

FIGURE 9.2 Parcel 3 (former site of the Athenian, Cristofaro, and Von Winkle properties)—May 2014. (Credit: Ilya Somin.)

FIGURE 9.3 Feral cat on Parcel 4A (former site of eleven of the condemned properties), March 2011. (Credit: Jackson Kuhl.)

stood empty for a decade or even longer, depriving the community of the economic benefits of a productive use of the land and the city of potential property tax revenue. Even from the standpoint of economic development, without reference to constitutional considerations or the intrinsic value of property rights, the Fort Trumbull condemnations have done a lot more harm than good. Governor Rowland was right to predict that Pfizer's move would "change the landscape of this community," even if it is not yet clear whether he was also right to predict that the effects will really last "for the next 100 years."[38] So far, at least, the effects have been very different from those supporters of the project had hoped for.

The Future of *Kelo* and Public Use

If the future of the properties condemned in the *Kelo* litigation remains uncertain, the same can be said for the future of *Kelo* as a legal precedent.

The controversial nature of the decision makes it possible that it will someday be narrowed or overruled. In October 2011, Justice Antonin Scalia, who had been one of the *Kelo* dissenters, called on the Court to overrule the decision and stated that he "do[es] not think that the *Kelo* opinion is long for this world."[39] He called the decision one of the Court's biggest "mistakes of political judgment, of estimating how far . . . it could stretch beyond the text of the Constitution without provoking overwhelming public criticism and resistance."[40] Scalia reiterated his view that "*Kelo* will not survive" in early 2014.[41] As we have seen, even Justice John Paul Stevens, the author of the *Kelo* majority opinion, has admitted that the ruling was in part based on a significant error, though he continues to defend the bottom-line result.[42]

Will Kelo *Be Overruled?*

It is difficult to predict whether the *Kelo* decision will prove to be a lasting precedent or not. At this time, all that can be safely said is that the close division on the Court and the controversy the decision has engendered render it more vulnerable to overruling than most other important cases. Historical evidence suggests that close, controversial decisions are far more likely to be overruled or narrowed than ones that command large majorities on the Court.[43]

Four of the nine justices who participated in the *Kelo* decision have since left the Court and been replaced, including two dissenters and two members of the majority. Since neither member of the majority was replaced by a jurist likely to vote the other way,[44] it is doubtful whether there are currently five votes for overruling *Kelo*. On the other hand, Justice Kennedy's ambiguous concurring opinion suggests that he might be open to narrowing the reach of *Kelo* in a future case. It is also possible that the massive negative public reaction to *Kelo* or some other factor will eventually lead Kennedy to have a change of heart similar to that which Justice Sandra Day O'Connor apparently experienced between her authorship of the ultradeferential *Midkiff* decision in 1984 and her forceful dissent in *Kelo*.[45]

For the moment, federal judicial opinion on public use issues remains sharply divided along ideological lines, with most liberal judges supporting the broad interpretation of public use adopted in *Berman, Midkiff,* and *Kelo* and most conservatives supporting the positions of the *Kelo* dissenters. What is true of federal judges is also true of most legal scholars, as left of center legal academics mostly support *Kelo,* while conservative and libertarian ones have been far more critical. This is not a positive trend for those who hope for robust judicial enforcement of the Public Use Clause in the future. As a general rule, strong judicial enforcement of a constitutional right is unlikely to occur without at least some substantial bipartisan, cross-ideological support for it.[46]

But widespread liberal opposition to *Kelo* outside the Supreme Court and the halls of academia might lead this to change in the future. Over time, it is possible that more left of center federal judges and legal scholars will adopt a perspective on public use in line with that expressed by Ralph Nader, the NAACP, the late Jane Jacobs, and other left of center critics of the modern Supreme Court's ultradeferential approach to public use issues.[47] As we have seen, state supreme court decisions in several states have recently adopted a more restrictive approach to public use issues than has the federal Supreme Court, including in moderate to liberal states such as Illinois, Michigan, Ohio, Maryland, and New Jersey.[48] Perhaps the next generation of liberal federal judges will be open to similar arguments. A small number of left of center legal scholars have also argued for a more restrictive approach to public use in recent years.[49] Whether they continue to be unusual exceptions remains to be seen.

The Supreme Court has not taken any new public use cases since *Kelo.* Perhaps the justices simply do not wish to return to this field in the near future, just as they went over twenty years without deciding a major public use case in the years before *Kelo.* But the deep division in the lower courts over the meaning of *Kelo*'s pretext standard could well force the Court to take a case on that issue sometime in the next few years.[50] Justice Samuel Alito, the conservative jurist appointed to replace Justice O'Connor in 2005, has at least once voted to hear a case that would enable the Court to address the issue.[51] Given his public advocacy of overruling *Kelo,* Justice Scalia may potentially be interested in taking another public use case as well.

If the Court does someday consider overruling *Kelo,* and a majority concludes that the case was wrongly decided, it could readily choose to reverse based on the Court's own standards for rejecting erroneous precedents. The Court has stated that it will "overrule an erroneously decided precedent . . . if: (1) its foundations have been 'ero[ded] by subsequent decisions'; (2) it has been subject to 'substantial and continuing' criticism; and (3) it has not induced 'individual or societal reliance' that counsels against overturning" it.[52] An additional factor that the Court considers is whether the original decision was "well reasoned."[53]

Since *Kelo* is a recent decision and the Court has not decided any other public use cases since then, it has not yet been "eroded" by subsequent Supreme Court rulings. But few Supreme Court cases have been subjected to as much "substantial and continuing criticism" as *Kelo*. Four justices forcefully dissented from the ruling. This is a significant factor since the Court has indicated that the overruling of a flawed precedent is more defensible if the initial ruling was "decided by the narrowest of margins, over spirited dissents challenging [its] basic underpinnings."[54] In addition, every state supreme court to have considered the question has repudiated *Kelo* as a guide to the interpretation of its state constitution's public use clause.[55] And the Court's decision has attracted numerous critics from across the political spectrum, outside the judiciary.

The quality of a precedent's reasoning is also a crucial factor in determining whether it should be overruled. The *Kelo* majority opinion's reasoning has grave deficiencies, some of which have become even more apparent since 2005.[56] Even Justice John Paul Stevens, author of the Court's opinion, has admitted that its reasoning was based in part on an "embarrassing" error: the assumption that a series of late nineteenth- and early twentieth-century "substantive" due process Supreme Court decisions applying a highly deferential approach to state government takings were actually decided under the Takings Clause of the Fifth Amendment. Few important Supreme Court decisions are based on reasoning so dubious that the author of the majority opinion admits to making an "embarrassing" mistake.

In addition, *Kelo* represents an unusual anomaly in the Court's jurisprudence on the Bill of Rights. In sharp contrast to its treatment of nearly every other individual right enumerated in the first ten amendments, the Court's decision in *Kelo* allows the very same governments whose abuses the Public Use Clause is intended to constrain to define the scope of the rights that are to be protected.[57]

Because it was decided only a few years ago, *Kelo* has not yet generated significant "individual or societal reliance."[58] And as we have seen in chapters 5 and 7, the dominant trend of both state legislation and state judicial decisions has actually gone against *Kelo*, with many states banning economic development takings, and several state supreme courts repudiating *Kelo* as a model for interpreting their state constitutions.

In fairness, however, *Kelo*'s reasoning was in large part derivative of that of *Berman v. Parker,* the 1954 Supreme Court decision upholding the validity of blight condemnations.[59] There is a strong case for overruling *Berman* as well as *Kelo,* because it is incompatible with the best interpretation of the Public Use Clause from the standpoint of both originalism and living Constitution theory.[60] But there is little doubt that *Berman* has generated far more "societal reliance" than *Kelo* has, with all but a handful of states still permitting at least some blight condemnations.[61] A Court wary of overruling such a long-standing precedent could potentially adopt the approach taken by Justice Sandra Day O'Connor in her *Kelo* dissent, which would have invalidated economic development takings but allowed blight condemnations to continue.[62] Although this approach has some weaknesses, I believe it is still preferable to leaving *Kelo* intact and allowing government officials to condemn property for virtually any potential "public purpose."[63]

The Court is far from consistent in following its own precepts on the criteria for overruling precedent. And those criteria do not actually require it to overrule decisions that meet them. The fact that *Kelo* fits the criteria well does not necessarily mean that it will be reversed. But it does reinforce the conclusion that the ruling is more vulnerable to reversal than most important Supreme Court decisions.

The Ongoing Legal and Political Struggle over Property Rights and Eminent Domain

Whether or not the Supreme Court chooses to hear another public use case in the near future, it is safe to predict that the political and legal controversy over public use issues will continue. In waging that fight, property rights advocates would do well to learn some key lessons from the *Kelo* case and its aftermath.

An important positive lesson is that, for constitutional reform movements, legal action and political action are not mutually exclusive strategies, but rather mutually reinforcing. Without the publicity generated by the *Kelo* case, there would never have been a massive political backlash that attracted widespread public attention to the problem of eminent domain abuse and generated numerous reform laws, some of which have greatly increased protection for property rights. At the same time, the *Kelo* case would not have gotten as far as it did if not for the careful work of a political movement that sought to make judicial protection for property rights more intellectually and politically respectable.[64]

If the Supreme Court someday overrules *Kelo,* it may be in part because of the hostile public reaction to the case. While the Court does not simply "follow the election returns," public opinion does significantly influence its decisions over time.[65] At the very least, the justices are less likely to hesitate in declaring economic development takings unconstitutional if they know that majority public opinion will be with them.

Even if future litigation fails to achieve the goal of getting *Kelo* overruled, it could potentially reinvigorate the property rights movement politically by attracting new public attention to the issue of eminent domain abuse. The *Kelo* backlash has begun to wane, with public attention moving on to other issues.[66] But another highly publicized case could refocus the public mind on the issue, especially if it reaches the Supreme Court and thereby attracts national media attention, as *Kelo* did. For this reason, among others, property rights advocates such as the Institute for Justice and the Pacific Legal Foundation have continued to look for potential cases that might serve as vehicles for pushing the public use issue further. They understand that they cannot rest on their laurels and that future progress depends on finding cases that can influence both judicial and public opinion.

The mutually reinforcing relationship between legal and political action is not unique to the property rights movement, of course. It was equally evident in the strategies adopted by previous movements seeking an expansion of constitutional rights, including the civil rights movement, the women's rights movement, the gun rights movement, and most recently the gay and lesbian community's struggle to secure legal recognition for same-sex marriage.[67] The strategy that the libertarian Institute for Justice pursued in *Kelo* and other cases was adapted from the methods pioneered by an earlier generation of liberal legal reformers. Like them, IJ seeks cases that can be effective in both the courtroom and the court of public opinion.[68]

A less hopeful lesson of *Kelo* is that the political process often cannot be relied on to protect even those constitutional rights that enjoy strong support from majority public opinion. In such cases, judicial intervention may still be a vital backstop to prevent rights violations facilitated by widespread political ignorance. Over time, political mobilization can help generate the necessary judicial intervention, but not render it completely unnecessary.

Perhaps the most important long-term consequence of *Kelo* was the breakdown of the post–New Deal consensus on judicial review of public use issues. Although the reigning orthodoxy in favor of judicial deference had begun to be challenged in the 1980s and 1990s,[69] most jurists and academic experts still considered it to be overwhelmingly dominant and obviously correct. *Kelo* dramatically demonstrated that such complacency was misplaced. The close 5-4 division in the Supreme Court and the negative reaction of public and elite opinion definitively showed that the meaning of public use is far from settled. This lesson was further underscored by the negative reaction to *Kelo* of those state supreme courts that repudiated it as a model for the interpretation of their state constitutional public use clauses.

Even a decade after the Supreme Court's decision the *Kelo* story still attracts widespread interest. It continues to resonate with activists and people interested in property rights issues in the United States and abroad. As this book goes to press, film producers Ted and Courtney Balaker are in the process of making a feature film based on the case, one that is likely to portray the plaintiffs sympathetically.[70] The continuing controversy surrounding the case further diminishes the likelihood that the post-New Deal conventional wisdom on public use will regain its previous dominance.

Defenders of the broad interpretation of public use are far from vanquished. Their position did, after all, prevail in the Supreme Court. And it still retains the support of numerous outstanding jurists and academics. But it has lost the privileged status of largely unquestioned orthodoxy. No longer can it be said that the broad view of public use "holds the field completely," as one scholar wrote in 1996.[71]

If the broad view of public use has lost ground, the narrow view has a long way to go to achieve the kind of dominance once enjoyed by its rival. Even if *Kelo* does get overruled, that would not necessarily lead to the complete establishment of the narrow view, which would also require overruling *Berman* and *Midkiff.* The former, at least, is a well-established precedent that can only be dislodged with great difficulty. Despite their many other disagreements, eight of the nine justices who heard the *Kelo* case still accepted its validity.[72]

But while *Berman* is safe from serious challenge in the near future, the shakiness of *Kelo* might over time infect it as well. Most of the arguments against *Kelo,* both originalist and living Constitution, also apply to *Berman.* Similarly, most of the pragmatic and moral objections to economic development takings also apply against blight condemnations. As a matter of technical legal doctrine, a decision overruling *Kelo* need not imperil *Berman*. But, in practice, any such ruling will, at the very least, raise questions about *Berman's* ultimate validity.

Even if *Kelo* and *Berman* are eventually overruled and the narrow definition of public use is restored, that will not completely put an end to the problem of harmful and abusive takings. Narrow public use takings can also sometimes cause more harm than good and enrich powerful interest groups at the expense of the general public.[73] Curbing such abuses will sometimes be difficult, in part because this is an area where—unlike in the case of blight and economic development takings—it may be impossible to dispense with the use of eminent domain entirely. Scholars and policy makers should search for new ways to address this issue. But though the reversal of decisions like *Kelo* and *Berman* is not a panacea for all the dangers of eminent domain, it would represent a major step forward.

Although this book is focused on eminent domain and public use issues in the United States, it is important to recognize that forcible displacement of property owners for economic development purposes is a major issue in other countries as well. In many developing nations, governments often displace poor and politically weak populations to make way for development projects.[74] As in the United States, such policies are often justified by the supposed need for expert government planning in order to alleviate poverty and promote economic growth.[75]

In China, some forty million rural farmers have been forced from their homes by economic development projects over the last several decades.[76] Approximately 1.25 million people were forcibly displaced just to facilitate construction for the 2008 Olympics in Beijing.[77] Such forcible displacements have been a major subject of public controversy in China, even in spite of the authoritarian nature of the government and its efforts to restrict dissent. The U.S. debate over *Kelo* and eminent domain more generally has attracted the attention of Chinese scholars and activists. I first became aware of this when—much to my surprise—my previous writings on the subject led to numerous inquiries from Chinese academics, an invitation to be a visiting professor at a Chinese university, and even an interview request from a Chinese television network.

The appropriate scope of public use restrictions on takings in other countries is a question beyond the focus of this book. But Americans should keep in mind that the treatment of these issues in the United States may have example effects beyond our borders. Political and legal battles over property rights and eminent domain have an international dimension as well as a purely domestic one.

In his 2006 book *The Audacity of Hope,* the soon-to-be President Barack Obama wrote that "[o]ur Constitution places the ownership of private property at the very heart of our system of liberty."[78] For far too long, unfortunately, the property rights protected by the Public Use Clause have been shunted to the furthest periphery of constitutional jurisprudence. The Supreme Court denied them even the most minimal constitutional protection, leaving them to the mercy of the very government officials that they were intended to constrain. This neglect was believed necessary to empower the democratic process and expert government planners to promote economic growth and protect the poor and vulnerable against the evils of blight and urban decay.

But far from facilitating social progress, the judiciary's neglect of property rights allowed powerful interest groups to use the grasping hand of government to expropriate property from the poor, minorities, and the politically weak. Far from promoting prosperity, it has all too often exacerbated the very economic deterioration it was intended to prevent. The *Kelo* case was by no means the first manifestation of these trends and certainly not the most egregious. But it did make them clear to far more people than ever before.

The grasping hand of eminent domain is far from shackled. But its iron fist has seen its legitimacy challenged. In many states, it is now subject to tighter restraint than previously. Whether that trend will continue remains to be seen. *Kelo* was far from the end of the struggle to confine the grasping hand to its proper, strictly limited, place. But by shattering the dominance of a misguided orthodoxy, it achieved a breakthrough that may in time be remembered as the end of the beginning.

Appendix A

Additional Tables

TABLE A1 **Post-*Kelo* Reform in States Ranked by Number of "Threatened" Private-to-Private Condemnations**

State	Number of Threatened Takings[1]	Effectiveness of Reform
Florida	2,055	Effective (L & LR)
Maryland	1,110	Ineffective (L)
California	635	Ineffective (L & CR)
New Jersey	589	Ineffective (L)
Missouri	437	Ineffective (L)
Ohio	331	Ineffective (L)
Michigan	173	Effective (L & LR)
Utah	167	Enacted Prior to *Kelo*
Kentucky	161	Ineffective (L)
Texas	118	Ineffective (L & LR)
Colorado	114	Ineffective (L)
Pennsylvania	108	Effective (L)
New York	89	No Reform
Minnesota	83	Effective (L)
Rhode Island	65	Ineffective (L)
Connecticut	61	Ineffective (L)
Indiana	51	Effective (L)
Arkansas	40	No Reform
Tennessee	37	Ineffective (L)
Virginia	27	Effective (L & LR)
Nevada	15	Effective (L & CR)
Vermont	15	Ineffective (L)
West Virginia	12	Ineffective (L)
Wisconsin	12	Effective (L)
Nebraska	11	Ineffective (L)
Arizona	10	Effective (CR)
Illinois	9	Ineffective (L)
Kansas	7	Effective (L)
South Carolina	7	Ineffective (LR)

(*continued*)

TABLE A1 **(continued)**

State	Number of Threatened Takings[1]	Effectiveness of Reform
Hawaii	5	No Reform
Massachusetts	4	No Reform
Oregon	2	Effective (CR)
Delaware	0	Effective (L)
Georgia	0	Effective (L & LR)
Idaho	0	Ineffective (L)
South Dakota	0	Effective (L)
Wyoming	0	Effective (L)
Alabama	0	Effective (L)
Alaska	0	Ineffective (L)
Iowa	0	Ineffective (L)
Louisiana	0	Effective (LR)
Maine	0	Ineffective (L)
Mississippi	0	Effective (CR)
Montana	0	Ineffective (L)
New Hampshire	0	Effective (L & LR)
New Mexico	0	Effective (L)
North Carolina	0	Ineffective (L)
North Dakota	0	Effective (CR)
Oklahoma	0	No Reform
Washington	0	No Reform

L = Reform enacted by state legislature; CR = Reform enacted by citizen-initiated referendum; LR = Reform enacted by legislature-initiated referendum.
1. Dana Berliner, *Public Power, Private Gain: A Five-Year, State-by-State Report Examining the Abuse of Eminent Domain* (2003), http://www.castlecoalition.org/pdf/report/ED_report.pdf. This data on known eminent domain condemnations by state includes developments from 1998 to 2002. Ibid., 8–9.

TABLE A2 **Post-*Kelo* Reform in States Ranked by Number of Private-to-Private Condemnations per 1 Million People**

State	2005 Population[1]	Takings[2]/1M people	Effectiveness of Reform
Pennsylvania	12,429,616	202.5	Effective (L)
Kansas	2,744,687	56.5	Effective (L)
Maryland	5,600,388	22.7	Ineffective (L)
Michigan	10,120,860	13.6	Effective (L & LR)
Rhode Island	1,076,189	11.2	Ineffective (L)
Connecticut	3,510,297	8.8	Ineffective (L)
Ohio	11,464,042	7.9	Ineffective (L)
Virginia	7,567,465	7.7	Effective (L &LR)
Oklahoma	3,547,884	6.5	No Reform
California	36,132,147	6.2	Ineffective (L & CR)
New Jersey	8,717,925	5.9	Ineffective (L)
Tennessee	5,962,959	4.9	Ineffective (L)
Colorado	4,665,177	4.9	Ineffective (L)
West Virginia	1,816,856	4.4	Ineffective (L)
Florida	17,789,864	3.8	Effective (L & LR)

TABLE A2 **(continued)**

State	2005 Population[1]	Takings[2]/1M people	Effectiveness of Reform
Missouri	5,800,310	3.1	Ineffective (L)
New York	19,254,630	3	No Reform
Arizona	5,939,292	1.9	Effective (CR)
Minnesota	5,132,799	1.8	Effective (L)
Alabama	4,557,808	1.8	Effective (L)
Washington	6,287,759	1.7	No Reform
Kentucky	4,173,405	1.7	Ineffective (L)
North Dakota	636,677	1.6	Effective (CR)
Maine	1,321,505	1.5	Ineffective (L)
Iowa	2,966,334	1.3	Ineffective (L)
Nevada	2,414,807	1.2	Effective (L & CR)
Louisiana	4,523,628	1.1	Effective (LR)
Mississippi	2,921,088	1	Effective (CR)
Massachusetts	6,398,743	0.8	No Reform
Illinois	12,763,371	0.6	Ineffective (L)
Indiana	6,271,973	0.6	Effective (L)
Nebraska	1,758,787	0.6	Ineffective (L)
Texas	22,859,968	0.5	Ineffective (L & LR)
Arkansas	2,779,154	0.4	No Reform
North Carolina	8,683,242	0.1	Ineffective (L)
Alaska	663,661	0	Ineffective (L)
Delaware	843,524	0	Effective (L)
Georgia	9,072,576	0	Effective (L & LR)
Idaho	1,429,096	0	Ineffective (L)
South Dakota	775,933	0	Effective (L)
Wyoming	509,294	0	Effective (L)
Hawaii	1,275,194	0	No Reform
Montana	935,670	0	Ineffective (L)
New Hampshire	1,309,940	0	Effective (L & LR)
New Mexico	1,928,384	0	Effective (L)
Oregon	3,641,056	0	Effective (CR)
South Carolina	4,255,083	0	Ineffective (LR)
Utah	2,469,585	0	Enacted Prior to *Kelo*
Vermont	623,050	0	Ineffective (L)
Wisconsin	5,536,201	0	Effective (L)

L = Reform enacted by state legislature; CR = Reform enacted by citizen-initiated referendum; LR = Reform enacted by legislature-initiated referendum.
1. United States Census Bureau, *Annual Estimates of the Population for the United States and States, and for Puerto Rico: April 1, 2000 to July 1, 2005* (2005), available at http://www.census.gov/popest/states/NST-ann -est2005.html.
2. Some takings affected more than one property.

State	2005 Population[1]	Threatened Takings[2] /1M people	Effectiveness of Reform
Maryland	5,600,388	198.2	Ineffective (L)
Florida	17,789,864	115.5	Effective (L & LR)
Missouri	5,800,310	75.3	Ineffective (L)
Utah	2,469,585	67.6	Enacted Prior to Kelo
New Jersey	8,717,925	67.6	Ineffective (L)
Rhode Island	1,076,189	60.4	Ineffective (L)
Kentucky	4,173,405	38.6	Ineffective (L)
Ohio	11,464,042	28.9	Ineffective (L)
Colorado	4,665,177	24.4	Ineffective (L)
Vermont	623,050	24.1	Ineffective (L)
California	36,132,147	17.6	Ineffective (L & CR)
Connecticut	3,510,297	17.4	Ineffective (L)
Michigan	10,120,860	17.1	Effective (L & LR)
Minnesota	5,132,799	16.2	Effective (L)
Arkansas	2,779,154	14.4	No Reform
Pennsylvania	12,429,616	8.7	Effective (L)
Indiana	6,271,973	8.1	Effective (L)
West Virginia	1,816,856	6.6	Ineffective (L)
Nebraska	1,758,787	6.3	Ineffective (L)
Nevada	2,414,807	6.2	Effective (L &CR)
Tennessee	5,962,959	6.2	Ineffective (L)
Texas	22,859,968	5.2	Ineffective (L & LR)
New York	19,254,630	4.6	No Reform
Hawaii	1,275,194	3.9	No Reform
Virginia	7,567,465	3.6	Effective (L & LR)
Kansas	2,744,687	2.6	Effective (L)
Wisconsin	5,536,201	2.2	Effective (L)
Arizona	5,939,292	1.7	Effective (CR)
South Carolina	4,255,083	1.6	Ineffective (LR)
Illinois	12,763,371	0.7	Ineffective (L)
Massachusetts	6,398,743	0.6	No Reform
Oregon	3,641,056	0.5	Effective (CR)
Delaware	843,524	0	Effective (L)
Georgia	9,072,576	0	Effective (L & LR)
Idaho	1,429,096	0	Ineffective (L)
South Dakota	775,933	0	Effective (L)
Wyoming	509,294	0	Effective (L)
Alabama	4,557,808	0	Effective (L)
Alaska	663,661	0	Ineffective (L)
Iowa	2,966,334	0	Ineffective (L)
Louisiana	4,523,628	0	Effective (LR)
Maine	1,321,505	0	Ineffective (L)
Mississippi	2,921,088	0	Effective (CR)
Montana	935,670	0	Ineffective (L)
New Hampshire	1,309,940	0	Effective (L & LR)
New Mexico	1,928,384	0	Effective (L)
North Carolina	8,683,242	0	Ineffective (L)
North Dakota	636,677	0	Effective (CR)
Oklahoma	3,547,884	0	No Reform
Washington	6,287,759	0	No Reform

L = Reform enacted by state legislature; CR = Reform enacted by citizen-initiated referendum; LR = Reform enacted by legislature-initiated referendum.
1. United States Census Bureau, *Annual Estimates of the Population for the United States and States, and for Puerto Rico*.
2. Some takings affected more than one property. Berliner, *Public Power, Private Gain*.

Appendix B

2007 *Saint Index Survey Questions on Post-*Kelo *Reform*[1]

Question 9.

In 2005, the US Supreme Court ruled that the government could take private property by eminent domain to give it to another private owner to promote economic development. Since that ruling, some states have passed new laws that restrict the government's power to take private property. Do you happen to know if your state is one of those that has passed such a law?

A. Yes, my state has enacted at least one such law
B. No, it has not enacted any laws like that
C. Don't know

Question 10 (asked only of those who chose answer A on Question 9).

Do you think that the new laws in your state will be effective in preventing the condemnation of private property for economic development?

A. Very effective
B. Somewhat effective
C. Mostly ineffective
D. Completely ineffective
E. Don't know

Note: For purposes of table 6.1, I counted the first two answers as "effective" and the second two as "ineffective" and marked "don't know"

as automatically mistaken. Respondents in states that had passed ineffective reforms were given credit for "correct" answers if they picked
either C or D. Those in states with effective laws similarly counted as
"correct" if they chose either A or B.

Notes

Introduction

1. Barack Obama, *The Audacity of Hope: Thoughts on Reclaiming the American Dream* (New York: Crown, 2006), 149.

2. Adam Smith, *An Inquiry into the Nature and Causes of the Wealth of Nations* (Chicago: University of Chicago Press, 1976 [1776]), 477.

3. 545 U.S. 469 (2005).

4. Ibid., 476–79.

5. *Hawaii Housing Authority v. Midkiff,* 467 U.S. 229, 241 (1984).

6. See discussion in chapter 4.

7. *Kelo,* 545 U.S. at 476–81.

8. Ibid., 518 (Thomas, J., dissenting).

9. See chapter 5.

10. See chapter 7.

11. This book was already in press when I learned of another forthcoming book on *Kelo,* a volume written by political scientist Guy F. Burnett. See Burnett, *The Safeguard of Liberty and Property: The Supreme Court,* Kelo. v. New London, *and the Takings Clause* (Lexington Books, forthcoming). I therefore cannot analyze its contributions to the literature in detail. It is, however, worth noting that Burnett's work does not consider most of the issues addressed in chapters 2–3 and 5–8 of the present book. In the section on relevance of originalism to public use (ibid., ch. 7), Burnett discusses only original intent originalism, while overlooking original meaning (the dominant school of originalism in recent decades). Burnett also neglects the holdout problem, the argument most commonly advanced as a justification for the use of eminent domain for private development. The present book extensively analyzes the holdout problem in chapter 3.

12. *Kelo,* 545 U.S. at 478 (quoting *Kelo v. City of New London,* 843 A.2d 500, 536 (Conn. 2004)). For the current state of Fort Trumbull, see the discussion in the conclusion of this book.

13. See, e.g., Robert D. Cooter and Hans-Bernd Schafer, *Solomon's Knot: How Law Can End the Poverty of Nations* (Princeton, NJ: Princeton University Press, 2012), ch. 6; Hernando de Soto, *The Mystery of Capital: Why Capitalism Triumphs in the West and Fails Everywhere Else* (New York: Basic Books, 2000), 49–63.

14. U.S. Const. amend. V.

15. For a broad view of what qualifies as a taking, see, e.g., Richard A. Epstein, *Takings: Private Property and the Power of Eminent Domain* (Cambridge, MA: Harvard University Press, 1985); for a narrow one, see, e.g., William Michael Treanor, "The Original Understanding of the Takings Clause and the Political Process," 95 *Columbia Law Review* 782 (1995).

16. For a well-written journalistic account that goes into greater detail, see Jeff Benedict, *Little Pink House: A True Story of Defiance and Courage* (New York: Grand Central Publishing, 2009).

17. U.S. Const. amend. XIV, § 1.

18. See, e.g., John Hart Ely, *Democracy and Distrust: A Theory of Judicial Review* (Cambridge, MA: Harvard University Press, 1980).

19. See, e.g., Cass R. Sunstein, *A Constitution of Many Minds: Why the Founding Document Doesn't Mean What It Meant Before* (Princeton, NJ: Princeton University Press, 2009); David A. Strauss, *The Living Constitution* (New York: Oxford University Press, 2010).

20. See, e.g., Larry D. Kramer, *The People Themselves: Popular Constitutionalism and Judicial Review* (Cambridge, MA, Harvard University Press, 2004); Matthew D. Adler, "Popular Constitutionalism and the Rule of Recognition: Whose Practices Ground U.S. Law?" 100 *Northwestern University Law Review* 719 (2006); Jack M. Balkin & Reva B. Siegel, "Principles, Practices, and Social Movements," 154 *University of Pennsylvania Law Review* 926 (2006).

21. See Ronald Dworkin, *Law's Empire* (Cambridge, MA: Harvard University Press, 1986), 377–99; Ronald Dworkin, *Freedom's Law: The Moral Reading of the American Constitution* (Cambridge, MA: Harvard University Press, 1996).

22. See John Paul Stevens, "*Kelo*, Popularity, and Substantive Due Process," Albritton Lecture, University of Alabama School, of Law, Nov. 16, 2011, at 16, available at http://www.supremecourt.gov/publicinfo/speeches/1.pdf.

23. *Kelo v. City of New London,* 545 U.S. 469, 483 (2005). The claim that the result in *Kelo* was required by a century of precedent was taken up by leading academic defenders of the decision as well. See, e.g., Kermit Roosevelt, *The Myth of Judicial Activism: Making Sense of Supreme Court Decisions* (New Haven, CT: Yale University Press, 2008), 138 (claiming that *Kelo* follows from "a line of cases extending back over a hundred years"); David Barron, "Eminent Domain Is Dead! (Long Live Eminent Domain!)," *Boston Globe*, Apr. 16, 2006, (claiming that it was backed by "a century of precedent.").

24. See *City of Norwood v. Horney*, 853 N.E.2d 1115, 1141 (Ohio 2006) (holding that "economic development" alone does not justify condemnation); *Board of County Commissioners of Muskogee County. v. Lowery*, 136 P.3d 639, 653–54 (Okla. 2006) (holding that "economic development" is not a "public purpose" under the Oklahoma State Constitution, and rejecting Kelo as a guide to interpretation of Oklahoma's State Constitution); *Benson v. State*, 710 N.W.2d 131, 146 (S.D. 2006) (concluding that the South Dakota Constitution gives property owners broader protection than *Kelo*).

25. 348 U.S. 26 (1954).

26. *Kelo*, 545 U.S. at 477–78.

Chapter One

1. Jeff Benedict, *Little Pink House: A True Story of Defiance and Courage* (New York: Grand Central Publishing, 2009).

2. Benedict, *Little Pink House*, 15–16.

3. Interview with Richard Beyer, Dec. 13, 2013.

4. Ibid.

5. Benedict, *Little Pink House*, 36–37; interview with Bill Von Winkle, Apr. 15, 2014.

6. Interview with Bill Von Winkle.

7. Ibid.

8. Benedict, *Little Pink House*, 5–8, 11–14.

9. Interview with Susette Kelo, Sept. 4, 2013.

10. See Benedict, *Little Pink House*.

11. Benedict, *Little Pink House*, 288. The house was officially listed in his mother's name. Interview with Scott Bullock and Dana Berliner, Feb. 7, 2014.

12. Interview with Michael Cristofaro, July 12, 2013.

13. Ibid.

14. E-mail from Michael Cristofaro to Ilya Somin, May 10, 2014.

15. Interview with Matthew Dery, July 31, 2013.

16. Ibid.

17. Ibid. See also Benedict, *Little Pink House*, 88.

18. Interview with Richard Beyer, July 13, 2013.

19. Benedict, *Little Pink House*, 45–46.

20. *Kelo v. City of New London*, 545 U.S. 469, 473 (2005).

21. Benedict, *Little Pink House*, 17–19.

22. Ibid., 9–10.

23. Ibid., 19–21.

24. Ibid., 24.

25. Ibid., 26–29.

26. Ibid., 28–29.

27. Ibid., 41–44.

28. Ibid., 44–51. Ellef later became the governor's chief of staff.

29. Ibid., 50–51.

30. Ted Mann, "Pfizer's Fingerprints on Fort Trumbull Plan," *The Day*, Oct. 16, 2005, http://www.theday.com/article/20051016/BIZ04/911119999.

31. Ibid.

32. Ibid.

33. Ibid.

34. Ibid.

35. Ibid.

36. Ibid.

37. Interview with Scott Bullock and Dana Berliner, Feb. 7, 2014.

38. Benedict, *Little Pink House*, 126, 134.

39. Quoted in ibid., 219.

40. Quoted in Lucette Lagnado, "Why New London, Conn., Still Waits for Its Ship to Come in: Pfizer's Vision for a Research Center Remains Far from Realized in Bitter Town," *Wall Street Journal*, Sept. 10, 2002.

41. Quoted in Ivar Peterson, "There Goes the Old Neighborhood, to Revitalization," *New York Times*, Jan. 30, 2005.

42. Interview with Richard Beyer.

43. Interview with Bill Von Winkle.

44. Benedict, *Little Pink House*, 41–51.

45. Interview with Claire Gaudiani, July 12, 2013. Unfortunately, Ms. Gaudiani would not permit me to quote the specific statements she made in the interview, preferring to leave them off the record. I believe, however, that it is permissible for me to record my own subjective impression on this point.

46. See discussion of this problem as it applies to the context of eminent domain, in chapter 4.

47. Quoted in Judy Benson, "Pfizer Digs in for Long Haul: Ground Officially Broken for $220 Million New London Project," *The Day*, Sept. 2, 1998.

48. Quoted in ibid.

49. New London Development Corporation, Fort Trumbull Municipal Development Plan, Aug. 1999.

50. Ibid., 5-1—5-4.

51. Benedict, *Little Pink House*, 146. By this point, Beachy was no longer the mayor but was still a member of the city council. He became mayor again in 2002.

52. For a detailed account, see ibid., chaps. 14–16.

53. Quoted in George Lefcoe, "Jeff Benedict's *Little Pink House*: The Back Story of the *Kelo* Case," 42 *Connecticut Law Review* 925, 941 n.85 (2010).

54. Ibid., 941.

55. U.S. Supreme Court Oral Argument Transcript, *Kelo v. City of New London*, No. 04-108, 2005 WL 529436, at *27 (argued Feb. 22, 2005).

56. Heather Vogell, "Fort Trumbull Residents Say they Want to Stay Put: Most in Favor of Plans for Revitalization, but Not if It Means Moving," *The Day*, Jan. 6, 1999 (emphasis in the original).

57. E.g., interview with Richard Beyer; interview with Susette Kelo; interview with Matthew Dery.

58. Interview with Marguerite Marley, July 23, 2013.

59. Benedict, *Little Pink House*, 216; interview with Bill Von Winkle.

60. Interview with Bill Von Winkle.

61. Ibid.

62. Interview with Richard Beyer.

63. Interview with Matthew Dery.

64. Interview with Michael Cristofaro.

65. Interview with Susette Kelo.

66. Benedict, *Little Pink House*, 288.

67. Interview with Bill Von Winkle.

68. Interview with Marguerite Marley.

69. Ibid.

70. Lucette Lagnado, "Why New London, Conn., Still Waits for its Ship to Come in: Pfizer's Vision for a Research Center Remains far from Realized in Bitter Town," *Wall Street Journal*, Sept. 10, 2002.

71. Ibid.

72. Quoted in Stan DeCoster, "The Battle of Eminent Domain: A 2005 Supreme Court Ruling Continues to Spark Debate in the College's Backyard," *Connecticut College Magazine*, Fall 2006, available at http://www.conncoll.edu /camelweb/index.cfm?fuseaction=publications&circuit=cconline&function =view&uid=21&id=419821961. On Sawyer's environmental lawsuit, see Benedict, *Little Pink House*, 162–63, 274–81.

73. Quoted in DeCoster, "The Battle of Eminent Domain."

74. Heather Vogell, "There Goes the Neighborhood: Residents Watch Redevelopment Devour Fort Trumbull Homes," *The Day*, Feb. 20, 1999.

75. Interview with Michael Cristofaro.

76. The *Kelo* plaintiffs themselves concede that some residents were willing to do so. Interview with Richard Beyer.

77. The Guretskys were in a somewhat different position from the other six property owners because the NLDC chose not to file an eminent domain action at the same time as the other six owners, due to the fact that their property was involved in a bankruptcy proceeding. *Kelo v. City of New London* (Conn. Super. Ct.), Plaintiff's Post-Trial Brief, Nov. 5, 2001, at 8–9. But they still were official parties to the case throughout, and were forced to give up their land after the federal Supreme Court ruled against the property owners.

78. Interview with Richard Beyer.

79. Interview with Matthew Dery; interview with Michael Cristofaro.

80. *Kelo v. City of New London,* 545 U.S. 469, 470 (2005).

81. Benedict, *Little Pink House,* 72–73, 81–83.

82. Quoted in Heather Vogell, "Will the NLDC Gain Broad Powers to Condemn Property?" *The Day,* June 13, 1999.

83. Quoted in Ibid.

84. Benedict, *Little Pink House,* 134–39; Interview with Frederick Paxton, June 11, 2014; interview with Peter Kreckovic, August 7, 2014.

85. For a detailed account of these efforts, see Benedict, *Little Pink House,* 123–63.

86. Ibid., 134–35; interview with Frederick Paxton.

87. Interview with Frederick Paxton.

88. Ibid.

89. Ibid., 65–66.

90. Interview with Richard Beyer; interview with Michael Cristofaro. One lawyer who turned down Beyer despite her sympathy for his cause recalled that she refused because the case was such an "uphill battle" that she "would not have felt comfortable taking Mr. Beyer's money." Interview with Margaret "Peggy" Little, Nov. 20, 2014.

91. Interview with Richard Beyer.

92. For a good discussion of the Institute for Justice's origins and objectives, see Steven M. Teles, *The Rise of the Conservative Legal Movement: The Battle for Control of the Law* (Princeton, NJ: Princeton University Press, 2008).

93. Interview with Peter Kreckovic, August 7, 2014; Benedict, *Little Pink House,* 157–58. Frederick Paxton confirms that it was Kreckovic who took the initiative to contact the Institute. Interview with Frederick Paxton.

94. *CRDA v. Banin,* 727 A.2d 102 (N.J. Super. Ct. 1998).

95. See the discussion of these cases in chapter 2.

96. Interview with Dana Berliner and Scott Bullock, June 11, 2012.

97. This paragraph summarizes points that Berliner and Bullock expressed to me in our first interview (ibid.).

98. 348 U.S. 26 (1954).

99. On this aspect of the Institute for Justice's strategy, see Teles, *Rise of the Conservative Legal Movement,* 244–46.

100. Quoted in ibid., 244.

101. Interview with Scott Bullock and Dana Berliner, June 11, 2012.

102. Interview with Michael Cristofaro; interview with Richard Beyer; interview with Matthew Dery; interview with Susette Kelo; interview with Bill Von Winkle.

103. Interview with Susette Kelo.

104. Interview with Bill Von Winkle.

105. Interview with Peter Kreckovic.

106. Interview with Scott Bullock, July 18, 2013.

107. Interview with Susette Kelo.

108. Interview with Matthew Dery.

109. Interview with Bill Von Winkle.

110. Quoted in *Kelo v. City of New London*, 843 A.2d 500, 537 (Conn. 2004), *aff'd*, 545 U.S. 469 (2005).

111. Benedict, *Little Pink House*, 261–63.

112. *Kelo v. City of New London*, 2002 Conn. Super. Lexis 789 (Conn. Super. Ct. 2002).

113. Ibid., *77–100.

114. Ibid., *111.

115. Ibid., *125.

116. See discussion above.

117. *Kelo*, 2002 Conn. Super. Lexis 789, at *231.

118. Ibid., *225–27.

119. Benedict, *Little Pink House*, 269.

120. Ibid.

121. *Kelo*, 2002 Conn. Super. Lexis 789, at *196–222.

122. Benedict, *Little Pink House*, 272.

123. Ibid., 271–72.

124. See, e.g., Lefcoe, "Jeff Benedict's Little Pink House," 944–47.

125. Benedict, *Little Pink House*, 272.

126. Ibid.

127. George Lefcoe argues that this was unlikely, because the NLDC would have had only nine months to make the necessary revisions. But even he concedes that the New London city council could have voted to extend the deadline. Lefcoe, "Jeff Benedict's Little Pink House," 946–47. Moreover, the NLDC and the city could simply have developed a new plan by the same process as the original one.

128. Quoted in Kathleen Edgecomb, "Vote Expected in New London, Conn., on Legal Fate of Four Neighborhood Homes," *The Day*, Mar. 15, 2002.

129. Interview with Matthew Dery.

130. Ibid.

131. Von Winkle told me that "you couldn't trust anything they [the NLDC] said." Interview with Bill Von Winkle.

132. Interview with Matthew Dery; interview with Bill Von Winkle.

133. Interview with Scott Bullock and Dana Berliner, Feb. 7, 2014.

134. Ibid.

135. *Kelo v. City of New London*, 843 A.2d 500, 500 (Conn. 2004), aff'd 545 U.S. 469 (2005).

136. Ibid., 519–36.

137. Ibid., 553–63, 569–74.

138. Ibid., 587 (Zarella, J., dissenting).

139. Ibid., 585.

140. Ibid., 596.

141. Ibid.

142. Ibid., 596–97.

143. Ibid., 597–602.

144. Ibid., 598–99.

145. See discussion in the conclusion.

146. *Kelo,* 843 A.2d at 521–22.

147. Ibid.

148. See *Kelo v. City of New London,* 843 A.2d 500 (Conn. 2004), Plaintiffs' Br. at 15–18. For Zarella's reliance on state precedent, see *Kelo,* 843 A.2d at 585–90.

149. Wesley W. Horton, *The History of the Connecticut Supreme Court,* (Thomson/West, 2008), 308.

150. Ibid. Horton also emphasized this point to me in one of our interviews. Interview with Wesley Horton, June 9, 2014.

151. See, e.g., *See Kelo v. City of New London,* 843 A.2d 500 (Conn. 2004),, Plaintiffs' Br. at 15-18.

152. Interview with Wesley Horton, July 15, 2013.

153. *Bugryn v. City of Bristol,* 774 A.2d 1042 (Conn. 2001). Ironically, Horton's client in the earlier case was strongly opposed to the New London takings and eventually joined an amicus brief supporting the property owners in the case. See Patricia Salkin Laura A. Lucero, and Allyson Phillips., "The Friends of the Court: The Role of Amicus Curiae in *Kelo v. City of New London,*" in *Eminent Domain Use and Abuse:* Kelo *in Context, ed.* Dwight H. Merriam and Mary Massaro Ross (Chicago: American Bar Association, 2006), 187–88 n.83.

154. Interview with Wesley Horton, July 15, 2013.

155. See chapter 2.

156. 467 U.S. 229 (1984). See the discussion of the *Midkiff* case in chapter 2.

157. See, e.g, Peterson, "There Goes the Old Neighborhood, to Revitalization," a detailed *New York Times* article about the case published in January 2005. The Westlaw data base of US newspapers includes 230 articles discussing *Kelo* published between the time the Supreme Court decided to hear the case on September 28, 2004 and the day before the Supreme Court issued its decision on June 23, 2005. Search conducted in the Westlaw data base of US Newspapers, Aug. 22, 2014. 122 of the articles appeared even before the Court heard oral argument on February 22.

158. Salkin et al., "Friends of the Court," 165–66.

159. Brief for the National Association for the Advancement of Colored People et al. as Amici Curiae Supporting Petitioners, *Kelo v. City of New London,* 545 U.S. 469 (2005) (No. 04-108), 2004 WL 2811057.

160. Brief of Jane Jacobs, as Amica Curiae Supporting Petitioners, *Kelo,* 545 U.S. 469 (2005) (No. 04-108), 2004 WL 2803191.

161. Salkin, et al., "Friends of the Court," 166, 173.

162. U.S. Supreme Court Oral Argument Transcript, *Kelo v. City of New London*, No. 04-108, *20–21 (argued Feb. 22, 2005) (available on Westlaw at 2005 WL 529436).

163. Ibid., *21.

164. *Kelo*, 545 U.S. at 503 (O'Connor, J., dissenting).

165. Interview with Dana Berliner and Scott Bullock, June 22, 2012.

166. Interview with Michael Cristofaro, July 12, 2013.

167. Interview with Wesley Horton, July 15, 2013.

168. Ibid.

169. For more on this point, see chapter 3.

170. See discussion in chapter 4.

171. Interview with Wesley Horton, July 15, 2013.

172. Ibid.

173. See discussion in chapter 4.

174. For examples of the many media accounts of the oral argument that highlighted this exchange, see, e.g., Charles Lane, "Defining Limits of Eminent Domain: High Court Weighs City's Claim to Land," *Washington Post*, Feb. 23, 2005; Jeff Jacoby, "Will Court Curb Eminent Domain?" *Boston Globe*, Feb. 27, 2005; and Stephen Henderson, "Private Land vs. Public Control: Phila. Area is Watching as Justices Weigh Conn. Eminent Domain Case," *Philadelphia Inquirer*, Feb. 23, 2005.

175. See, e.g., Linda Greenhouse, "Justices Appear Unlikely to Increase Land-Use Oversight," *New York Times*, Feb. 23, 2005; Dahlia Lithwick, "Condemn-Nation," Slate, Feb. 22, 2005.

176. Interview with Wesley Horton, July 15, 2013; interview with Wesley Horton, June 9, 2014.

Chapter Two

1. See, e.g., Eric R. Claeys, "Public-Use Limitations and Natural Property Rights," 2004 *Michigan State Law Review* 877 (2004); Lawrence Berger, "The Public Use Requirement in Eminent Domain," *57 Oregon Law Review* 203, 207–12 (1977); Philip Nichols, "The Meaning of Public Use in the Law of Eminent Domain," 20 *B.U. Law Review* 615 (1940).

2. For an overview of early nineteenth century state court jurisprudence on other constitutional property rights issues, see Bernard H. Siegan, *Property Rights: From Magna Carta to the Fourteenth Amendment,* (New Brunswick, Transaction Publishers, 2001), 123-80. Unfortunately, this book includes very little discussion of state public use jurisprudence during the relevant period.

3. John Adams, "Discourses on Davila," in *The Works of John Adams*, ed. Charles Francis Adams (Boston: Little, Brown, 1851), 6:280.

4. Max Farrand, *The Records of the Federal Convention of 1787* (New Haven, CT: Yale University Press, 1937), 1:534.

5. On Madison's key role in drafting and enacting the Takings Clause, see Akhil Reed Amar, *The Bill of Rights: Creation and Reconstruction* (New Haven, CT: Yale University Press, 1998), 77–78.

6. James Madison, "Property," [1792], in Philip Kurland and Ralph Lerner, eds., *The Founders Constitution*, (Chicago: University of Chicago Press, 1987), 1:598.

7. Madison, "Federalist 10," in Alexander Hamilton et al., *The Federalist Papers, ed.* Clinton Rossiter (New York: Mentor, 1961), 58.

8. James W. Ely, Jr., *The Guardian of Every Other Right: A Constitutional History of Property Rights, 3rd ed.* (New York: Oxford University Press, 2008), 42–59; Jennifer Nedelsky, *Private Property and the Limits of American Constitutionalism* (Chicago: University of Chicago Press, 1990), 103–04, 152–53; Buckner F. Melton, Jr. "Eminent Domain, 'Public Use,' and the Conundrum of Original Intent," 36 *Natural Resources Journal* 59, 77–79 (1996).

9. See, e.g., Melton, "Eminent Domain, 'Public Use,' and the Conundrum of Original Intent," 77–79.

10. Amar, *Bill of Rights*, 77–78.

11. For a detailed pathbreaking discussion of this point, see William Baude, "Rethinking the Federal Eminent Domain Power, 122 *Yale Law Journal* 1738 (2013).

12. *Kohl v. United States*, 91 U.S. 367 (1875).

13. 2 U.S. (2 Dall.) 304, 311 (1795).

14. Ibid., 312.

15. Ibid., 312–16.

16. 3 U.S. (3 Dall.) 386, 388 (1798) (Chase, J.). Chase's opinion was one of four separate opinions issued by each of the four justices who heard the case.

17. Ibid., 393–94.

18. *Vanhorne's Lessee* addressed a complicated title dispute connected with a territorial dispute between Connecticut and Pennsylvania.

19. For citations to numerous works on Locke's influence on the Founders's and the American legal tradition's perception of property rights, see, e.g., Steven Menashi, "Cain as His Brother's Keeper: Property Rights and Christian Doctrine in Locke's Two Treatises of Government," 42 *Seton Hall Law Review* 185, 186–87 (2012).

20. John Locke, *Two Treatises of Government,* rev. ed., ed. Peter Laslett (Cambridge: Cambridge University Press, 1963), § 138.

21. Ibid., § 140.

22. Ibid., § 139.

23. William Blackstone, *Commentaries on the Laws of England* (Chicago: University of Chicago Press, 1979 [1765]), 1:134.

24. Ibid.

25. Ibid., 134–35. For a good discussion of Blackstone's position on this issue, and other relevant British legal thought of the era, see Claeys, "Public-Use Limitations and Natural Rights," 895–96.

26. Melton, "Eminent Domain," 85; for similar conclusions, see, e.g., Nathan Sales, Note, "Classical Republicanism and the Fifth Amendment's 'Public Use' Requirement," 49 *Duke Law Journal* 339 (1999); Nichols, "The Meaning of Public Use," 616–18; Berger, "The Public Use Requirement," 205–08; and William Stoebuck, "A General Theory of Eminent Domain, 47 *Washington Law Review* 553, 590–97 (1972).

27. See sources cited in the previous note, all of which reference one or both of these types of takings for support.

28. For a detailed discussion of the relevant history, see Morton J. Horwitz, "The Transformation in the Conception of Property in American Law, 1780–1860," 40 *University of Chicago Law Review* 248, 270–79 (1973).

29. For a helpful short explanation of this dynamic, see Melton, "Eminent Domain," 73.

30. Sales, "Classical Republicanism," 372–73.

31. Berger, "The Public Use Requirement," 206. For a detailed survey, see Henry Walcott Farnam, *Chapters in the History of Social Legislation in the United States to 1860* (Washington, DC: Carnegie Foundation, 1938), 94–100; see also Morton J. Horwitz, *The Transformation of American Law, 1780–1860* (Cambridge, MA: Harvard University Press, 1977), 49.

32. Farnam, *Chapters in the History of Social Legislation*, 95–97.

33. See, e.g., Berger, "Public Use Requirement," 206; Sales, "Classical Republicanism," 373–74; see also John Lewis, *A Treatise on the Law of Eminent Domain in the United States* (Chicago: Callaghan, 1888), 246–47, which cites numerous statutes.

34. Sales, "Classical Republicanism," 373–74.

35. See, e.g., Berger, "The Public Use Requirement," 205–06.

36. This point is recognized by Sales, "Classical Republicanism," 375.

37. See the discussion later in this chapter.

38. See, e.g., Sales, "Classical Republicanism," 375–79; Berger, "Public Use Requirement," 207–08.

39. See Sales, "Classical Republicanism"; Berger, "Public Use Requirement."

40. For citations to relevant cases, see Philip Nichols, *The Law of Eminent Domain: A Treatise on the Principles Which Affect the Taking of Property for the Public Use,* 2nd ed. (Albany, NY: Matthew Bender, 1917), 1:234–35.

41. Ibid., 235.

42. *In re Hickman*, 4 Harr. 580, 581 (Del. 1847).

43. See, e.g., *Brewer v. Bowman*, 9 Ga. 37, 41–42 (1850); *Robinson v. Swope*, 75 Ky. (12 Bush) 21, 25 (1876).

44. Sales, "Classical Republicanism," 379.

45. *Brewer,* 9 Ga. at 42.

46. See, e.g., Sales, "Classical Republicanism," 352–65; Stoebuck, "General Theory of Eminent Domain," 564–69; For a discussion of this "republican" assumption and its historical importance, see Gordon S. Wood, *The Creation of the American Republic, 1776–89* (Chapel Hill: University of North Carolina Press, 1969), 54–58.

47. For arguments that the founders were heavily influenced by liberalism, see, e.g., Bernard Bailyn, *The Ideological Origins of the American Revolution,* rev. ed. (Cambridge, MA: Harvard University Press, 1992); for arguments that republican views were dominant, see, e.g., J. G. A. Pocock, *The Machiavellian Moment: Florentine Political Thought and the Atlantic Republican Tradition* (Princeton, NJ: Princeton University Press, 1975), 506.

48. For a discussion of Madison's concerns about the fate of property rights in the democratic process, see Nedelsky, *Private Property and the Limits of American Constitutionalism,* chap. 2.

49. Ibid., 78.

50. Farrand, *The Records of the Federal Convention of 1787,* 1:512.

51. Nedelsky, *Private Property and the Limits of American Constitutionalism,* 80–81.

52. On the possibly exceptional nature of the Fifth Amendment, see, e.g., Amar, *Bill of Rights,* 77–79; Morton J. Horwitz, "Republicanism and Liberalism in American Constitutional Thought," 29 *William and Mary Law Review* 57, 68 (1987).

53. Sales, "Classical Republicanism," 367. See Pennsylvania Constitution of 1776, art. VIII; Virginia Constitution of 1776, Bill of Rights, § 6.

54. 32 U.S. (7 Pet.) 243 (1833).

55. Ibid., 243–44.

56. Berger, "The Public Use Requirement in Eminent Domain," 209.

57. Comment, "The Public Use Limitation on Eminent Domain: An Advance Requiem," 58 *Yale Law Journal* 599, 605–06 (1949).

58. John Lewis, *A Treatise on the Law of Eminent Domain in the United States* (Chicago: Callaghan, 1888).

59. Thomas Cooley, *A Treatise on the Constitutional Limitations Which Rest Upon the Legislative Power of the States of the American Union* (Boston: Little, Brown, 1868).

60. See *Sadler v. Langham,* 34 Ala. 311, 333–37 (Ala. 1859), which struck down a private road statute based on the narrow view, while minimizing the significance of *Aldridge v. T. C. & D. R. R. Co.,* 2 Stew. & Por. 199 (Ala. 1832), which had adopted the broad view that any "public benefit" could be a "public use".

61. See, e.g., *Sadler v. Langham,* 34 Ala. 311 (1859).

62. *Whiteman v. Wilmington & S.R. Co.*, 2 Harr. 514, 519 (Del. 1839).

63. See discussion later in this chapter.

64. See, e.g., *Dayton Gold and Silver Min. Co. v. Seawell*, 11 Nev. 394 (1876).

65. *Seely v. Sebastia*, 4 Ore. 25 (1870).

66. *City of Pittsburgh v. Scott*, 1 Pa. 309 (1845).

67. Ibid., 314.

68. Ibid.

69. See, e.g., *Smedley v. Erwin*, 51 Pa. 445 (1866), which discusses *Scott* and applies the rule it establishes but fails to clarify this ambiguity; *Waddell's Appeal*, 84 Pa. 90 (1877), which struck down a private road taking but again without clarifying the ambiguity in precedent. The court eventually adopted the narrow view in *Twelfth St. Market Co. v. Philadelphia & R. T. R. Co.*, 21 A. 989 (Pa. 1891).

70. 5 George 227, 239 (Miss. 1857).

71. The taking in question in *Brown* itself was one for the benefit of a railroad corporation, and railroads are common carriers required to serve the public; thus, the taking qualified even under the narrow view of public use. What is not clear is whether the court restricted itself to the narrow view or not.

72. See, e.g., Eric Foner, *Reconstruction: America's Unfinished Revolution, 1863–1877* (New York: Harper, 1988).

73. See *In re Rhode Island Suburban Ry. Co.*, 48 A. 591 (R.I. 1901); *Varner v. Martin*, 21 W.Va. 534 (1883); *Riley v. Charleston Union Station Co.*, 51 S.E. 485 (S.C. 1905); *Fallsburg Power & Manufacturing Co. v. Alexander*, 101 Va. 98 (1903); *Jenel v. Green Island Drain Co.*, 12 Neb. 163 (1881); *Twelfth St. Market Co. v. Philadelphia & R. T. R. Co.*, 21 A. 989 (Pa. 1891); *Healy Lumber Co. v. Morris* 74 P. 681 (Wash. 1903); *Kyle v. Texas & N.O. Ry. Co.*, 3 Willson 518 (Tex. Ct. App. 1889); *Hancock Fence & Stock Law Co. v. Adams*, 9 S.W. 246 (Ky. App. 1888).

74. See *Pioneer Irrigation Dist. v. Bradbury*, 68 P. 295 (Idaho 1902); *St. Louis, I. M. & S. Ry. Co. v. Petty*, 21 S.W. 884 (Ark. 1893).

75. See, e.g., Lewis, *Treatise on the Law of Eminent Domain*, 248–50; Berger, "Public Use Requirement," 206.

76. Berger, "Public Use Requirement," 207; see also Harry N. Scheiber, "Property Law, Expropriation, and Resource Allocation by Government: The United States, 1789–1910," 33 *Journal of Economic History* 232, 239–44 (1973).

77. See cases cited in Lewis, *Treatise on the Law of Eminent Domain*, 230. Lewis also cites Indiana as a state that upheld a mill act on this basis. Ibid. But the case he refers to actually upheld the act without clearly endorsing the broad interpretation of public use. See *Hankins v. Lawrence*, 8 Blackf. 266 (Ind. 1846), which merely states that the power mills are a public use comparable to grist mills but without explaining why. The same goes for the Indiana Supreme Court's earlier 1819 decision upholding the taking of property for grist mills. *Kepley v. Taylor*, 1 Blackf. 492 (Ind. 1819). Later, in 1873, the Indiana Supreme Court endorsed the narrow view. *Wild v. Deig*, 43 Ind. 455 (1873).

78. See cases cited in Lewis, *Treatise on the Law of Eminent Domain*, 231–32.

79. See *Jordan v. Woodward*, 40 Me. 317, 323 (1855); *Miller v. Troost*, 14 Minn. 365, 369 (1869); *Fisher v. Horicon Iron & Mfg. Co.*, 10 Wis. 351 (1860).

80. *Jordan*, 40 Me. at 323.

81. Ibid., 324.

82. *Fisher*, 10 Wis. at 358.

83. Ibid.

84. The court emphases the mere existence of potential economic "benefits, though great, are merely incidental, and such as flow, to a greater or less degree, from all great industries, and would not alone justify the appropriation of private property to secure them." *Miller* 14 Minn. at 369.

85. For relevant citations, see Lewis, *Treatise on the Law of Eminent Domain*, 252. Some of these cases did not directly address mill act condemnations but merely concluded that they are unconstitutional in the course of addressing cases involving other issues. The 1871 Georgia decision, *Loughbridge v. Harris*, 42 Ga. 501 (1871) is notable because the Georgia Supreme Court adopted the broad view of eminent domain just a few years later, in 1877, without overruling *Loughbridge*. Because the 1871 case contains almost no analysis and does not make clear what overall theory of public use it is endorsing, I have chosen to classify Georgia as a state endorsing the broad theory of public use, even though *Loughbridge* cuts the other way.

86. *Head v. Amoskeag Manufacturing Co.*, 113 U.S. 9, 21 (1885). The approach adopted by the Supreme Court was pioneered by Chief Justice Lemuel Shaw of the Massachusetts Supreme Judicial Court. See *Murdock v. Stickney*, 8 Cush. 113, 116 (Mass. 1851). For a strong critique of this reasoning, see Richard A. Epstein, *Takings: Private Property and the Power of Eminent Domain* (Cambridge, MA: Harvard University Press, 1985), 171–72 (though Epstein ultimately endorses the result in *Head*, though not the Court's reasoning).

87. I do not count here cases that upheld mill acts on the basis of usage and precedent without endorsing either the broad or the narrow view of public use in the process.

88. The Supreme Court's opinion in *Head* gives the impression that the predominant view was that mill acts were constitutional. But it does so by downplaying the significance of several cases where, in the view of the Court, state judges ruled that mill acts were unconstitutional only in dicta, and ignoring the significance of cases where they were upheld only on the basis of precedent or long usage, even as the court endorsed the narrow view of public use as the general rule. See *Head*, 113 U.S. at 19–20.

89. *Kohl v. United States*, 91 U.S. 367 (1875).

90. See Bryan H. Wildenthal, "The Road to *Twining*: Reassessing the Disincorporation of the Bill of Rights," 61 *Ohio State Law Journal* 1457 (2000); Before

the 1940s, the Supreme Court almost never applied the Bill of Rights against state governments. Gerard Magliocca, "Becoming the Bill of Rights," Indiana University Robert H. McKinney School of Law Research Paper No. 2013-16 (2013), 13–17, available at http://papers.ssrn.com/sol3/papers.cfm?abstract_id=2236457&rec=1 &srcabs=2166569&alg=1&pos=2.

91. *Fallbrook Irrigation District v. Bradley*, 164 U.S. 112, 158 (1896).

92. See the discussion of this issue in chapter 4.

93. *Wilkinson v. Leland*, 27 U.S. (2 Pet.) 627, 658 (1829). Like *Calder v. Bull* and *Vanhorne's Lessee*, this case did not involve an actual dispute over eminent domain, but rather a different issue to which the extent of state power to take property was tangentially relevant.

94. Ibid., 657.

95. Joseph Story, *Commentaries on the Constitution of the United States: With a Preliminary Review of the Constitutional History of the Colonies and States, before the Adoption of the Constitution* (1833), bk. 3, chap. 38, § 1784.

96. *West River Bridge Co. v. Dix*, 47 U.S. 507 (1848).

97. U.S. Const. art. 10, cl. 1.

98. *West River Bridge*, 47 U.S. 507, at 533–35.

99. Ibid., 546 (Woodbury, J.).

100. 160 U.S. 668 (1896).

101. Ibid., 679–80.

102. Ibid., 680–81.

103. See, e.g., James W. Ely, Jr., "The Fuller Court and Takings Jurisprudence," 2 *Journal of Supreme Court History* 120, 127 (1996), which cites *Gettysburg* as an example of the Court's "reluctan[ce] to treat the public use requirement as a significant restraint on the exercise of eminent domain."

104. *Kelo v. City of New London*, 545 U.S. 469, 517 (2005) (quoting *Gettysburg*, 160 U.S. at 680) (Thomas, J., dissenting).

105. *Gettysburg*, 160 U.S. at 680.

106. Ibid. (emphasis added).

107. For an overview of the 1835–36 debate, see David P. Currie, *The Constitution in Congress: Descent into the Maelstrom, 1829–1861* (Chicago: University of Chicago Press, 2006), 12–17. On the 1862 debate, see Michael J. Kurtz, "Emancipation in the Federal City," 24 *Civil War History* 250, 251–54 (1978).

108. *Dred Scott v. Sandford*, 60 U.S. (19 How.) 393 (1857).

109. For a detailed recent analysis of the legal rationale for the Proclamation, see James Oakes, *Freedom National: The Destruction of Slavery in the United States, 1861–65* (New York: Norton, 2013), 342–59.

110. 24 *Cong. Deb.*, 1st Sess., 4018. For other similar arguments in the 1835–36 debates, see e.g., ibid., 2245–46 (statement of Rep. Francis Pickens); ibid., 2225 (statement of Rep. James Bouldin); ibid., 2029–30 (statement of Rep. Henry Wise);

ibid., 753 (statement of Sen. Felix Grundy); ibid., 786 (statement of Sen. Benjamin
W. Leigh); ibid., 77–78 (statement of Sen. Alexander Porter); ibid., 693–94 (statement of Sen. Robert J. Walker).

111. *Cong. Globe*, 37th Cong., 2d Sess., 1523; see also ibid., 1335 (statement of
Sen. Garrett Davis).

112. See Robert M. Cover, *Justice Accused: Antislavery and the Judicial Process* (New Haven, CT: Yale University Press, 1975), 86–99.

113. Ibid., 87–88.

114. Oakes, *Freedom National*, 18–20.

115. *Cong. Globe*, 37th Cong., 2d Sess., 1497.

116. Ibid.

117. See, e.g., ibid., 1447 (statement of Sen. Charles Sumner); ibid., 1285–86
(statement of Sen. Samuel Pomeroy); ibid., 1503–04 (statement of Sen. James
McDougall). For similar arguments in the 1835–36 debate, see, e.g., 24 *Cong. Deb.*,
1st Sess., 669–71 (statement of Sen. Samuel Prentiss).

118. Alison Goodyear Freehling, *Drift toward Dissolution: The Virginia Slavery
Debate of 1831–32* (Baton Rouge: Louisiana State University Press, 1982), 144–45.

119. 24 *Cong. Deb.*, 1st Sess., 670.

120. Some advocates of emancipation in the 1862 debate did in fact argue
against compensation. See, e.g., *Cong. Globe*, 37th Cong., 2d Sess., 1285–86 (statement of Sen. Samuel C. Pomeroy).

121. Kurtz, "Emancipation in the Federal City," 255–56. Whether this level of
compensation was constitutionally adequate was a point of debate in Congress at
the time. See, e.g., *Cong. Globe*, 37th Cong., 2d Sess., 1283–86.

122. It is equivalent to $6,976 in 2014 dollars, according to the inflation cal-
culator at DaveManuel.com, available at http://www.davemanuel.com/inflation
-calculator.php, and $6,902 in 2013 dollars, according the inflation calculator at
Westegg.com, available at http://www.westegg.com/inflation/infl.cgi.

123. For discussions of Cooley's extensive influence, see Alan Robert Jones,
*The Constitutional Conservatism of Thomas McIntyre Cooley: A Study in the
History of Ideas* (New York: Garland, 1987); James W. Ely, Jr., "Thomas Cooley,
'Public Use,' and New Directions in Takings Jurisprudence," 2004 *Michigan
State Law Review* 845, 845 (2004).

124. On Lewis's status as an influential treatise writer, see, e.g., Robert Jay
Goldstein, *Ecology and Environmental Ethics: Green Wood and the Bundle of
Sticks* (Burlington, VT: Ashgate, 2004), 43–44 n.89. Goldstein states that "there
is no doubt that Lewis's *Treatise* was influential," noting that it was quickly cited
in state supreme court litigation, and by the U.S. Supreme Court in an important
1897 decision, as well as numerous other cases. Ibid. See also Morton J. Horwitz,
*The Transformation of American Law, 1870–1960: The Crisis of Legal Ortho-
dox,* (New York: Oxford University Press, 1992), 147; William Michael Treanor,

"The Original Understanding of the Takings Clause and the Political Process,"
95 *Columbia Law Review* 782, 799 (1995).

125. Cooley, *Constitutional Limitations,* 531.

126. Ibid., 532.

127. Ibid., 532, 534–35.

128. Ibid., 536.

129. Lewis, *Treatise on the Law of Eminent Domain,* 224–25.

130. Ibid., 217, 228–84.

131. See, e.g., Henry E. Mills and Augustus L. Abbott, *Mills on the Law of Eminent Domain,* 2nd ed. (St. Louis, MO: Gilbert Book Co., 1888), 93–94; Carman Fitz Randolph, *The Law of Eminent Domain in the United States* (Cambridge: John Wilson & Son, 1894), 52–53. It is worth noting that the first edition of the Mills treatise is less clear on this point than the second and seems to equivocate between the two interpretations. See Henry E. Mills, *A Treatise upon the Law of Eminent Domain* (St. Louis, MO: F. H. Thomas 1879), 15–17.

132. Christopher Gustavus Tiedeman, *A Treatise on the Limitations of the Police Power in the United States* (St. Louis, MO: F. H. Thomas, 1886), 387–91.

133. Fitz Randolph, *The Law of Eminent Domain,* 53. This treatise still, however, endorsed the narrow definition of public use. Ibid., 52–53.

134. On the Progressive critique of property rights, see, e.g., Morton J. Horwitz, *The Transformation of American Law, 1870–1960: The Crisis of Legal Orthodoxy* (Cambridge, MA: Harvard University Press, 1992), chaps. 2, 5; Barbara Fried, *The Progressive Assault on Laissez-Faire: Robert Hale and the First Law and Economics Movement* (Cambridge, MA: Harvard University Press, 2001); and James W. Ely, Jr., "The Progressive Era Assault on Individualism and Property Rights," 29 *Social Philosophy and Policy* 255 (2012).

135. See David E. Bernstein, *Rehabilitating Lochner: Defending Individual Rights against Progressive Reform* (Chicago: University of Chicago Press, 2011), 40–44, 90–102.

136. See Ely, *Guardian of Every Other Right,* 125–42.

137. Sheldon Goldman, *Picking Federal Judges: Lower Court Selection from Roosevelt to Reagan* (New Haven, CT: Yale University Press, 1997), chaps. 2–3.

138. For an excellent overview, see Wendell E. Pritchett, "The 'Public Menace' of Blight: Urban Renewal and the Private Uses of Eminent Domain," 21 *Yale Law & Policy Review* 1 (2003).

139. Nichols, "The Meaning of Public Use," 629. Nichols, Jr., was an eminent domain practitioner, an attorney with the Lands Division of the Department of Justice, and the son of Philip Nichols, Sr., the originator of *Nichols on Eminent Domain,* which remains arguably the leading treatise in the field.

140. Comment, "The Public Use Limitation on Eminent Domain," 599, 614.

141. See, e.g., *Walker v. Shasta Power Co.*, 160 F. 856, 861 (9th Cir. 1908); *United States, v. Brown*, 279 F. 168, 169–70 (D. Idaho 1922), *aff'd, Brown v. United States*, 263 U.S. 78 (1923).

142. *Mt. Vernon-Woodberry Cotton Duck Co. v. Alabama Interstate Power Co.*, 240 U.S. 30, 32 (1916).

143. All of the cases cited by Holmes in support of this statement were previous federal Due Process Clause challenges to condemnations.

144. See Stuart Banner, *American Property: A History of How, Why, and What We Own* (Cambridge, MA: Harvard University Press, 2011), 271–72.

145. *International Paper Co. v. United States*, 282 U.S. 399 (1931).

146. Ibid., 400–405.

147. Ibid., 408.

148. The lower court ruled that there was no exercise of eminent domain because the government "did not take control of the product and output of the Niagara Falls Power Company [the International Paper Company's supplier] without its consent, but, on the contrary, with and by its consent, by contract, and not for the public use of the United States in its corporate capacity but for the use of certain citizens thereof in the aid of national security and defense." *International Paper Co. v. United States*, 68 Ct. Cl. 414 (Ct. Cl. 1929), *rev'd*, 282 U.S. 399 (1931).

149. 327 U.S. 546, 552 (1946).

150. Ibid., 553.

151. Ibid., 557 (Frankfurter, J., concurring).

152. 348 U.S. 26 (1954). For a discussion of *Berman* and its history, see Amy Lavine, "Urban Renewal and the story of *Berman v. Parker*," 42 *Urban Lawyer* 423 (2010).

153. See *Berman*, 348 U.S. at 30, noting that "64.3% of the dwellings [in the area] were beyond repair, 18.4% needed major repairs, only 17.3% were satisfactory."

154. Ibid., 32.

155. Ibid.

156. Ibid., 33–34.

157. See discussion in chapter 3.

158. Ibid.

159. Pritchett, "Public Menace of Private Blight," 6.

160. Ibid., 46.

161. *New York City Housing Authority v. Muller*, 1 N.E.2d 153 (N.Y. 1936). For examples of similar decisions in other states soon after, see Nichols, "Meaning of Public Use," 630 n.80.

162. For examples of blight and other state court rulings based on Berman's interpretation of public use, see, e.g., *Arco Pipeline Co. v. 3.60 Acres, More or Less*, 539 P.2d 64, 69 (Alaska 1975); *City of Phoenix v. Fehlner*, 363 P.2d 607, 609 (Ariz. 1961); *In re Bunker Hill Urban Renewal Project*, 61 Cal.2d 21

(1964); *Rabinoff v. District Court in and for City and Cnty. of Denver*, 360 P.2d 114 (Colo. 1961); *Wilmington Housing Authority v. Numbers 500, 502, and 504*, 254 A.2d 856, 858–59 (Del. Super.1969); *Boise Redevelopment Agency v. Yick Kong Corp.*, 499 P.2d 575 (Idaho 1972); State ex rel. *Fatzer v. Urban Renewal Agency of Kansas City*, 296 P.2d 656, 660 (Kan. 1956). *Dilley v. City of Des Moines*, 247 N.W.2d 187 (Iowa 1976); *Monroe Redevelopment Agency v. Faulk*, 287 So. 2d 578, 583 (La. Ct. App. 1974); *Bowker v. City of Worcester*, 136 N.E.2d 208, 213 (Mass. 1956); *Paulk v. Housing Authority of City of Tupelo*, 195 So. 2d 488 (Miss. 1967); *City of Helena v. DeWolf*, 508 P.2d 122, 127 (Mont. 1973); *Redevelopment Commission of Greensboro v. Sec. National Bank*, 114 S.E.2d 688 (N.C. 1960); *Isaacs v. Oklahoma City*, 437 P.2d 229 (Okla. 1966); *Davis v. City of Lubbock*, 326 S.W.2d 699 (Texas 1959).

163. 304 N.W.2d 455, 457, 459 (Mich. 1981), overruled by *Cnty. of Wayne v. Hathcock,* 684 N.W.2d 765 (Mich. 2004). For a detailed analysis of *Poletown* and *Hathcock*, see Ilya Somin, "Overcoming *Poletown*: *County of Wayne v. Hathcock*, Economic Development Takings, and the Future of Public Use," 2004 *Michigan State Law Review* 1005 (2004).

164. See Jeanie Wylie, *Poletown: Community Betrayed* (Urbana, IL: University of Illinois Press, 1989), 92–102.

165. Ibid., 99–100.

166. See discussion of Justice Ryan's dissent in chapter 3.

167. 467 U.S. 229 (1984).

168. Ibid., 232.

169. See Sumner Lacroix and Louis Rose, "Public Use, Just Compensation, and Land Reform in Hawaii," 17 *Research in Law and Economics* 7 (1995) (presenting evidence that there was no real exercise of monopoly power in the Hawaii land market). Even if there was an oligopoly problem, Hawaii's use of eminent domain did little to increase the availability of land on the housing market. See Eric Young and Kerry Kamita, "Extending Land Reform to Leasehold Condominiums in Hawaii," 14 *University of Hawaii Law Review* 681 (1992) (arguing that the land reform program upheld in *Midkiff* did little to make more land available to tenant farmers); William R. Fischel, *Regulatory Takings* (Cambridge, MA: Harvard University Press, 1995), 72. However, the Supreme Court did not appear to doubt either the existence of an oligopoly or the appropriateness of eminent domain as a solution to the problem.

170. *Midkiff,* 467 U.S. at 242.

171. Ibid., 240–41.

172. Bruce A. Ackerman, *Private Property and the Constitution* (New Haven, CT: Yale University Press, 1977), 190–91 n.5.

173. Melton, "Eminent Domain," 62.

174. Thomas W. Merrill and David A. Dana, *Property: Takings* (New York: Foundation Press, 2002), 196.

175. See, e.g., Ellen Frankel Paul, *Private Property and Eminent Domain* (New Brunswick, NJ: Transaction Publishers, 1987), 101–03.

176. See *Baycol, Inc. v. Downtown Development Authority* 315 So. 2d 451, 457 (Fla. 1975) (holding that a "'public [economic] benefit' is not synonymous with 'public purpose' as a predicate which can justify eminent domain"); *Owensboro v. McCormick*, 581 S.W.2d 3, 8 (Ky. 1979) ("No 'public use' is involved where the land of A is condemned merely to enable B to build a factory"); *Karesh v. City of Charleston*, 247 S.E.2d 342, 345 (S.C. 1978) (striking down taking justified only by economic development); *City of Little Rock v. Raines*, 411 S.W.2d 486, 495 (Ark. 1967) (private economic development project not a public use); *Hogue v. Port of Seattle*, 341 P.2d 171, 181–91 (Wash. 1959) (denying condemnation of residential property so that agency could "devote it to what it considers a higher and better economic use"); Opinion of the Justices, 131 A.2d 904, 905–06 (Me. 1957) (condemnation for industrial development to enhance economy not a public use).

177. *Edens v. City of Columbia*, 91 S.E.2d 280 (S.C. 1956).

178. On the rise of the property rights movement, see, e.g., Nancie G. Marzulla, *"The Property Rights Movement: How It Began and Where it is Headed," in Land Rights: The 1990s' Property Rights Rebellion, ed.* Bruce Yandle (Lanham, MD: Rowman & Littlefield, 1995), 1, 13–19; Ely, *Guardian of Every Other Right,* 155–70 (describing increased support for property rights during this period).

179. See generally Steven Teles, *The Rise of the Conservative Legal Movement* (Princeton, NJ: Princeton University Press, 2008).

180. See *Southwestern Illinois Development Authority v. National City Environmental, L.L.C.*, 768 N.E.2d 1, 9, 11 (Ill. 2002) (holding that a "contribu[tion] to positive economic growth in the region" is not a public use justifying condemnation); *County of Wayne v. Hathcock*, 684 N.W.2d 765, 770, 778 (Mich. 2004) (invalidating economic development takings under the Michigan Constitution); *City of Bozeman v. Vaniman*, 898 P.2d 1208, 1214 (Mont. 1995) (holding that a condemnation that transfers property to a private business is unconstitutional unless the transfer to the business is insignificant and incidental to a public project); *Georgia Department of Transportation v. Jasper County*, 586 S.E.2d 853, 856 (S.C. 2003) (holding that even a substantial "projected economic benefit . . . cannot justify a condemnation").

181. *Hathcock*, 684 N.W.2d at 778.

182. See *City of Jamestown v. Leevers Supermarkets, Inc.*, 552 N.W.2d 365, 374 (N.D. 1996) (upholding economic development takings so long as the "primary object" of the taking is "economic welfare"). In 2003, the Kansas Supreme Court reaffirmed longstanding previous decisions to that effect. See *General Building Contractors v. Board of Shawnee City Commissioners*, 66 P.3d 873, 882–83 (Kan. 2003).

183. For an overview of the Court's evolution on property rights issues during this period, see Ilya Somin, "Taking Property Rights Seriously: The Su-

preme Court and the 'Poor Relation' of Constitutional Law," George Mason University Law and Economics Paper 08-53 (2008), available at http://ssrn.com /abstract=1247854.

184. For numerous examples, see Ilya Somin, "Originalism and Political Ignorance," 97 *Minnesota Law Review* 625, 625–27 (2012).

185. See James E. Ryan, "Laying Claim to the Constitution: The Promise of New Textualism," 97 *Virginia Law Review* 1524, 1524–26 (2011).

186. See examples cited in Somin, "Originalism and Political Ignorance," 628 n.16.

187. Confirmation Hearing on the Nomination of Elena Kagan to Be an Associate Justice of the Supreme Court of the United States: Hearing before the Senate Committee on the Judiciary, 111th Cong., 62 (2010) (statement of Elena Kagan).

188. See, e.g., Calvin Johnson, *Righteous Anger at the Wicked States: The Meaning of the Founders' Constitution* (Cambridge: Cambridge University Press, 2005); Larry Alexander and Saikrishna Prakash, "'Is That English You're Speaking?' Why Intention-Free Interpretation Is an Impossibility," 41 *San Diego Law Review* 967, 974–77 (2004).

189. For a discussion of the rise of original meaning of originalism, see Lawrence B. Solum, "What Is Originalism? The Evolution of Contemporary Originalist Theory, Apr. 28, 2011, available at http://papers.ssrn.com/sol3/papers.cfm?abs tract_id=1392961, at 6–17. For cites to numerous prominent works advocating original meaning originalism, see Somin, "Originalism and Political Ignorance," 625–27.

190. See Amar, *Bill of Rights,* chaps. 7–12; Kurt T. Lash, *The Fourteenth Amendment and the Privileges and Immunities of American Citizenship* (Cambridge: Cambridge University Press, 2014), 296–97. Michael Rappaport, "Originalism and Regulatory Takings: Why the Fifth Amendment May Not Protect against Regulatory Takings, but the Fourteenth Amendment May," 45 *San Diego Law Review* 729 (2008).

191. Rappaport, "Originalism and Regulatory Takings."

192. The Court most recently reaffirmed this approach in *McDonald v. City of Chicago,* 130 S. Ct. 3020 (2010).

193. Ibid., 3032 (quotations omitted); see also *Duncan v. La.,* 391 U.S. 145, 149 (1968).

194. These include the Third Amendment, which bans the quartering of troops in private homes in peacetime, the Seventh Amendment, which creates a right of trial by jury in civil cases, and the Fifth Amendment's requirement of grand jury indictment for criminal defendants. *McDonald,* 130 s. Ct. at 3032.

195. For an extensive overview, see Ryan C. Williams, "The One and Only Substantive Due Process Clause," 120 *Yale Law Journal* 408 (2010).

196. U.S. Const. amend. XIV, § 1. For Thomas's defense of this approach, see *McDonald,* 130 S. Ct. at 3058–79 (Thomas, J., concurring). For an important

recent academic defense, see Lash, *Privileges and Immunities,* 288–97. I use the term "incorporation" to describe Lash's theory, even though he himself rejects it (ibid., 296–97), because it is the standard terminology used in discussions of this issue. Lash rejects the term because he believes that the adoption of the Fourteenth Amendment "reconfigured the meaning and scope of the original Bill of Rights" instead of just incorporating the 1791 meaning. In my view, the term "incorporation" is broad enough to include both theories claiming that the Fourteenth Amendment merely applies an unchanged 1791 meaning against the states, and theories which posit that it applies a potentially different meaning.

197. Lash, *Privileges and Immunities,* 293; see also ibid., 296–97.

198. See discussion of Madison's views earlier in this chapter. See also Laura S. Underkuffler, "On Property: An Essay," 100 *Yale Law Journal* 127, 134 (1990), which discusses Madison's emphasis on the need to protect property rights against majoritarian hostility.

199. Nedelsky, *Private Property and the Limits of American Constitutionalism,* 22–31.

200. Ibid.

201. For an excellent recent account of Bingham's crucial role in drafting the amendment and shepherding it through Congress, see Gerard Magliocca, *American Founding Son: John Bingham and the Invention of the Fourteenth Amendment* (New York: NYU Press, 2013).

202. 39th Cong., 1st Sess., *Cong. Globe* 1065 (1866) (statement of Rep. John Bingham).

203. On the centrality of property rights in nineteenth-century conceptions of civil rights, see, e.g., Harold Hyman & William Wiecek, *Equal Justice Under Law: Constitutional Development, 1835–75* (New York: Harper & Row, 1982), 395–97.

204. See, e.g., Robert H. Bork, *The Tempting of America* (New York: Free Press, 1990), 144.

205. Antonin M. Scalia, *A Matter of Interpretation: Federal Courts and the Law* (Princeton, NJ: Princeton University Press, 1997), 17; Randy E. Barnett, *Restoring the Lost Constitution* (Princeton, NJ: Princeton University Press, 2004), 92.

206. For a discussion of this possibility, see Somin, "Originalism and Political Ignorance," 633–34, 636–37.

207. 554 U.S. 570, 576–77 (2008) (quoting *United States v. Sprague,* 282 U.S. 716, 731 (1931))

208. Gary Lawson and Guy Seidman, "Originalism as a Legal Enterprise," 23 *Constitutional Commentary* 47, 72–73 (2006).

209. Ibid.

210. For a recent overview of modern political ignorance, see Ilya Somin, *Democracy and Political Ignorance: Why Smaller Government Is Smarter* (Stanford, CA: Stanford University Press, 2013), chap. 1.

211. For a summary of the evidence on political knowledge in these periods, see Somin, "Originalism and Political Ignorance," 642–47.

212. Comment, "The Public Use Limitation on Eminent Domain," 603. For other academic supporters of the broad view who recognize that the narrow view coheres better with the text, see, e.g., Sales, "Classical Republicanism," 345; Stoebuck, "General Theory of Eminent Domain," 590. For similar arguments by defenders of the narrow view, see Lewis, *Treatise on the Law of Eminent Domain,* 223–24; Roger Clegg, "Reclaiming the Text of the Takings Clause," 46 *South Carolina Law Review* 531, 537 (1995).

213. For a more detailed discussion of this issue, see Somin, "Originalism and Political Ignorance," 665–66.

214. See chapter 5.

215. Lawson and Seidman, "Originalism as a Legal Enterprise," 72–73.

216. *Holmes v. Jennison*, 39 U.S. 540, 570–71 (1840).

217. Lewis, *Treatise on Eminent Domain,* 221.

218. *McQuillen v. Hatton*, 42 Ohio St. 202, 204 (1884).

219. See discussion earlier in this chapter.

220. See discussion of treatises earlier in this chapter.

221. See discussion earlier in this chapter.

222. See discussion of their views earlier in this chapter.

223. See discussion in chapter 8.

224. See, e.g., the discussion of this question as applied to public use in Lewis, *Treatise on Eminent Domain,* 225–26.

225. On the view of judicial duty on this issue during the Founding era, see Philip Hamburger, *Law and Judicial Duty* (Cambridge, MA: Harvard University Press, 2008), esp. chap. 5; and Scott D. Gerber, *A Distinct Judicial Power: The Origins of Judicial Review 1606–1787* (New York: Oxford University Press, 2011), chap. 16.

226. Hamilton, "Federalist 78," in Alexander Hamilton et al., *The Federalist Papers*, ed. Clinton Rossiter (New York: Mentor, 1961), 466.

227. Ibid.

228. 347 U.S. 54 (1954).

229. 388 U.S. 1 (1967).

230. For prominent originalist justifications of *Brown* that acknowledge these points, see Michael McConnell, "Originalism and the Desegregation Decisions," 81 *Virginia Law Review* 947 (1995); Steven G. Calabresi and Michael Perl, "Originalism and *Brown v. Board of Education,*" Northwestern Public Law Research Paper No. 13-26 (2013), available at http://papers.ssrn.com/sol3/papers.cfm?abstract_id=2307651. For leading originalist defenses of *Loving* that make similar acknowledgements, see Steven G. Calabresi and Andrea Matthews, "Originalism and *Loving v. Virginia*," 2012 *BYU Law Review* 1393 (2012); David Upham, "Interracial Marriage and the Original Understanding of the Privileges

and Immunities Clause," unpublished paper (Mar. 27, 2013), available at http://papers.ssrn.com/sol3/papers.cfm?abstract_id=2240046.

231. For an examination of Bork's thought on this point, see Ilya Somin, "The Borkean Dilemma: Robert Bork and the Tension between Originalism and Democracy," 80 *University of Chicago Law Review Dialogue* 243 (2013).

232. Robert H. Bork, "Tradition and Morality in Constitutional Law," in Robert H. Bork, *A Time to Speak: Selected Writing and Arguments* (New York: ISI Books, 2008), 402.

233. For an exploration of this tension in Bork's thought, see Somin, "Borkean Dilemma."

234. Amar, *Bill of Rights,* 163–206; Michael Kent Curtis, *No State Shall Abridge: The Fourteenth Amendment and the Bill of Rights* (Durham, NC: Duke University Press, 1986).

235. See the discussion of the Supreme Court's acceptance of the incorporation of the Takings Clause under its selective incorporation approach earlier in this chapter. Advocates of incorporation under the Privileges or Immunities Clause generally hold that all individual rights created by the Bill of Rights are incorporated. See, e.g., Lash, *Privileges and Immunities,* 288–97.

236. See, e.g., Raoul Berger, *The Fourteenth Amendment and the Bill of Rights* (Norman: University of Oklahoma Press, 1989).

237. Jed Rubenfeld, "Usings," 102 *Yale Law Journal* 1077, 1078–80 (1993). For a rare similar view advanced by a different scholar, see Harry N. Scheiber, "The 'Takings Clause' and the Fifth Amendment: Original Intent and Significance in American Legal Development," in *The Bill of Rights: Original Meaning and Current Understanding,* ed. Eugene Hickock (Charlottesville: University Press of Virginia, 1991), 233, 235.

238. Ibid.

239. See John Paul Stevens, "*Kelo,* Popularity, and Substantive Due Process," Albritton Lecture, University of Alabama School, of Law, Nov. 16, 2011, at 15–17, available at http://www.supremecourt.gov/publicinfo/speeches/1.pdf.

240. See discussion earlier in this chapter.

241. For more detailed criticism of Rubenfeld on this point, see Sales, "Classical Republicanism," 344–45 n.23; Melton, "Eminent Domain," 76–77; and Treanor, "Original Understanding," 839 & n.292.

242. James Madison to Robert Evans, June 15, 1819, in Kurland and Lerner, eds., *The Founders Constitution,* 1:573.

Chapter Three

1. The housing market collapse and recession of 2007-2008 has, however, led to novel proposals for the use of eminent domain to transfer property to private

parties, most notably a plan to condemn "underwater" mortgages and transfer them to homeowners, in order to prop up the housing market. For this proposal, see Robert C. Hockett, "Paying Paul and Robbing No One: An Eminent Domain Solution for Underwater Mortgage Debt," 19 *Current Issues in Economics and Finance* 1 (2013). So far, only one small city, Richmond, California, has adopted this policy. See Lorelai Laird, "California City Seeks Eminet Domain to Bail Out Foreclosures," *ABA Journal,* Mar. 1, 2014, available at http://www.abajournal .com/magazine/article/california_city_seeks_eminent_domain_to_bail_out_fore closures/. For my critique of Richmond's plan, see Ilya Somin, "Richmond, Calif. Runs Amok with Eminent Domain," *USA Today,* Aug. 12, 2013.

2. 684 N.W.2d 765, 786 (Mich. 2004) (emphasis in original).

3. In 2002, the Supreme Court of Illinois refused to allow a "contribu[tion] to economic growth in the region" to justify a taking because such a standard could justify virtually any condemnation that benefited private industry, since "every lawful business" contributes to economic growth to some degree, *Southwestern Illinois Development Authority v. National City Environmental., L.L.C,* 768 N.E.2d 1, 9 (Ill. 2002). Similarly, the Supreme Court of Kentucky forbade the economic development rationale in 1979 largely because "[w]hen the door is once opened to it, there is no limit that can be drawn." *Owensboro v. McCormick,* 581 S.W.2d 3, 8 (Ky. 1979) [quoting 26 Am. Jur. 2d *Eminent Domain* § 34, at 684–85 (1966)].

4. *Poletown Neighborhood Council v. City of Detroit,* 304 N.W.2d 455, 458 (Mich. 1981), *overruled by County of Wayne v. Hathcock,* 684 N.W.2d 765 (Mich. 2004).

5. This, indeed, is what the *Poletown* court tried to do when it held that the benefit must be "clear and significant." Ibid.

6. See discussion later in this chapter.

7. U.S. Supreme Court Oral Argument Transcript, *Kelo v. City of New London,* No. 04-108, *20–21 (argued Feb. 22, 2005), 2005 WL 529436. See discussion of this part of the oral argument in chapter 1.

8. Ibid., at *5.

9. Gregory S. Alexander, "Eminent Domain and Secondary Rent-Seeking," 1 *NYU Journal of Law and Liberty* 958 (2005); Daniel B. Kelly, "Acquiring Land through Eminent Domain: Justifications, Limitations, and Alternatives," in *Research Handbook on the Economics of Property Law,* ed. Kenneth Ayotte and Henry E. Smith (Northampton, MA: Edward Elgar, 2011), 344, 354; Thomas W. Merrill, "The Economics of Public Use," 72 *Cornell Law Review* 61, 85-86 (1986).

10. Kelly, "Acquiring Land through Eminent Domain," 354.

11. See ibid., and Alexander, "Eminent Domain and Secondary Rent-seeking."

12. See, e.g., *Mayor of the City of Vicksburg v. Thomas,* 645 So. 2d 940, 943 (Miss. 1994) (holding that property may only be condemned for transfer to

"private parties subject to conditions to insure that the proposed public use will continue to be served"); *Krauter v. Lower Big Blue Natural Resource District,* 259 N.W.2d 472, 475–76 (Neb. 1977) (holding that "a condemning agency must have a present plan and a present public purpose for the use of the property before it is authorized to commence a condemnation action. . . . The possibility that the condemning agency at some future time may adopt a plan to use the property for a public purpose is not sufficient."); *Casino Reinvestment Development Authority v. Banin,* 727 A.2d 102, 111 (N.J. Super. Ct. 1998) (holding that when a "public agency acquires . . . property for the purposes of conveying it to a private developer," there must be advance "assurances that the public interest will be protected").

13. *Poletown Neighborhood Council v. City of Detroit,* 304 N.W.2d 455, 459 (Mich. 1981), *overruled by County of Wayne v. Hathcock,* 684 N.W.2d 765 (Mich. 2004).

14. Ibid.

15. Ibid., 480 (Ryan, J., dissenting) (noting that "there will be no public control" over the GM plant scheduled to be built on the Poletown site).

16. 442 N.W.2d 730, 731-32 (Mich. Ct. App. 1989).

17. *Poletown,* 304 N.W.2d at , 467 (Ryan, J., dissenting).

18. Ibid., 467–68 (citing statement of Mayor Young and reprinting a letter from Thomas A. Murphy, Chairman of the Board, General Motors, to Coleman A. Young, sent on October 8, 1980).

19. Ibid., 480.

20. Ibid.

21. Ibid.

22. Marie Michael, "Detroit at 300: New Seeds of Hope for a Troubled City," *Dollars & Sense* (2001), 24, 25.

23. Ibid.

24. See chapter 1.

25. See, e.g., *General Building Contractors v. Board of Shawnee City Commissioners,* 66 P.3d 873, 881–83 (Kan. 2003) (upholding economic development condemnation for purpose of building industrial facility for later transfer to private owners with whom no development agreements had as yet been reached); *City of Jamestown v. Leevers Supermarkets, Inc.,* 552 N.W.2d 365, 373–74 (N.D. 1996) (following *Poletown* approach and concluding that economic development takings will be upheld so long as the "primary object" of the taking is "economic welfare"); *City of Minneapolis v. Wurtele,* 291 N.W.2d 386, 390 (Minn. 1980) (holding, in a case endorsing the constitutionality of economic development takings, that "a public body's decision that a [condemnation] project is in the public interest is presumed correct unless there is a showing of fraud or undue influence"); *Vitucci v. New York City School Construction Authority,* 289 A.D.2d 479, (N.Y. App. Div. 2001) (holding that an economic development taking passes

muster despite the fact that the property was originally condemned to build a school, because "as long as the initial taking was in good faith, there appears to be little limitation on the condemnor's right to put the property to an alternate use upon the discontinuation of the original planned public purpose"). The Maryland Court of Appeals decision endorsing economic development condemnations was partly based on the fact that the government "will maintain significant control over the industrial park" that the new owner used the condemned property to build. *Prince George's County v. Collington Crossroads*, 339 A.2d 278, 283 (Md. 1975). However, the control in question involved merely the right to regulate the facility to ensure "health, safety, and welfare, control . . . hazards and nuisances, and guidelines for assuring a high quality physical environment"; and a guarantee that part of the project would be used as "open space." Ibid. It did not create a binding obligation to produce any actual economic benefits for the community of the kind that were used to justify condemnation in the first place.

26. *Poletown Neighborhood Council v. City of Detroit*, 304 N.W.2d 455, 458–59 (Mich. 1981), overruled by *Cnty. of Wayne v. Hathcock*, 684 N.W.2d 765 (Mich. 2004).

27. See discussion of this issue later in this chapter and in chapter 4.

28. Steven Pinker, *How the Mind Works* (New York: W.W. Norton, 1999), 421–23.

29. *Poletown Neighborhood Council v. City of Detroit*, 304 N.W.2d 455, 470 (Mich. 1981), overruled by *Cnty. of Wayne v. Hathcock*, 684 N.W.2d 765 (Mich. 2004) (Ryan, J., dissenting).

30. Ibid.

31. Ilya Somin, "Overcoming *Poletown*: *County of Wayne v. Hathcock*, Economic Development Takings, and the Future of Public Use," 2004 *Michigan State Law Review* 1005, 1018 (2004).

32. Michael, "Detroit at 300." The estimate of the number of businesses eliminated in the *Poletown* takings is in fact unclear. While Marie Michael cites a figure of 600, other sources cite much lower numbers, in the range of 140 to 160. See Somin, "Overcoming *Poletown*," 1017 n.52. If the lower estimates are correct, it would be much less likely that the number of jobs lost from the businesses shut down was equal to that created by the new factory. However, it is important to remember that the lost jobs were wiped out immediately whereas the new ones did not begin to appear for four years after the 1981 condemnations and that the job losses suffered from wiping out the businesses do not include jobs eliminated by the destruction of Poletown's churches, schools, and hospitals, nor those lost as a result of the expulsion of over four thousand residents.

33. At the time, opponents of the condemnations claimed that nine thousand jobs would be lost because of them. John Bukowczyk, "The Decline and Fall of a Detroit Neighborhood: *Poletown vs. GM and the City of Detroit*," 41 *Washington & Lee Law Review* 49, 68 (1984). This partisan estimate, like GM's promise that six thousand jobs would be created, must be viewed with skepticism.

34. According to data compiled by the city, some one-third of the affected businesses closed down immediately, while two-thirds of the remainder (approximately 40 to 45 percent of the original total) relocated to other parts of Detroit. Bryan D. Jones et al., *The Sustaining Hand: Community Leadership and Corporate Power* (Lawrence: University Press of Kansas, 1986), 100. Even if we assume—implausibly—that those relocated businesses that stayed in Detroit continued to employ as many workers as before, the area would have suffered a net job loss if the approximately 350 businesses that either shut down or moved outside of the city employed an average of just seven workers each. And, obviously, this does not even consider the job losses and other economic costs inflicted by the destruction of schools, churches, and other nonprofit institutions.

35. See Somin, "Overcoming *Poletown*," 1017 n.52.

36. *Poletown Neighborhood Council v. City of Detroit*, 304 N.W.2d 455, 459 (Mich. 1981), overruled by *County of Wayne v. Hathcock*, 684 N.W.2d 765 (Mich. 2004).

37. Ibid.

38. See *Kelo v. City of New London*, 843 A.2d 500, 511 (Conn. 2004), *aff'd*, 545 U.S. 469 (2005) (noting that two of the plaintiffs' families have "lived in their homes for decades and others had put enormous amounts of time, effort, and money into their property").

39. Ibid., 596–600 (Zarella, J., dissenting).

40. Ibid., 541 n.58.

41. Jane Jacobs, *Death and Life of Great American Cities* (New York: Random House, 1961), 5.

42. See, e.g., Mindy Thompson Fullilove, *Root Shock: How Tearing up City Neighborhoods Hurts America, and What We Can Do About It* (New York: One World/Ballantine Books, 2004); Herbert J. Gans, *The Urban Villagers*, rev. ed. (New York: Free Press, 1982), 362–86 (same); Bernard J. Frieden and Lynne B. Sagalyn, *Downtown Inc: How America Rebuilds Cities* (Cambridge, MA: M.I.T. Press, 1989), 20–35; Merrill, "Economics of Public Use," 82–85.Margaret Jane Radin, "The Liberal Conception of Property: Cross Currents in the Jurisprudence of Takings," 88 *Columbia Law Review* 1667, 1689–91 (1988); David R.E. Aladjem, "Public Use and Treatment as an Equal: An Essay on *Poletown Neighborhood Council v. City of Detroit* and *Hawaii Housing Authority v. Midkiff*," 15 *Ecology Law Quarterly* 671, 673–74 (1988); Richard A. Epstein, "Property, Speech and the Politics of Distrust," 59 *University of Chicago Law Review* 41, 62 n.60 (1992).

43. For a detailed discussion of the psychological harm suffered by people forced to leave Fort Trumbull, see Carol L. Zeiner, "*Kelo* through the Lens of Therapeutic Jurisprudence," *Phoenix Law Review* (forthcoming), available at papers.ssrn.com/sol3/papers.cfm?abstract_id=2292066.

44. For a summary and analysis of the literature on rent-seeking and capture, see Dennis C. Mueller, *Public Choice III* (Cambridge: Cambridge University Press, 2003), 337–48.

45. For a recent summary of the available evidence, see Ilya Somin, *Democracy and Political Ignorance: Why Smaller Government Is Smarter* (Stanford, CA: Stanford University Press, 2013), chap. 1. For earlier surveys, see, e.g., Michael X. Delli Carpini and Scott Keeter, *What Americans Know about Politics and Why It Matters* (New Haven, CT: Yale University Press, 1996); Richard Shenkman, *Just How Stupid Are We? Facing the Truth About the American Voter* (New York: Basic Books, 2008); Scott Althaus, *Collective Preferences in Democratic Politics* (New York: Cambridge University Press, 2003); Ilya Somin, "Political Ignorance and the Countermajoritarian Difficulty: A New Perspective on the Central Obsession of Constitutional Theory," 89 *Iowa Law Review* 1287, 1290–1304 (2004); Ilya Somin, "Voter Ignorance and the Democratic Ideal," 12 *Critical Review* 413, 413–19 (1998).

46. Somin, *Democracy and Political Ignorance,* chap. 1.

47. For a more detailed discussion, see ibid., 62–77.

48. Jeanie Wylie, *Poletown: Community Betrayed* (Urbana: University of Illinois Press, 1989), 214.

49. Ibid., 214–15; Michael, "Detroit at 300."

50. See Dick M. Carpenter and John K. Ross, "Testing O'Connor and Thomas: Does the Use of Eminent Domain Target Poor and Minority Communities?," 46 *Urban Studies* 2447 (2009).

51. Ibid.

52. See discussion in chapter 1.

53. See William A. Fischel, *The Homevoter Hypothesis: How Home Values Influence Local Government Taxation, School Finance, and Use Policies* (Cambridge, MA: Harvard University Press, 2001); see also Naomi Lamoreaux, "The Mystery of Property Rights: A US Perspective," 71 *Journal of Economic History* 275 (2011), and the discussion of Judge Richard Posner's views later in this chapter.

54. One recent study defends Philadelphia's use of eminent domain in part on the grounds that only 240 of over 4300 condemnations for transfer to private parties met with any "official resistance" (defined as litigation or revestment) between 1992 and 2007. Debbie Becher, *Private Property and Public Power: Eminent Domain in Philadelphia,* (New York: Oxford University Press, 2014), 58.

55. In discussing specific cases, Becher acknowledges that sometimes owners gave in because they believe resistance was hopeless, and recognizes that similar things may have occurred in other cases where those displaced did not reveal their motives for deciding not to resist. Ibid., 223–24.

56. See Robert K. Fleck and F. Andrew Hanssen, "Repeated Adjustment of Delegated Powers and the History of Eminent Domain," 30 *International Review of Law and Economics* 99, 105 (2010).

57. 348 U.S. 26, 32 (1954). "Slum clearance" was upheld as a public use to justify condemnation under the Michigan state constitution in 1951. *In re Slum Clearance*, 50 N.W.2d 340 (Mich. 1951).

58. Ibid., 32.

59. *In re West 41st St. Realty v. New York State Urban Development Corp.*, 744 N.Y.S.2d 121 (N.Y. App. Div. 2002).

60. 76 P.3d 1, 12–15 (Nev. 2003),

61. Ibid., 13. In a recent report on eminent domain produced by the US Commission on Civil Rights, a statement by one member of the Commission claims that this blight designation was justified because "the major hotels and casinos of the strip do not reside in the City of Las Vegas, but rather outside the city's jurisdiction in Clark County." United States Commission Civil Rights, Briefing Report, The Civil Rights Implications of Eminent Domain Abuse, (2014), available at http://www.usccr.gov/pubs/FINAL_FY14_Eminent-Domain-Report.pdf (Statement of Commissioner David Kladney), 36. In fact, however, there are numerous casinos in downtown Las Vegas, and the condemnation upheld in *Pappas* was for a parking lot intended to be used by a consortium of casinos located in the area. *Pappas*, 76 P.3d at 7. Commissioner Kladney also claimed that the area in question was genuinely blighted. in various ways but without citing any evidence to support these assertions. USSCR, Civil Rights Implications of Eminent Domain Abuse, 37, In striking down the takings, the trial court in *Pappas* found that the City had also failed to provide any evidence of genuine blight, and that its blight alleviation plan was " not based on empirical data; instead it is a hollow shell merely mimicking the words of the enabling statutes." *City of Las Vegas Redevelopment Authority v. Pappas*, 1996 WL 34464336 (Nev. Dist. Ct. July 3, 1996), rev'd 76 P.3d 1 (Nev. 2003). The trial court also found that "No [blight] survey was completed in its entirety. Not one survey indicated whether the property was blighted or non-blighted." Ibid. In reversing the trial court's ruling, the state Supreme Court did not contest these factual findings, but nonetheless concluded that the blight designation was still permissible under Nevada's then extremely broad definition of blight. It also reiterated the Redevelopment Authority's claims that the downtown area was suffering from various bad conditions, such as a higher crime rate than the rest of the city, but did not contest the point that these claims were not based on any systematic surveys proving the presence of blight. *Pappas*, 76 P.3d at 14-15. Commissioner Kladney also claims that the City's efforts to redevelop the downtown area led to an "economic renaissance" in Las Vegas. USSCR, *Civil Rights Implications of Eminent Domain Abuse*, 37, He cites no evidence indicating that the taking upheld in Pappas helped cause that "renaissance" in any way.

62. *Matter of Goldstein v. New York State Urban Development Corp.*, 921 N.E.2d 164, 172–73 (N.Y. 2009). This standard was reaffirmed in *Matter of Kaur v. N.Y. State Urban Development Co.*, 933 N.E.2d 721 (N.Y. 2010).

63. N.Y. Const. art. XVIII, §§ 1, 9.

64. For a much more detailed discussion of the blight determinations in these cases, see Ilya Somin, "Let There Be Blight: Blight Condemnations in New York after *Goldstein* and *Kaur*," 38 *Fordham Urban Law Journal* 1193, 1201–10 (2011). See also the discussion of these cases in chapter 7.

65. *Pappas*, 76 P.3d at 13.

66. Ibid.

67. Colin Gordon, "Blighting the Way: Urban Renewal, Economic Development, and the Elusive Definition of Blight," 31 *Fordham Urban Law Journal* 305, 307 (2004).

68. Ibid., 306.

69. Wendell E. Pritchett, "Beyond *Kelo:* Urban Redevelopment in the 21st Century," 22 *Georgia State University Law Review* 895, 910–12 (2006).

70. Gordon, "Blighting the Way," 307.

71. See chapter 5.

72. For a good review of the relevant history, see Wendell E. Pritchett, "The 'Public Menace' of Blight: Urban Renewal and the Private Uses of Eminent Domain," 21 *Yale Law & Policy Review* 1, 5–23 (2003).

73. Ibid., 17.

74. See, e.g., ibid., 3–4, 16–18; Lawrence Friedman, *Government and Slum Housing: A Century of Frustration* (New York: Rand McNally, 1969), 169.

75. Quoted in Pritchett, "Public Menace," 18.

76. *Berman v. Parker*, 348 U.S. 26, 34 (1954).

77. See, e.g.,, Jacobs, *Death and Life of Great American Cities,* 5, 270–90, 311–14; Martin Anderson, *The Federal Bulldozer* (New York: McGraw-Hill, 1967); Gans, *Urban Villagers*, 362–84; Scott Greer, *Urban Renewal and American Cities: The Dilemma of Democratic Intervention* (Indianapolis, IN: Bobbs-Merrill, 1965), 3–5.; Chester W. Hartman, "Relocation: Illusory Promises and No Relief," 47 *Virginia Law Review* 745 (1971).

78. Pritchett, "The 'Public Menace' of Blight," 47.

79. Anderson, *Federal Bulldozer*, 8, 54.

80. Ibid., 57–70.

81. Fullilove, *Root Shock*; Frieden and Sagalyn, *Downtown Inc.*, 20–35.

82. A 1994 summary of the evidence on urban redevelopment takings concludes that

> In essence, the powers and internal pressures [of the blight condemnation process] create a mandate to gentrify selected areas, resulting in a de facto concentration of poverty elsewhere, preferably outside the decision makers' jurisdiction. The net result is that a neighborhood of poor people is replaced by office towers, luxury hotels, or retail centers. The former low-income

residents, displaced by the bulldozer or an equally effective increase in rents, must relocate into another area they can—
perhaps—afford. The entire process can be viewed as a strategy
of poverty concentration and geographical containment to protect the property values—and entertainment choices—of downtown elites.

    Benjamin B. Quinones, "Redevelopment Redefined: Revital-
izing the Central City with Resident Control," 27 *University of
Michigan Journal of Law & Reform*, 680, 740–41 (1994).

83. See Somin, "Overcoming *Poletown*," 1006–07.

84. *Berman v. Parker*, 348 U.S. 26, 30 (1954).

85. Pritchett, "Public Menace," 44. See also ibid., 37–41, for documentation of
widespread support for such takings.

86. Gans, *Urban Villagers*, 385–86.

87. Anderson, *Federal Bulldozer*, 54.

88. Pritchett, "Public Menace," 37. Not all of these were necessarily federally
sponsored takings.

89. *County of Wayne v. Hathcock*, 684 N.W.2d 765, 783 (Mich. 2004).

90. See the discussion of O'Connor's dissent in chapter 4.

91. Gans, *Urban Villagers*, at 368.

92. Ibid., 369–71, 378–81.

93. Howard Gillette, Jr., *Between Justice and Beauty: Race, Planning, and the
Failure of Urban Policy in Washington, D.C.* (Baltimore: John Hopkins University Press, 1995), 163–64.

94. Gans, *Urban Villagers*, 370.

95. Pritchett, "Public Menace," 47.

96. PBS transcript, available at http://www.pbs.org/wgbh/amex/mlk/sfeature
/sf_video_pop_04_tr_qry.html.

97. Pritchett, "Public Menace," 47.

98. Frieden and Sagalyn, *Downtown Inc.*, 28.

99. Mindy Thompson Fullilove, *Eminent Domain and African-Americans*
(Washington, D.C. Institute for Justice, 2007), 2.

100. Anderson, *Federal Bulldozer*, 64–65.

101. Alan Altshuler and David Luberoff, *Mega-Projects: The Changing Politics of Urban Investment* (Washington, DC: Brookings Institution, 2003), 25–26.

102. See, e.g., see Robert Dreher and John Echeverria, "Kelo's Unanswered
Questions: The Policy Debate Over the Use of Eminent Domain for Economic
Development," Georgetown Environmental Law and Policy Institute, (2006),
28–32, available at http://www.gelpi.org/gelpi/current_research/documents/GEL
PIReport_Kelo.pdf.

103. See, e.g., Dick M. Carpenter and John K. Ross, "Testing O'Connor and Thomas: Does the Use of Eminent Domain Target Poor and Minority Communities?," 46 *Urban Studies* 2447 (2009).

104. Altshuler and Luberoff, *Mega-Projects*, 44.

105. Brief for the National Association for the Advancement of Colored People et al. as Amici Curiae Supporting Petitioners, *Kelo v. City of New London*, 545 U.S. 469 (2004) (No. 04-108), 2004 WL 2811057.

106. Ibid., 7–12.

107. See Steven J. Eagle, "Does Blight Really Justify Condemnation?" 39 *Urban Lawyer* 833 (2007); and Steven J. Eagle, "Assembling Land for Urban Redevelopment: The Case for Owner Participation," in Bruce Benson, ed., *Property Rights: Eminent Domain and Regulatory Takings Re-Examined*, (New York: Palgrave Macmillan, 2010), 8, 17–23.

108. See, e.g. Becher, *Private Property and Public Power,* 58–70, 238.

109. Ibid., 64–67.

110. As Becher herself notes, "[a]bandoned properties in run-down neighborhoods seem to have little to no value to anyone in their current state. The owners, if they are even around to notice, may experience the value of such properties as nothing more than sources of additional property taxes, and perhaps, headaches." Ibid. 65. She makes this point as a justification for condemning them. But it is at least equally compelling as a reason why developers or the government should be able to easily acquire them without resorting to eminent domain.

111. For a review of various strategies for dealing with tax delinquent properties, including proposals for reform, see Frank S. Alexander and Leslie A. Powell, "Neighborhood Stabilization Strategies for Vacant and Abandoned Properties," 34 *Zoning and Planning Law Report* 1 (2011).

112. For a review of possible strategies, see ibid., 4–6. For example, the authors note that jurisdictions can make it easier to deal with tax delinquencies by permitting in rem judicial foreclosure, and by streamlining the number of procedural steps in the foreclosure process.

113. For a discussion of some proposals of this type, see chapter 8.

114. See ibid., 2–3.

115. See, e.g., Robert D. Cooter and Hans-Bernd Schafer, *Solomon's Knot: How Law Can End the Poverty of Nations* (Princeton, NJ: Princeton University Press, 2012), chap. 6; Hernando de Soto, *The Mystery of Capital: Why Capitalism Triumphs in the West and Fails Everywhere Else* (New York: Basic Books, 2000), 49–63. For a helpful recent overview, see Peter J. Boettke and Rosolino Antonio Candela, "Property Rights, Exchange, and the Production of Economic Development," in *Encyclopedia of Law and Economics*, ed. Jürgen Backhaus (Springer, forthcoming), available at http://papers.ssrn.com/sol3/papers.cfm?abstract_id=2478167.

116. For an overview of the holdout problem and associated literature, see. Kelly, "Acquiring Land through Eminent Domain," 345–48. For a detailed recent discussion of the holdout problem as a rationale for eminent domain, see Thomas J. Miceli, *The Economic Theory of Eminent Domain: Private, Property, Public Use* (Cambridge: Cambridge University Press, 2011), 27–34. See also Michael Heller, *The Gridlock Economy: How Too Much Ownership Wrecks Markets, Stops Innovation, and Costs Lives* (New York: Basic Books, 2008), 108–17; Merrill, "The Economics of Public Use," 72–81; Guido Calabresi and A. Douglas Melamed, "Property Rules, Liability Rules and Inalienability Rules: One View of the Cathedral," 85 *Harvard Law Review* 1089, 1106–08 (1972); Lloyd R. Cohen, "Holdouts and Free Riders," 20 *Journal of Legal Studies* 351 (1991). For a defense of economic development takings that heavily emphasizes the holdout rationale, see Dreher and Echeverria, "Kelo's Unanswered Questions," 28–32.

117. Heller, *Gridlock Economy,* 108.

118. This computes to $50,000−$5000 (paid to the holdout)−$4900 (paid to the other forty-nine owners who, by assumption, sell at the market price of $100).

119. See, e.g., Thomas Merrill and John Echeverria, Amicus Brief of American Planning Association, Connecticut Chapter of the American Planning Association, and National Congress for Economic Community Development, *Kelo v. City of New London*, 545 U.S. 469 (2005), 2005 WL 166929, 18–19.

120. Some scholars refer to this type of property owner as an "honest holdout." See Steven Shavell, "Eminent Domain vs. Government Purchase of Land Given Imperfect Information about Owners' Valuations," 53 *Journal of Law and Economics* 1 (2010).

121. See discussion in chapter 1; Wylie, *Poletown: Community Betrayed*, 83.

122. U.S. Supreme Court Oral Argument Transcript, *Kelo v. City of New London*, No. 04-108, 2005 WL 529436, at *27 (argued Feb. 22, 2005).

123. See, e.g., Kelly, "Acquiring Land through Eminent Domain," 348.

124. For a good discussion of this point, see Samuel R. Staley, "The Proper Uses of Eminent Domain for Urban Redevelopment: Is Eminent Domain Necessary?" in Bruce Benson, ed., *Property Rights: Eminent Domain and Regulatory Takings Re-Examined*, (New York: Palgrave Macmillan, 2010), 27, 41–42, 48–49.

125. Ibid., 41–42.

126. Ibid., 42.

127. See discussion in chapter 1.

128. *Kelo v. City of New London*, 545 U.S. 469 (2005), Amicus Brief of Richard Epstein and Cato Institute, 23, available at https://www.ij.org/images/pdf_folder/private_property/kelo/cato01.pdf.

129. See, e.g., Roderick Hills, Jr., "Rethinking Balancing Tests in Blight Condemnation Jurisprudence," 39 *Fordham Urban Law Journal City Square* 29, 33

(2012); Dreher and Echeverria, *Kelo's Unanswered Questions*, 28. For examples of architectural holdouts, see, e.g., Andrew Alpern and Seymour Durst, *New York's Architectural Holdouts,* (New York: Dover, 1997).

130. This point is adapted from Ilya Somin, "Blight Pretext, and Eminent Domain in New York," 39 *Fordham Urban Law Journal City Square* 57, 69–70 (2012).

131. Kelly, "Acquiring Land Through Eminent Domain," 346–47.

132. Cohen, "Holdouts and Free Riders," 359.

133. Ibid.

134. Richard A. Posner, *Economic Analysis of Law, 2nd ed.* (Chicago: Little, Brown, 1977), 43–44; Patricia Munch, "An Economic Analysis of Eminent Domain," 84 *Journal of Political Economy* 473, 479 (1976).

135. Michael Wheeler and Georgia Levenson, *Disney (A): From Disneyland to Disney World—Learning the Art of Land Assembly,* Harvard Business School, Case Study No 9-898-018, rev. ed., Sept. 27, 2000, at 3–4, available at http://www.hbs.edu/faculty/Pages/item.aspx?num=25439.

136. Ibid., 2. While the plan for the Virginia park was eventually shelved due to local opposition, ibid., 11–12, the failure was not due to land assembly problems but to the threat to Disney's public image caused by its plan to build in the vicinity of historic Civil War sites. See ibid., 7–8, 11–12; and David S. Hilzenrath, "Disney's Land of Make Believe: Acquisition Agent Used Ruse to Prevent Real Estate Speculation," *Washington Post*, Nov. 12, 1993, at A1.

137. Daniel B. Kelly, "The 'Public Use' Requirement in Eminent Domain Law: A Rationale Based on Secret Purchases and Private Influence," 92 *Cornell Law Review* 1, 6, 22–24 (2006).

138. Ibid., 23–24.

139. Ibid., 6–7.

140. Ibid., 25.

141. Ibid., 31–32; Merrill, "The Economics of Public Use," 81–82.

142. Bruce Benson, "Eminent Domain For Private Use: Is it Justified by Market Failure or an Example of Government Failure," in Bruce Benson, ed., *Property Rights: Eminent Domain and Regulatory Takings Re-Examined*, (New York: Palgrave Macmillan, 2010), 149, 151.

143. Kelly, "The 'Public Use' Requirement in Eminent Domain Law," 32; Merrill, "The Economics of Public Use," 81.

144. Kelly, "The 'Public Use' Requirement in Eminent Domain Law," 20; ibid., n.108.

145. For an argument challenging the conventional wisdom on this issue, William A. Fischel, *Regulatory Takings: Law, Economics, and Politics* (Cambridge, MA: Harvard University Press, 1995), 68–70.

146. Bruce L. Benson, "The Mythology of Holdout as Justification for Eminent Domain and the Public Provision of Roads," 10 *Independent Review* 165, 170–71 (2005).

147. For the classic explanation of the ways in which tying one's own hands can be an advantage in negotiations, see Thomas C. Schelling, *The Strategy of Conflict* (Cambridge, MA: Harvard University Press, 1960), 35–43, 120–31; see also Donald J. Kochan, "'Public Use' and the Independent Judiciary: Condemnation in an Interest-Group Perspective," 3 *Texas Review of Law & Policy* 49, 88–90 (1998), which explains how precommitment strategies used to prevent holdouts in corporate transactions can be applied to economic development projects that might otherwise need to resort to eminent domain.

148. Cohen, "Holdouts and Free Riders," 359.

149. Kelly, "Acquiring Land through Eminent Domain," 349–50.

150. For a discussion of such requirements, see chapter 8.

151. Kelly, "Acquiring Land through Eminent Domain," 350.

152. See Miceli, *Economic Theory of Eminent Domain,* 152–53.

153. Thomas Merrill and John Echeverria, Amicus Brief of American Planning Association, Connecticut Chapter of the American Planning Association, and National Congress for Economic Community Development, *Kelo v. City of New London*, 545 U.S. 469 (2005), 2005 WL 166929, 18–19.

154. Robert Bruegmann, *Sprawl: A Compact History* (Chicago: University of Chicago Press, 2005). Bruegmann also argues that many of the conventional criticisms of sprawl are overstated. Ibid., 138–55.

155. See Ilya Somin and Jonathan Adler, "The Green Costs of *Kelo*: Economic Development Takings and Environmental Protection," 84 *Washington University Law Review* 623, 657 (2006).

156. See Edward Glaeser et al., "Why Have Housing Prices Gone Up?," 95 *American Economic Review* 329 (2005); Edward Glaeser and Joseph Gyourko. "The Impact of Building Restrictions on Housing Affordability," 9 *Economic Policy Review* 21 (2003); Edward Glaeser et al., "Why Is Manhattan so Expensive? Regulation and the Rise in Housing Prices," National Bureau of Economic Research Working Paper No. 10124 (Nov. 2003).

157. For additional discussion of this issue, see chapter 8.

158. See discussion earlier in this chapter.

159. John Hart Ely, *Democracy and Distrust: A Theory of Judicial Review* (Cambridge, MA: Harvard University Press, 1980).

160. See, e.g., David A. Strauss, *The Living Constitution* (New York: Oxford University Press, 2010); Cass R. Sunstein, *A Constitution of Many Minds: Why the Founding Document Doesn't Mean What It Meant Before* (Princeton, NJ: Princeton University Press, 2009).

161. Ronald Dworkin, *Law's Empire* (Cambridge, MA: Harvard University Press, 1986), 379; see also Ronald Dworkin, *Freedom's Law: The Moral Reading of the American Constitution* (Cambridge, MA: Harvard University Press, 1996).

162. See, e.g., Larry D. Kramer, *The People Themselves: Popular Constitutionalism and Judicial Review* (Cambridge, MA: Harvard University Press,

2004); Matthew D. Adler, "Popular Constitutionalism and the Rule of Recognition: Whose Practices Ground U.S. Law?" 100 *Northwestern University Law Review* 719 (2006); Jack M. Balkin and Reva B. Siegel, "Principles, Practices, and Social Movements," 154 *University of Pennsylvania Law Review* 926 (2006); William N. Eskridge, Jr., "Some Effects of Identity-Based Social Movements on Constitutional Law in the Twentieth Century," 100 *Michigan Law Review* 2062 (2002); Reva B. Siegel, "Constitutional Culture, Social Movement Conflict, and Constitutional Change: The Case of the de Facto ERA," 94 *California Law Review* 1323 (2006).

163. See, e.g., Ely, *Democracy and Distrust,* chap. 6; Kermit Roosevelt, *Myth of Judicial Activism: Making Sense of Supreme Court Decisions* (New Haven, CT: Yale University Press, 2008), 29–37.

164. 304 U.S. 144, 152–53 n.4 (1938).

165. Ely, *Democracy and Distrust,* chap. 6.

166. Ibid., 74.

167. For an earlier argument that representation-reinforcement theory justifies invalidation of some private-to-private takings under the Public Use Clause, see Paul Boudreaux, "Eminent Domain, Property Rights, and the Solution of Representation-Reinforcement," 83 *Denver University Law Review* 1 (2005). Boudreaux's analysis differs from in that he argues only that the taking of property from the poor to transfer it to private parties should be deemed unconstitutional. In my view, the same reasoning applies to takings that victimize racial and ethnic minorities, and other politically weak groups. I also address several other aspects of the relationship between eminent domain and representation-reinforcement theory that Boudreaux's article does not.

168. E.g., Roosevelt, *Myth of Judicial Activism,* 137–39.

169. Richard A. Posner, *How Judges Think* (Cambridge, MA: Harvard University Press, 2008), 319.

170. See discussion earlier in this chapter.

171. See, e.g., the discussion earlier in this chapter, and Fullilove, *Root Shock.*

172. *Kelo v. City of New London,* 545 U.S. 469, 521–22 (2005) (Thomas, J., dissenting) [quoting *United States v. Carolene Prods.,* 304 U.S. 144, 152–53 n.4 (1938)].

173. Ely, *Democracy and Distrust,* 88–101.

174. Ibid., 97.

175. On this point, see, e.g., Bruce Ackerman, "Beyond Carolene Products," 98 *Harvard Law Review* 713 (1985); Laurence Tribe, "The Puzzling Persistence of Process-Based Constitutional Theory," 89 *Yale Law Journal* 1063 (1980).

176. See Strauss, *The Living Constitution*; David Strauss, "Common Law Constitutional Interpretation," 96 *University of Chicago Law Review* 877 (1996).

177. See the discussion of *Berman* in chapter 2.

178. Strauss, *The Living Constitution,* 79–80.

179. Ibid., 83–84.

180. 467 U.S. 229, 241 (1984). [quoting *Thompson v. Consol. Gas Corp.,* 300 U.S. 55, 80 (1937)].

181. *Kelo v. City of New London,* 545 U.S. 469, 477 (2005).

182. *Midkiff,* 467 U.S. at 241.

183. See the discussion of O'Connor's approach in chapter 4 and the discussion of *Kelo* and precedent in the conclusion.

184. See discussion of Stevens's new view in chapter 2.

185. See discussion of the history of public use in chapter 2.

186. Strauss, *The Living Constitution,* 92.

187. See discussion of these cases in chapters 2 and 6.

188. See Noga Morag-Levine, "Judges, Legislators, and Europe's Law: Common Law Constitutionalism and Foreign Precedents," 65 *Maryland Law Review* 32 (2006).

189. Dworkin, *Law's Empire,* 398.

190. Dworkin, *Freedom's Law:,* 2.

191. Dworkin, *Laws Empire,* 380–81; See also Dworkin, *Freedom's Law,* 8–9.

192. Dworkin, *Freedom's Law,* 7.

193. Dworkin, *Law's Empire,* 379.

194. Ibid., 297–306.

195. Dworkin, *Law's Empire,* 297.

196. Ibid., 398.

197. Ibid.

198. See, e.g., Ronald Dworkin, *A Matter of Principle* (Cambridge, MA: Harvard University Press, 1985), 209–11.

199. See, e.g., Larry D. Kramer, *The People Themselves: Popular Constitutionalism and Judicial Review* (Cambridge, MA: Harvard University Press, 2004); Matthew D. Adler, "Popular Constitutionalism and the Rule of Recognition: Whose Practices Ground U.S. Law?" 100 *Northwestern University Law Review* 719 (2006); Balkin and Siegel, "Principles, Practices, and Social Movements."

200. See, e.g., Barry Friedman, *The Will of the People: How Public Opinion Has Influenced the Supreme Court and Shaped the Meaning of the Constitution* (New York: Farrar, Straus, & Giroux, 2009).

201. See, e.g., Kramer, *The People Themselves;* Balkin and Siegel, "Principles, Practices, and Social Movements"; Eskridge, "Some Effects of Identity-Based Social Movements on Constitutional Law in the Twentieth Century."

202. On feminism as a popular constitutionalist movement, see, e.g., Siegel, "Constitutional Culture, Social Movement Conflict, and Constitutional Change: The Case of the de Facto ERA." On the gun rights case, see Adam Winkler, *Gun Fight: The Battle over the Right to Bear Arms in America* (New York: Norton, 2013).

203. For an analysis of the Tea Party movement in terms of popular constitutionalism, see Ilya Somin, "The Tea Party Movement and Popular Constitutionalism," 105 *Northwestern University Law Review Colloquy* 300 (2011).

204. See discussion in chapter 5.

205. See survey data compiled in ibid.

206. A 2009 poll on the subject found almost exactly the same degree of opposition as was evident in surveys conducted in the immediate aftermath of the taking. See ibid.

207. For an overview, see Somin, *Democracy and Political Ignorance,* chap. 1.

208. See, e.g., Mark Tushnet, *Taking the Constitution Away from the Courts* (Princeton, NJ: Princeton University Press, 1999).

209. This theory dates back to an influential 1893 article by James Bradley Thayer. See James Bradley Thayer, "The Origin and Scope of the American Doctrine of Constitutional Law," 7 *Harvard Law Review* 129 (1893). For a recent history and evaluation of the theory, see Richard A. Posner, "The Rise and Fall of Judicial Self-Restraint," 100 *California Law Review* 519 (2012).

210. See, e.g., Thomas W. Merrill, "The Conservative Case for Precedent," 31 *Harvard Journal of Law and Public Policy* 977 (2008).

211. 347 U.S. 54 (1954).

212. See Gerald Gunther, *Learned Hand: The Man and the Judge* (New York: Knopf, 1994), 654–57; Herbert Wechsler, "Toward Neutral Principles of Constitutional Law," 73 *Harvard Law Review* 1 (1959).

213. See, e.g., *Lawrence v. Texas,* 539 U.S. 558 (2003) (striking down laws banning "homosexual sodomy" and overruling a 1986 precedent in order to do so).

214. See Bruce Ackerman, *We the People: Foundations* (Cambridge, MA: Harvard University Press, 1991); Bruce Ackerman, *We the People: Transformations* (Cambridge, MA: Harvard University Press, 1998); Bruce Ackerman, *We the People: The Civil Rights Revolution* (Cambridge, MA: Harvard University Press, 2014).

215. Ackerman, *Foundations,* chap. 3.

216. See discussion of *Berman* earlier in this chapter.

217. See Ackerman, *Foundations,* chap. 10.

218. Ibid., 266.

219. In previous scholarship, I have argued that even some of the much better-known New Deal–era changes in constitutional doctrine may have lacked the kind of broad public understanding that Ackerman's theory requires. See Ilya Somin, "Voter Knowledge and Constitutional Change: Assessing the New Deal Experience," 45 *William & Mary Law Review* 595 (2003).

220. See Ackerman, *Civil Rights Revolution,* pt. II.

221. See ibid., and Ackerman, *Foundations,* chap. 4.

222. *Kelo v. City of New London,* 545 U.S. 469, 518 (2005) (Thomas, J., dissenting). I discuss Thomas's comparison between takings and searches in greater detail in chapter 4.

223. See discussion in chapter 8. On the significance of business ownership for personal autonomy, see John Tomasi, *Free Market Fairness* (Princeton, NJ: Princeton University Press, 2012), 77–79.

Chapter Four

1. *Kelo v. City of New London*, 545 U.S. 469, 478–86 (2005).

2. *Hawaii Housing Authority v. Midkiff*, 467 U.S. 229, 241 (1984).

3. *Kelo*, 545 U.S. at 499–506 (O'Conner, J., dissenting); ibid., 518–23 (Thomas, J., dissenting).

4. See the discussion of *Berman* and *Midkiff* in chapter 2.

5. Kelo, 545 U.S. at 480.

6. Ibid., 485.

7. Ibid., 487–89.

8. Ibid., 488.

9. Ibid., 478–83, including notes 9–11.

10. See discussion later in this chapter.

11. See, for example, *Kelo,* 545 U.S. at 480–82, 487–89 (relying on these two precedents extensively).

12. *Hawaii Housing Authority v. Midkiff*, 467 U.S. 229, 241 (1984).

13. Ibid., 240.

14. *Kelo*, 545 U.S. at 484.

15. Ibid., 487.

16. Ibid.

17. Ibid., 488–89.

18. Scott Bullock, "The Inadequacy of the Planning Process for Protecting Property owners from the Abuse of Eminent Domain for Economic Development," in Bruce Benson, ed., *Property Rights: Eminent Domain and Regulatory Takings Re-Examined* (New York: Palgrave Macmillan, 2010), 89, 91.

19. *Kelo*, 545 U.S. at 487 n.17.

20. The case involved condemnation powers established pursuant to the Amargosa Redevelopment Plan. 99 Cents Only Store v Lancaster Redevelopment Agency, 237 F. Supp. 2d 1123, 1125–26 (C.D. Cal. 2001).

21. *Kelo,* 545 U.S. at 477–78.

22. See discussion of this disagreement in chapter 7.

23. *Kelo*, 545 U.S. at 490 (Kennedy, J., concurring).

24. Ibid. (citing *Hawaii Housing Authority v. Midkiff*, 467 U.S. 229, 241 (1984)).

25. Ibid.

26. Ibid., 491.

27. Ibid.

28. Ibid.

29. Ibid. [citing *Cleburne v. Cleburne Living Center, Inc.*, 473 U.S. 432, 446–47 (1985); *Department of Agriculture v. Moreno*, 413 U.S. 528, 533–36 (1973)].

30. Ibid., 493 (Kennedy, J., concurring).

31. Ibid.

32. Judge Richard Posner criticizes Kennedy for not concurring in the judgment only because he left "the reader uncertain whether the majority opinion or the concurring opinion should be regarded as the best predictor of how the Court would decide a similar case in the future." Richard Posner, "Foreword: A Political Court," 119 *Harvard Law Review* 31, 95 (2005).

33. *Kelo*, 545 U.S. at 490 (Kennedy, J., concurring).

34. Ibid., 492 (Kennedy, J., concurring).

35. See discussion later in this chapter.

36. See discussion in chapter 3.

37. See discussion of this view in chapter 2.

38. See chapter 3.

39. *Kelo*, 545 U.S. at 477; *Hawaii Housing Authority v. Midkiff*, 467 U.S. 229, 245 (1984) (noting that "a purely private taking could not withstand the scrutiny of the public use requirement").

40. *Kelo*, 545 U.S. at 482.

41. See discussion in chapter 3.

42. James W. Ely, Jr., " 'Poor Relation' Once More: The Supreme Court and the Vanishing Rights of Property Owners," 2005 *Cato Supreme Court Review* 39, 62.

43. U.S. Const. amend. IV.

44. *Kelo*, 545 U.S. at 518 (Thomas, J., dissenting).

45. Ely, " 'Poor Relation' Once More," at 63.

46. *United States v. 564.54 Acres of Land*, 441 U.S. 506, 511 (1979) (noting that "the Court . . . has employed the concept of fair market value to determine the condemnee's loss" and the amount of compensation due).

47. For an extensive overview, see Yun-Chien Chang, *Private Property and Takings Compensation: Theoretical Framework and Empirical Analysis* (Northampton, UK: Edward Elgar, 2013); See also Glenn S. Lunney, "Compensation for Takings: How Much is Just?," 42 *Catholic University Law Review* 721 (1993).

48. US Senate Committee on the Judiciary, *The* Kelo *Decision: Investigating Takings of Homes and Other Private Property*, (testimony of Professor Thomas W. Merrill), (Sept. 20, 2005), available at http://www.judiciary.senate.gov/hear ings/testimony.cfm?renderforprint=1&id=e655f9e2809e5476862f735da10a 78d5&wit_id=e655f9e2809e5476862f735da10a78d5-2-5. See also Lee Anne Fennell, "Picturing Takings," 57 *Notre Dame Law Review* 85–86 (2012), which suggests that the rationale for judicial deference on public use is "institutional competence."

49. *Kelo,* 545 U.S. at 482 (quoting *Hairston v. Danville & W. R. Co.*, 208 U.S. 598, 606–07 (1908)). For the argument that *Kelo* represents a "shift in favor of

federalism" by the liberal wing of the Court, see David L. Callies, *"Kelo v. City of New London:* Of Planning, Federalism, and a Switch in Time, "28 *University of Hawaii Law Review* 327, 328 (2006).; for a critique of that view, see Mark Fenster, "The Takings Clause, Version 2005: The Legal Process of Constitutional Property Rights," 9 *University of Pennsylvania Journal of Constitutional Law* 667, 719–25 (2007).

50. *Ornelas v. United States*, 517 U.S. 690, 699 (1996); see also *United States v. Brown*, 310 Fed. App'x 776, 778 (6th Cir. 2009) (noting relevance of "understanding [of] local conditions" in determining whether a search is reasonable); *United States v. Atchley*, 474 F.3d 840, 847 (6th Cir. 2007) (same).

51. For a more detailed discussion of the parallels between these cases and property rights, see Ilya Somin, "Federalism and Property Rights," 2011 *University of Chicago Legal Forum* 53, 80–84.

52. See ibid., 67–71.

53. For a discussion of this point, see ibid., 84–86.

54. I discuss some potential complications in chapter 8.

55. *Kelo v. City of New London*, 545 U.S. 469, 472–74 (2005). On the role of confidence in the planning process in Justice Stevens's opinion, see Nicole Stelle Garnett, "Planning as Public Use?," 34 *Ecology Law Quarterly* 443 (2007).

56. *Kelo,* 545 U.S. at 491 (Kennedy, J., concurring).

57. See discussion of the *99 Cents* case earlier in this chapter.

58. *Kelo*, 545 U.S. at 488.

59. Ibid., 478 (asserting that "there was no evidence of illegitimate purpose in the case"); ibid., 493 (Kennedy, J., concurring) (stating that there is no evidence of "an impermissible private purpose" in *Kelo*); ibid., 495 (O'Connor, J., dissenting) (stating that the NLDC had acted "[c]onsistent[ly] with its mandate" to "assist the city council in economic development planning"); *Kelo v. City of New London*, 843 A.2d 500, 538–41 (Conn. 2004) (concluding that the NLDC and New London were not motivated by a desire to advance Pfizer's interests); ibid., 595 (Zarella, J., dissenting) (stating that "[t]he record clearly demonstrates that the development plan was not intended to serve the interests of Pfizer, Inc., or any other private entity, but rather, to revitalize the local economy").

60. See discussion in chapter 1, and Ted Mann, "Pfizer's Fingerprints on Fort Trumbull Plan," *The Day* (Oct. 16, 2005), http://www.theday.com/article/20051016/BIZ04/911119999.

61. Ibid., 493 (Kennedy, J., concurring) (noting that "[t]his is not the occasion for conjecture as to what sort of cases might justify a more demanding standard of review").

62. Ibid.

63. Ibid.

64. *Kelo*, 545 U.S. at 502 (O'Connor, J., dissenting).

65. Had Kennedy concurred in judgment, his concurrence might have had controlling precedential force under *Marks v United States*, 430 U.S. 188 (1977). *Marks* held that "[w]hen a fragmented Court decides a case and no single rationale explaining the result enjoys the assent of five justices, the holding of the Court may be viewed as that position taken by those Members who concurred in the judgments on the narrowest grounds." Ibid., 193.

66. See chapter 7.

67. Interview with Wesley Horton, June 9, 2014.

68. *Kelo,* 545 U.S. at 483.

69. Ibid., 480.

70. See, e.g., Kermit Roosevelt, *Myth of Judicial Activism: Making Sense of Supreme Court Decisions* (New Haven, CT: Yale University Press, 2008), 138, which claims that *Kelo* follows from "a line of cases extending back over a hundred years"); David Barron, "Eminent Domain Is Dead! Long Live Eminent Domain!" *Boston Globe*, Apr. 16, 2006, which states that it was backed by "a century of precedent."

71. See Thomas Merrill and John Echeverria, Amicus Brief of American Planning Association, Connecticut Chapter of the American Planning Association, and National Congress for Economic Community Development, *Kelo v. City of New London*, 545 U.S. 469 (2005), 2005 WL 166929, 8–12.

72. *Kelo,* 545 U.S. at 480. I first pointed out this error in the Court's analysis in Ilya Somin, "Controlling the Grasping Hand: Economic Development Takings After *Kelo*," 15 *Supreme Court Economic Review* 183, 241–44 (2007).

73. For a detailed discussion of the Court's refusal to incorporate the Takings Clause in the early twentieth century, see Bradley C. Karkkainen, "The Police Power Revisited: Phantom Incorporation and the Roots of the Takings 'Muddle,'" 90 *Minnesota Law Review* 826, 844–55 (2006).

74. 198 U.S. 45 (1905).

75. On these points, see David E. Bernstein, *Rehabilitating Lochner: Defending Individual Rights against Progressive Reform* (Chicago: University of Chicago Press, 2011), chaps. 1–2.

76. Ibid. (citing *Fallbrook Irrigation District v. Bradley*, 164 U.S. 112, 158–64 (1896)).

77. *Fallbrook,* 164 U.S. at 156.

78. Ibid., 158.

79. *Kelo,* 545 U.S. at 480–82 [citing *Mt. Vernon-Woodberry Cotton Duck Co v. Alabama Interstate Power Co.*, 240 U.S. 30 (1916); *O'Neill v. Leamer*, 239 U.S. 244 (1915); *Strickley v. Highland Boy Goldmining Co.*, 200 US 527 (1906); *Clark v. Nash*, 198 U.S. 361 (1905)].

80. *Mt. Vernon-Woodberry*, 240 U.S. at 31 (stating that the case is based on a claim that an Alabama condemnation statute "contravene[s] the 14th Amendment

of the Constitution of the United States"); *O'Neill*, 239 U.S. at 249 (noting that the condemnation considered in that case was challenged on the ground that it was "contrary to the 14th Amendment, as amounting to a deprivation of property without due process of law"); *Strickley*, 200 U.S. at 531 (upholding a challenged condemnation because "there is nothing in the 14th Amendment which prevents a state from requiring such concessions"); *Clark v. Nash* did not explicitly state the precise constitutional basis of the challenge, but did cite *Fallbrook's* Fourteenth Amendment analysis as a controlling precedent. *Clark,* 198 U.S. at 369–70.

81. *Clark,* 198 U.S. at 369.

82. See *Wight v. Davidson*, 181 U.S. 371, 384 (1901). (ruling that a Fourteenth Amendment Due Process Clause precedent is inapplicable because "it by no means necessarily follows [from the fact that Congress's powers in the District are limited by the Takings Clause] that a long and consistent construction put upon the 5th Amendment, and maintaining the validity of the acts of Congress relating to public improvements within the District of Columbia, is to be deemed overruled by a decision concerning the operation of the 14th Amendment as controlling state legislation").

83. Bernstein, *Rehabilitating Lochner,* 48–50.

84. *Kelo,* 545 U.S. at 515–19 (Thomas, J., dissenting).

85. For a discussion of the history behind the Fuller Court's rejection of incorporation, see Bryan H. Wildenthal, "The Road to Twining: Reassessing the Disincorporation of the Bill of Rights," 61 *Ohio State Law Journal* 1457 (2000).

86. See Lawrence Berger, "Public Use, Substantive Due Process, and Takings—An Integration," 74 *Nebraska Law Review* 843, 862–66 (1995) (noting the longstanding tendency of jurists to conflate substantive due process and public use challenges to takings).

87. See, e.g., Michael G. Collins, "October Term, 1896—Embracing Due Process," 45 *American Journal of Legal History* 71, 73–82 (2001) (citing extensive evidence that *Fallbrook* and other early Supreme Court takings cases were part of a more general movement toward expansion of economic substantive due process).

88. See John Paul Stevens, "*Kelo*, Popularity, and Substantive Due Process," Albritton Lecture, University of Alabama School of Law, Nov. 16, 2011, 16, available at http://www.supremecourt.gov/publicinfo/speeches/1.pdf.

89. Ibid., 17.

90. Ibid., 15–18. Justice Stevens does acknowledge some very modest "substantive due process" constraints on the purposes for which property might be condemned. Ibid.

91. See discussion in chapter 2.

92. See discussion of these cases in chapter 2.

93. *Kelo v. City of New London*, 545 U.S. 469, 483 (2005).

94. For the view that revulsion against the *Lochner* era motivates much of the opposition to strong enforcement of the Public Use Clause that led to the Court's decision in *Kelo*, see, e.g., Richard Fallon, *The Dynamic Constitution: An Introduction to American Constitutional Law and Practice,* 2d ed. (Cambridge: Cambridge University Press, 2013), 104-05, 115-22.

95. See discussion of *Midkiff* in chapter 2.

96. *Kelo*, 545 U.S. at 493 (O'Connor, J., dissenting).

97. *Kelo v. City of New London*, 843 A.2d 500, 596–603 (Conn. 2004), *aff'd*, 545 U.S. 469 (2005) (Zarella, J., dissenting). See discussion of this dissent in chapter 1.

98. *Kelo,* 545 U.S. at 503 (O'Connor, J., dissenting).

99. See chapter 1.

100. *Kelo,* 545 U.S. at 494 (O'Connor, J., dissenting).

101. See discussion in chapter 3.

102. *Kelo,* 545 U.S. at 505 (O'Connor, J., dissenting).

103. See ibid.

104. Ibid., 501.

105. See the discussion earlier in this chapter.

106. *Kelo*, 545 U.S. at 501 (O'Connor, J., dissenting).

107. Ibid. (repudiating *Berman v. Parker*, 348 U.S. 26, 32 (1954), and *Hawaii Housing Authority v. Midkiff*, 467 U.S. 299, 240 (1984)).

108. Ibid., 500 (O'Connor, J., dissenting).

109. See *County of Wayne v. Hathcock*, 684 N.W.2d 765, 782–85 (Mich. 2004); see also the discussion of *Hathcock* in chapter 2; Ilya Somin, "Overcoming *Poletown*: *County of Wayne v. Hathcock*, Economic Development Takings, and the Future of Public Use," 2004 *Michigan State Law Review* 1005.

110. Benjamin Barros, "Nothing 'Errant' About It: The Berman and Midkiff Conference Notes and How the Supreme Court Got to *Kelo* with Its Eyes Wide Open," in *Private Property, Community Development, and Eminent Domain, ed.* Robin Paul Malloy (Burlington, VT: Ashgate, 2008), 69–72.

111. For a recent analysis of O'Connor's public use jurisprudence that reaches a similar conclusion, see James W. Ely, J., "Two Cheers for Justice O'Connor," 1 *Brigham-Kanner Property Rights Conference Journal* 149, 169–74 (2012). Ely suggests that O'Connor's change of heart may have been influenced by the Michigan Supreme Court's *Hathcock* decision, which adopted a similar approach to the one she advocated in her *Kelo* dissent. Ibid., 174.

112. See discussion in chapter 3.

113. See Debra Pogrund Stark, "How Do You Solve a Problem Like in *Kelo*?," 40 *John Marshall Law Review* 609, 624–30 (2007).

114. See discussions of this issue in chapters 2 and 5.

115. See Ilya Somin, "What if *Kelo v. City of New London* Had Gone the Other Way?," 45 *Indiana Law Review* 21, 30–31 (2011).

116. See examples given in chapters 2 and 7.

117. See discussion in chapters 2 and 3.

118. 347 U.S. 54 (1954).

119. *Kelo v. City of New London*, 545 U.S. 469, 521–22 (2005) (Thomas, J., dissenting).

120. Ibid., 521–22.

121. Ibid., 521 (Thomas, J., dissenting).

122. Ibid., 511–19 (Thomas, J., dissenting).

123. Ibid., 506.

124. See discussion in chapter 2.

125. *Kelo,* 545 U.S. at 518 (Thomas, J., dissenting).

126. Interview with Wesley Horton, June 9, 2014.

127. See numerous academic works and judicial opinions advocating a broad interpretation of public use cited in chapter 2, most of which were ignored by Thomas.

128. *Kelo,* 545 U.S. at 508 (Thomas, J., dissenting).

129. Ibid., 509.

130. Ibid.

131. Ibid.

132. On the relatively narrow original meaning of "general welfare," see, e.g., John C. Eastman, "Restoring the 'General' to the General Welfare Clause," 4 *Chapman Law Review* 63 (2001).

133. See discussion in chapter 2.

134. *Kelo,* 545 U.S. at 513–14 (Thomas, J., dissenting).

135. Ibid., 514.

136. See ibid., 514–15, where Thomas cites a few of the mill act cases but does not consider the many other state court public use decisions of the era.

137. I tried to address this gap in the literature in chapter 2.

138. *Kelo,* 545 U.S. at 515–17 (Thomas, J., dissenting).

139. Ibid., 516.

140. *Clark v. Nash*, 198 U.S. 361, 369 (1905). See also the discussion of *Clark* earlier in this chapter.

141. Julia D. Mahoney, "*Kelo*'s Legacy: Eminent Domain and the Future of Property Rights," 2005 *Supreme Court Review* 103, 132 (2005).

Chapter Five

1. There have been several previous analyses of the *Kelo* backlash. The most comprehensive is probably my own article on the subject, which this chapter updates. See Ilya Somin, "The Limits of Backlash: Assessing the Political Response to *Kelo*," 93 *Minnesota Law Review* 2100 (2009). For other discussions, all of which do not cover the full range of post-*Kelo* legislation, as this chapter does,

see Kyle Scott, *The Price of Politics: Lessons from* Kelo v. City of New London (Lanham, MD: Lexington Books, 2010), 119–33; John P. Hoehn and Kwami Adanu, "What Motivates Voters' Support for Eminent Domain Reform: Ownership, Vulnerability, or Ideology," 37 *International Review of Law and Economics* 90 (2014); Marc Mihaly and Turner Smith, *"Kelo's* Trail: A Survey of State and Federal Legislative and Judicial Activity Five Years Later," 38 *Ecology Law Quarterly* 703 (2011); Janice Nadler and Shari Seidman Diamond, "Government Takings of Private Property," *in Public Opinion and Constitutional Controversy,* ed. Nathaniel Persily et al. (New York: Oxford University Press, 2008), 286; Edward J. López et al., "Pass a Law, Any Law: State Legislative Responses to the *Kelo* Backlash," 5 *Review of Law and Economics* 101 (2009); Andrew Morriss, "Symbol or Substance? An Empirical Assessment of State Responses to *Kelo,"* 17 *Supreme Court Economic Review* 237 (2009); James W. Ely, Jr., "Post-*Kelo* Reform: Is the Glass Half-Full or Half-Empty?," 17 *Supreme Court Economic Review* 127 (2009); Elaine B. Sharp and Donald Haider-Markel, "At the Invitation of the Court: Eminent Domain Reform in State Legislatures in the Wake of the *Kelo* Decision," 38 *Publius: Journal of Federalism* 556 (2008); Timothy Sandefur, "The 'Backlash' So Far: Will Americans Get Meaningful Eminent Domain Reform?," 2006 *Michigan State Law Review* 709; and Lynn Blais, "Urban Revitalization in the Post-*Kelo* Era," 34 *Fordham Urban Law Journal* 657 (2007).

2. 408 U.S. 238, 256–67 (1972).

3. See *Gregg v. Georgia,* 428 U.S. 153, 179–80 & n.23 (1976) (noting that "at least 35 states" and the federal government had enacted new death penalty statutes in response to *Furman* and listing the state laws in question).

4. 798 N.E.2d 941, 969 (Mass. 2003). For a list of states enacting constitutional bans on same-sex marriage, see National Conference of State Legislatures, *Same Sex Marriage, Civil Unions and Domestic Partnerships* (2008), available at http://www.ncsl.org/programs/cyf/samesex.htm.

5. *In re Marriage Cases,* 183 P.3d 384, 450–52 & n.70 (Cal. 2008), *superseded by* Cal. Const. art. I, § 7.5; *Kerrigan v. Commissioner of Public Health,* 957 A.2d 407, 481 (Conn. 2008).

6. *Kelo v. City of New London,* 545 U.S. 469, 489 (2005).

7. Richard A. Posner, "The Supreme Court, 2004 Term–Foreword: A Political Court," 119 *Harvard Law Review* 31, 98 (2005). At his confirmation hearing before the Senate, then-Judge John Roberts commented that the legislative reaction to *Kelo* shows that "this body [Congress] and legislative bodies in the States are protectors of the people's rights as well" and "can protect them in situations where the Court has determined, as it did 5-4 in *Kelo,* that they are not going to draw that line." Confirmation Hearing on the Nomination of John G. Roberts, Jr. to Be Chief Justice of the United States: Hearing before the Senate Committee on the Judiciary, 109th Cong. 286 (2005). For a prescient early prediction that the political response would likely prove to be inadequate, see Julia D. Ma-

honey, "*Kelo's* Legacy: Eminent Domain and the Future of Property Rights," 2005 *Supreme Court Review* 103, 126–29 (2005).

8. Posner, "The Supreme Court, 2004 Term—Foreword," 98.

9. See Richard A. Posner, *How Judges Think* (Cambridge, MA: Harvard University Press, 2008), 319.

10. John Paul Stevens, "Judicial Predilections," 6 *Nevada Law Journal* 1, 4 (2005).

11. For perhaps the best-known modern statement of this argument, see John Hart Ely, *Democracy and Distrust: A Theory of Judicial Review* 87–88 (Cambridge, MA: Harvard University Press, 1980) (arguing that judicial review should focus on protecting citizens' rights to participate in the political process and minority groups against oppression by the majority).

12. James Madison, "Federalist 10," in Alexander Hamilton, James Madison, and John Jay, *The Federalist Papers, ed.* Clinton Rossiter (New York: Mentor, 1961), 83.

13. Ibid.

14. See Somin, "Limits of Backlash."

15. Nader has been a long-standing critic of economic development takings. See, e.g., Ralph Nader and Alan Hirsch, "Making Eminent Domain Humane," 49 *Villanova Law Review* 207 (2004). For his statement denouncing *Kelo*, see Ralph Nader, Statement, June 23, 2005, http://ml.greens.org/pipermail/ctgp-news/2005-June/000507.html Nader said that "the U.S. Supreme Court's decision in *Kelo v. City of New London* mocks common sense, tarnishes constitutional law and is an affront to fundamental fairness." For Limbaugh's denunciation of *Kelo*, see "Rush Limbaugh: Liberals Like Stephen Breyer Have Bastardized the Constitution" (radio transcript Oct. 12, 2005), http://www.freerepublic.com/focus/f-news/1501453/posts. Limbaugh stated that "Government can kick the little guy out of his and her homes and sell those home [sic] to a big developer who's going to pay a higher tax base to the government. Well, that's not what the takings clause was about. It's not what it is about. It's just been bastardized, and it gets bastardized because you have justices on the court who will sit there and impose their personal policy preferences rather than try to get the original intent of the Constitution."

16. H.R. Res. 340, 109th Cong., 151 *Congressional Record* H5,592–93 (2005); Adam Karlin, "A Backlash on Seizure of Property," *Christian Science Monitor,* July 6, 2005.

17. See Eric Kriss, "More Seek Curbs on Eminent Domain," *Syracuse Post-Standard,* July 31, 2005, A16.

18. "Howard Dean Speaks to Utah Democrats" (KSL television broadcast July 16, 2005), available at http://tv.ksl.com/index.php?nid=148&sid=76641.

19. Charles Hurt, "Congress Assails Domain Ruling," *Washington Times,* July 1, 2005, at A1.

20. Quoted in ibid. In 2006, Sanders was elected to the Senate.

21. Brief for the National Association for the Advancement of Colored People et al. as Amici Curiae Supporting Petitioners, *Kelo v. New City of London*, 545 U.S. 469 (2004) (No. 04-108).

22. U.S. Senate Committee on the Judiciary, *The* Kelo *Decision: Investigating Takings of Homes and Other Private Property* (testimony of Hilary O. Shelton) (Sept. 20, 2005), available at http://www.gpo.gov/fdsys/pkg/CHRG-109shrg24723 /pdf/CHRG-109shrg24723.pdf, 139, 141; Shelton reiterated the NAACP's opposition to economic development takings in testimony before the US Commission on Civil Rights in 2011. See United States Commission on Civil Rights, *Briefing Report, The Civil Rights Implications of Eminent Domain Abuse* (2014), available at http://www.usccr.gov/pubs/FINAL_FY14_Eminent-Domain-Report.pdf (statement of Hilary O. Shelton), 54–57.

23. See Patricia Salkin et al., "The Friends of the Court: The Role of Amicus Curiae in *Kelo v. City of New London*," in *Eminent Domain Use and Abuse: Kelo in Context, ed.* Dwight H. Merriam and Mary Massaron Ross (Chicago: American Bar Association, 2006),

24. See David de Sola, "Souter's Home an Activist Target," CNN.com, Jan. 22, 2006, available at http://edition.cnn.com/2006/LAW/01/21/eminent.domain/

25. See table 5.1. The differences between the two surveys are likely due to a difference in question wording.

26. The Zogby survey question asked respondents whether they agreed "with the recent Supreme Court ruling that allowed a city in Connecticut to take the private property of one citizen and give it to another citizen to use for *private development?*" Zogby International, American Farm Bureau Federation Survey 27, question 28 (Nov. 2, 2005) (emphasis added). This wording ignores the fact that the legal rationale for *Kelo* is that the takings are intended to promote "public" development. By contrast, the Saint Index survey asked respondents whether they supported or opposed the Court's decision "that local governments can take homes, business and private property to make way for private economic development if officials believe it *would benefit the public.*" Saint Index 2005, question 10 (emphasis added).

27. Saint Index 2005, question 10.

28. Center for Economic & Civic Opinion at University of Massachusetts/ Lowell, The Saint Index Poll, question 9 (2006) (hereinafter Saint Index 2006); see also Ilya Somin, "Is Post-*Kelo* Eminent Domain Reform Bad for the Poor?," 101 *Northwestern University Law Review* 1931, 1940 table. 2 (2007).

29. The wording is favorable to the pro-*Kelo* side because it mentions the rationale for the taking ("benefit [to] the local economy") and notes that the owners will get a "fair market price." Respondents who are not experts in this field might believe that the latter actually means a "fair price" that takes account of the full extent of the owners' losses, even though it only actually means "fair

market value," which is often not enough to fully compensate owners for the loss of subjective value. On the other hand, the question does not mention any of the arguments against such takings such as the likelihood that they will destroy more economic value than they create.

30. This figure does not include the state of Utah, which enacted effective eminent domain reform prior to *Kelo*.

31. See Mihaly and Smith, *"Kelo's* Trail"; Morriss, "Symbol or Substance?" For the Institute for Justice study, see Institute for Justice, *50 State Report Card: Eminent Domain Reform Legislation Since* Kelo, available at http://castleco alition.org/index.php?option=com_content&task=view&id=2412&Itemid=129 (last visited July 5, 2014). My scoring significantly differs from the Institute for Justice's with respect to only one state, Iowa. The Institute for Justice rates Iowa favorably because the new reform law requires that 75 percent of the properties in an area must be designated as blighted before condemnation. But I believe this to be ineffective for reasons discussed later in the chapter (primarily because it is so easy to designate a property as blighted that the 75 percent figure is not much of an obstacle). In my previous article on this subject, I also rated two marginal cases significantly differently from IJ: Idaho (which I rated as "effective," while IJ gave it a D+ grade); and Wisconsin, which I rated as ineffective, while IJ gave it a C+, but still considered its improvements "significant." See Somin, "Limits of Backlash." I have since changed my ratings for both cases, though both remain close calls.

32. Dana Berliner, *Public Power, Private Gain: A Five-Year, State-by-State Report Examining the Abuse of Eminent Domain* (2003), http://www.castlecoali tion.org/pdf/report/ED_report.pdf. Berliner was one of the two Institute for Justice lawyers who represented Susette Kelo and the other New London property owners. *Kelo v. City of New London*, 545 U.S. 469, 469 (2005).

33. Berliner, *Public Power, Private Gain*, 2.

34. Ibid., 3.

35. See tables A1–A3 in the appendix.

36. See table A1 in the appendix.

37. See table A2 in the appendix.

38. Utah Code Ann. § 17B-4-202 (2004) (current version at Utah Code Ann. § 17C-1-202 (2006)); Henry Lamb, "Utah Bans Eminent Domain Use by Redevelopment Agencies," 8 *Environmental & Climate News*, June 2005, at 1. (describing the politics behind the Utah law). In March 2006, Utah partially rescinded its ban on blight condemnations See. Utah Code Ann. § 17c-2-503 (amended 2007).

39. For discussion of the role of blight designations in post-*Kelo* reform laws that reaches similar conclusions to mine, but without considering each state in as much detail, see Martin E. Gold and Lynne B. Sagalyn, "The Use and Abuse of Blight in Eminent Domain, " 38 *Fordham Urban Law Journal* 1119, 1150–60 (2011).

40. Mihaly and Smith, *"Kelo's* Trail."; Hudson Hayes Luce, "The Meaning of Blight: A Survey of Statutory and Case Law," 35 *Real Property Probate & Trusts Journal* 389, 394–96 (2000) (describing definitions of blight used in various states); Colin Gordon, "Blighting the Way: Urban Renewal, Economic Development, and the Elusive Definition of Blight," 31 *Fordham Urban Law Journal* 305, 305–07 (2004) (describing very broad use of blight designations to facilitate condemnation).The latter two articles are partly out-of-date because they do not account for the abolition of private-to-private blight condemnations by Florida, Nevada, New Mexico, North Dakota, South Dakota, and Utah, as well as the tightening of the definition of blight by other states in the aftermath of *Kelo.* Utah, however, later partly reversed itself. See discussion later in this chapter.

41. Gordon, "Blighting the Way," 320–23; Luce, "The Meaning of Blight," 397–400.

42. Alaska Stat. § 09.55.240(a)(2) (2008) (exempting preexisting public uses declared in state law from a ban on economic development takings); Alaska Stat. § 18.55.950(2) (2008) ("'[B]lighted area' means an area, other than a slum area, that by reason of the predominance of defective or inadequate street layout, faulty lot layout in relation to size, adequacy, accessibility, or usefulness, unsanitary or unsafe conditions, deterioration of site or improvements, tax or special assessment delinquency exceeding the fair value of the land, improper subdivision or obsolete platting, or the existence of conditions that endanger life or property by fire and other causes, or any combination of these factors, substantially impairs or arrests the sound growth of the municipality, retards the provision of housing accommodations, or constitutes an economic or social liability and is a menace to the public health, safety, morals, or welfare in its condition and use."); Colo. Rev. Stat. § 31-25-103(2) (2008) (defining "blight" to include any condition that "substantially impairs or arrests the sound growth of the municipality, retards the provision of housing accommodations, or constitutes an economic or social liability, and is a menace to the public health, safety, morals, or welfare"); Colo. Rev. Stat. § 38-1-101(2)(b) (2008) (allowing condemnation for the "eradication of blight"); Mo. Rev. Stat. § 353.020.2 (2008) (defining "blighted area" as "that portion of the city . . . that by reason of age, obsolescence, inadequate or out-moded design or physical deterioration have become economic and social liabilities, and that such conditions are conducive to ill health, transmission of disease, crime or inability to pay reasonable taxes"); Mo. Rev. Stat. § 523.271.2 (2008) (exempting blight condemnations from ban on "economic development" takings); Mont. Code. Ann. § 7-15-4206(2) (2007) ("'Blighted area' means an area that is conducive to ill health, transmission of disease, infant mortality, juvenile delinquency, and crime, that substantially impairs or arrests the sound growth of the city or its environs, that retards the provision of housing accommodations, or that constitutes an economic or social liability or is detrimental or constitutes a menace to the public health, safety, welfare, and morals in its present condition

and use by reason of: (a) the substantial physical dilapidation, deterioration, age obsolescence, or defective construction, material, and arrangement of buildings or improvements, whether residential or nonresidential."); Mont. Code Ann. § 70-30-102 (2007) (banning economic development condemnations but retaining most of the broad definition of blight outlined in Montana Code Annotated section 7-15-4206(2)(a)); Neb. Rev. Stat. § 18-2103 (2007) (defining blight as any area in a condition that "substantially impairs or arrests the sound growth of the community, retards the provision of housing accommodations, or constitutes an economic or social liability" and has "deteriorating" structures); Neb. Rev. Stat. § 76-701 (2007) (exempting "blight" condemnations from ban on economic development takings); N.C. Gen. Stat. § 160A-503(2) (2007) ("'Blighted area' shall mean an area in which there is a predominance of buildings or improvements (or which is predominantly residential in character), and which, by reason of dilapidation, deterioration, age or obsolescence, inadequate provision for ventilation, light, air, sanitation, or open spaces, high density of population and overcrowding, unsanitary or unsafe conditions, or the existence of conditions which endanger life or property by fire and other causes, or any combination of such factors, substantially impairs the sound growth of the community, is conducive to ill health, transmission of disease, infant mortality, juvenile delinquency and crime, and is detrimental to the public health, safety, morals or welfare."); N.C. Gen. Stat. § 160A-515 (2007) (exempting blight condemnations from restrictions on economic development takings); Ohio Rev. Code Ann. § 1.08, 303.26(E) (LexisNexis 2008) ("'Blighted area' and 'slum' mean an area in which at least seventy per cent of the parcels are blighted parcels and those blighted parcels substantially impair or arrest the sound growth of the state or a political subdivision of the state, retard the provision of housing accommodations, constitute an economic or social liability, or are a menace to the public health, safety, morals, or welfare . . . ."). To qualify as a "blighted parcel," a parcel must meet at least two of seventeen vague and general conditions such as "deterioration," "age and obsolescence," "faulty lot layout," being "located in an area of defective or inadequate street layout," and "overcrowding of buildings." Ohio Rev. Code Ann. §§ 108.(B)(2)(a-p) (LexisNexis 2008). Virtually any area is likely to meet two or more of these criteria. S.B. 167, § 2(A), 126th Gen. Assem. (Ohio 2005) (exempting blight condemnations from temporary moratorium on economic development takings); Tex. Gov't Code Ann. § 2206.001(b)(3) (Vernon 2008) (exempting condemnations "to eliminate an existing affirmative harm on society from slum or blighted areas" from the ban on economic development takings); Tex. Loc. Gov't Code Ann. § 374.003(3) (Vernon 2005) ("'Blighted area' means an area that is not a slum area, but that, because of deteriorating buildings, structures, or other improvements; defective or inadequate streets, street layout, or accessibility; unsanitary conditions; or other hazardous conditions, adversely affects the public health, safety, morals, or welfare . . . or results in an economic or social liability to the municipality."); Vt. Stat. Ann. tit. 12, § 1040 (2008) (exempting blight condemnations from ban on economic development takings); Vt. Stat. Ann. tit. 24, § 3201(3) (2008) (defining "blighted area" to include any planning or layout condition that "substantially impairs or arrests the sound growth of a municipality, retards the provision of housing accommodations or constitutes an economic or social liability and is a menace to the public health, safety, morals, or welfare"); W. Va. Code Ann. § 16-18-3 (LexisNexis 2006) (defining "blighted area" as an area that, due to a number of factors such as deterioration or inadequate street layout, "substantially impairs or arrests the sound growth of the community, retards the provision of housing accommodations or constitutes an economic or social liability and is a menace to the public health, safety, morals, or welfare in its present condition and use"); W. Va. Code Ann. § 16-18-6 (LexisNexis 2006) (exempting blight condemnation from ban on redevelopment takings). A 2010 Nebraska appellate decision ruled that the Nebraska reform law also does not forbid the condemnation of property for publicly owned deceleration lanes, even if the project provides "incidental" economic benefits to a private interest. See *City of Omaha v. Tract No. 1*, 778 N.W.2d 122 (Neb. Ct. App. 2010).

43. See statutes summarized in notes above.

44. *Panama City Beach Community Redevelopment Agency v. State*, 831 So. 2d 662, 668–69 (Fla. 2002).

45. *City of Phoenix v. Superior Court*, 671 P.2d 387, 391–93 (Ariz. 1983). The language was present in Arizona's pre-*Kelo* blight law, which has since been superseded by the state's post-*Kelo* reforms.

46. A 2007 Missouri Supreme Court decision might be considered an exception to this generalization. It construed section 353.020 of Missouri's blight law as requiring separate proof of "social liability" that goes beyond merely showing the existence of an "economic liability," in the sense of an obstacle to future growth and reduction of tax revenue. *Centene Plaza Redevelopment Corp. v. Mint Properties.*, 225 S.W.3d 431, 433 (Mo. 2007). The decision notes, however, that proof of the existence of "social liability" might be demonstrated by providing evidence "concerning the public health, safety, and welfare," which in this case was totally absent from the record. Ibid., 433–35. In any event, Missouri local governments also had the power to condemn property based on the definition of blight in another statute that defines the concept as requiring proof of the existence of either an "economic" or a "social liability." State *ex rel. Atkinson v. Planned Industrial Expansion Authority*, 517 S.W.2d 36, 41 (Mo. 1975) (noting that industrial development projects undertaken in accordance with this section include the power to acquire property through the use of eminent domain). A more recent Missouri Supreme Court decision has ruled that the Missouri post-*Kelo* reform statute, which includes a broad definition of blight, does not allow the condemnation of property in a case where a port authority sought to condemn property for a train track for which "[t]he record demonstrates that the

only manner in which the taking will 'improve river commerce' is by drawing more economic development into the area." Missouri *ex rel. Jackson v. Dolan,* 398 S.W.3d 472, 482 (Mo. 2013). However, the case did not involve any claim that the property in question was blighted. The court noted that its ruling was based on the fact that "economic development" was "the *sole* purpose" of the taking in question, which leaves open the possibility that similar condemnations might be permissible under a broad definition of blight. Ibid. Nevertheless, this ruling does create the possibility that Missouri's statute might end up restricting eminent domain more than I originally expected.

47. S.B. 3086, 94th Gen. Assem., § 1-1-5 (Ill. 2006).

48. 65 Ill. Comp. Stat. 5/11-74.4-3(a)(1) (2006).

49. Ibid.

50. The statute does require that at least five of the listed factors be present. Ibid. However, this is little obstacle to obtaining a blight declaration because so many are conditions that exist in almost any area.

51. See Idaho Code Ann. § 7-701A(2)(b) (Supp. 2008) (forbidding condemnations "[f]or the purpose of promoting or effectuating economic development" and for the acquisition of nonblighted property, and defining blight as a condition that poses physical risks to the occupants of a building, spreads disease or crime, or poses "an actual risk of harm" to public safety, health, morals, or welfare).

52. Ibid., § 7-701A(2)(b)(ii).

53. Ibid., § 7-701A(2)(b)(iii).

54. Idaho Const. art. I, § 14.

55. *Cohen v. Larson,* 867 P.2d 956, 969 n.3 (Idaho 1993).

56. Nev. Rev. Stat. § 37.010(1)(q) (2007).

57. Ibid., § 279.388.

58. They are "economic dislocation, deterioration or disuse," "subdividing and sale of lots of irregular form and shape and inadequate size for proper usefulness and development," "[t]he laying out of lots in disregard of the contours and other physical characteristics of the ground," "[t]he existence of inadequate streets, open spaces and utilities," "[a] growing or total lack of proper utilization of some parts of the area, resulting in a stagnant and unproductive condition of land," and "[a] loss of population and a reduction of proper use of some parts of the area, resulting in its further deterioration and added costs to the taxpayer. Ibid.

59. See discussion of Nevada's referendum initiative later in this chapter.

60. Ky. Rev. Stat. Ann. § 99.340(2) (LexisNexis 2004).

61. Ibid., § 99.370(6).

62. Ibid., § 99.340.

63. Me. Rev. Stat. Ann. tit. 30-A, § 5101 (1964); Me. Rev. Stat. Ann. tit. 1, § 816 (2008) (exempting blight condemnations from ban on economic development condemnations).

64. Me. Rev. Stat. Ann. tit. 30-A, § 5101 (1964).

65. Ibid., § 5102.
66. Ibid., § 5201.
67. Tenn. Code Ann. § 13-20-201(a) (2008).
68. Ibid.
69. R.I. Gen. Laws § 42-64.12-7 (Supp. 2008).
70. Ibid., § 45-31-6 (1999).
71. Ibid., § 45-31-8. An "arrested blighted area" is defined as

[A]ny area which, by reason of the existence of physical conditions including, but not by way of limitation, the existence of unsuitable soil conditions, the existence of dumping or other insanitary or unsafe conditions, the existence of ledge or rock, the necessity of unduly expensive excavation, fill or grading, or the necessity of undertaking unduly expensive measures for the drainage of the area or for the prevention of flooding or for making the area appropriate for sound development, or by reason of obsolete, inappropriate, or otherwise faulty platting or subdivision, deterioration of site improvements, inadequacy of utilities, diversity of ownership of plots, or tax delinquencies, or by reason of any combination of any of the foregoing conditions, is unduly costly to develop soundly through the ordinary operations of private enterprise and impairs the sound growth of the community.

Ibid., § 45-31-8(2). A "deteriorated blighted area" is

[A]ny area in which there exist buildings or improvements, either used or intended to be used for living, commercial, industrial, or other purposes, or any combination of these uses, which by reason of:

(i) Dilapidation, deterioration, age, or obsolescence;

(ii) Inadequate provision for ventilation, light, sanitation, open spaces, and recreation facilities;

(iii) High density of population and overcrowding;

(iv) Defective design or unsanitary or unsafe character or conditions of physical construction;

(v) Defective or inadequate street and lot layout; and

(vi) Mixed character, shifting, or deterioration of uses to which they are put, or any combination of these factors and characteristics, are conducive to the further deterioration and decline of the area to the point where it may become a slum blighted area as defined in subdivision (18), and are detrimental to the public health, safety, morals, and welfare of the inhabitants of the community and of the state generally. A deteriorated blighted area need not be restricted to, or consist entirely of, lands, buildings, or improvements which of themselves are detrimental or inimical to the public health, safety, morals, or welfare, but may consist of an area in which these conditions exist and injuriously affect the entire area.

Ibid., § 45-31-8(6). Finally, a "slum blighted area" is

[A]ny area in which there is a predominance of buildings or improvements, either used or intended to be used for living, commercial, industrial, or other purposes, or any combination of these uses, which by reason of: (i) dilapidation, deterioration, age, or obsolescence; (ii) inadequate provision for ventilation, light, sanitation, open spaces, and recreation facilities; (iii) high density of population and overcrowding; (iv) defective design or unsanitary or unsafe character or condition of physical construction; (v) defective or inadequate street and lot layout; and (vi) mixed character or shifting of uses to which they are put, or any combination of these factors and characteristics, are conducive to ill health, transmission of disease, infant mortality, juvenile delinquency, and crime; injuriously affect the entire area and constitute a menace to the public health, safety, morals, and welfare of the inhabitants of the community and of the state generally. A slum blighted area need not be restricted to, or consist entirely of, lands, buildings, or improvements which of themselves are detrimental or inimical to the public health, safety, morals, or welfare, but may consist of an area in which these conditions predominate and injuriously affect the entire area.

Ibid., § 45-31-8(18). The Rhode Island reform law explicitly reaffirms the power of local redevelopment agencies to condemn property under these blight statutes. Ibid., § 42-64.12-6(d) (Supp. 2008) (noting the power to condemn property in order to "[e]liminat[e] an identifiable public harm and/or correct[] conditions adversely affecting public health, safety, morals, or welfare, including, but not limited to, the elimination and prevention of blighted and substandard areas, as defined by chapter 45–31").

72. Ibid.

73. N.J. Assembly Bill 3615/Senate Bill 2447 (enacted Sept. 9, 2013).

74. Ibid. The decision in question is *Gallenthin Realty Development, Inc. v. Borough of Paulsboro*, 924 A.2d 447 (N.J. 2007). See the discussion of this ruling in chapter 7.

75. John Ross, "New Jersey Enacts Ponderous, Self-Negating Eminent Domain 'Reform,'" *Reason*, Sept. 13, 2013, available at http://reason.com/blog/2013/09/14/new -jersey-enacts-ponderous-self-negatin.

76. Ibid.

77. Iowa Code § 6A.22 (2008).

78. Ibid. (emphasis added).

79. Ibid.

80. S.53, 1206, 1210, 1650, 1809, 2006 Leg. (Cal. 2006).

81. S.53, 1210, 1650, 1809, 2006 Leg. (Cal. 2006).

82. Timothy Sandefur, "Governor Schwarzenegger Signs Mealy-Mouthed Property Rights Protection," *PLF on Eminent Domain*, Sept. 29, 2006, available at http://eminentdomain.typepad.com/my_weblog/2006/09/gov_schwarzeneg .html.

83. S.1206 § 2(b)(2) (requiring that blighted areas meet physical and economic conditions defined in section 3).

84. The list of "physical conditions" includes "conditions that prevent or substantially hinder the viable use or capacity of buildings or lots," and "[a]djacent or nearby incompatible land uses that prevent the development of those parcels or other portions of the project area." Since "viable use" and "development" are left undefined, local officials will have broad discretion to designate areas as they see fit. Ibid., § 3. The list of "economic conditions" is similar. Among other things, it includes "[d]epreciated or stagnant property values," "[a]bnormally high business vacancies," and "abnormally low lease rates." Ibid. Since almost any area occasionally experiences stagnation or decline in property values and a declining business climate, this list too puts no meaningful restrictions on blight designations.

85. See Roger Showley, "Court Ruling Kills State's Redevelopment Agencies," *San Diego Union-Tribune,* Dec. 29, 2011.

86. Conn. Gen. Stat. § 8-193(b)(1) (2009).

87. Ibid., § 8-124 (allowing use of eminent domain by redevelopment agencies); ibid., § 8-125(2) (stating that "redevelopment areas" can be declared in any "area within the state that is deteriorated, deteriorating, substandard or detrimental to the safety, health, morals or welfare of the community"). The concept of "deteriorating" area is defined extremely broadly. Ibid., § 8-125(7) (providing a list of numerous conditions only one of which must be met for an area to qualify as "deteriorating." Even this list is not exhaustive, since the statute says that possible conditions qualifying an area as "deteriorating" are "not limited" to those enumerated). *Kelo v. City of New London*, 545 U.S. 469, 475 (2005) (noting that Connecticut law permitted condemnation of the New London properties despite the fact that they were not "blighted" and only because they were located in the development area).

88. Conn. Gen. Stat. §§ 8-125–33 (2009) (outlining procedures for condemning property in "redevelopment areas").

89. Md. Code Ann. Real Prop. § 12-105.1(a) (West 2007).

90. Md. Const. art. III, § 61. The Maryland Constitution allows the use of eminent domain in "slum or blighted areas" and defines these terms as follows:

The term "slum area" shall mean any area where dwellings predominate which, by reason of depreciation, overcrowding, faulty arrangement or design, lack of ventilation, light or sanitary facilities, or any combination of these factors, are detrimental to the public safety, health or morals. The term "blighted area" shall mean an area in which a majority of buildings have declined in productivity by reason of obsolescence, depreciation or other causes to an extent they no longer justify fundamental repairs and adequate maintenance.

91. An Act to Establish a Moratorium on Eminent Domain, S.B. 167 § 2, Ohio Gen. Assem. (Ohio 2005) [codified at Ohio Rev. Code Ann. § 1426 (LexisNexis 2005 Bulletin #5)].

92. Ibid.

93. Ibid.

94. Ohio Rev. Code Ann. § 303.26(E) (LexisNexis 2003) (defining blight to include deteriorating structures or where the site "substantially impairs or arrests the sound growth of a county, retards the provision of housing accommodations, or constitutes an economic or social liability and is a menace to the public health, safety, morals, or welfare").

95. An Act to Establish a Moratorium on Eminent Domain, S.B. 167 § 3, Ohio Gen. Assem. (Ohio 2005) (codified at Ohio Rev. Code Ann. 1426 (LexisNexis 2005 Bulletin #5)).

96. For a detailed analysis of the commission's composition, see Somin, "Controlling the Grasping Hand," 249.

97. *Final Report of the Task Force to Study Eminent Domain* 12, Aug. 1, 2006 (on file with author). The new definition of blight advocated by the commission would allow the designation of an area as "blighted" so long as it was characterized by any two of seventeen different conditions. Ibid., attachment 2. Many of these are vaguely defined and could apply to almost any property. For example, one of the seventeen conditions is "[f]aulty lot layout in relation to size, adequacy, accessibility, or usefulness." Ibid. Others include "[e]xcessive dwelling unit density" (without defining what constitutes "excessive"), and "[a]ge and obsolescence" (also undefined). Ibid. Like the old definition, the new one would still permit virtually any property to be designated as "blighted."

98. Ohio Rev. Code Ann. §§ 1.08, 303.26 (LexisNexis 2008).

99. Tex. Gov't Code Ann. § 2206.001(b) (Vernon 2008).

100. Ibid.

101. Ibid.

102. See discussions in chapter 4 and chapter 7.

103. Tex. Gov't Code Ann. § 2206.001(b)(3) (Vernons 2008).

104. Tex. Loc. Gov't Code Ann. § 373.005(b)(1)(A) (Vernons 2005).

105. Ibid.

106. Ibid., § 2206.001(e).

107. Ibid., § 2206.001(b)(3) (referencing other Texas laws allowing takings for community development or improving blighted areas). These statutes are listed as the only broad exceptions to the bill's ban on takings "for economic development purposes." Ibid., § 2206.001(b).

108. Ibid., § 373.005(b)(1)(A).

109. Sandefur is more optimistic about these two provisions, calling them "significant improvements." Sandefur, "The 'Backlash' So Far," at 734. He does not, however, consider the possibility that they can be circumvented by means of the "community development" exception.

110. Act of Apr. 17, 2007, ch. 68, 2007 Wash. Sess. Laws 268 (codified in scattered sections of Wash. Rev. Code ch. 8 (2007)).

111. *Central Puget Sound Regional Transit Authority v. Miller*, 128 P.3d 588 (Wash. 2006). The state's Senate Committee on the Judiciary cited this decision as the reason for passing the new Washington law. S. Report, Substitute H.B. 1458, 60th Leg. (Wash. 2007), available at http://www.leg.wa.gov/pub/billinfo/2007-08 /Pdf/Bill%20Reports/Senate/1458-S.SBR.pdf.

112. See *Hogue v. Port of Seattle*, 341 P.2d 171, 187 (Wash. 1959), which forbids condemnation of private property so that an agency could "devote it to what it consider[ed] a higher and better economic use."

113. Wash. Rev. Code § 35.80A.010 (2008) (defining blight narrowly for purposes of condemnation).

114. Act of May 11, 2006, ch. 2006–11, 2006 Fla. Laws 214 (codified in scattered sections of Fla. Stat.); Act of Apr. 3, 2007, 2007 N.M. Laws 3873, ch. 330 (codified in scattered sections of N.M. Stat.). The New Mexico bill does still permit the condemnation of property that is characterized by "obsolete or impractical planning and platting" and "(a) was platted prior to 1971; (b) has remained vacant and unimproved; and (c) threatens the health, safety and welfare of persons or property due to erosion, flooding and inadequate drainage." Act of Apr. 3, 2007, 2007 N.M. Laws 3873, ch. 330, § 3-18-10(B)(3) (codified in scattered sections of N.M. Stat.).

115. See discussion above. However, Utah partially rescinded its ban on blight condemnations in a more recent bill. Act of Mar. 21, 2007, ch. 379, 2007 Utah Laws 2326 (codified in scattered sections of Utah Code Ann. §17C) (permitting blight condemnations if approved by a supermajority of property owners in the affected area).

116. A report prepared by the Institute for Justice, the libertarian public interest law firm that represented the property owners in *Kelo*, does not list a single private-to-private condemnation in Utah during the entire five-year period from 1998 to 2002. Berliner, *Public Power, Private Gain*, 196. The Institute for Justice report concluded (two years before the enactment of the 2005 reform law) that

"Utah has done fairly well in avoiding the use of eminent domain for private parties." Ibid. New Mexico did not have any private-to-private condemnations during the 1998–2002 period. Ibid., 143.

117. Ibid., 52–58.

118. S.D. Codified Laws § 11-7-22.1(1)) (Supp. 2008).

119. Act of May 18, 2006, ch. 192, 2006 Kan. Sess. Laws 1345, §§ 1–2 (codified at Kan. Stat. Ann. §§ 26-501a, 26-501b (Supp. 2008)).

120. Kan. Stat. Ann. § 26-501a(b) (Supp. 2008).

121. Ibid., § 26-501b(e).

122. Ala. Code § 24-2-2(c) (2008) (limiting definition of blight to a relatively narrow range of situations, such as property that is "unfit for human habitation," poses a public health risk, or has major tax delinquencies); Ibid., § 11-47-170(b) (forbidding condemnations that "transfer" nonblighted property to private parties); Del. Sen. Bill 7 (signed into law Apr. 9, 2009), available at http://legis.delaware.gov/LIS/LIS145.NSF/vwLegislation/SB+7?Opendocument; Ga. Code Ann. § 22-1-1(1), (10) (Supp. 2008) (forbidding economic development takings, and defining blight to include primarily risks to health, the environment, and safety, while excluding "esthetic" considerations); Ind. Code § 32-24-4.5-7 (Supp. 2008) (forbidding most private-to-private condemnations and defining blight as an area that "constitutes a public nuisance," is unfit for habitation, does not meet the building code, is a fire hazard, or is "otherwise dangerous"); Mich. Comp. Laws § 213.23(1), (3), (8) (Supp. 2008) (banning condemnations for "general economic development" and limiting the definition of "blight" to property that is a "public nuisance," an "attractive nuisance," poses a threat to public safety, such as a fire hazard, or is abandoned). The law does have a potential loophole insofar as it permits the condemnation of property as "blighted" if it "is not maintained in accordance with applicable local housing or property maintenance codes or ordinances." Ibid., § 213.23(8)(g); N.H. Rev. Stat. Ann. § 205:3-b (Supp. 2008) (defining public use as "exclusively" limited to government ownership, public utilities and common carriers, and blight-like condemnations needed to "remove structures beyond repair, public nuisances, structures unfit for human habitation or use, and abandoned property when such structures or property constitute a menace to health and safety"); Va. Code Ann. § 1-219.1 (2008) (permitting condemnation of private property only if "(i) the property is taken for the possession, ownership, occupation, and enjoyment of property by the public or a public corporation; (ii) the property is taken for construction, maintenance, or operation of public facilities by public corporations or by private entities provided that there is a written agreement with a public corporation providing for use of the facility by the public; (iii) the property is taken for the creation or functioning of any public service corporation, public service company, or railroad; (iv) the property is taken for the provision of any authorized utility service by a government utility corporation; (v) the property is taken for the elimination of blight provided that

the property itself is a blighted property; or (vi) the property taken is in a re-development or conservation area and is abandoned or the acquisition is needed to clear title where one of the owners agrees to such acquisition or the acquisition is by agreement of all the owners"). The new law also narrows the definition of "blight" to include only "property that endangers the public health or safety in its condition at the time of the filing of the petition for condemnation and is (i) a public nuisance or (ii) an individual commercial, industrial, or residential structure or improvement that is beyond repair or unfit for human occupancy or use." Ibid., § 1-219.1(B); Wyo. Stat. Ann. § 1-26-801(c) (2007) ("As used in and for purposes of this section only, 'public purpose' means the possession, occupation and enjoyment of the land by a public entity. 'Public purpose' shall not include the taking of private property by a public entity for the purpose of transferring the property to another private individual or private entity except in the case of condemnation for the purpose of protecting the public health and safety . . .".). Technically, this law seems to forbid blight condemnations. However, the provision permitting condemnations for the purpose of protecting "public health and safety" is functionally equivalent to allowing condemnation under an extremely narrow definition of blight.

Delaware previously enacted a highly ineffective reform law in 2006. For a discussion of that earlier Delaware law, see Somin, "Limits of Backlash," 2133.

123. See John Ross, "Alabama Brings Back Eminent Domain for Private Gain," *Reason,* Mar. 31, 2013, available at http://reason.com/blog/2013/03/31/ala bama-brings-back-eminent-domain-for-p.

124. Ala. Senate Bill 96 (enacted Mar. 30, 2013). I discussed the issue in Ilya Somin, "Don't Believe the Denials—Alabama Really Did Undermine It's Post-*Kelo* Eminent Domain Reform Law," *Volokh Conspiracy,* Apr. 7, 2013, available at http://www.volokh.com/2013/04/07/dont-believe-the-denials-alabama-really-did -undermine-its-post-kelo-eminent-domain-reform-law/.

125. *PKO Ventures, LLC v. Norfolk Redevelopment and Housing Authority,* 747 S.E.2d 826, 830 (Va. 2013) (holding that "The plain meaning of Code § 1-219.1 makes it clear that redevelopment and housing authorities no longer have the authority to condemn individual properties within a redevelopment area determined to be a blighted area when the properties are not themselves blighted").

126. 26 Pa. Cons. Stat. § 204(a) (Supp. 2008).

127. Ibid., § 203(4) (excluding areas designated as blighted within "a city of the first or second class," which under law turns out to be Pittsburgh and Philadelphia).

128. Berliner, *Public Power, Private Gain,* 173, 179–81 (describing major condemnation projects in the two cities).

129. See Nick Sibilla, "Philadelphia Wants to Use Eminent Domain to Turn an Artist's Studio into a Parking Lot and Supermarket," *Forbes,* Dec. 3, 2013, available at http://www.forbes.com/sites/instituteforjustice/2013/12/03/philadelphia

-wants-to-use-eminent-domain-to-turn-an-artists-studio-into-a-parking-lot-and
-supermarket/. In December 2014, the city abandoned its efforts to condemn
the studio after a prolonged legal and political battle in which the artist was
represented by the Institute for Justice. See Ilya Somin, "Philadelphia Aban-
dons Misguided Effort to Condemn Successful Artist's Studio," Volokh Conspiracy, *Washington Post*, Dec. 23, 2014, available at http://www.washingtonpost
.com/news/volokh-conspiracy/wp/2014/12/23/philadelphia-abandons-effort-to
-condemn-successful-artists-studio/.

130. Ibid.

131. Minn. Stat. § 117.025 (2008) (defining "public use" to mean exclusively
direct public use, or mitigation of blight, or a public nuisance, and *not* "the public
benefits of economic development," and defining a "blighted area" as an urban
area where more than half of the buildings are "structurally substandard" in the
sense of having two or more building code violations).

132. Ibid., § 117.011 (2006) (setting out exceptions for tax increment financing
districts), *repealed by* Minn. Stat. § 117.012 (West 2009 Electronic Update). A
survey by the pro-*Kelo* League of Minnesota Cities found that twenty-seven of
the thirty-four Minnesota cities that had used private-to-private takings for economic development purposes between 1999 and 2005 are located in the Twin Cities
area, which was exempt from the state's 2006 post-*Kelo* reform law. League of
Minnesota Cities, *Research on Cities' Use of Eminent Domain* (2005); Eric Wil-
lette, "LMC Study Finds Cities Use Eminent Domain Judiciously," *League of
Minnesota Cities Bulletin*, Nov. 30, 2005, 1.

133. Minn. Stat. § 117.011 (2008).

134. Minn. Stat. § 117.012 (West 2009 Electronic Update).

135. Wis. Stat. § 32.03(6)(a) (2007–08).

136. Ibid.

137. See Berliner, *Public Power, Private Gain*, 10–11, which notes that Alabama "has mostly refrained from abusing the power of eminent domain in recent
years" and had only one documented private-to-private condemnation in 2002;
Ibid., 59 (noting that Georgia is "one of a handful of states with no reported instances" of such condemnations between 1998 and 2002); Ibid., 189 (discussing
South Dakota).

138. These are the seven states that did so despite ranking in the top twenty
on the Institute for Justice's survey of private-to-private condemnations between
1998 and 2002. See table 5.5.

139. For a complete list and other details, see National Conference of State
Legislatures, *Property Rights Issues on the 2006 Ballot*, Nov. 12, 2006, available
at http://www.ncsl.org/statevote/prop_rights_06.htm.

140. Ibid. Only two post-*Kelo* ballot initiatives were defeated—one in Idaho
and one in California. *Id.* Both lost primarily because they were tied to controversial measures limiting "regulatory takings." See, e.g., Timothy Sandefur, "The

California Crack-up," *Liberty*, Feb. 2007, available at http://liberty unbound. com/archive/2007_02/sandefur-california.html. No stand-alone post-*Kelo* public use referendum initiative was defeated anywhere in the country.

141. Ga. Amendment 1 (enacted on Nov. 7, 2006, and amending Ga. Const. art. IX, § 2); N.H. Question 1 (enacted on Nov. 7, 2006, and amending N.H. Const. art. 12-a).

142. S.C. Amendment 5 (amending S.C. Const. art. I, § 13); Tex. Amendment 11 (enacted Nov. 3, 2009).

143. La. Amendment 5 (amending La. Const. art. I, § 4(B), art. VI, § 21(A) and adding art. VI, § 21(D)).

144. Ariz. Proposition 207 (enacted on Nov. 7, 2006, and codified at Ariz. Rev. Stat. Ann. §§ 12-1131 to -1138) (forbidding condemnations for "economic development" and limiting blight-like condemnations to cases where there is "a direct threat to public health or safety caused by the property in its current condition"); La. Amendment 5 (enacted on Sept. 30, 2006, and amending La. Const. art. I, § 4(B), art. VI, § 21(A) and adding art. VI, § 21(D)) (forbidding condemnations for "economic development" and tax revenue purposes, and confining blight condemnations to cases where there is a threat to public health or safety); Miss. Measure 31 (enacted Nov. 8, 2011) (forbidding economic development takings and limiting blight takings to areas that are seriously dilapidated or pose a threat to public safety). For a more detailed discussion of Measure 31, see Ilya Somin, "Referendum Initiatives Prevent Eminent Domain Abuse, " *Daily Caller,* Nov. 9, 2011, available at http://dailycaller.com/2011/11/09/referendum -initiatives-prevent-eminent-domain-abuse/; Or. Measure 39 (enacted on Nov. 7, 2006, and codified at Or. Rev. Stat. § 35.015) (forbidding most private-to-private condemnations and limiting blight-like condemnations to cases where they are needed to eliminate dangers to public health or safety).

145. *New Orleans Redevelopment Authority v. Johnson*, 16 So. 3d 569, 578–84 (La. Ct. App. 2009).

146. Miss. Measure 31 (enacted Nov. 8, 2011).

147. Nev. Ballot Question 2 (enacted on Nov. 7, 2006, reenacted on Nov. 4, 2008, and amending Nev. Const. art. I, § 22) (forbidding the "direct or indirect transfer of any interest in property taken in an eminent domain proceeding from one private party to another private party"); N.D. Measure 2 (amending N.D. Const. art. I, § 16) (mandating that "public use or a public purpose does not include public benefits of economic development, including an increase in tax base, tax revenues, employment, or general economic health. Private property shall not be taken for the use of, or ownership by, any private individual or entity, unless that property is necessary for conducting a common carrier or utility business"). The Nevada law did not take effect until it was approved by the voters a second time in November 2008. Nev. Ballot Question 2 (enacted on Nov. 7, 2006, reenacted on Nov. 4, 2008).

148. See discussion of Florida's reform earlier.

149. Fla. Amendment 8 (enacted on Nov. 7, 2006, and amending Fla. Const. art. X, § 6).

150. Va. Question 1 (enacted Nov. 7, 2012). For an account of the political struggle over Question 1 by a supporter of the initiative, see Jeremy P. Hopkins, "Obtaining Eminent Domain Reform: A View through the Lens of Virginia's Constitutional Amendment," American Law Institute Continuing Legal Education Program, Jan. 23–25, 2014.

151. Va. Question 1.

152. See the discussion of that law earlier in this chapter.

153. Va. Question 1.

154. Ga. Amendment 1 (enacted on Nov. 7, 2006, and amending Ga. Const. art. IX, § 2).

155. N.H. Question 1 (enacted on Nov. 7, 2006, and amending N.H. Const. art. 12-a).

156. Ibid.

157. S.C. Amendment 5 (enacted Nov. 7, 2006).

158. *Karesh v. City Council of Charleston*, 247 S.E.2d 342, 345 (S.C. 1978).

159. S.C. Amendment 5 (amending S.C. Const. art. I, § 13(B)).

160. Cal. Proposition 99 (enacted on June 3, 2008, and amending Cal. Const. art. I, § 19).

161. Ilya Somin, "Prop. 99's False Promise of Reform," *Los Angeles Times*, May 19, 2008, at A15. Proposition 99 includes a provision that would negate any conflicting eminent domain reform passed the same day, so long as Proposition 99 got more votes than its competitor. Cal. Proposition 99, § 9 (enacted June 3, 2008). Samantha Young, "Voters Reject Prop. 98, Endorse Prop. 99," *Long Beach Press-Telegram*, June 4, 2008, (noting that the California League of Cities placed Proposition 99 on the ballot and spent eleven million dollars on promoting it and working to defeat Proposition 98).

162. Cal. Proposition 99 § 2, (enacted on June 3, 2008, and amending Cal. Const. art. I, § 19(b), (e)(3)) (exempting from protection owner-occupied residences where the owner has resided for less than one year).

163. Somin, "Prop. 99's False Promise of Reform."

164. Ibid.

165. Cal. Proposition 99 (enacted on June 3, 2008, and amending Cal. Const. art. I, § 19(e)(5)) (exempting takings of homes that are "incidental" to a variety of "public work[s] or improvement[s]"). The text of this section reads as follows:

> Public work or improvement" means facilities or infrastructure
> for the delivery of public services such as education, police, fire
> protection, parks, recreation, emergency medical, public health,
> libraries, flood protection, streets or highways, public transit,

railroad, airports and seaports; utility, common carrier or other similar projects such as energy-related, communication-related, water-related and wastewater-related facilities or infrastructure; projects identified by a State or local government for recovery from natural disasters; and private uses incidental to, or necessary for, the public work or improvement.

166. Mich. Ballot Proposal 06-04 (enacted on Nov. 7, 2006, and amending Mich. Const. art. X, § 2).

167. 684 N.W.2d 765, 779–86 (Mich. 2004); the status of blight condemnations under *Hathcock* is analyzed in Ilya Somin, "Overcoming *Poletown: County of Wayne v. Hathcock*, Economic Development Takings, and the Future of Public Use," 2004 *Michigan State Law Review* 1005 (2004).

168. See discussion earlier in this chapter.

169. The five are Arizona, Mississippi, Nevada, North Dakota, and Oregon.

170. The four are Georgia, New Hampshire, South Carolina, and Texas.

171. Ibid.

172. H.R. 4128, 109th Cong. (enacted Nov. 4, 2005).

173. Scott Bullock, "The Specter of Condemnation," *Wall Street Journal*, June 24, 2006.

174. The PRPA was renamed as the "Strengthening the Ownership of Private Property Act of 2007," available at http://thomas.loc.gov/home/gpoxmlc110/h926 _ih.xml.

175. See Christina Walsh, "Congress Can Halt Eminent Domain Abuse," *Washington Times*, Feb. 15, 2012, available at http://www.washingtontimes.com /news/2012/feb/15/congress-can-halt-eminent-domain-abuse/;See H.R. 1433, Bill Summary and Status, available at http://thomas.loc.gov/cgi-bin/bdquery/z?d112 :HR01433:@@@X.

176. Ibid.

177. See H.R. 1944, Bill Summary and Status, available at http://thomas.loc .gov/cgi-bin/bdquery/D?d113:1:./temp/~bdUTss:@@@X|/home/LegislativeData .php?n=BSS;c=113|.

178. H.R. 4128, 109th Cong. § 2(a) (2005).

179. Ibid., § 2(b).

180. Ibid., § 8(1). The Act goes on to establish several exemptions, but these are relatively narrow. Ibid., § 8(1)(A–G) (exempting condemnations that transfer property to public ownership and several other traditional public uses).

181. Ibid., § 2(b).

182. Ibid., § 8(2).

183. Ibid.

184. Robert Meltz, *Condemnation of Private Property for Economic Development: Legal Comments on the House-Passed Bill (H.R. 4128) and Bond Amendment* (Congressional Research Service, 2005), 4. The report bases this

conclusion on section 5(a)(2) of the PRPA, which requires the attorney general to compile a list of economic development grants but does not explicitly state that the list should be used as a guide for determining which funds to cut off in the event of PRPA violations. Ibid., 4 & n.7 (citing H.R. 4128, 109th Cong. § 5(a)(2) (2005)). Section 11 of the Act does require that the Act "be construed in favor of a broad protection of private property rights." H.R. 4128, § 11. However, it is unclear whether this requirement would bind the attorney general in his determination of the range of programs covered by the Act's funding cutoff.

185. For a detailed calculation, see Somin, "Limits of Backlash," 2150–51.

186. Act of Nov. 30, 2005, Pub. L. No. 109-115, § 726, 119 Stat. 2396, 2494–95 (2005).

187. Ibid., 2495.

188. Ibid.

189. See discussion in chapter 4.

190. § 726, 119 Stat. at 2495, *reprinted in* Meltz, *Condemnation of Private Property for Economic Development*, at 12.

191. Ibid.

192. Exec. Order No. 13,406, 71 Fed. Reg. 36,973 (June 23, 2006).

193. Ibid.

194. Such claims were made by the New London authorities in *Kelo* itself, and accepted by virtually all the justices, including the dissenters. See *Kelo v. City of New London*, 545 U.S. 469, 484–85 (2005); ibid., 501 (O'Connor, J., dissenting).

Chapter Six

1. See table 6.1 on page 168.

2. See discussion in chapter 5.

3. See, e.g., Timothy Sandefur, "The 'Backlash' So Far: Will Americans Get Meaningful Eminent Domain Reform?," 2006 *Michigan State Law Review* 709, 769–72.

4. See Ilya Somin, *Democracy and Political Ignorance: Why Smaller Government Is Smarter* (Stanford, CA: Stanford University Press, 2013), chap. 3.

5. Center for Economic & Civic Opinion at University of Mass./Lowell, The Saint Index Poll, question 9 (2007) (on file with author) [hereinafter Saint Index 2007]. The survey included one thousand respondents in a nationwide random sample.

6. See table 6.1.

7. For the exact wording of the two questions involved, see appendix B.

8. Saint Index 2007, question 9.

9. See discussion of the difficulty of classifying the effectiveness of these two states' reforms in chapter 5; 28 of the 36 respondents in Idaho and Wisconsin were

simply unaware of the existence of post-*Kelo* reform laws in their states. Changing the classification of those of the remaining eight who gave answers on effectiveness would have no statistically significant effect on the national results.

10. Saint Index 2007, question 10.

11. Only 17 percent of respondents expressed any opinion at all about the effectiveness of post-*Kelo* reform in their states. Saint Index 2007, question 10.

12. Question 10 on the Saint Index survey has four possible answers in addition to "don't know." See appendix B. However, as described in appendix B, in each case I coded two different answers as "correct" for purposes of table 6.1. Respondents living in states that had passed effective laws could get a "correct" answer by choosing either A or B, while those in states with ineffective reforms could pick either C or D.

13. For the classic survey result showing that many respondents will express opinions even about completely fictitious legislation invented by researchers rather than admit ignorance, see Stanley Payne's famous finding that 70 percent of respondents expressed opinions regarding the nonexistent "Metallic Metals Act." Stanley Payne, *The Art of Asking Questions* (Princeton, NJ: Princeton University Press,1951), 18.

14. Michael X. Delli Carpini and Scott Keeter, *What Americans Know about Politics and Why It Matters* (New Haven, CT: Yale University Press, 1996), 157.

15. See Martin P. Wattenberg, *Is Voting for Young People?* (New York: Pearson, 2007), 79–91.

16. Somin, *Democracy and Political Ignorance,* 22, tbl. 1.1.

17. Saint Index 2007.

18. Ibid.

19. Ibid., question 9. Standard tests showed that the difference between the 26 percent and 20 percent figures is not statistically significant; the relevant data is available from the author.

20. Ibid., questions 9, 10.

21. For a defense of the theory, see Vincent L. Hutchings, *Public Opinion and Democratic Accountability* (Princeton, NJ: Princeton University Press, 2003).

22. Saint Index 2007.

23. See discussion earlier in this chapter.

24. Saint Index 2006; Ilya Somin, "Is Post-*Kelo* Eminent Domain Reform Bad for the Poor?" 101 *Northwestern University Law Review* 1931, 1940 (2007).

25. Saint Index 2007.

26. See, e.g., Philip E. Converse, "Popular Representation and the Distribution of Information," *in Information and Democratic Processes,* ed. John A. Ferejohn and James Kuklinski (Urbana: University of Illinois Press, 1990); Donald A. Wittman, *The Myth of Democratic Failure* (Chicago: University of Chicago Press, 1995). For criticism of the theory, see, e.g., Somin, *Democracy and Political Ignorance,* 110–17.

27. Saint Index 2007.

28. Ibid.

29. The 43 percent figure is based on data from Saint Index 2006. The 1.3 percent figure is calculated by taking 10 percent of the 13 percent who could correctly identify the status of post-*Kelo* reform in their state. Saint Index 2007.

30. For the argument that reliance on opinion leaders can alleviate the problem of political ignorance, see, e.g., Arthur Lupia and Mathew D. McCubbins, *The Democratic Dilemma: Can Citizens Learn What They Need to Know?* (Cambridge: Cambridge University Press, 1998), 206–08.

31. See Somin, *Democracy and Political Ignorance,* 97–100; Ilya Somin, "Resolving the Democratic Dilemma?," 16 *Yale Journal on Regulation* 401, 408–11 (1999).

32. On the utility of such cues, see, e.g., Lupia and McCubbins, *The Democratic Dilemma,* 206.

33. Quoted in Michael Gardner, "Lawmakers Rethink Land-Seizure Laws," *San Diego Union-Tribune,* Aug. 17, 2005, at A1.

34. Saint Index 2007, question 9.

35. David R. Mayhew, *Congress: The Electoral Connection* (New Haven, CT: Yale University Press, 1974), 61–73, 114–15, 121–25.

36. Dan Walters, "Eminent Domain Bills Are Stalled—Except One for Casino Tribe," *Sacramento Bee,* Sept. 16, 2005, at A3.

37. Ibid.

38. Ibid.

39. See discussion of California's reforms in chapter 5.

40. Interview with Steven Miller, Vice President for Policy, Nev. Policy Research Institute, (Mar. 14, 2007) (on file with author). Nevada eventually passed effective eminent domain reform by referendum. See discussion of Nevada's reform law in chapter 5.

41. See discussion of Proposition 99 in chapter 5.

42. See ibid.

43. See table 5.3.

44. Ibid.

45. See discussion in chapter 5.

46. The Arizona initiative was undertaken by an activist group known as the Arizona HomeOwners' Protection Effort. Arizona Secretary of State, *Proposition 207,* available at http://www.azsos.gov/election/2006/Info/PubPamphlet /english/Prop207.htm (last visited Mar. 5, 2009). The Nevada law was put on the ballot by the People's Initiative to Stop the Taking of Our Land (PISTOL), along with other individuals. See *Nevadans for the Protection of Property Rights, Inc. v. Heller,* 141 P.3d 1235, 1238–39 (Nev. 2006) (listing the respondents to the initiative petition of "Nevada Property Owners' Bill of Rights," which sought to amend the Nevada Constitution with respect to eminent domain). In North

Dakota, the ballot initiative was sponsored by a group known as Citizens to Restrict Eminent Domain) (C-RED). National Institute on Money in State Politics, *2006 Ballot Measure Overview* 37, 48 (2007), available at http://www.policyar chive.org/bitstream/handle/10207/5780/2007110512006BallotReport_Overview .pdf?sequence-1 (demonstrating that C-RED raised all of the contributions in support of Measure 2, which prohibits government takings of private property for economic development). In Oregon, the post-*Kelo* initiative was filed by the Oregonians in Action Political Action Committee. Measure Argument for State Voters' Pamphlet for Measure 39 (on file with author). Oregonians in Action is a property rights activist group. Oregonians in Action, *Background Information*, available at http://www.oia.org/index.php/about-us (last visited Mar. 13, 2009).

47. See discussion of Proposition 99 earlier in this chapter.

48. Samantha Young, "Voters Reject Prop. 98, Endorse Prop. 99," *Long Beach Press-Telegram*, June 4, 2008.

49. Ibid.

50. For defenses of the interest group explanation, see Martin E. Gold and Lynne B. Sagalyn, "The Use and Abuse of Blight in Eminent Domain, " 38 *Fordham Urban Law Journal* 1119, 1159–63 (2011);); Elaine B. Sharp and Donald Haider-Markel, "At the Invitation of the Court: Eminent Domain Reform in State Legislatures in the Wake of the *Kelo* Decision," 38 *Publius: The Journal of Federalism* 556 (2008); and Sandefur, "The 'Backlash' So Far," 768–72.

51. Jeremy P. Hopkins, "Obtaining Eminent Domain Reform: A View through the Lens of Virginia's Constitutional Amendment," American Law Institute Continuing Legal Education Program, Jan. 23–25, 2014.

52. Sandefur, "The 'Backlash' So Far," 768–72.

53. Interview with Brooke Rollins, President & CEO, Tex. Pub. Policy Found. (Mar. 17, 2007) (on file with author).

54. See Edward J. López et al., "Pass a Law, Any Law: State Legislative Responses to the *Kelo* Backlash," 5 *Review of Law and Economics* 101 (2009); Andrew Morriss, "Symbol or Substance? An Empirical Assessment of State Responses to *Kelo*," 17 *Supreme Court Economic Review* 237 (2009); see also Thomas J. Miceli, *The Economic Theory of Eminent Domain: Private Property, Public Use* (Cambridge: Cambridge University Press, 2011), 54–55.

55. The National Association of Homebuilders filed an amicus brief supporting the property owners in *Kelo*. See Patricia Salkin et al., "The Friends of the Court: The Role of Amicus Curiae in *Kelo v. City of New London*," in *Eminent Domain Use and Abuse:* Kelo *in Context,* ed. Dwight H. Merriam and Mary Massaron Ross (Chicago: American Bar Association, 2006), 179.

56. See chapter 4.

57. See discussion in chapter 5.

58. Somin, "Is Post-*Kelo* Eminent Domain Reform Bad for the Poor?," 1940, tbl. 2.

59. See Lopez et al., "Pass a Law, Any Law"; Morris, "Symbol or Substance." On the greater propensity of Republicans and conservatives to oppose *Kelo*, see table 5.1.

60. For example, growth rates and urbanization are relatively crude measures of the extent to which developers and other interest groups have an incentive to try to use eminent domain to acquire property.

61. James Madison, "Federalist 10," in Alexander Hamilton et al., *The Federalist Papers*, ed. Clinton Rossiter, (New York: Mentor, 1961), 75.

62. Ibid.

63. This issue is discussed in more detail in the conclusion.

64. Stephen Ansolabahere and Nathaniel Persily, *Field Report: Constitutional Attitudes Survey* 61 (Knowledge Networks, July 2010). For a more detailed breakdown of this data, see table 5.1.

65. See data in table 5.1.

66. Ansolabahere and Persily, *Constitutional Attitudes Survey*, 66.

67. The states are Delaware, Mississippi, New Jersey, Texas, and Virginia. See discussion of their reform laws in chapter 5. Three of the five (Delaware, Texas, and Virginia) were following up or revising earlier post-*Kelo* reform laws.

68. Interview with Richard Beyer, July 13, 2013.

69. Ibid.

70. On the Illinois law, see 65 Ill. Comp. Stat. § 5/11-74.3-1 et seq.; On the Alabama rollback, see the discussion in chapter 5. See also Dana Berliner, "Trends in Eminent Domain Legislation and Use," American Law Institute-CLE (Jan. 24, 2013); Dana Berliner, "Eminent Domain Abuse Is Making a Comeback," *Wall Street Journal*, May 16, 2014. The Illinois rollback is probably less significant than the others because that state never enacted a genuinely effective post-*Kelo* reform law to begin. See discussion of the Illinois law in chapter 5.

71. See Minn. Stat. § 473J.09 (2012). Subdivision 5 of this law allows the use of eminent domain for private as well as publicly owned stadiums. Ibid., subd. 5.

72. See discussion of *Poletown* in chapter 2.

Chapter Seven

1. *Kelo*, 545 U.S. at 478 (noting that government is not "allowed to take property under the mere pretext of a public purpose, when its actual purpose was to bestow a private benefit.").

2. See works cited in chapter 5.

3. The most thorough discussion is my own 2011 article on the subject, which this chapter revises and updates. See Ilya Somin, "The Judicial Reaction to

Kelo," 4 *Albany Government Law Review* 1 (2011) (Introduction to the Symposium on Eminent Domain in the United States). Daniel B. Kelly has published an excellent analysis of judicial interpretations of *Kelo*'s anti-pretextual taking rule. Kelly, however, does not consider the other issues raised in post-*Kelo* litigation. Daniel Kelly, "Pretextual Takings: Of Private Developers, Local Governments, and Impermissible Favoritism," 17 *Supreme Court Economic Review* 173 (2009).

4. *City of Norwood v. Horney*, 853 N.E.2d 1115, 1136 (Ohio 2006) (holding that "economic development" alone does not justify condemnation); *Board of County Commissioners of Muskogee County v. Lowery*, 136 P.3d 639, 650–51 (Okla. 2006) (holding that "economic development" is not a "public purpose" under the Oklahoma state constitution and rejecting *Kelo* as a guide to interpretation of Oklahoma's state constitution); *Benson v. State*, 710 N.W.2d 131, 146 (S.D. 2006) (concluding that the South Dakota constitution gives property owners broader protection than *Kelo*).

5. *Mayor of Baltimore v. Valsamaki*, 916 A.2d 324, 356 (Md. 2007); *Sapero v. Mayor of Baltimore*, 920 A.2d 1061, 1079–80 (Md. 2007); *Rhode Island Economic Development Corp. v. The Parking Co.*, 892 A.2d 87, 102 (R.I. 2006).

6. *Kaur v. New York State Urban Development Corp.*, 933 N.E.2d 721, 731–32 (N.Y. 2010); *Goldstein v. New York State Urban Development Corp.*, 921 N.E.2d 164, 170–72 (N.Y. 2009).

7. *City of Norwood v. Horney*, 853 N.E.2d 1115, 1141 (Ohio 2006); *Board of County Commissioners of Muskogee County v. Lowery*, 136 P.3d 639, 653–54 (Okla. 2006).

8. *Norwood*, 853 N.E.2d at 1136. For a more detailed analysis of *Norwood*, see Ilya Somin, "Blight Sweet Blight," *Legal Times*, Aug. 14, 2006, 42–44, available at http://www.law.gmu.edu/assets/files/faculty/Somin_LegalTimesBlight_8 -14-06.pdf.

9. Ibid., 1137 (O'Connor, J., dissenting) [quoting *Kelo v. City of New London*, 545 U.S. 469, 498 (2005)].

10. Ibid., 1141.

11. *Lowery*, 136 P.3d at 651.

12. 710 N.W.2d 131, 146 (S.D. 2006).

13. The court wrote that "[t]he reasons which incline us to this view are, first, that it accords with the primary and more commonly understood meaning of the words; second, it accords with the general practice in regard to taking private property for public use in vogue when the phrase was first brought into use in the earlier Constitutions; third, it is the only view which gives the words any force as a limitation or renders them capable of any definite and practical application" Ibid.

14. *Kelo*, 545 U.S. at 489.

15. See discussion of this issue in chapter 4.

16. *City of Norwood v. Horney*, 853 N.E.2d 1115, 1136–47 (Ohio 2006); *Benson*, 710 N.W.2d at 146.

17. *Board of County Commissioners of Muskogee County v. Lowery*, 136 P.3d 639, 652 (Okla. 2006) (quoting Oklahoma Const. art. 2, § 23).

18. *Mayor of Baltimore v. Valsamaki*, 916 A.2d 324, 356 (Md. 2007); *Sapero v. Mayor of Baltimore*, 920 A.2d 1061, 1080 (Md. 2007); *Rhode Island Economic Development Corp. v. The Parking Co.*, 892 A.2d 87, 107–08 (R.I. 2006).

19. *Valsamaki*, 916 A.2d at 336, 356; *Sapero*, 920 A.2d at 1080; *Parking Co.*, 892 A.2d at 104.

20. *Parking Co.*, 892 A.2d at 99.

21. *Valsamaki*, 916 A.2d at 327 n.1 (quoting *Black's Law Dictionary* 310 (8th ed. 2004)).

22. *Parking Co.*, 892 A.2d at 107.

23. Ibid., 105–06.

24. Ibid., 106.

25. Ibid., 92–94.

26. *Kelo v. City of New London*, 545 U.S. 469, 488–89 (2005).

27. *Parking Co.*, 892 A.2d at 101 (quoting *In re* Rhode Island Suburban Railway Co. 48 A. 590, 591 (R.I. 1901)).

28. Ibid.

29. 348 U.S. 26, 32 (1954).

30. See, e.g., *Kelo*, 545 U.S. at 480–81.

31. See discussion of pretextual takings later in this chapter.

32. *Mayor of Baltimore v. Valsamaki*, 916 A.2d 324, 356 (Md. 2007) (emphasis in original).

33. Ibid.

34. *Sapero v. Mayor of Baltimore City*, 920 A.2d 1061, 1072 (Md. 2007).

35. *Valsamaki*, 916 A.2d at 352.

36. Ibid., 328–30.

37. See discussion in chapter 4.

38. *City of Norwood v. Horney*, 853 N.E. 2d 1115, 1146–47 (Ohio 2006).

39. Ibid., 1146.

40. 924 A.2d 447, 460 (N.J. 2007).

41. Ibid.

42. For a discussion of this problem, see Ilya Somin and Jonathan Adler, "The Green Costs of *Kelo*: Economic Development Takings and Environmental Protection," 84 *Washington University Law Review* 623, 641–52 (2006).

43. *In re Condemnation by Redevelopment Authority*, 962 A.2d 1257, 1263 (Pa. Commw. Ct. 2008). These cases were litigated under Pennsylvania's broader pre-*Kelo* definition of blight, which has since been displaced by a narrower one enacted in its post-*Kelo* reform law. See the discussion of the new law in chapter 5.

44. *In re Redevelopment Authority*, 962 A.2d at 1263.

45. Ibid.

46. *Kaur v. New York State Urban Development Corp.*, 933 N.E.2d 721 (N.Y. 2010); *Goldstein v. New York State Urban Development Corp.*, 921 N.E.2d 164 (N.Y. 2009). For a more detailed discussions of *Kaur* and *Goldstein*, see Ilya Somin, "Let There Be Blight: Blight Condemnations in New York After *Goldstein* and *Kaur*," 38 *Fordham Urban Law Journal* 1193 (2011) (symposium on eminent domain in New York). Some of the material in this section is adopted from that article, as is a portion of the discussion of these cases later in the chapter. For other academic commentary on the two cases, see Amy Lavine and Norman Oder, "Urban Redevelopment Policy, Judicial Deference to Unaccountable Agencies, and Reality in Brooklyn's Atlantic Yards Project," 42 *Urban Lawyer* 287 (2010); Keith Hirokawa and Patricia Salkin, "Can Urban University Expansion and Sustainable Development Co-Exist? A Case Study in Progress on Columbia University," 37 *Fordham Urban Law Journal* 637, 684–89 (2010).

47. *Kaur*, 933 N.E.2d at 724, 731–32; *Goldstein*, 921 N.E.2d at 170–71.

48. Only about one-third of the over 5,300 housing units to be constructed would be affordable for middle- or low-income residents. *Goldstein*, 921 N.E.2d at 166. See also *In re* Develop Don't Destroy (Brooklyn), 874 N.Y.S.2d 414, 424 (App. Div. 2009) (holding the construction of the basketball stadium was a permissible "public purpose").

49. New York Const. art. XVIII, § 1; *Goldstein*, 921 N.E.2d at 170–71.

50. For accounts of the area and its characteristics, see Neil deMause and Joanna Cagan, *Field of Schemes: How the Great Stadium Swindle Turns Public Money into Private Profit* (London: University of Nebraska Press, 2008) 279–80, which notes that the area in question was "prime Brooklyn real estate" at the nexus of several "booming neighborhoods"; see also Damon Root, "When Public Power Is Used for Private Gain," *Reason*, Oct. 8, 2009, available at http://reason.com/archives/2009/ 10/08/when-public-power-is-used-for.

51. *Goldstein*, 921 N.E.2d at 189–90 (Smith, J., dissenting).

52. Ibid., 171.

53. Ibid., 172 [quoting *Yonkers v. Community Development Agency v. Morris*, 335 N.E.2d 327, 331 (N.Y. 1975)].

54. Ibid.

55. N.Y. Const. art. XVIII, § 1 (this is the provision of the constitution that authorizes blight condemnations). For a discussion of the original meaning of Article XVIII, see Somin, "Let There be Blight."

56. *Goldstein*, 921 N.E.2d at 189 (Smith, J., dissenting).

57. Ibid.

58. Ibid., 166.

59. Root, "When Public Power Is Used for Private Gain" (quoting the firm's report): Lavine and Oder, "Urban Redevelopment Policy," at 298–99.

60. Ibid.; *Goldstein*, 921 N.E.2d at 189 (Smith, J., dissenting).

61. Root, "Urban Redevelopment Policy."

62. *Goldstein*, 921 N.E.2d at 190 (Smith, J., dissenting).

63. See Brief for Respondent at 25–34, *Goldstein v. New York State Urban Development Corp.*, 921 N.E.2d 164 (N.Y. 2009), 2009 WL 3810844.

64. *Goldstein*, 921 N.E.2d at 172.

65. Ibid.

66. *Kaur v. New York State Urban Development Corp.*, 933 N.E.2d 721, 724 (N.Y. 2010).

67. *Kaur v. New York State Urban Development Corp.*, 892 N.Y.S.2d 8, 28 (App. Div. 2009), *rev'd*, 933 N.E.2d 721 (N.Y. 2010).

68. Ibid., 20.

69. Ibid.

70. Ibid., 19–21.

71. *Kaur*, 933 N.E.2d at 726 n.6; *Goldstein v. New York State Urban Development Corp.*, 921 N.E. 164, 166–67 (N.Y. 2009).

72. *Kaur*, 892 N.Y.S.2d at 22. Later, another firm was hired to conduct an independent blight study, but it was required to use "the same flawed methodology." Ibid.; Damon Root, "Holding Justice Kennedy to His Word: Why the Supreme Court Must Put a Stop to Columbia University's Eminent Domain Abuse," *Reason*, Sept. 29, 2010, available at http://reason.com/archives/2010/09/29/holding-justice -kennedy-to-his (providing more details on the biases and flaws in the blight study); see also Damon Root, "College Cheats," *New York Post*, Feb. 16, 2009 available at http://www.nypost.com/p/news/opinion/opedcolumnists/item_oZsTv770 SurlH I5f5BJlQO;jsessionid=DD25B89035A1B3D03970A76560585183.

73. *Kaur*, 892 N.Y.S.2d at 22.

74. Columbia already owned 76 percent of the land in the area at the time of the study and "the university refused to perform basic and necessary repairs— thereby both pushing tenants out of Columbia-owned buildings and manufacturing the ugly conditions that later advanced the school's real-estate interests" See Root, "College Cheats."

75. *Kaur*, 892 N.Y.S.2d at 30, 32 (Richter, J., concurring).

76. *Kaur*, 933 N.E.2d at 733. Judge Smith, the sole dissenter in *Goldstein*, concurred in *Kaur* only because of the force of the earlier precedent. Ibid., 737 (Smith, J., concurring).

77. Ibid., 732.

78. Ibid.

79. Ibid., 733.

80. *Kaur*, 892 N.Y.S.2d at 12–13, 21. The New York Court of Appeals incorrectly stated that the First Department had ignored the Urbitran study. *Kaur*, 933 N.E.2d at 733.

81. *Uptown Holdings, LLC v. City of New York*, 908 N.Y.S.2d 657, 660–61 (App. Div. 2010).

82. Presumably, New York courts would still invalidate a condemnation where the authorities openly admit that the purpose was to benefit a well-connected private interest.

83. See, e.g., Barry Friedman, *The Will of the People: How Public Opinion Has Influenced the Supreme Court and Shaped the Meaning of the Constitution* (New York: Farrar, Straus and Giroux, 2009).

84. Thomas W. Merrill and Henry E. Smith, *Property* (New York: Oxford University Press, 2010), 248.

85. See discussion of these cases in chapter 2.

86. Matthew J. Streb, "The Study of Judicial Elections," in *Running for Judge: The Rising Political, Financial, and Legal Stakes of Judicial Elections,* ed., Matthew J. Streb (New York: New York University Press, 2007), 5–6.

87. See discussion in chapter 6.

88. *Kelo v. City of New London*, 545 U.S. 469, 477–78 (2005) (noting that government is not "allowed to take property under the mere pretext of a public purpose, when its actual purpose was to bestow a private benefit").

89. *Goldstein v. Pataki*, 488 F. Supp. 2d 254, 288 (E.D.N.Y. 2007), *aff'd*, 516 F.3d 50 (2d Cir. 2008).

90. *Kelo*, 545 U.S. at 487.

91. See discussion of this point in chapter 4.

92. *Kelo*, 545 U.S. at 491 (Kennedy, J., concurring).

93. Ibid.

94. Kelly, "Pretextual Takings," at 184–99. Kelly finds fault with the three tests, and proposes an alternative approach of his own. Ibid., 215–20.

95. *Middletown Township v. Lands of Stone*, 939 A.2d 331, 337 (Pa. 2007).

96. *In re O'Reilly*, 5 A.3d 246, 258 (Pa. 2010).

97. 198 P.3d 615, 642 (Haw. 2008).

98. *County of Hawai'i v. C&J Coupe Family Ltd. Partnership*, 242 P.3d 1136, 1148 (Haw. 2010).

99. Ibid., 1148–58.

100. *New England Estates v. Town of Branford*, 988 A.2d 229, 253 n.28 (Conn. 2010)

101. *Kaur v. New York State Urban Development Corp.*, 892 N.Y.S. 2d 8, 18, 20 (App. Div. 2009), *rev'd*, 933 N.E.2d 721 (N.Y. 2010).

102. *49 WB, LLC v. Village of Haverstraw*, 839 N.Y.S. 2d 127, 141 (App. Div. 2007).

103. See discussion of *Kaur's* implications for pretext doctrine later in this chapter.

104. Lior Strahilevitz and Eduardo Penalver, "Judicial Takings or Due Process," 97 *Cornell Law Review* 305, 322 (2012).

105. *Armendariz v. Penman*, 75 F.3d 1311, 1321 (9th Cir. 1996) (en banc) (invalidating a taking because the official rationale of blight alleviation was a

mere pretext for "[a] scheme . . . to deprive the plaintiffs of their property . . . so a shopping-center developer could buy [it] at a lower price"); *Aaron v. Target Corp.*, 269 F. Supp. 2d 1162, 1174–75 (E.D. Mo. 2003), *rev'd on other grounds*, 357 F.3d 768 (8th Cir. 2004) (holding that a property owner was likely to prevail on a claim that a taking ostensibly to alleviate blight was actually intended to serve the interests of the Target Corporation*); 99 Cents Only Store v. Lancaster Redevelopment Agency*, 237 F. Supp. 2d 1123, 1129 (C.D. Cal. 2001) (holding that "[n]o judicial deference is required . . . where the ostensible public use is demonstrably pretextual" and that the condemnation must be invalidated because "Lancaster's condemnation efforts rest on nothing more than the desire to achieve the naked transfer of property from one private party to another"); *Cottonwood Christian Center v. Cypress Redevelopment Agency*, 218 F. Supp. 2d 1203, 1229 (C.D. Cal. 2002) ("Courts must look beyond the government's purported public use to determine whether that is the genuine reason or if it is merely pretext."). For a discussion of *99 Cents* case and its use by the *Kelo* majority, see chapter 4.

106. *Franco v. National Capital Revitalization Corp.*, 930 A.2d 160, 173–74 (D.C. 2007).

107. This court should not be confused with the federal D.C. Circuit Court of Appeals.

108. *Franco*, 930 A. 2d at 173.

109. *Kelo v. City of New London*, 545 U.S. 469, 490 (2005) (Kennedy, J., concurring).

110. *Franco v. District of Columbia,* 39 A.3d 890, 894 (D.C. 2012).

111. 2006 WL 3507937, at *14 (N.D. Cal. Dec. 5, 2006), *rev'd*, 714 F.3d 1118 (9th Cir. 2013). (alterations in original) (quoting *Kelo*, 545 U.S. at 491 (Kennedy, J., concurring)).

112. The nonbinding nature of Kennedy's opinion was recognized by the *Franco* court:

> We apply the decision of the *Kelo* majority, written by Justice Stevens. Although Justice Kennedy's concurrence discusses at some length a court's role when presented with allegations of a pretextual public purpose, that discussion is not the holding of the court. Five justices, including Justice Kennedy, . . . agreed with Justice Stevens' reasoning, and that opinion is the Court's holding.
>
> *Franco*, 930 A.2d at 169 n.8.

113. 714 F.3d 1118 (9th Cir. 2013). See discussion of this case later in this chapter.

114. *Mayor of Baltimore v. Valsamaki*, 916 A.2d 324, 352–53 (Md. 2007) (noting absence of a clear plan for the use of the condemned property, and contrasting with *Kelo*); *Middletown Township v. Lands of Stone*, 939 A.2d 331, 338 (Pa.

2007) (concluding that "evidence of a well-developed plan of proper scope is significant proof that an authorized purpose truly motivates a taking"); *Rhode Island Economic Development Corp. v. The Parking Co.*, 892 A.2d 87, 104 (R.I. 2006) (emphasizing that "[t]he City of New London's exhaustive preparatory efforts that preceded the takings in *Kelo,* stand in stark contrast to [the condemning authority's] approach in the case before us").

115. Nicole Garnett argues that planning is the main focus of *Kelo*'s pretext analysis, and under its reasoning, the presence of significant planning "almost always precludes a finding of pretext." Nicole Stelle Garnett, "Planning as Public Use?," 34 *Ecology Law Quarterly* 443, 454 (2007).

116. 550 F.3d 302, 311 (3d Cir. 2008).

117. Ibid., 305–06.

118. Ibid., 311.

119. Ibid.

120. Ibid., 310–11.

121. See discussion in chapter 1.

122. 516 F.3d 50 (2d Cir. 2008). See the discussion of the state decision earlier in this chapter.

123. Ibid., 55, 62.

124. Ibid., 62.

125. Ibid., 58.

126. Ibid., 55–56.

127. Ibid., 63.

128. Ibid. The court makes clear that its definition of "classic public use" is extremely broad by noting that private-to-private blight takings and "the creation of affordable housing" qualify. Ibid., 58.

129. 173 F. Appendix 931 (2d Cir. 2006).

130. Ibid., 932.

131. For a detailed discussion of *Didden*, see Ilya Somin, "Judge Sonia Sotomayor's Record on Constitutional Property Rights," Testimony before the U.S. Senate Committee on the Judiciary, July 16, 2009, at 5–8, available at http://www.law .gmu.edu/assets/files/news/2009/Somin_TestimonySotomayor.pdf. See also *Didden*, 173 F. Appendix at 932.

132. *Didden*, 173 F. Appendix at 932. The opinion is unsigned and unpublished. But then-Judge Sotomayor was the senior judge on the panel, and the senior judge usually drafts such opinions.

133. Ibid., 933 (citations omitted).

134. *Didden v. Village of Port Chester*, 304 F. Supp. 2d 548, 553, 556 (S.D.N.Y. 2004). This district court ruling addressed a different issue arising from the same transaction.

135. See Somin, "Judge Sonia Sotomayor's Record on Constitutional Property Rights," 6–8.

136. 2d Cir. R. 32.1.1(b)(2), available at http://www.ca2.uscourts.gov/clerk /Rules/LR/Local_Rule_32_1_1.htm.

137. For details, see Somin, "Let There Be Blight."

138. *Kaur v. New York State Urban Development Corp.*, 892 N.Y.S.2d 8, 10–16 (App. Div., 2009), *rev'd*, 933 N.E.2d 721 (N.Y. 2010).

139. *MHC Financing Ltd. Partnership v. City of San Rafael*, 714 F.3d 1118 (9th Cir. 2013).

140. Ibid., 1129 (quoting *Kelo v. City of New London*, 545 U.S. 469, 490 (2005)) (Kennedy, J., concurring).

141. 2011 Guam 17 (2011). I use the title of this case under which a petition for certiorari was filed in the Supreme Court rather than the title used in the Guam courts: *Government of Guam v. 162.04 Acres of Land*.

142. For a detailed discussion of this case, see the amicus brief I wrote on behalf of numerous public interest organizations unsuccessfully urging the Supreme Court to take the case. *Ilagan v. Ungacta*, Amicus brief of National Federation of Independent Business Small Business Legal Center et al. (Jan. 7, 2013), available at http://www.cato.org/sites/cato.org/files/pubs/pdf/ilagan_filed_brief.pdf.

143. *Kelo,* 545 U.S. at 488–89.

144. See Kelly, "Pretextual Takings," 188–89, and discussion in chapter 3.

145. See chapter 4, and Kelly, "Pretextual Takings," 198.

146. Kelly, "Pretextual Takings," 191–92.

147. See, e.g., *Church of Lukumi Babalu Aye v. City of Hialeah*, 508 U.S. 520 (1993) (religious discrimination); *Washington v. Davis*, 426 U.S. 229 (1976) (racial discrimination).

148. *Kelo,* 545 U.S. at 493 (Kennedy, J., concurring).

149. For a detailed discussion of such an approach, see Kelly, "Pretextual Takings."

150. See discussion of this problem in the analysis of Justice Kennedy's opinion in chapter 4.

151. See the conclusion.

152. See chapter 2.

Chapter Eight

1. See, e.g., David Dana, "The Law and Expressive Meaning of Condemning the Poor after *Kelo*," 101 *Northwestern University Law Review* 365 (2007); Debbie Becher, *Private Property and Public Power: Eminent Domain in Philadelphia,* (New York: Oxford University Press, 2014), 239; US Senate Committee on the Judiciary, *The Kelo Decision: Investigating Takings of Homes and Other Private Property* (Sept 20, 2005), (testimony of Professor Thomas W. Merrill), available at http://www.gpo.gov/fdsys/pkg/CHRG-109shrg24723/pdf/CHRG-109

shrg24723.pdf; Thomas Merrill and John Echeverria, Amicus Brief of American Planning Association, Connecticut Chapter of the American Planning Association, and National Congress for Economic Community Development, *Kelo v. City of New London*, 545 U.S. 469 (2005), 2005 WL 166929, 17.

2. See chapter 2.

3. See Ilya Somin, "Overcoming *Poletown*: *County of Wayne v. Hathcock*, Economic Development Takings, and the Future of Public Use," 2004 *Michigan State Law Review* 1005, 1020–21, and discussion in chapter 3.

4. See, e.g., Yun-Chien Chang, *Private Property and Takings Compensation: Theoretical Framework and Empirical Analysis* (Northampton, UK: Edward Elgar, 2013), 167–72; Debbie Becher, *Private Property and Public Power: Eminent Domain in Philadelphia,* (New York: Oxford University Press, 2014), 228-31; Margaret Jane Radin, "The Liberal Conception of Property: Cross Currents in the Jurisprudence of Takings," 88 *Columbia Law Review* 1667, 1689–96 (1988); Gideon Parchomovsky and Peter Siegelman, "Selling Mayberry: Communities and Individuals in Law and Economics," 92 *California Law Review* 75, 139–42 (2004). Aaron N. Green, "Takings, Just Compensation, and Efficient Use of Land, Urban, and Environmental Resources," 33 *The Urban Lawyer* 517 (2001); Richard A. Epstein, "Property, Speech and the Politics of Distrust," 59 *University y of Chicago Law Review* 41, 62 n.60 62–63 (1992); Gideon Kanner, "Condemnation Blight: Just How Just Is Just Compensation?," 48 *Notre Dame Law Review* 765 (1973).

5. U.S. Supreme Court Oral Argument Transcript, *Kelo v City of New London*, No. 04-108 (argued Feb 22, 2005), 2005 WL 529436, at *15, 30, 32–34.

6. Ibid., *32–33.

7. Ibid., *15.

8. See, e.g., James Krier and Christopher Serkin, "Public Ruses," 2004 *Michigan State Law Review* 859, 865–75 (2004); US Senate Committee on the Judiciary, *The* Kelo *Decision: Investigating Takings of Homes and Other Private Property,* at 6 (Sept. 20, 2005), available at http://judiciary.senate.gov/testimony .cfin?id=1612&wit_id=4661) (testimony of Professor Thomas W. Merrill). For citations to other advocates of increasing compensation, see Chang, *Private Property and Takings Compensation,* 168–69.

9. For some related criticism of increasing compensation as a solution to the problem of eminent domain abuse, see Julia D. Mahoney, *"Kelo's* Legacy: Eminent Domain and the Future of Property Rights," 2005 *Supreme Court Review* 103, 129–30 (2005).

10. For a summary of this issue, see Thomas W. Merrill, "The Economics of Public Use," 72 *Cornell Law Review* 61, 82–84 (1986).

11. For a recent argument that fair market value compensation does in fact capture most types of subjective value, see Brian Angelo Lee, "Just Undercompensation: The Idiosyncratic Premium in Eminent Domain," 113 *Columbia Law*

Review 593 (2013). However, even Lee recognizes that the fair market value formula undercompensates for the owner's loss of "autonomy" (ibid.). Moreover, Lee's argument has been subjected to strong criticism by Lee Ann Fennell, "Just Enough," 113 *Columbia Law Review Side Bar* 109 (2013), which points out some important aspects of subjective value that Lee's analysis underestimates or overlooks.

12. See Parchomovsky and Siegelman, "Selling Mayberry," 139–42

13. See Abraham Bell and Gideon Parchomovsky, "Taking Compensation Private," 59 *Stanford Law Review* 871 (2007). For an insightful analysis and critique of proposals to improve eminent domain compensation by incentivizing owners to reveal their true valuations, see Richard A. Epstein, "The Use and Limits of Self-Valuation Systems," 81 *University of Chicago Law Review* 109 (2014).

14. Bell and Parchomovsky argue that most owners would be able to readily foresee these changes. Bell and Parchomovsky, "Taking Compensation Private," 902-03. I am skeptical that this is true, especially in the case of owners who hold on to their property for many years.

15. See Yun-chien Chang, "Self-Assessment of Takings Compensation: An Empirical Study," 28 *Journal of Law, Economics, and Organization* 265 (2010).

16. Ibid.

17. Bell and Parchomovsky, "Taking Compensation Private," 891–92.

18. According to the Supreme Court, some of the landowners had avoided selling their land voluntarily because they would thereby incur "significant federal tax liabilities." They lobbied the state legislature to condemn their properties instead, so as to "mak[e] the federal tax consequences less severe." *Hawaii Housing Authority v. Midkiff*, 467 U.S. 229, 233 (1984).

19. *Kelo* Oral Argument, at *32–33.

20. See Nicole Stelle Garnett, "The Neglected Political Economy of Eminent Domain," 105 *Michigan Law Review* 101, 142–43 (2006).

21. But see Daryl Levinson, "Making Governments Pay: Markets, Politics, and the Allocation of Constitutional Costs," 67 *University of Chicago Law Review* 345, 345 (2000) (pointing out that "[g]overnment actors respond to political incentives, not financial ones—to votes, not dollars. We cannot assume that government will internalize social costs just because it is forced to make a budgetary outlay"); Garnett, "Neglected Political Economy,'" 138–43 (arguing that political incentives will often lead to condemnations whose costs exceed their benefit, even if compensation levels are increased); Louis Kaplow, "An Economic Analysis of Legal Transitions," 99 *Harvard Law Review* 509, 560–66 (1986).

22. See the discussion of *Poletown* in chapter 3, and Somin, "Overcoming *Poletown*."

23. Wallace Kaufman, "How Fair is Market Value? An Appraiser's Report of Temptations, Deficiencies, and Distortions in the Condemnation Process," in

Bruce Benson, ed., *Property Rights: Eminent Domain and Regulatory Takings Re-Examined*, (New York: Palgrave Macmillan, 2010), 77, 79.

24. Somin, "Overcoming *Poletown*," 1017–18. While the owners of the condemned businesses and other institutions received compensation payments, the cost of the destruction of these institutions to the community at large was not compensated in any way.

25. See discussion in chapter 1.

26. See chapter 3.

27. William A. Fischel, "The Political Economy of Public Use in *Poletown*: How Federal Grants Encourage Excessive Use of Eminent Domain," 2004 *Michigan State Law Review* 929.

28. For example, about half the projected cost of the *Poletown* condemnation was paid for by state and federal funds. Somin, "Overcoming *Poletown*," 1018.

29. For the argument that requiring sufficiently high compensation will deter inefficient takings and render eminent domain "self-limiting," see for example William Fischel, *Regulatory Takings* (Cambridge, MA: Harvard University Press, 1995), 74.

30. See discussion in chapter 3.

31. See Chang, *Private Property and Takings Compensation*, chaps. 5–8. Chang finds that wealthier and more politically influential property owners are systematically overcompensated and others undercompensated in Taiwan (ibid., chaps. 5–6). In New York City, undercompensation is prevalent in cases that are settled (ibid., chap. 7), while overcompensation occurs far more often in cases that go to court, which are usually cases involving larger and wealthier landowners (ibid., chap. 8), perhaps because these types of owners can more readily afford a prolonged legal battle. For an early study reaching similar conclusions, see Patricia Munch, "An Economic Analysis of Eminent Domain," 84 *Journal of Political Economy* 473 (1976).

32. For a discussion of several such factors, see Kaufman, "How Fair is Market Value?," 79–86.

33. See, e.g., Thomas W. Merrill and David A. Dana, *Property: Takings* (New York: Foundation Press, 2002), 173–79; Richard A. Epstein, *Supreme Neglect: How to Revive Constitutional Protection for Property Rights* (New York: Oxford University Press, 2008), 91.

34. U.S. Senate Committee on the Judiciary, *The Kelo Decision: Investigating Takings of Homes and Other Private Property*, at 6 (testimony of Professor Thomas W. Merrill) (Sept. 20, 2005), available at http://www.gpo.gov/fdsys/pkg /CHRG-109shrg24723/pdf/CHRG-109shrg24723.pdf [hereinafter Merrill Testimony]; Thomas W. Merrill, "The Misplaced Flight to Substance," 19 *Probate & Property* 16, 18 (2005); Gerald E. Frug and David J. Barron. "Making Planning Matter: A New Approach to Eminent Domain," 71 *Harvard Design Magazine*

(2005); David J. Barron and Gerald E. Frug, "Make Eminent Domain Fair for All," *Boston Globe*, Aug. 12, 2005.

35. Merrill Testimony, 6.

36. Merrill,"The Misplaced Flight to Substance," 18. For an early version of the same argument, see Merrill, "The Economics of Public Use," 80–81.

37. Merrill,"The Misplaced Flight to Substance," 18.

38. Ibid.

39. See discussion in chapter 3.

40. Merrill, "The Misplaced Flight to Substance," 18.

41. Merrill Testimony, 4.

42. See discussion in chapter 3.

43. See, e.g., Akhil Reed Amar, *America's Unwritten Constitution: The Precedents and Principles We Live By* (New York: Basic Books, 2012), 131–32; Daniel Farber, *The Rights Retained by the People: The "Silent" Ninth Amendment and the Constitutional Rights Americans Don't Know they Have* (New York: Basic Books, 2007), 168–69; Radin, "The Liberal Conception of Property," 1689–93; Margaret Jane Radin, "Property and Personhood," 34 *Stanford Law Review* 957 (1982); D. Benjamin Barros, "Home as a Legal Concept," 46 *Santa Clara Law Review* 255 (2006); Eduardo Penalver, "Eminent Domain Reform Takes an Interesting Turn in California," *Prawfsblawg,* June 5, 2008, available at http://prawfsblawg.blogs.com/prawfsblawg/2008/06/eminent-domain.html. Penalver would also extend heightened protection to some types of commercial property and long-term residential leases. Ibid.

44. See works cited in the previous note. For an important challenge to the conventional wisdom on this point, see Stephanie Stern, "Residential Protectionism and the Legal Mythology of Home," 107 *Michigan Law Review* 1093 (2009).

45. See ibid., 1133–39.

46. See chapter 1.

47. On the targeting of churches and synagogues for economic development takings, see, e.g., Brief for Becket Fund for Religious Liberty as Amicus Curiae in Support of Petitioners, *Kelo v. City of New London*, 545 U.S. 469 (2005), 2004 WL 2787141, at *8–11 & n.20.

48. See Garnett, "Neglected Political Economy," 106.

49. See Stern, "Residential Protectionism."

50. See discussion of this point in chapter 3.

51. For an example of such legislation, see Wisconsin's post-*Kelo* reform, discussed in chapter 5.

52. See, e.g., cases cited in chapter 3.

53. *Poletown Neighborhood Council v. City of Detroit*, 304 N.W.2d 455, 459 (Mich. 1981), *overruled by County of Wayne v. Hathcock*, 684 N.W.2d 765 (Mich. 2004).

54. Ibid.

55. *See Wilmington Parking Authority v. Land with Improvements*, 521 A.2d 227, 231 (Del. 1987) (holding that "when the exercise of eminent domain results in a substantial benefit to specific and identifiable private parties, a court must inspect with heightened scrutiny a claim that the public interest is the predominant interest being advanced").

56. *Kelo v. City of New London*, 843 A.2d 500, 585–90 (Conn. 2004), *aff'd*, 545 U.S. 469 (2005) (Zarella, J., dissenting). See the discussion of this dissent in chapter 1.

57. See, e.g., *Tolksdorff v. Griffith*, 626 N.W.2d 163, 167–69 (Mich. 2001) (invalidating legislation that allows condemnation of limited amounts of property in order to build roads for the benefit of landlocked property owners); *City of Lansing v. Edward Rose Realty, Inc.*, 502 N.W.2d 638, 643–46 (Mich. 1993) (invalidating taking of two apartment complexes for the benefit of a cable television company); *City of Center Line v. Chmelko*, 416 N.W.2d 401, 402, 404–407 (Mich. Ct. App. 1987) (invalidating condemnation of "two parcels of property" in order to facilitate expansion of a "local car dealership").

58. *City of Detroit v. Vavro*, 442 N.W.2d 730 (Mich. Ct. App. 1989).

59. Ibid., 731.

60. Ibid., 731–32. A 1995 court of appeals decision reaffirmed this holding. See *Detroit Edison Co. v. City of Detroit*, 527 N.W.2d 9, 11 (Mich. Ct. App. 1995).

61. Somin, "Overcoming *Poletown*," 1006.

62. Dana Berliner, *Public Power, Private Gain: A Five Year, State-by-State Report Examining the Abuse of Eminent Domain* 100 (2003), available at http://www.ij.org/publications/castle/.

63. Ibid., 2.

64. Berliner, *Public Power, Private Gain*, at 2. Detroit condemnations included takings for casinos and sports teams, and one in which a developer with ties to the mayor was able to obtain a condemnation that resulted in the destruction of an entire African American neighborhood. Ibid., 102–06.

65. I briefly discussed this issue in Ilya Somin, "Eminent Domain and the Decline of Detroit," *Volokh Conspiracy*, July 22, 2013, available at http://www.volokh.com/2013/07/22/eminent-domain-and-the-decline-of-detroit/.

66. For a discussion of those limitations, see chapter 5.

67. See, e.g., Nicole Stelle Garnett, "The Public Use Question as a Takings Problem," 71 *George Washington Law Review* 934, 963–69 (2003); Amicus Brief of Professors David L. Callies, James T. Ely, Paula A. Franzese, Nicole Stelle Garnett, James E. Krier, Daniel R. Mandelker, John Copeland Nagle, John Nolon, J.B. Ruhl, Shelley Ross Saxer, A. Dan Tarlock, Laura Underkuffler, and Edward F. Ziegler, *Kelo v. City of New London*, No. 04-108, *15–27, 2004 WL 2803192.

68. Garnett, "The Public Use Question as a Takings Problem," 966.

69. Brief for Petitioners, *Kelo v. City of New London*, 545 U.S. 469 (2005) (No. 04-108), 2004 WL 369341 at *4–5.

70. See discussion in chapter 3.

71. See Richard A. Epstein, *The Classical Liberal Constitution: The Uncertain Quest for Limited Government* (Cambridge, MA: Harvard University Press, 2014), 357–59; Richard A. Epstein, *Supreme Neglect: How to Revive Constitutional Protection for Property Rights* (New York: Oxford University Press, 2008), 83–86; *Kelo v. City of New London*, 545 U.S. 469 (2005), amicus brief of Richard Epstein and Cato Institute, 12–16, available at https://www.ij.org/im ages/pdf_folder/private_property/kelo/cato01.pdf; see also Richard A. Epstein, *Takings: Private Property and Eminent Domain* (Cambridge, MA: Harvard University Press, 1985), 169–74, which presents some related ideas. For a view similar to Epstein's, see Samuel R. Staley, "The Proper Uses of Eminent Domain for Urban Redevelopment: Is Eminent Domain Necessary?" in Bruce Benson, ed., Property Rights: Eminent Domain and Regulatory Takings Re-Examined, (New York: Palgrave Macmillan, 2010), 27, 40–42, Staley argues that eminent domain should be used for private development projects only if it is a "last resort" needed to overcome genuine holdout problems whose existence has been established by a higher level of scrutiny.

72. Epstein, *Classical Liberal Constitution,* 358.

73. See Thomas J. Miceli, *The Economic Theory of Eminent Domain: Private Property, Public Use* (Cambridge: Cambridge University Press, 2011), chap. 2.

74. Epstein, *Supreme Neglect,* 85.

75. See discussion above.

76. For a more detailed critique of Epstein's proposal along these lines, see Ilya Somin, "Libertarianism and Originalism," in *The Classical Liberal Constitution," NYU Journal of Law and Liberty* (forthcoming) (symposium on *The Classical Liberal Constitution*).

77. Epstein, *Supreme Neglect,* 85.

78. See discussion of subjective value earlier in this chapter.

79. See discussion in chapter 3.

80. Michael Heller and Roderick Hills, "Land Assembly Districts," 121 *Harvard Law Review* 1465 (2008); for a critique of this proposal, which focuses on issues different from those I address here, see Daniel B. Kelly, "The Limitations of Majoritarian Land Assembly," 122 *Harvard Law Review Forum* 7 (2009). For other proposals for increased community control over takings that, in my view, have shortcomings similar to those of the Heller-Hills LAD plan, see Becher, *Private Property and Public Power,* 231-35.

81. Heller and Hills, "Land Assembly Districts," 1488–93.

82. Ibid.

83. Ibid., 1503–05.

84. Ibid., 1497–99.

85. Ibid., 1499–1502.

86. See the discussion of rational political ignorance in chapter 3, and in Ilya Somin, *Democracy and Political Ignorance: Why Smaller Government Is Smarter* (Stanford, CA: Stanford University Press, 2013), chap. 3.

87. See Kelly, "Limitations of Majoritarian Land Assembly."

88. Becher, 234–35.

89. Ibid., 235.

90. See discussion in chapter 3.

91. See Robert C. Ellickson, "Federalism and *Kelo*: A Question for Richard Epstein," 44 *Tulsa Law Review* 751, 762 (2009).

92. Ibid., 762–63. See also Vicki L. Been, "'Exit' as a Constraint on Land Use Exactions: Rethinking the Unconstitutional Conditions Doctrine," 91 *Columbia Law Review* 473, 509 (1991); Anup Malani, "Valuing Laws as Local Amenities," 121 *Harvard Law Review* 1273 (2008) (providing evidence showing that the effects of various laws are capitalized into home prices, which local governments have incentives to keep high).

93. Ellickson, "Federalism and *Kelo*," 762–63 & n.66.

94. Been, "'Exit' as a Constraint on Land Use Exactions," 509.

95. For some of the better-known works along these lines, see Charles M. Tiebout, "A Pure Theory of Local Expenditures," 64 *Journal of Political Economy* 416 (1956); Geoffrey Brennan and James M. Buchanan, *The Power to Tax: Analytical Foundations of a Fiscal Constitution* (New York: Cambridge University Press, 1980), 173–86; Albert Breton, *Competitive Governments: An Economic Theory of Politics and Public Finance* (Cambridge: Cambridge University Press, 1996); Thomas R. Dye, *American Federalism: Competition among Governments* (Lexington, MA: Lexington Books, 1990); James M. Buchanan, "Federalism as an Ideal Political Order and an Objective for Constitutional Reform," 25 *Publius* 19 (1995); Wallace E. Oates, "An Essay on Fiscal Federalism," 37 *Journal of Economic Literature* 1120, 1134–37 (1999); Wallace E. Oates and Robert Schwab, "Economic Competition among Jurisdictions: Efficiency Enhancing or Efficiency Distorting?," 35 *Journal of Public Economies* 333 (1988); Barry Weingast, "The Economic Role of Political Institutions: Market-Preserving Federalism and Economic Development," 11 *Journal of Law, Economics, and Organization* 1 (1995). I have contributed to this literature myself. See Somin, *Democracy and Political Ignorance*, chap. 5.

96. See, e.g., Richard A. Epstein, "Exit Rights under Federalism," 55 *Law & Contemporary Problems* 147, 154–59 (1992); William Fischel, *Regulatory Takings: Law, Economics, and Politics* (Cambridge, MA: Harvard University Press, 1995), 282–88.

97. See, e.g., David Wildasin, "Labor-Market Integration, Investment in Risky Human Capital, and Fiscal Competition," 90 *American Economic Review* 73 (2000).

98. See, e.g., Nathan Ashby, "Economic Freedom and Migration Flows between U.S. States," 73 *Southern Economic Journal* 677 (2007).

99. Richard Schragger, "Mobile Capital, Local Economic Regulation, and the Democratic City," 123 *Harvard Law Review* 482 (2009).

100. For a discussion of the relevance of moving costs to foot voting, see Somin, *Democracy and Political Ignorance,* 144–45.

101. Melvyn R. Durchslag, "Forgotten Federalism: The Takings Clause and Local Land Use Decisions," 59 *Maryland Law Review* 464, 511 (2000).

102. For the classic analysis, see Gideon Kanner, "Condemnation Blight: Just How Just Is Just Compensation?," 48 *Notre Dame Law Review* 765 (1973).

103. Ellickson, "Federalism and *Kelo,*" 763 n.66.

104. Ibid.

105. Ibid.

106. William Fischel, *The Homevoter Hypothesis: How Home Values Influence Local Government, Taxation, School Finance, and Land-Use Policies* (Cambridge, MA: University of Harvard Press, 2001).

107. See discussion in chapter 3; Dick M. Carpenter & John K. Ross, "Testing O'Connor and Thomas: Does the Use Of Eminent Domain Target Poor and Minority Communities?," 46 *Urban Studies* 2447 (2009).

108. See discussion in chapter 3. For the classic formulation of voice and exit as alternative responses to bad policy, see Albert O. Hirschman, *Exit, Voice, and Loyalty* (Cambridge, MA: Harvard University Press, 1971).

109. See discussion in chapter 3.

110. *City of Oakland v. Oakland Raiders,* 646 P.2d 835 (Cal. 1982). A California appellate court later ruled that this eminent domain action was barred by the Commerce Clause of the federal Constitution because of the resulting burden on interstate commerce. *City of Oakland v. Oakland Raiders,* 174 Cal. App. 3d 414 (Cal. App. 1st Dist. 1985). However, the basis for the ruling—that the city's plan would create an injunction preventing the team from moving forever and that it would affect an entire nationwide league rather than just the Raiders—would not extend to most other types of mobile property. Ibid., 421.

111. See discussion in chapter 2.

112. The California court that ultimately invalidated the attempted condemnation of the Oakland Raiders noted that "eminent domain cases have traditionally concerned real property, rarely implicating commerce clause considerations which deal primarily with products in the flow of interstate commerce. Whether the commerce clause precludes taking by eminent domain of intangible property, however, is a novel question posed, it seems, for the first time in this case." *City of Oakland,* 174 Cal. App. 3d at 419.

113. *Mayor and City Council of Baltimore v. Baltimore Football Club, Inc.,* 624 F. Supp. 278, 283 (D. Md. 1985).

114. Ibid., 282–84.

115. See discussion in chapter 2.

116. *Dayton Gold and Silver Min. Co. v. Seawell*, 11 Nev. 394, 404–05 (1876).

117. See, e.g., Carol Zeiner, "Eminent Domain Wolves in Sheep's Clothing: Private Benefit Masquerading as Classic Public Use," 28 *Virginia Environmental Law Journal* 1 (2010); Julia D. Mahoney, "*Kelo's* Legacy: Eminent Domain and the Future of Property Rights," 2005 *Supreme Court Review* 103, 121–22 (2005). For the Nevada Supreme Court's preference for a necessity test, see ibid., 405.

118. See Zeiner, "Eminent Domain Wolves in Sheep's Clothing." I raised a similar possibility in Somin, "Overcoming *Poletown*," 1031–32.

119. See discussion in chapter 3.

120. This possibility is raised in Somin, "Overcoming *Poletown*," 1031–32, and Zeiner, "Wolves in Sheep's Clothing."

121. See, e.g., *Yick Wo v. Hopkins*, 118 U.S. 356 (1886).

122. See, e.g., *Tolksdorff v. Griffith*, 464 Mich. 1 (2001).

123. *City of Springfield v. Dreison Investments, Inc.*, 2000 WL 782971, at *50 (Mass. Super. Ct. Feb. 25, 2000).

124. *Texas Rice Land Partners, Ltd. v. Denbury-Green Pipeline*, 363 S.W.3d 192 (Tex. 2011).

125. For some additional discussion of this issue, see the conclusion.

126. See Alexandra Klass, "Takings and Transmission," 91 *North Carolina Law Review* 1079 (2013); Klass, "The Frontier of Eminent Domain," 79 *University of Colorado Law Review* 651 (2008). For a condensed version of the latter article, see Klass, "The Frontier of Eminent Domain," 31 *Regulation–20* (2008). Further citations to "Frontier of Eminent Domain" reference the longer *University of Colorado Law Review* version.

127. For a more extensive discussion see Ilya Somin, "Using Eminent Domain to Take Property for Universities," Volokh Conspiracy, Sept. 19, 2012, available at http://www.volokh.com/2012/09/19/using-eminent-domain-to-take-property -for-universities/. See also Kevin Kiley, "Change is Eminent," Chronicle of Higher Education, Sept. 19, 2012, available at https://www.insidehighered.com /news/2012/09/19/ball-state-use-eminent-domain-spotlights-rare-potent-tool-state -universities.

128. See Steven Chen, "Keeping Public Use Relevant in Stadium Eminent Domain Takings; The Massachusetts Way," 40 *Boston College Environmental Affairs Law Review* 453, 467–71 (2013). See also the discussion of the new Minnesota law to that effect in chapter 6.

129. *City of Arlington v. Golddust Twins Realty Corp.*, 41 F.3d 960, 962 (5th Cir. 1994).

130. See David Schultz, *American Politics in the Age of Ignorance: Why Lawmakers Choose Belief Over Research* (New York: Palgrave Macmillan, 2012), chap. 3.

131. Alan Altshuler and David Luberoff, *Mega-Projects: The Changing Politics of Urban Investment* (Washington, DC: Brookings Institution, 2003), 33.

132. For some possible reforms, see Klass, "Takings and Transmission," 1134–53 and Klass, "Frontier of Eminent Domain.," 691–700.

133. Klass recognizes that interest group power may be an obstacle to effective reform in this area because "natural resource companies still wield significant political power in the region." Klass, "Frontier of Eminent Domain," 694.

134. For this type of argument, see Abraham Bell and Gideon Parchomovsky, "The Uselessness of Public Use," 106 *Columbia Law Review* 1412 (2006).

135. Ibid.

136. See, e.g., *Loretto v. Teleprompter CATV Corp.* 458 U.S. 419, 426 (1982) (permanent physical occupation); *Lucas v. Carolina Coastal Commission*, 505 U.S. 1003, 1015 (1992) (complete loss of economic value).

137. Richard A. Posner, *How Judges Think* (Cambridge, MA: Harvard University Press, 2008), 319.

138. See Abraham Bell, "Private Takings," 76 *University of Chicago Law Review* 517, 574–77 (2009).

139. See discussion in chapter 3.

140. See, e.g., David Dana, "The Law and Expressive Meaning of Condemning the Poor after *Kelo*," 101 *Northwestern University Law Review* 365 (2007); Becher, *Private Property and Public Power*, 239; U.S. Senate Committee on the Judiciary, *The* Kelo *Decision: Investigating Takings of Homes and Other Private Property*, (testimony of Professor Thomas W. Merrill) (Sept 20, 2005) available at http://www.gpo.gov/fdsys/pkg/CHRG-109shrg24723/pdf/CHRG-109 shrg24723.pdf.

141. See discussion of these states' reforms in chapter 5.

142. I expand on this issue in greater detail in Ilya Somin, "Is Post-*Kelo* Eminent Domain Reform Bad for the Poor?" 101 *Northwestern University Law Review* 1931, 1936–38 (2007).

143. Dana, "The Law and Expressive Meaning of Condemning the Poor after *Kelo*," 365.

144. For a detailed discussion of the relevant survey data, see Somin, "Is Post-*Kelo* Eminent Domain Reform Bad for the Poor," 1937–41.

Conclusion

1. For a detailed examination of the possible consequences of a victory for the property owners in *Kelo*, which concludes that it would probably have done more for the property rights cause than was accomplished by the political backlash against *Kelo*, see Ilya Somin, "What If *Kelo v. City of New London* Had Gone the Other Way?," 45 *Indiana Law Review* 21 (2011) (Symposium on What If Counterfactuals in Constitutional History). For an argument that the prop-

erty rights movement's defeat in *Kelo* "eventually became a victory of a different sort," see Ben DePoorter, "The Upside of Losing," 113 *Columbia Law Review* 817, 831–32 (2013).

2. Jeff Benedict, *Little Pink House: A True Story of Defiance and Courage* (New York: Grand Central Publishing, 2009), 331, 363.

3. Ibid., 370–75; E-mail from Susette Kelo, June 17, 2014; e-mail from Scott Bullock, July 17, 2014.

4. E-mail from Susette Kelo, June 17, 2014; e-mail from Scott Bullock, July 17, 2014.

5. Benedict, *Little Pink House,* 372; interview with Michael Cristofaro, July 12, 2013.

6. Discussion with Michael Cristofaro, May 30, 2014.

7. Interview with Michael Cristofaro, July 12, 2013.

8. Benedict, *Little Pink House,* 357.

9. Ibid.

10. Ibid., 374; see also George Lefcoe, "Jeff Benedict's *Little Pink House*: The Back Story of the *Kelo* Case," 42 *Connecticut Law Review* 925, 954–55 (2010).

11. Interview with Michael Cristofaro, July 12, 2013.

12. Benedict, *Little Pink House,* 147–48, 154–56, 187–90.

13. Ibid., 187–88; Interview with Frederick Paxton, June 11, 2014.

14. Benedict, *Little Pink House,* 217–19, 230–31.

15. See chapter 1.

16. Jon Lender, "Inglorious Anniversary: What's Become of the Players 5 Years after Rowland's Fall? Legacy of a Scandal, "*Hartford Courant,* July 1, 2009.

17. Alison Leigh Cowan, "Connecticut Official and State Contractor are Each Sentenced to 30 Months in Prison," *New York Times,* Apr. 26, 2006.

18. Some of the *Kelo* plaintiffs raised this connection in interviews with me. Interview with Richard Beyer, July 13, 2013; Interview with Matthew Dery, July 31, 2013.

19. Jeff Benedict, "Apology Adds an Epilogue to *Kelo* Case," *Hartford Courant,* Sept. 16, 2011.

20. Quoted in ibid.

21. Ibid.

22. *Kelo v. City of New London,* 843 A.2d 500, 596–602 (Conn. 2004) (Zarella, J., dissenting), *aff'd,* 545 U.S. 469 (2005). See also discussion in chapter 1.

23. Interview with Richard Beyer, July 13, 2013.

24. Interview with Susette Kelo, Sept. 4, 2013.

25. Interview with Bill Von Winkle, Apr. 15, 2014.

26. Interview with Frederick Paxton, June 11, 2014.

27. Quoted in Kathleen Edgecomb, "NLDC Getting a New Identity," *The Day,* Feb. 1, 2012.

28. Quoted in Paul Choinere, "Take the Steps to Pursue Fort Trumbull Dreams," *The Day,* Dec. 8, 2013.

29. Ibid.

30. Kathleen Edgecomb, "'It Still Hurts': Fight to Save Home Scars One Fort Trumbull Family," *The Day,* June 23, 2013; see also Charlotte Allen, "'*Kelo*' Revisited," *Weekly Standard,* Feb. 10, 2014, available at http://www.weeklystandard .com/articles/kelo-revisited_776021.html.

31. Edgecomb, "'It Still Hurts.'"

32. David Collins, "Feral Cats Ignore Eminent Domain," *The Day,* Dec. 10, 2008; John Carney, "The Famous 'Kelo House' Property Is Now a Vacant Lot," *Business Insider,* Nov. 10, 2009, available at http://www.businessinsider.com/the -famous-kelo-house-property-is-now-a-vacant-lot-2009-11

33. William Yardley, "After Eminent Domain Victory, Disputed Project Goes Nowhere," *New York Times,* Nov. 21, 2005.

34. Kate Moran, "Developer Says Fort Trumbull Hotel Plan Not Viable Since 2002; Project Became Unrealistic without Pfizer Commitment," *The Day,* June 12, 2004.

35. Lefcoe, "Jeff Benedict's *Little Pink House*," 939; Patrick McGeehan, "Pfizer to Leave City That Won Eminent Land-Use Case," *New York Times,* Nov. 12, 2009.

36. McGeehan, "Pfizer to Leave City."

37. Lefcoe, "Jeff Benedict's *Little Pink House*," 936.

38. Quoted in Judy Benson, "Pfizer Digs in for Long Haul: Ground Officially Broken for $220 Million New London Project," *The Day,* Sept. 2, 1998.

39. Quoted in Abdon M. Pallasch, "Scalia Offers Ruling: *Deep Dish v. Thin Crust*," *Chicago Sun-Times,* Oct. 18, 2011.

40. Quoted in ibid.

41. Quoted in Nathan Eagle, "Supreme Court Justice Scalia Talks Eminent Domain, Internment Camps," *Hawaii Civil Beat,* Feb. 4, 2014, available at http:// hawaii.news.blogs.civilbeat.com/post/75652335571/supreme-court-justice-scalia -talks-eminent-domain.

42. See discussion of this point in chapters 2 and 3.

43. See, e.g., Thomas G. Hansford and James F. Spriggs, *The Politics of Precedent on the US Supreme Court* (Princeton, NJ: Princeton University Press, 2006), 83-90.

44. See chapter 4.

45. See discussion of O'Connor's changing views in chapter 4.

46. For my analysis of the relevance of this historical trend to prospects for judicial protection of property rights generally, see Ilya Somin, "Taking Property Rights Seriously: The Supreme Court and the 'Poor Relation' of Constitutional Law," George Mason Law & Economics Research Paper No. 08-53 (2008), available at http://ssrn.com/abstract=1247854, pp. 38–41.

47. See discussion of the NAACP and Nader's views in chapter 5.

48. See chapter 7.

49. See, e.g., Wendell E. Pritchett, "The 'Public Menace' of Blight: Urban Renewal and the Private Uses of Eminent Domain," 21 *Yale Law & Policy Review* 1, 5–23 (2003); Julia D. Mahoney, "*Kelo's* Legacy: Eminent Domain and the Future of Property Rights," 2005 *Supreme Court Review* 103, 132 (2005).; Paul Boudreaux, "Eminent Domain, Property Rights, and the Solution of Representation-Reinforcement," 83 *Denver University Law Review* 1 (2005); and Maya Yxta Murray, "Peering," unpublished paper (Nov. 2013).

50. See cases from those states cited in chapters 3 and 7.

51. See *Goldstein v. Pataki*, 516 F.3d 50 (2d Cir. 2008).

52. *Lawrence v. Texas*, 539 U.S. 558, 587–88 (2003).

53. *Montejo v. Louisiana*, 556 U.S. 778, 793 (2009).

54. *Payne v. Tennessee*, 501 U.S. 808, 828–29 (1991).

55. See chapter 7.

56. See discussion in chapter 4.

57. See ibid.

58. *Lawrence*, 539 U.S. at 577.

59. See discussion in chapter 4.

60. See discussion in chapters 2 and 3.

61. See discussion in chapter 5.

62. *Kelo v. City of New London*, 545 U.S. 469. 499–501 (2005) (O'Connor, J., dissenting).

63. See the discussion of O'Connor's approach in chapter 4.

64. See discussion in chapter 2.

65. For an extensive historical overview, see Barry Friedman, *The Will of the People: How Public Opinion Has Influenced the Supreme Court and Shaped the Meaning of the Constitution* (New York: Farrar, Straus & Giroux, 2009).

66. See chapter 6.

67. On the NAACP's combined political and legal strategy in the civil rights struggle, see, e.g., Mark Tushnet, *The NAACP's Legal Strategy Against Segregated Education, 1925–50*, rev. ed. (Chapel Hill: University of North Carolina Press, 2005); On future Supreme Court Justice Ruth Bader Ginsburg's efforts to combine litigation and political strategy in promoting women's rights in the 1970s, see Amy Leigh Campbell, *Raising the Bar: Ruth Bader Ginsburg and the ACLU's Women's Rights Project* (Princeton, NJ: Xlibris, 2003). On gun rights, see Adam Winkler, *Gunfight: The Battle over the Right to Bear Arms in America* (New York: Norton, 2012). For a good recent discussion of the interaction between legal and political action in the gay marriage movement, see Michael J. Klarman, *From the Closet to the Altar: Courts, Backlash, and the Struggle for Same-Sex Marriage* (New York: Oxford University Press, 2012).

68. On this point, see Steven M. Teles, *The Rise of the Conservative Legal Movement: The Battle for Control of the Law* (Princeton, NJ: Princeton University Press, 2008), 237–45.

69. See discussion in chapter 2.

70. Ted Balaker and Courtney Balaker, "Culture Can Help Tame Eminent Domain Abuse," *USA Today*, June 222, 2014, available at http://www.usatoday.com/story /opinion/2014/06/22/court-working-class-eminent-domain-column/10629613/

71. Buckner F. Melton, Jr. "Eminent Domain, 'Public Use,' and the Conundrum of Original Intent," 36 *Natural Resources Journal*, 59, 62 (1996).

72. See chapter 4.

73. See discussion in chapter 8.

74. See, e.g., William Easterly, *The Tyranny of Experts: Economists, Dictators, and the Forgotten Rights of the Poor* (New York: Basic Books, 2013), 1–6.

75. Ibid.

76. Kent Ewing, "China Goes Back to the Land," *Asia Times,* Mar. 9, 2006.

77. Maureen Fan, "As Beijing Olympics Near, Homes and Hope Crumble," *Washington Post*, July 12, 2008.

78. Barack Obama, *The Audacity of Hope: Thoughts on Reclaiming the American Dream* (New York: Crown, 2006), 149.

Appendix B

1. 2007 Saint Index, questions 9, 10.

Index